# THE BOY WITH NO SHOES

*Novels by William Horwood*

The Stonor Eagles
Callanish
Skallagrigg

*The Duncton Chronicles*
Duncton Wood
Duncton Quest
Duncton Found

*The Book of Silence*
Duncton Tales
Duncton Rising
Duncton Stone

*The Wolves of Time*
Journeys to the Heartland
Seekers at the WulfRock

*Tales of the Willows*
The Willows in Winter
Toad Triumphant
The Willows and Beyond
The Willows at Christmas

WILLIAM HORWOOD

# THE BOY WITH NO SHOES

## A MEMOIR

review

First published in 2004 by                  .
HEADLINE BOOK PUBLISHING

10 9 8 7 6 5 4 3 2 1

Cataloguing in Publication Data is available from the British Library

ISBN 0 7553 1317 8

Typeset in AGaramond by Avon DataSet Ltd, Bidford on Avon, Warwickshire
Printed and bound in Great Britain by Clays Ltd, St Ives plc

Headline's policy is to use papers that are natural, renewable and recyclable
products and made from wood grown in sustainable forests. The logging
and manufacturing processes are expected to conform to the environmental
regulations of the country of origin.

Headline Book Publishing
A division of Hodder Headline
338 Euston Road
London NW1 3BH

www.headline.co.uk
www.hodderheadline.com

# CONTENTS

Prologue 1

## PART ONE: JIMMY

1. Running 5
2. Darktime 10
3. My Wake-up Call 23
4. The Head Who Listened 32
5. The Man Who Wasn't 44
6. Hobnail Boots 54
7. The House of a Thousand Rooms 67
8. Mr Mee 77
9. My First Mountain 87
10. The Battle of San Romano 102
11. Granny and the African Gentleman 124
12. Mr Coalman Moves On 132
13. Newfoundland 149

## PART TWO: NORTH END

14. Treasures of the Sea 167
15. Eleven Plus 179
16. Failing Children 192

17. Lessons of History  203

18. Listening to Tides  219

19. Music Lessons  237

20. Breakdown  249

21. Flowers of the Dunes  270

22. Tidal Currents  280

23. Drowning  293

24. Grandfather's Legacy  304

25. Captain Flax  316

26. Mr Wharton  329

27. Harriet  351

28. Top Cup  359

29. Tormentil  374

## PART THREE: LOOKING BACK

30. Crocodile  401

31. The Open Sea  411

32. The World Turning  424

33. Looking Back  437

# AUTHOR'S NOTE

When I was thirty-four and had been iller than I knew for two long years, my recovery began in the strangest and most magical of ways. I woke one day from dreaming and saw myself when very young, as clearly as in a black-and-white Kodak photograph. I saw how desperately the little boy I once was had needed someone to talk to in a world where no one wanted to listen. I decided there and then to travel back in time and let myself as adult be listener to the child. This book and my final healing is the result of that imaginative listening over very many years.

Because the boy that I was seemed someone other than myself, it proved easier – in fact essential – to give him a different name and to change the names of those who most influenced him for good and ill. I even changed the name of his home town, which was, of course, my own. Adopting such disguise, I have been able to fill gaps, paper over cracks and visit distant places of emotion I would never otherwise have reached.

I have decided to leave things that way. For one thing it protects the dignity and innocence of others in the story, most of them now dead, whose perceptions of the same events would inevitably be different from my own. For another, though there is still someone left alive who calls me Billy, the fact is that the boy I listened to changed in the telling and will now always be Jimmy to me.

WH, Oxford, 2004

# PROLOGUE

My name is Jimmy and there was a man in my time long ago, before the Boy and the Girl, before my Darktime, before Granny came to help me; and that man held my hand and took me out of our cold house into the sun and then along a street to a great big place with a sign outside.

It was dark and deep, with lots of boxes and all sorts of things piled up and everything warm, with dust rising slowly, endlessly. He let me watch the dust caught shining in the sun. He didn't hurry me or shout.

That was the place and that was the day when the Man Who Was gave me the pair of shoes.

I know he did.

I know it was him.

I can remember that.

It is the very first thing I remember.

'Do you want them, Jimmy?' he said, squatting down and showing them to me.

I'm sure he said that.

When I nodded, he smiled. I can remember the feel of the smile all around me but I can't remember his face or the smile itself. The name on that smile was love.

Then he said, 'You will have to learn to tie these laces. Look!'

I tried to copy what he did but I was all fingers and thumbs.

'You'll learn,' he said, tying the laces for me one after the other, and I felt the good tightness of them on my feet and looked at my shoes in wonder.

He was the man who gave me the shoes.

There was sun, so warm and everything so good.

I remember that day because it entered my heart and stayed there, never to go away, never, even at the worst of times, even when I was dying.

The Man Who Was gave me the shoes.

I'm sure it was him.

Then came the day when it rained. It drummed on my head and into my hair as the train drew in, huffing and puffing and noisy with steam. The rain drummed down onto my T-shirt. It made my shorts sopping wet and ran down my bare legs and turned me cold, as cold as ice. I couldn't move and I couldn't run and I couldn't find my way beyond the rain towards the train he got on, that terrible day when the train door was shut and he was lost behind the reflections in the glass beyond the rain.

The rain was a cage I could not break out of.

I only had one hand to rattle its bars.

Ma held the other so painfully tight that it cracked my bones. She didn't want me to break out of the cage of the rain that drummed.

'You stay here,' she said. 'Just do as you're told for once.'

So I couldn't run to the train and ask him never, never to go.

I was unable to move as the rain drummed into me a terrible fear, enough to stop my breath and freeze my mind. And the fear was this: that when it cleared and I could see through the tears it made on my face, he would not be there to take my hand and keep me safe from Ma, and I would always, always be alone.

Then the rain was gone and so was he, gone for good along with the train, and I knew I had been right to feel that fear.

So all that was left were the shoes on my feet, which he gave me that day when he kneeled on the ground before me in a shaft of dusty sunlight and spoke my name like no one else, ever again.

# PART ONE

# JIMMY

# 1

# RUNNING

The park keeper in his uniform and hat shouted at me and grabbed one of my ears and pulled me towards him.

'KEEP OFF THE GRASS!' he yelled, so close it made my eardrums ache.

Then he said, 'I'll cut off your ears with my garden shears. I'll cut the bloody things off, seeing as you don't use them.'

That was what set me running across the grass I should never have walked on.

Out through the black iron gates with the spikes and shadows and spiders on top . . .

Down, and up, and across the streets, running away from the fat man, away from the shears that cut when they shut . . .

Past a black car that squealed and shouted . . .

Past a black dog that growled and snarled as I passed, so I had to run faster still . . .

Because the man was still coming.

'You little bugger, you . . .'

The man with the shears was coming, out of the park where he normally stayed. That's why I was certain that this time my aching ears would be cut right off my head.

Round Dumpton Road and up into the street where I lived, past the old woman's house at the end, with its familiar wall and railings. Past that was almost to safety – but when I looked back he was still coming.

'I'll tell your mum, you little . . .'

Ma was busy, so I knew he wasn't going to talk to her; but still he was coming.

So, as fast as I could, I was running, my breathing desperate and painful, for the fat man was coming and his feet were drumming like rain on my head, telling me something bad was going to happen.

I turned onto the concrete path of No 15, up towards the big wooden gate, to try to open it before the man got there with the shears for my ears.

Running and banging on the gate, shouting for Ma, who was busy inside with a man but would help, might help, must help.

'Ma! *Help!*'

The gate was shut, the gate was shut fast.

'*Ma! Maaaaa!*'

Beyond the gate I heard the back door open. She growled out in anger like a dog, did Ma when roused, which was often, and it was that growling I heard. But better that than the shears. Above my head the latch shot up, the gate banged open and out of my yard Ma's red raw hand crashed down and then straight across my face, one, two and three: SLAP! SLAP! *SLAPPPP!*

'Ma . . .'

'I told you to stay away; I *told* you . . .'

She was all dolled up and smelt of powder and perfume and her face was red.

'Ma, there's a man coming . . .'

'I told you,' she snarled, 'not to come back yet.'

Then the gate crashed shut, leaving me outside, and I knew I was wrong to come back early, but the man with the shears said he would cut off my ears; and now he had reached the concrete path and the gate was locked and the back door slammed shut and there was nowhere to go.

What could I do?

I sank down on my knees and put my cheek against the warm wood of the gate and felt its soft roughness as a caress.

I put up my hand on the wood because it was the nearest I could get to Ma.

Then I bowed my head and felt my knees grazed on the concrete path. But that didn't hurt. My breathing was so fast I began to choke as I huddled down to wait for the man with the shears to come those last few steps to cut off my ears.

Then I looked at my legs and my feet and there I saw the only thing I owned that someone might want.

Not my khaki shorts, which were hand-me-downs from another boy whose Ma, Ma knew.

Not my shirt, which was the Boy's.

But my canvas shoes with white rubber on the front and laces that I had learnt to tie so that one day I could show the Man Who Was how clever I was, if he ever came back.

They were my own shoes, my very own, the only thing to call my own. Not hand-me-down shoes from the Boy or woollen gloves from the Girl. My own.

So then I knew what I had to do to save my ears.

My hands were shaking like my breath, and in the silence of my fear I took off my shoes and laid them neatly on the path as an offering, a gift, the only thing I had to give; my greatest thing.

I had walked on the grass and so had to lose my shoes.

Then I looked up and heard my terror thumping in my chest because there was the man with the shears, come to cut off my ears.

He shouted through his blubber mouth and yellow teeth, 'I'm sick and tired, I'm sick and tired of all you boys. So you see these shears . . . *look at me* . . .'

I tried but I couldn't. I was too afraid to look up at him. Then the man reached down and grabbed my ear and I felt the cold of metal on the side of my head.

The gate crashed open and I saw the black boots of the man with Ma.

'What's he done now?'

'He's walked on the grass once too often, that's what he's done, so I'm going to cut off an ear right close to his head.'

The other man laughed high, high above my head and I smelt the stink of the parkman's trousers.

'Cut 'em both off, for all I care . . .'

'*Maaaa . . .*'

And in straining my head to try and see Ma, searching past the man at the gate towards the back door, hoping she would come to help, I felt the root of my ear beginning to burn and the *snip snip snip* of their laughter just before the cutting was to start.

That was the moment I screamed and caught my first glimpse of that great dark place which is betwixt and between, the place that was Darktime and is. Because I knew if Ma wasn't coming to save my ears, she was a ma who would never come, not ever.

Then the gate slammed shut and silence fell as my screams died away. When I dared look up, the park keeper had gone and I was alone, except for my shoes. So I picked them up and held them close to my chest, and since there was nowhere in all the world to go I stayed where I was until the sun dropped out of the sky and evening came and I grew cold.

Once in a while people came and went along the pavement at the bottom of our concrete path. I stared into the face of each and every one because I thought that maybe one of them might be the Man Who Was come to take me away. Right until darkness I waited, growing cold enough to shiver. The Man never came, but the shoes he gave me, held tight to my chest, as tight as tight could be, were a comfort all the same.

He was the one who gave me the shoes.

I know he did.

I know it was him. I can remember that.

Even in Darktime that was one thing that never left me.

Sitting there shivering, I made a wish for him to come to get me one day.

I made a wish to feel his hand holding mine again.

I made a wish that one day I would be allowed to show him how clever I was to be able to tie my laces all by myself.

I fell asleep whispering those wishes, not knowing that wishes are never granted when you expect or how you expect.

I fell asleep locked out by Ma, not knowing that there was a long road to travel between the wishing and the granting: there was

Darktime to get through, and long times alone, and the only way to reach the end of the road and still be alive was to find others to help you along. Nobody can travel so far alone, not without dying first.

That night, when I fell asleep in the cold outside No 15, when I was five and Ma forgot I was still out there because she was so busy with the man inside, I didn't know anything, or hardly anything at all.

But I did know this: I had the shoes and they were mine and so long as I could wear them or hold them close I would never be completely alone, not ever, and I would always be safe.

I knew that; and I knew as well that I couldn't remember anything about the man who gave me the shoes except the feel of his hand in mine and that big place of boxes and sun and the rising dust caught in light; and that once upon a time in the time long ago I was loved enough to be given some shoes that were mine alone and all for me.

# 2

# DARKTIME

Darktime never goes away. It is always waiting to summon me back into its terrible depth.

That's why it is 'is' and never 'was'.

Darktime is the void between the Man Who Was and my Ma not wanting me, the place of being lost in the dark, the place of me being no one, where even the memory of the Man Who Was and the shoes he gave me begins to slip away, slips fast away into the spiralling darkness around me, where I may never be able to find it again and I am left alone for ever.

Jimmy Rova, who I was once, was a skinny boy in khaki shorts and a striped T-shirt and a short-back-and-sides, hardly noticeable at all: you wouldn't have seen what was inside his head; you would never have guessed in a month of Sundays that Darktime was there.

Darktime was the dying place where I couldn't remember that my name was once Jimmy Rova.

It was the vast and limitless agony of knowing I once lost something, something I needed, but not being able to remember what it was and so never knowing where to find it again. Darktime was knowing for ever the feeling of loss, and it was a place of terrible loneliness.

I started falling into that place when I was five, more than a year after the Rainday, when the rain drummed down on my head and froze my mind and limbs, putting into me the fear that the Man would leave and never come back.

\* \* \*

It was another hot day and I was crouching by a bramble bush with my bow and arrow.

'What are you doing?' said the Boy.

'Shooting the bumblebee.'

The Boy laughed and the bumblebee, tracked all morning, caught in the sun, ready to be shooted with an arrow, was gone when I looked again. It was then I began my discovery that when the Boy came, joy often flew away.

'Who are you?' I asked, which I did not often do in that aftertime of grieving the Man's departure. I didn't speak much. I couldn't read or write. But that hot day I dared ask him who he was.

'Don't you even know your own brother!?'

That sentence was followed by mocking laughter, which I heard then for the very first time. A bit of trust in me lay down and died. I had done something wrong: I had forgotten the Boy and forgotten that he was my brother.

'What's your name?' I asked.

'Michael,' he said and we stood in the hot sun by the bramble bush staring at each other. For a moment, just an instant, there was hope in me flying up towards the blue sky.

But then he said, '. . . but don't think you're my *real* brother – or anyone else's,' and hope became a white bird whose wings stopped so suddenly that it fell from the sky.

It was a long time before I said anything to Ma.

'Ma, *Ma . . .*'

'What is it now?' said Ma, dabbing at her nose with a powder puff, the dust cascading through a shaft of sunlight towards the floor.

'Is Mikey my brother?'

'Yes.'

'He isn't.'

I watched in surprise as her red raw hitting hand came raging through the scented dust and slapped me hard.

'Never say such things.'

\*   \*   \*

Darktime wasn't sudden like Ma's hand, it crept up on me by degrees, a shadow advancing from behind, until in the end it came much faster than I could run.

Ma's pinking shears – the Boy who others called Michael had them. I couldn't escape him all the time, and sometimes he tracked me down and put his snot in my mouth; sometimes he caught me in the sun and pinned me down or cuffed me.

'*Ma . . .*'

'Oh Jimmy, for God's sake stop whingeing; I'm busy.'

Her red raw hitting hand was fretting at the page of her book, so I slipped away.

That day he had another big boy with him.

'Let's cut off Jimmy's willy with Ma's pinking shears.'

They caught me by the apple tree and held me tight and pulled down my khaki shorts and then my pants. I felt the pain of the other boy's hand too hard at my willy. I felt his fingers hold it and pull it out so it hurt at the roots.

I saw the pinking shears snip-snipping in the sun above me and then cutting down *snap! snap! snap!* just like those shears the park keeper held. Then I was nothing but a struggling scream, which was one long dark corridor of a scream, and I was running down it towards Darktime.

Suddenly Ma's hand came crashing out of the sun and hit the Boy and his friend, who cried and snivelled.

'It was only a joke,' said the Boy, but his eyes weren't laughing; his eyes were cruel.

Ma's hand hit me as well for good measure and when she was gone with the pinking shears the Boy came back and snarled like a dog, his teeth twisted and bent, 'We'll *bite* it off when the day comes that she's not looking.'

That opened the door wide onto another fear.

One day I put on my shoes. Ma said they were sneakers really, because they were made across the ocean blue, but I didn't mind. They had been given to me and me alone. They were made of faded blue canvas with white rubber round the edges and a star at each side.

Then we all set off for a day on the beach, the boys and Ma, and a new man called Ralph.

The day was hot and when the level of the sea dropped it left the jetty above green and slippery with seaweed.

I put my shoe on that part by mistake and the shoe slipped down, towards the rise and fall of the sea below.

Then my foot followed my shoe, and my leg my foot and my body my leg and I fell straight in, straight down, down into the sea.

It was not dark at all down there but bluebottle green, and I reached up towards the light above, to where the sun was; reached up and up as high as I could, but still my hand couldn't break through the surface, and my feet couldn't touch the bottom.

Yet I wasn't scared. I felt free of them all down there, stretched-out free, where nobody was, where my shoes were still safe on my feet, and I was all by myself and no Boy snipped and snapped and laughed his mocking laughter.

Then suddenly the surface above, which was filled with a beautiful trembling light, broke apart and a black hand reached down and grabbed my hair. I was pulled out even straighter than I fell in by the man with Ma called Ralph, back to the world of the laughter where my Darktime was at its beginning.

Except there was one thing, one good thing.

That day when I nearly drowned I discovered I wasn't afraid of the sea any more. Down on the shore, I went straight back in and learnt to swim in no time at all. The sea held no fear for me because I had known its embrace and I knew that it wasn't bad.

My swimming was just doggy-paddling in the waves, in wonder that my body did not touch the bottom, in joy at the floating of it. But I didn't want to tell anyone what I could do. I feared that if the Boy knew, he would cut off my arms to stop me swimming, like he was going to bite off my willy.

But I *could* swim, and it wasn't long before they all found out.

'Don't go out so far, Jimmy,' cried Ma, when she finally bothered to look.

I paddled back in, slowly so as not to be noticed, while Ralph gave the Boy a lesson in swimming, which he didn't like, because he cried and his cheeks went pale and his lips blue. That was one rare time I found myself grinning, but not for long.

Ralph shouted at the Boy not to be soppy and Michael struggled and cried. Then I felt something strange: it was as if I saw as clear as sunlight that the Boy was weaker than me and that he needed protecting, just like I did.

'He's my *brother*,' I thought, accepting that he was and always would be, whatever he said and did. Somewhere in the landscape of my mind, off on a distant horizon, that thought was a mountain, big as anything, and it wasn't all bad.

The Girl appeared one day of that long summer.

'Who are you?' I asked, because though I didn't have faith in anyone I knew, I still had faith in strangers.

'The little squit doesn't even know he has a cousin,' she said, turning her back on me, her mocking laughter even harsher than the Boy's it joined, making a terrible duet.

I had done something wrong again: I should have remembered I had a cousin. She came to stay from her boarding school.

'He can go to the party with you,' said Ma.

'We don't want him.'

'Well, nor do I, not this afternoon.'

Her hard red hand grew restless. She had put rouge on her cheeks and put her best frock on and straightened her seams and wanted us all right out of the way, as she often did.

'You're to take him or else until five o'clock. Get your shoes, Jimmy, you're to go with them.'

I went for my shoes but they had gone.

I always left them by the door, because that's where they lived. I thought they might die anywhere else.

'He can't come with us because he's got no shoes!'

Their laughter and mockery was in double time.

'Jimmy! Come here! Where are your shoes?'

'I . . .' but her hand crashed down.

'He's gone and lost them, Ma.'

'Well, then,' she said, snapping with impatience, 'take him all the same, just as he is, with no shoes. *Just as he is, or I'll . . . !*'

Out on the street, out of sight of the house, the Boy said, 'You're to walk thirteen paces behind us, because we'll not be seen with you if you've got no shoes. Not eleven not fourteen but thirteen, see?'

He liked his numbers and he knew I couldn't count, however hard I tried. And I tried that day. One and two and five and more. I couldn't count to thirteen, but I knew it was more than five and less than a million, so I moved my lips and said what numbers I could think of. Sometimes the Boy and the Girl turned round to see if I was nearer or further than thirteen paces away. I didn't want to be with them, but I didn't want to be alone.

Towards the end of that long walk up Star Hill they stopped bothering to look round, shouting over their shoulders, 'You're coming too near. Get back, get back!'

So I slowed down and listened miserably to them as they danced and sang their way along: *'He's got no shoes. He's got no shoes . . .'* And I tried so hard to count, my bare feet hurting on the paving stones.

After a while, all I could think of was where my shoes had gone; all I could think of was getting home to find them. The blood and the bruises on my shoeless feet didn't worry me at all. But when we got back to the house the shoes were still not there. Nor the next day, nor the day after that. Somewhere I knew they were dying, and calling my name because they needed my help.

I looked and I looked and I looked again and eventually I was so tired from looking that I sat down and cried on the step where they had been.

\* \* \*

For three days I hunted for them in every place I knew, snivelling to myself while the Boy and the Girl laughed at me, whispering their secrets, glancing their smirks my way. Not once did they help.

From time of waking to time of sleeping I searched, into the darkest corners of our house, into the darkness of their laughter.

I called out for my shoes quietly, from place to place, but they never came.

At the end of each day I went back to where I knew I had put them, where I always put them, hoping they had come back by themselves while I was looking in all the other places.

One evening, before I turned my head into my grief for the night, I took my clothes off right where I had left the shoes, where they lived. I put down the khaki shorts, the ones that my shoes knew, and then my striped T-shirt and my underpants, and I begged them to help to bring back my shoes.

'Please,' I said into the dark.

*Please come back*, I whispered.

In the morning I heard again the laughter of the Boy and Girl downstairs and their no-good scampering, but I still believed them when they called, 'Jimmy, Jimmy, your shoes have come home! Come and see what's here!'

I ran downstairs in a tumbling of joy, but there were no shoes and the Boy and Girl had gone. There were just my shorts and my shirt and my pants, and they had been wiped in fresh dog muck, brown and smelly and hardening into brown-black.

I stood staring, and I could hear my breathing thumping like my heart.

From far off came the sound of the Girl and the Boy out in the street, dancing and singing, dancing and singing.

But I just stood staring, and something in me cracked and began to die.

That was the true beginning of Darktime.

In the drumming of the silence I bent down and picked up my hand-me-downs, which were stained with dog muck, even my pants, and I put them on. Then I went out of the house and walked off down the road, away from the Boy and Girl, away from the house, away from Ma with her angry hitting hand.

Darktime was suddenly everywhere and all about for ever, and it didn't matter if I stayed or went. So I set off in my smelly clothes to see if there was someone somewhere who could help me find my shoes, so that my shoes could help me run away. That someone I was looking for was the Man Who Was. Then I began to run because the great sky broke after all the days of blue and large blobs of rain drummed on my head and my back and my thighs. I ran for my life, but it was too late. The rain caught me in its cage and I froze to the spot, terrified.

I stood there for a long, long time, sopping wet and getting wetter still, while thunder and lightning circled about me and I shook with fear.

Finally, a policeman appeared, with a big hat and a dark-blue uniform with silver buttons.

'What's your name, son?'

I stayed silent and shook my bent-down head.

I didn't even know my own name, that's how wrong I was to have lost my shoes and how much I smelt.

The policeman took me home.

'Your lad got lost, Mrs Rova, wandering by himself. He's got himself into a mess. He needs a wash and a drink and a good warm bed.'

When he was gone the hands of Ma hit me and dragged me upstairs and locked the door on the box room with me beyond it.

'You can stay like that, just as you are. You're a filthy, filthy boy.'

Later their laughter was sent through the keyhole of the door that was shut, and the dented brass door handle rattled to the tune: '*He's got no shoes. He's got no shoes. Jimmy's the boy who likes dog muck.*'

I looked around the little room, but there was nothing there I knew, nothing at all. I stood by the door with my head against it, as I did once by the garden gate in the time long ago, but this time I didn't call for Ma. I stood so long I wet my pants, my thighs shivering once the warmth of it turned to cold.

I stood so long I grew tired. Then I sat down in my wet shorts and reached for my feet and held them tight, because that was where my shoes had once been.

Then even memory slipped and slid and I could no longer remember what my shoes had looked like, or who it was who once held my hand long before, or even if he had, and I began to cry from the depths of the dark.

I was in Darktime and Jimmy was no more.

Raised voices out of the darkness.

Hushed voices.

A hairbrush rapped on knuckles.

The Boy and the Girl leaving for school. The Girl taken by a black shiny car to the railway station with her big case and Ma going with her.

'That's that then,' said Ma with satisfaction when she came back. Ma enjoyed saying goodbye to her own children and others'; she liked to see the back of them.

'What's the Girl's name, Ma?'

'Don't be silly.'

'I can't remember it.'

'Her name's Hilary.'

'Where's she gone?'

'She's boarding. You know that.'

'Where's the B . . . Where's Mikey?'

'Boarding now as well.'

'Oh.'

'One day you'll be old enough, you'll . . .'

But I didn't want to hear the rest. Didn't want to hear anything. Didn't know I had a brother. Didn't know I had a cousin. Didn't hardly know my own name.

I was in the house alone tap-tapping at the windowsill to drown out the sound of the wind in the cellar below, which tap-tap-tapped where the Coalman lived.

'Don't turn out the light. *Please*. Don't close the door. *Please*.'

'You deserve it shut and no light.'

These days the Coalman stalked me, and the Coalman could open the cellar door at night.

More and more when I awoke at night I woke into Darktime where there was no one but me.

'Ma, *Ma* . . .'

But I didn't shout, except in my mind, where I screamed as the Coalman, as black as everything else in my world, reached out to touch my shoulder.

A letter arrived from Africa.

'Jimmy, Granny's coming home and we're moving house.'

I only knew that when we moved it was certain and for ever that my shoes would be no more.

Wooden packing cases lined with silver paper; tea in their corners; hands and feet as busy as bees and no time for anything at all. Everything into the pantechnicon at last and the house empty everywhere.

'Where are you going now, Jimmy? I told you. Come down here! We're all waiting!'

'Looking.'

I searched through the echoing house for my shoes one final time, but they were nowhere to be found.

I went downstairs and then outside to the doorstep where they had once lived. I said my last goodbye to my shoes and left a stone on the step so they'd know I had waited as long as I could.

'Come on, Jimmy.'

Then the house disappeared behind us and was gone from my life for ever and ever.

I looked back one last time and, as the sun broke out of the sky and shone on the grey slates of the house, I saw myself reflected in the window of the black shiny car. My eyes were shadowed and dead; they looked as black as coal and I knew that behind them there was Darktime. I couldn't get it out of my head.

'I never, ever want to come back to Ramsgate again,' said Ma. 'It's a horrid place.'

A bugle call early in the morning from somewhere near the new house. Except it wasn't new but old, and big. The bugle sound rose way up into the sky, up high where Ma couldn't reach it with her voice and hands to despoil it; where the big ones couldn't steal it and hide it for ever.

Every morning that bugle call sounded, and it became my friend.
'Who's Granny?'
'My mother.'
'Has she come from Africa?'
'She's not come yet. It takes a long time to come from Africa.'
'When's she coming?'
The Boy and the Girl came in and when Ma was gone they said together, 'Granny'll never speak to *you*, because you don't know your name and you don't have shoes and you smell of dog muck.'
'Not ever?'
'*Never!*'

I could swim and I could hear the bugle sound, but it was not enough to stop Darktime deepening further still.
Sometimes I hid in the shrubbery.
I kept out of the way.
I wet my bed at night for the comfort of the warmth of it.
By day I was ignored and wandered by myself, and saw the world nearby and far off, nobody noticing that I had gone and come back again.
'Hello, Jimmy,' voices said, but I never said much. It was safer saying nothing.

There came a time when once a day and many times I went across the Green and stood at the edge of the shingle to look out across the sea for Granny's ship. But I began to think it never would.
There came a time when I began to stop thinking that it might.

I felt a shiver and a weakening.

My body was sickening to die.

I could swim in the sea but not in Darktime, and its tide was rising and soon would drown me.

'Jimmy's ill,' said someone up there in the light.

'Yes, I think he is.'

A journey by bus with a little leather suitcase.

A room, waiting alone.

A window onto blue, blue sky.

A man and a table and a carpet with holes and brown linoleum.

*Jimmy's going to the loony bin,'* the Girl had laughed and the Boy had repeated.

That's why I needed the suitcase.

Darktime got darker.

I was wandering through drumming silence already. Didn't want no loony bin.

'What's your name, son?' said the policeman.

I did something wrong: I didn't know my own name.

'You're Jimmy Rova, aren't you? You know that, don't you?'

'Am I?' I heard myself say.

Then I said, 'My granny was going to come home.'

I was trying to make a beam of light in my mind to lighten the lonely darkness.

'Was she?'

'I think so. She was going to help me find my shoes.'

'Are you sure?'

I didn't want to answer.

*No* is for ever, and *don't know* is nothing, and *yes* may never be.

'Your granny's coming over the sea?'

My name was Jimmy Rova and I looked past the policeman's legs to the far horizon where the ships went back and forth. Some went to London, some were on journeys to the Seven Seas, and a few went to Dover.

I saw a ship come sailing by with smoke coming from its funnels.

'Yes,' I said, trying to pull myself out of the darkness, 'she's on *that* ship.'

So there I stood looking, the policeman at my side.

'Come on, son, I'll walk you home.'

'She'll come one day,' whispered the Jimmy boy who was me, the boy with no shoes. I often whispered to myself. There was no one else to whisper to. Words made no sense in a world of silence.

I took the policeman's hand and turned from the horizon to begin the long familiar trudge back into Darktime.

I had three things I could call my own.

I could swim.

I had a bugle sound that was my friend.

I had a granny who I believed one day might come.

All of which were true: I *could* swim; every morning at 6.15 sharp the bugle *did* sound beyond the darkness, to remind me of what could be . . . and one great day in my life Granny *did* come, right out of Africa, across the Seven Seas, in a ship that puffed black smoke and did not go to London Town and did not go to Dover but came straight towards our shingly shore, nearer and nearer, bigger and bigger, so huge it scared everyone as it crashed right up the beach to where I had stood waiting for so long, waiting until Granny came to rescue me.

It was Granny who brought light into my Darktime and taught me what to do.

# 3

# MY WAKE-UP CALL

The house we moved to was near the home of the Band of the Royal Marines, all five hundred and fifty-one of them. They practised music every day, and every Sunday morning they marched through our town on their way to the Garrison Church: left right, left right, left right.

Their drums drummed and their piccolos trilled and the big pom-pom marched in the middle of the second rank. Out in front the Drum Major tossed his great silver stick high up into the air to catch the sun, and he never dropped it once.

Every morning at 6.15 sharp, the Royal Marine bugler, with bright brass buttons that went in a line right up his tunic, would march across the parade ground and stand to attention by the flagpole, which had rattled in the wind all night long. Then he would sound his bugle and wake up the Marines, and me.

I would lie waiting in my bed, sometimes shivering with cold because we had no heating in our house, and we had no carpets, only cracked and freezing lino, which tore at my bare feet when I went to the bathroom. Then I would listen to my wake-up call and imagine I was one of the notes the bugler blew, flying up into the sky, right past the top of the pole, so that I was looking down over our town.

There below me I could see the fishermen pushing out their boats. There were the miners in Upper Stoning coming home tired after a nightshift at Nunnestone colliery. There was the milkman from Stoning Dairies and his cart pulled by a horse. There was a lamp-lighter who went round with a ladder and a pole at dawn to turn down the streetlamps. This was not olden times; this was nearly yesterday.

There was the Pier reaching out to sea with a flag at the end. The flag was always frayed from the constant wind, which sometimes blew so hard it made seahorses of the waves, who galloped away to where I had never been but dreamed I might one day go.

Up our way – we lived in South Stoning then – I could see the lifeboat on its ramp on the Promenade, tilted towards the shingle and the sea. It was always ready to be launched for those in peril on the sea.

And down on the shore, where the shingle shifted and roared even on calm days, there were the longshoremen, walking beside the dangerous waves in their thick jackets and boots, searching for driftwood and treasure.

One day the bugler woke me but I wasn't able to fly up with his sound. I couldn't even see the daylight or raise my head. Behind my eyes there was a cruel drum beating – *thump, thump, THUMP!* – and my feather pillow felt as hard as a kerbstone and made my neck ache. I couldn't seem to breathe.

I was so ill I was too weak to cry. Ma came and put her hand to my forehead and sent for Dr Test, the famous lifeboat doctor. He had a thin mouth and Brylcreemed hair. He poked me and put cold fingers on my chest. He opened my mouth. He looked at my eyes. He said I had diphtheria and that I might die.

Days and weeks went by. I was so ill I could hardly see or hear. I no longer heard the bugler sound his bugle to wake me up. I grew weaker and weaker.

One day an ambulance came to take me into hospital and Ma said, 'When you come out Granny'll be here. She's coming home from staying with Auntie Ellie in Africa.'

'Why?'

Ma said, 'Because no one else wants her. I can't say I do, but duty calls.'

'What does she look like?'

Ma said, 'Like me, only older.'

I knew then that Granny would be pasty-faced and the oldest person I would ever know.

* * *

The hospital had rows and rows of metal beds painted blue-grey to match the walls. They put me in a bed with movable sides, which Nurse pulled up at night so I wouldn't fall out. I was in a room all by myself and when Ma walked away and left me I thought the world had ended.

I remember a boy crying.

Even now, even today, when I sometimes wake up in the night, I hear him crying still and find his voice in my throat.

Nurse wore a white mask and a silver buckle on her belt and opened the window in the afternoon at three. She closed it again at six.

One evening she forgot to close the window. The wind blew at the curtain and made it move, but I didn't mind. I could smell the sea and hear the seagulls call. I felt the fresh night air on my face and arms. It was the best night I had.

Then, when dawn came, something happened better still. I heard the bugle again. It was a long way away but it was the bugle all the same, so I knew the bugler was still alive and that my home must still be there.

That evening I said, 'Please leave the window open.'

Nurse said, 'Don't be silly.'

'*Please*,' I said.

Nurse said nothing, but her silver buckle shone as bright as needles as she closed it.

When dawn came I got out of bed by climbing over its high sides, which rattled and squeaked. That took me a long time, I was so weak. I tried to reach up to the window but it was too high. I pulled the chair over and climbed up. I was so weak my legs shook and the chair rat-tat-tatted against the wall. I opened the window and put my ear to the gap. The cold hurt but the air was good.

I heard Nurse walk back and forth outside.

I knew I wasn't strong enough to wait for long.

The curtains fluttered over my face and then I heard the bugle sound the wake-up call to tell me he was there.

I did that for five dawns running before they caught me because I fell off the chair and I was too weak to get back into bed. They took the chair away to stop me doing it again, and I was allowed to hear the bugle call no more.

After that, I got worse. People came to stare at me, and Dr Test as well. They all stood whispering at the foot of my bed and then went outside into the corridor. Then their whispers died away and I was alone.

I heard the boy whimpering every night and growing weaker and weaker like me. I knew that boy. He was the Boy With No Shoes and I was crying for him. I knew that even if they brought the chair back I wouldn't be able to climb out of bed to open the window again.

One day Nurse came with Dr Test and a man in black clothes. Ma arrived and they brought a chair for her to sit on, so I knew it was serious. They poked and prodded me as if I wasn't there and shook their heads as if to say it was my fault. Ma didn't seem to know what to say or do. Then everyone went but her. I could tell she wanted to go too, and I knew that when she did I was going to die.

When night came Ma suddenly got up and, after a whispered conversation at the door, she left and someone else sat in the chair.

I felt a hand on my forehead and heard words spoken that were as soft as summer days. 'Sleep now, my dear,' were those magical words.

Later, I woke up in the middle of the dark night, but I was not alone because the hand that had comforted me now held my hand. There was a smell I had never smelt before. It was mothballs. It was my granny's smell. She held my hand all night, and then all day, and then all night after that.

I heard her say to someone, 'Jimmy needs something to hold on to. He needs a helping hand to bring him to the shore.'

Her voice was old and cracked like china, but it was strong, much stronger than any voice I had ever known.

She had arrived in the ship on the shingly shore and when someone had told her I was dying she would have none of it. She didn't take off her coat or open her suitcase or stop for a meal. She came straight away to see me and she gave me a hand that felt like home.

When dawn came, a long time later, I opened my eyes. That was when I saw my granny for the first time. She had grey-white hair held in a net. Her eyes were dark and sharp. She had a silver brooch on her blouse and a thin gold ring on a bent and swollen finger on her right hand. She had a nose that was as long and sharp as a darning needle.

'Jimmy,' she said, 'I'm your granny and you're not getting better and you've got to tell me why.'

I didn't have an answer.

Then she said, 'Why are you looking at the window?'

I didn't reply.

Then she said, 'Do you want it opened?'

I said, 'It's not allowed.'

'Who said?'

'Nurse.'

'Well,' said Granny, 'she's Nurse and I'm your granny and you're going to find there's a world of difference.'

She got up with a look on her face like walls would fall down if they got in her way, and she opened the window. Then she sat down again.

I smelt the sea air and I heard the gulls.

'Granny,' I said, 'is the bugler still alive?'

'Which bugler, my dear?'

As she spoke, the Royal Marine bugler blew his wake-up call. It was far off but strong. I held my granny's hand tighter still for joy.

After that the window was kept open every night and my granny never left. She slept as best she could in the chair by the bed. They brought her food and grumbled, but she stayed exactly where she was. She told me stories about her life, but still I did not get better.

One day Granny said, 'What do you want most in all the world?'

My heart sank because I thought she was asking so that she could get me a present before she went away again.

'Are you going back to Auntie Ellie in Africa?'

'Not in a month of Sundays,' she said firmly; 'not for one hundred gold sovereigns. Your home is my home now and always will be. Now, what do you want most in the world?'

'I don't know,' I said.

'You better know or you'll never get it,' she said. 'So think and tell me when I come back tomorrow.'

Then she took off her silver brooch and she gave it to me to hold instead of her hand so that she could go and get some sleep. She had sat by my bed for nearly six days and nights to make sure I stayed alive.

'Granny,' I said when she came back, 'could you get me *anything* in the whole world?'

'No, my dear, I certainly could not, and you wouldn't want it if I could! But I dare say I could lead you to the things that matter.'

'I know what I want.'

'Tell me.'

'You can't get it, though.'

Granny stayed silent.

I said, 'What I want most is for the Royal Marine bugler to play in my room.'

I told her about the Royal Marine Band and all they did. I told her about how I had listened every morning to the wake-up call before I got ill. I think that was the first time I told my granny everything.

When I was finished she stood up and put on her hat and coat and got her stick. That look was back in her eyes, the same as when she opened the window.

'Where are you going, Granny?'

'To see somebody,' she said.

She did not come back the next day, or the day after that, but she sent a message to say that she would be back very soon.

An afternoon passed, then an evening. Night came and with it a rising wind so strong that it brought the sound of the waves and shingle right to the bottom of my bed. The curtains shifted in the draught and banged but still Nurse didn't close the window. She was afraid of what my granny would say.

I slept deep and long because I knew Granny was coming back; I knew she would.

But the next thing I heard was the sound of marching steps.

Left right, left right, left right!

*LEFT RIGHT, LEFT RIGHT, LEFT RIGHT!*

Then, even before I could open my eyes, I heard the bugle call. It was right there in my room, right above me.

I have never in all my life been so surprised.

The bugler was so tall he went up to the ceiling. He was so wide he blocked out half the room. In his shiny bugle I could see the reflection of the rising sun. His bright brass buttons caught the sunlight too.

As the bugler played the wake-up call its notes bounced all around the room, over the bed and into my head, through one ear and out the other and then back again.

'Lad,' he said when he was finished, with the bugle sound echoing all about, 'it's time to get up.'

I said, 'But I'm ill.'

'No shirkers in the Royal Marines,' he said, 'and no excuses.'

Then came the second surprise.

He put his bugle beside my bed, leant down and heaved me up and took me to the window. He opened it as wide as it would go and he held me there.

'Listen!' he said.

I listened but there was no sound.

I said, 'I can't hear anything, sir.'

'That's right,' he said. 'And that's because I'm here and not out on the parade ground. Now listen to me, Sonny Jim. There's five hundred and fifty-one lads getting up this morning without Reveille being sounded, so what do you think about that?'

'I don't know,' I said.

'When you've worked it out you write to me and let me know the answer.'

'I'll try, sir,' I said, looking at his shiny bugle.

'Do you want me to play again and wake up the whole hospital?'

'Yes, please,' I said.

So he did, so loud that I had to put my hands to my ears.

Then he said, 'I've got to go, and as I can't leave my bugle here I'll give you this instead.'

That was when I got my third surprise.

He grasped one of the brass buttons on his tunic and he pulled it right off, just like that.

He held it out and gave it to me.

'If five hundred and fifty-one lads can get up *without* a bugler, you can get up *with* one in your room! That's the answer I was looking for, but write to me when you're better all the same.'

'Yes, sir,' I said.

Then he tucked his bugle under his arm, stood to attention, saluted, and marched out of the room *LEFT RIGHT, LEFT RIGHT, LEFT RIGHT.*

Then all down the corridor . . .

*Left right, left right, left . . .*

Granny came back later that day.

'Well?' she said.

I told her the bugler had been there and I showed her the bright brass button to prove it.

'When can I go home?' I asked.

'When you're better.'

'I *am* getting better.'

Two weeks later, I went home.

Granny was there to meet me.

'I've got to write a letter,' I said, 'but I can't write and I can't read.'

'You soon will,' she said firmly. 'Meanwhile, you can draw.'

I drew a picture of the bugler by the flagpole with a brass button missing on his tunic because it was after he had visited me. I posted it in the red pillar box on the Front.

A week later I got a letter back. Inside was a white card with black printing on it. It was an invitation for Granny and me – to a concert to be given by the Royal Marine Band. The invitation came from Colonel Sir Richard Marquand, the commanding officer.

It had blue handwriting on it. Granny read it and smiled, which she didn't often do.

'It's to you, and says, "I am glad to hear you are getting better. I hope you will be well enough to escort your grandmother to our concert, since ladies cannot come unaccompanied." '

I could hardly sleep the night before. When I did wake it was six-fifteen and the bugler was bugling. I listened just as I did before I was ill and once again I flew up into the air like one of the notes.

I saw across my town. I saw the fishermen, the miners and the longshoremen. I saw the Pier, and the seahorses racing over the sea. The only difference now was that Granny was walking along the Promenade wearing her hat and coat and carrying her stick.

When the wake-up call was over and the last note brought me back down to my bed, I got up and ran across the cracked lino out into the corridor and along to my granny's bedroom.

I knocked on the door until she called me in.

I said, 'Granny, it's time to get up because we've got a busy day. Did you hear the bugler call?'

'I do not hear as well as I used,' she said, 'so when you hear the bugle you come and tell me, and I'll know the long night is over and it's time to get up. Will you do that for me?'

I said I would, and I always did until the time came for us to leave that house.

# 4

# THE HEAD WHO LISTENED

One July Granny and Ma agreed about something for once, and that was my education.

It was the end of the summer term and my school report said that because of my not being able to read and write I was still a backward child and must be kept behind for a second year running in the junior class. Ma could see the point, but Granny could not. But both agreed on this: if I was kept down another year things would never improve.

As Ma was tired and had other things on her mind, it was Granny herself who went to talk to Mr Thompson, the Headmaster. She took me with her but told me to stay silent until I was asked to speak. Which she didn't need to as I rarely spoke anyway and then only to her.

'My grandson is not stupid,' she said.

'He cannot benefit from lessons in the next class up if he cannot read or write,' replied Mr Thompson, closing the file and getting up. He was a busy man and wanted to get rid of Granny, but it was never that easy.

'Why not?' said Granny, not moving, and making him sit down again. 'And what exactly, may I ask, does "benefit" mean? More goes into his head than comes out of it, of that I am sure.'

'Are you a trained educationalist?' Mr Thompson asked my granny.

'I am a Baptist, which is a great deal better,' said Granny sharply, 'and I have lived in Africa where many people cannot read or write but grow up to be a lot wiser and more humane than people from Great Britain who can.'

'You are referring to the natives?' said Mr Thompson.

'I am referring to the indigenous peoples,' said Granny, 'most of whom are sensible enough not to put reading, writing, Shakespeare, the Houses of Parliament, the British Monarchy and its Established Church very high on their list of priorities.'

'Yes, but how can we possibly know that your grandson is taking things in if he cannot read or write and never talks?' said Mr Thompson, growing exasperated with Granny, as people often did.

'If I find a way for you to know, will you allow him to move up?'

Mr Thompson sighed and said he might.

'To his proper year?' said Granny, who never gave up.

'It is unlikely that your grandson will be able to do anything in the next three months that will demonstrate to his teachers and myself that he should be promoted to his own age group. But if he can, none will be happier than I.'

'Oh?' said Granny.

'Yes. Children who are kept down tend to be disruptive influences.'

'Jimmy is as quiet as a mouse, perhaps too quiet, and he has never been disruptive, I believe?' said Granny.

'True,' said Mr Thompson, rising for a final time. 'But he'll have to prove the abilities you claim for him by the Friday before the start of the autumn term, which is when we draw up the final class list. That's the third of September.'

'We will find a way,' said Granny grimly, 'won't we, Jimmy?'

'Er, yes,' I said, which were the only words I uttered in Mr Thompson's hearing.

That was the same summer Granny decided to stop eating meat for a time. She joined the Society for Vegetarians and started boiling carrots and growing lettuces so much that Ma grew very cross.

'We have teeth,' said Ma, 'and are carnivores.'

'I have false teeth now,' said Granny, 'and eating meat, apart from being morally wrong, is growing more difficult for me.'

They agreed to differ and talked about how I was going to show I could take things in.

'Well, I don't know,' said Ma, 'and I've got to go to work. You've taken up this battle, Mother, and you should see it through.'

'Humph!' said Granny.

The reason Ma was anxious to go to work was that she had just become farm secretary to Mr Jardey of Wingham, whose business was livestock and whose cheeks looked like mutton chops. He was a widower and Ma often did not come home till late, he worked her so hard.

'Humph!' Granny would say that summer when Ma came home with rouge on her cheeks and smelling of scent.

The spring had been very warm and that summer turned into a heat wave which went on and on and on. It was so hot that the tar on the road melted and ruined Granny's shoes. As I often wore no shoes it stuck to my feet and got between my toes, and we had to get it off with turpentine.

There was no rain for weeks on end, so I was happy. Rain always troubled me. The grass on the Green by the Promenade turned yellow and dry so that the earth showed through. Everything in the greenhouse died for lack of water. All Granny's lettuces shrivelled up and died and she only kept her tomatoes alive by sprinkling them at dawn with the water from the glass in which she kept her false teeth.

The one place you could get cool was in the sea, so that was where the whole town seemed to go, morning, noon and night. Ma came and sat on the shingle with salty egg sandwiches and home-made ginger beer.

This was the first time I remember Uncle Max visiting. He was a scientist and lived in London, which Ma said was even hotter than Stoning. Ma invited him to came down to stay with us, so he did. He had his new car and his new fiancée Antonia, who was always doing her hair and nails and wore rouge on her cheeks like a film star.

I wore nothing but khaki shorts and got as brown as a berry. My brother Michael stayed as white as a sheet. When my cousin Hilary turned up she sat gracefully here and gracefully there but never took many clothes off. She just got hot and bad-tempered.

Everybody else said, 'There's never been a summer like it; let's enjoy it while we can.'

At weekends, trippers came by train from London Town. They bought Mr Gelato's ice cream, which was the Best in Britain, and candyfloss. They sat on the shingle with handkerchiefs on their heads and shrimped in the waves at low tide when the sand was exposed. Men unbuttoned their shirts and ladies took off their cardigans and blouses down to their bras and pulled up their skirts to their knickers.

They all turned lobster pink and the St John Ambulance Brigade was kept busy with fainting ladies and lost children. A dog went mad in Nelson Road and attacked the tyre of the No 80 Dover bus, owned by the East Kent Road Car Company.

Then the Great White Shark came and ruined it all.

He was washed up on the beach opposite our house and was so big and heavy that nobody could move him.

That was not the worst of it. With the sun being so hot he began to rot and he sent a pong all over Stoning. Wherever you went there was no escape from that dreadful smell.

Also, people said there might be other sharks about, live ones this time, so it was not safe to swim. Mothers wouldn't allow their children into the water any more, so there seemed no escape from either the smell or the heat, and all because of the Great White Shark.

But I found that there was one place where it was possible to escape. It was on the windward side of the shark, which was usually between it and the falling tide. So, as Granny said it was all stuff and nonsense about there being other sharks, I used to go down there and loll in the water and watch the shark rotting more and more and see the people staring and holding their noses.

Granny told me a lot about sharks because she had seen them off the coast of Africa.

'We had one that terrorized the coast and ate people, and your Auntie Ellie nearly died of fright, the silly girl.'

I asked, 'What happened?'

'Ellie did not do as she was told,' said Granny darkly, pursing her mouth and frowning.

'Why didn't you tell somebody to go and kill the shark?'

'For the very good reason that sharks have the right to live like the rest of us. Unfortunately, they are sometimes inclined to overdo things and eat people, which is not very nice. Perhaps they need to be taught the error of their ways.'

I began to feel sorry for the dead shark, which had not had the benefit of Granny telling it the error of its ways and so had probably eaten too many people. If it had had the benefit of her advice, it might still be alive.

Lolling in the sea, looking at the shark, I suddenly had an idea and got out of the water and went straight inside to get on with it.

'Granny,' I said, 'I need a pencil and paper so I can draw the shark.'

'What a good idea,' she said.

After that you could not stop me drawing that shark and other sharks like it. I drew them on the beach and in the sea. I drew them having ice cream and taking tea with Granny in the garden. I drew them big and small. But most of all I drew the Great White Shark swimming in the sea and eating things, back in the days when if it had learnt the error of its ways it would not have died.

'Granny,' I said, 'I've run out of drawing paper again.'

She bought me some more sheets, and coloured crayons and charcoal. That summer I lost myself in drawing, and in every picture there was that shark. Sometimes I drew people I knew, like the Royal Marines and the Armed Forces men who came to study how to move the shark; and Freddie Hammel, coxswain of the lifeboat, who liked to pass the time of day with Granny. But always there was the shark, and always it was alive again.

One day I came back from watching tennis through the hedge in Fitzroy Square and I found the fire brigade had come to take the shark away. Men in black rubber suits and masks climbed on it and hacked it with axes as if it was just wood and had not once been a living, breathing shark.

Then they put the head and fin and other bits on a lorry and sprayed disinfectant where it had been. When they went, it seemed to me they left behind a great hole that could never be filled again, and I was sad.

That evening Granny asked, 'What's wrong?'

I said I had nothing to draw any more. I said I hadn't said goodbye to the shark. I said . . . and I cried. I felt I had lost a friend.

Michael said, 'It's just a smelly lump of fish meat and bones and you're just stupid. So stupid you can't even read or write, so I don't know what you're crying for. At least it means we won't have a pong in our noses or any more of your stupid drawings littering the place.'

I stopped drawing for a time.

After a few days Granny said, 'You know where your drawing things are, Jimmy, so if you change your mind . . .'

Three days later I did change my mind because another good idea came into my head. I took my paper and crayons and I went along the beach to where the great brambles grow, where I knew a hiding place nobody else knew. I crawled in there and I began to draw the pictures in my mind. I called all the pictures I drew 'Granny and the Great White Shark' and I put numbers on them, starting with 1 and going on past 30.

When they were finished I put them on the bramble bushes in my hidey-hole one after another, like a cartoon story in the *Beano* or the *Dandy*. I would go there whenever I wanted and pull them out and put them in a row and just sit looking at them, adding bits when I felt like it to make my story better.

'What have you been doing today? Where have you been?' Ma would ask when she got home from work. But I said nothing because I didn't know how to explain about the picture story.

'On the beach,' I said.

Not even Granny knew about the pictures, just me alone.

That summer when it was so hot and it never rained, Granny tried to teach me to read so that I could go up to the next class. But I could not learn, I just could not. The printed page was double Dutch to me.

I preferred to listen to Granny and Ma and Uncle Max; and to hear the talk of Freddie Hammel and the other fishermen. Granny said I was safe with them and they just let me be. They didn't mind my silence.

Then September came and Granny said, 'Well, my dear, I am very much afraid that we have nothing to show for the summer except those drawings you made when the shark was here. We'll have to do the best we can with those. Come along.'

We walked up to school and found Mr Thompson and Granny showed him my pictures. To her surprise, he thought they were interesting and he called in the art master. All the teachers were there that day to discuss the form lists for the new term starting later that week. We had gone in early as their meeting was starting at eleven.

The art master and Mr Thompson looked and looked at my pictures and then asked me questions about them. I didn't know how to reply and said next to nothing. It was as if they didn't believe I had drawn them, so the more they asked, the less I said.

'He *can* talk if only you give him time,' said Granny. She was like a seabird on Dover cliffs protecting her chicks against the rooks. But it did no good.

'If only he had more to show than just these few pictures, Mrs Drickner,' he said finally. 'I mean . . . they do show good observation and considerable persistence in one so young, but by themselves . . . I'm sorry, but he'll have to stay down next term. Perhaps in the spring . . .'

I could see that Granny was very disappointed. She didn't like to admit defeat. But what more could she say?

I was thinking about that and feeling I had let her down as we went out of Mr Thompson's room. Then I thought of something I could say myself. It was almost the first time I said anything by myself in that school.

'I did some more drawings, lots.'

'Pardon?' said the art master.

'More pictures,' I said. 'There are lots and lots of them.'

'Where?' said the art master, interested now and glancing at Mr Thompson. 'I would like to see them.'

'Where are they, Jimmy?' asked Granny.

I said, 'They're in my den among the blackberry brambles on the Seafront. I must have done them, because no one else but me knows where it is, so I'm not pretending or telling fibs. I could show them to you if you like.'

'It's not me that matters now, Jimmy,' said Granny.

Mr Thompson looked at his watch and said, 'I haven't much time as there's a meeting at eleven, but if they're not too far . . . ?'

Granny looked grateful for once.

'In all the time I've known young Jimmy Rova,' said Mr Thompson, 'this is the first time he has volunteered anything at all. What are we teachers for if we can't listen when our pupils start talking? That's what I tell new teachers and I should practise what I preach. I think we should give him the benefit of the doubt and see what he has to offer. My deputy can take the meeting in my place.'

Mr Thompson and I walked all the way to the Front and then along past our house towards South Stoning Castle and my den. Granny and the art master came as well.

'There's not much room,' I said when we got to the tunnel in the brambles that led to my den, 'and you can only get in on your hands and knees.'

The brambles grew much higher than them, and were thicker than barbed wire.

Mr Thompson said the art master should come and look first as he was the youngest and fittest. He crawled in after me but only looked for a few moments at my pictures before he said, 'You stay here, Jimmy, and I'll ask Mr Thompson to . . . to crawl in too.'

I heard them talking to each other. Then Mr Thompson knelt on the ground near the entrance to the tunnel and peered in at my den. We looked at each other. I didn't say anything but he did.

'I'm a bit chubby and a bit stiff and a bit old for this sort of thing, Jimmy.'

'It's not hard,' I said; 'just bend low and don't mind the thorns.'

'Er, right,' he said, huffing and puffing as he shoved himself in and I tried to untangle the brambles from his hair and jacket as he crawled along.

He grinned when he finally reached my den and looked up at the brambles all around.

'How I'm going to get out I can't imagine!' he said. 'So . . . these are your pictures, are they?'

One by one he looked at them, saying not a word.

'Shall I explain them to you?' I said.

He said he would be grateful if I would.

'It might take long,' I said.

He said it didn't matter.

'It's a story,' I said, 'that I made up myself.'

'I like stories,' he said. 'My meeting will be all the better for me not being there. Some things can wait and some things can't. This can't. This is about the shark that was washed up on the shore at Stoning this summer, isn't it?'

I nodded.

'I didn't want it to die,' I said. 'I nearly died once and it's not very nice. Sometimes . . .'

'Sometimes what, Jimmy?'

The way he said it I knew he was on my side. He looked funny in my den all squatted down but I liked him there. I had no friends to show my place and my things to, and Granny wasn't the same.

So first I showed him my collection of flints and told him how flints were made, like Granny explained. I showed him my dried wood from the beach and the patterns of animals and places they made. I showed him where the red ants were and we watched them carrying bits of decayed blackberries. I gave him the string of knots that Freddie Hammel taught me to tie and told him all the names and all their uses. I talked about dynamos in motorcars, like Uncle Max taught me. I told him lots of things I knew.

'Now, Jimmy,' he said finally, 'tell me the story of the shark you've drawn.'

'All right,' I said, turning to the first picture, 'this is where it starts . . .'

I could talk to him then like I talked to Granny, because he didn't hurry me and I knew he was listening. Sometimes he asked questions but mostly he just listened.

'Oh dear, have I said too many words?' I said towards the end.

'Not at all,' he said. 'Now we had got up to the bit where . . .'

Right to the end he was patient, right to the last picture of all.

He looked at me and I looked at him.

'There isn't any more,' I said. 'That's the end.'

'Yes,' he said, looking at my pictures one by one again. 'Jimmy, you were sad about the shark.'

I nodded and said I was. Then I thought a bit and I found myself say, 'But not any more. Not now I've told you the story. So it's all right.'

I thought he was worried about me, but I had known worse things than the shark dying and ponging and being taken away.

When it was all over and we were out of my den and back on the Seafront again, I found more than an hour and a half had passed. Granny and the art master were up on the Promenade, sitting on a bench.

'I don't think I could crawl in there very easily,' said Granny, looking back at the brambles and pretending to hitch up her skirt, 'but if I must, I must . . .'

'There's no need,' said Mr Thompson. 'I have seen and heard what I needed to and I've been thinking about things as Jimmy talked. I don't think that it is to Jimmy's advantage . . .'

My heart sank.

'. . . that he remains in a lower class. He has a lot to learn but also a lot to contribute to his peers, more than I appreciated. The thought he's put into the drawings he's done this summer shows that. I shall recommend he goes into his proper class with his own age group. I am sure he will learn to read and write in his own good time, and in his own way. Meanwhile, he must work hard, very hard, at everything else . . .'

My heart was filled with joy to see Granny look so proud and pleased.

'Do you think, gentlemen, it would be wise if one of you retrieved my grandson's pictures and we took them in. I do believe it is coming on to rain.'

I looked at Mr Thompson and he looked at me. He smiled and I grinned. Rain was how my story ended, because the shark dies and the last thing was rain, big black bars of rain, like a cage, like Darktime, out of which that shark never could go until I came and rescued him into the world of my picture, where he was forever free.

I fetched the pictures myself, but as we went back to the Promenade the sky began to darken and rain started, so I grew really scared. Mr Thompson and the art master left at the double and Granny said that she hoped they wouldn't get wet.

Granny knew I was frightened of rain, so she held my arm tight and guided me into someone's doorway until the rain lessened and we could walk home. Then she made me a celebratory cup of cocoa and opened a special tin of biscuits. She began to look through the pictures I had rescued from my den.

'Now,' she said finally, 'perhaps you can explain to me exactly what they are about?'

So I told Granny the story I had drawn, the way I told it to Mr Thompson, but what she said at the end was different from what he said.

'Jimmy . . . do you know why you're so afraid of rain?'

I shook my head. I couldn't really remember much about the past, just the Man and the shoes that once had been. I didn't want to remember any more and if Granny knew, I didn't want her to tell me.

There was a drumming against the window pane as the rain started up again.

'I don't like being scared, Granny, but . . .'

I stared at the window. The rain running down caught the light of the sky clearing over the sea and it made a cage.

'But what, Jimmy?'

Granny didn't like unfinished sentences. She said that sloppy sentences came from sloppy minds.

'I made the shark live again so he could be free and swim wherever he wanted. That's what I want for me.'

'It's what most people want,' said Granny, quietly smiling a little and putting her hand on my arm, 'but so few find.'

'Did you find it?'

'It was right in front of my nose,' she said.

# 5

# THE MAN WHO WASN'T

There was a man who came visiting Ma at Christmas and sometimes in the holidays, when he had nowhere better to go.

He travelled by train from his ancient university town and carried a worn brown suitcase with books in it, and a leather briefcase with clinking bottles, which were full of gin. I remember him just once before Darktime, wearing a khaki uniform and an officer's hat, and a Sam Browne. That was his shiny leather belt, which was the only belt I ever knew which had a Christian name.

He never kissed me, but sometimes he would rub his cheek against mine just to show it was like sandpaper, which it was. It is the smell of gin and cigarettes I remember most, and the dry red scabs on his elbows and legs which left trails of dry skin on the carpets. Not many in my class knew the word *psoriasis*.

His coming and going was not often or regular, not like the sun and the moon and the tides; it was sometimes, like gales in the winter and showers in summer – and like Ma's tempers. Ma always had her hair done when he was coming, and got out the powder puff and rouge, and took more trouble with the food and got fussed up and angry.

He didn't kiss her much either. He slept in the best room, the one next to Granny's, which overlooked the sea. The others called it Daddy's room, but I didn't.

He was the man who wasn't Daddy to me.

Ma called him Scup because his name was Howard Scupple, and though he was her husband, so she said and so did he, she called herself Mrs Rova and never explained why. The Boy and the Girl were from the Scupple family but I was a Rova, which just went to show something no one ever explained.

'Why?'

'Because.'

So I never knew the cause of my name, but one thing I did know: Scupple wasn't it and didn't feel like it.

There were Kodak snaps of Howard Scupple near a camp with the big boy, and his hair was dark then.

But he never went camping with me.

He never climbed the sycamore near our front door. So he never smelt the lichen on his hands.

He never went down onto the beach. So he never skimmed flat stones on the sea.

He never came to sports day. So he never knew that I could throw the cricket ball.

He never once sat and watched the waves with me. So he never knew the many things I knew, or heard the things I heard, or saw the things I saw.

In his room, which they called Daddy's, there was a desk at which he read and wrote and drank. In the bottom drawer on the right, under a book, there was a Colt revolver with a brown wooden handle all criss-cross scored for gripping, and a barrel, dark but shiny.

In another drawer was a cardboard box in which there were bullets wrapped up in greaseproof paper. I didn't know the bullets were for the gun but I did know that bullets went off.

This man called Daddy who wasn't mine had a voice like the shingly shore and chuckled more than he laughed. He could tell stories till kingdom come to which the adults would listen and laugh but which passed high over my head like honking geese on a night in autumn.

Some evenings he drank gin and his eyes changed and seemed not to be eyes but points: hard flinty points like pebbles on the beach that have gone red and cracked in a fire.

He still talked when he drank, but he didn't chuckle so much, and I didn't speak because if I did it provoked a joke and a laugh that seemed a part of Darktime and felt in my mind like a slap. His words came out of his mouth like unfriendly armies and his books were like their castle keeps, and his room smelt of stale cigarettes.

Once, when I had nothing to do and his door was open, I watched him writing with a cigarette smoking in his mouth and a glass of gin caught in the sun. He sat there as sharp and clear as an icicle.

I watched him and my heart beat hard before I dared to go in.

'What are you writing?' I asked.

'It's a poem,' he said. It was only then that I saw his eyes were gin-hard and his mouth wore its cruel and crooked smile.

'What's a pome?' I asked, waiting, but he wouldn't say. Daddy was a scholar and a teacher but he never learnt the language children speak, so he couldn't teach them.

'A *poem*!' he said, irritable like Ma, his hand reaching for the glass as he frowned. He spoke in a voice that wanted to push me out of the room.

'I know a poem,' I said carefully.

'Do you?' he let his voice say.

He looked at me so hard, so cold, his eyes so filled with flint, that try as I might I couldn't even remember the first line. I crept away, and never tried to tell him a poem again.

> *Bobby had a shilling*
> *All his very own*
> *Should he buy a whistle*
> *Or an ice cream cone?*

That was the poem that man who wasn't my Daddy never heard from me.

This man came to our house every Christmas Eve when all the work was done. He didn't see the shopping coming in or the turkey being carried through the door on the 23rd. He didn't know the scrimping and the saving my Ma had to do to get his presents, or see the firelight dancing in her eyes in the nights before as she dreamed her dreams of what Christmas ought to be but never was.

No, he arrived as late as possible on the 24th, or so it seemed to me, on the last train down, with his briefcase of drink bottles, and the work in his big case so important that he had to go straight to his room to begin.

I called him Daddy but I knew he wasn't. There could be no love lost because none had ever been found.

He acted Father Christmas after the Queen's speech, giving out the presents from under the tree, reading the labels, and making us thank out loud whoever sent us things.

'Thank you, Uncle Max,' I would say and I meant it.

'Thank you, Mrs Kreble, for the pound note,' I would say and wonder what she looked like.

Mrs Kreble was my godmother but I never saw her until years later. She was another who never came to walk the beach with me.

'Thank you, Auntie Ellie in Salisbury, Rhodesia,' I had to say each Christmas. It sounded exciting and made me think of sharks. At the mention of Ellie's name Granny pursed her lips but Ma looked indifferent.

'Thank you, Mr Sawyer, for the crinkly five-pound note,' I said just the once, since I never heard from him again. Cecil Sawyer was my godfather, but he never stood on the beach as dusk drew in and felt the wind at his cheeks as he looked at the lights of the ships sheltering offshore.

The annual coming of the Man Who Wasn't My Father meant there were always arguments at Christmas. Always. And one year a silence descended inside our heads after he opened the present that was from his friends in Oxford who he lodged with. Their present was a dressing gown made of silk with a twisted cord of silk as well. It shimmered by the firelight and was beautiful. Our house was make-do-and-mend, not beautiful.

There was silence because the next present he opened was the one from Ma for which she had saved and saved from money from her farm secretary work. She had made lists of what to get the Man Who Wasn't and finally chosen something from Marks and Spencer: it was a dressing gown with a cord with tassels on the end. But it wasn't of silk and it didn't shimmer in the firelight.

'Well . . .' said the Man Who Wasn't into our sudden silence, 'I'll keep one here and one in Oxford and . . .'

The spirit of Christmas died in the house that day.

Sometimes she would go to him where he sat at the head of the table and try to give him a hug. He always looked as if he would be glad when it was over. Always.

One day when he had been gone a long, long time after Christmas I found a marble in the road. It was smoky blue and flecked with red and worn rough where it had rolled. I kept it in the pocket of my shorts. I used to play with it on the beach with pebbles for its friends and enemies, against myself. First I'd be Me and then I'd be Myself, and the one wanted to beat the other so much it hurt. Me got better and better, and so did Myself, and the game went on for hours and days.

One day there was a Dinky car in Mr Newing's shop window that I wanted, so I needed some money. I looked around for what I had to sell and found my marble.

But nobody wanted to buy that as nobody played marbles any more.

I had my book *Bobby Had a Shilling*, but no one wanted a book with rhymes.

So as the Man Who Wasn't was away I went into his room and took the box of bullets from his drawer.

I thought I could sell them, but first I decided to try one out to see if it worked as I might not have another chance. I found two bricks and put the bullet in between and stood on top. Then I found an old nail, put its point against the cap, which someone once told me was how bullets worked, and bashed it again and again with a stone. But I wasn't heavy enough to hold the bullet in place so it moved beneath my feet each time I bashed it and never went off. I didn't know I was having a brush with death.

After that I took the box of bullets around the back streets and sold them for a penny halfpenny each to boys. A Royal Marine boy who knew about live rounds said he was going to tell his dad and I would be in trouble, so I stopped before I ever made enough for the Dinky car. It was blue and had windows and bumpers, and two doors so small you could only open them with your nails. I knew that because Mr Newing let me pick it up once.

That evening some mothers came around to see Ma in a deputation and had words. They were in a deputation because Ma was educated and wore glasses and they were afraid of her. They all sat around the drawing room with severe faces and after a lot of talking and raised voices I had to come and answer questions.

Granny was there too, looking even more severe, and pouring cups of tea into the best china teacups.

I thought I would get hit or sent to bed but I didn't, though it felt like what I did was bad. Instead Ma suddenly got tired of the tea and sitting about and being polite and said in a loud voice, 'Guns! I am sick and tired of them! The war is long over! It's us ladies who must make the peace because men never will. Wait here!'

All the ladies looked very startled and sipped their tea while we heard her banging about upstairs in the Man Who Wasn't's room. Suddenly she came back into the room carrying a gun and everybody jumped up thinking she had flipped her lid and was going to shoot them.

Instead she shouted, 'Follow me!'

Everybody followed after her as quick as lightning, Granny included, and Ma led us out onto the green opposite our house.

I wondered who she was going to shoot. I knew it couldn't be the Man Who Wasn't, as he was back living with the friends who gave him the silk dressing gown – away from children and Ma. I didn't think it was going to be me. It turned out to be nobody, and that day Ma did something better than murder.

With the gun held high above her head, and all of us running behind her, she strode straight onto the beach and down towards the waves.

This was unusual for Ma, who didn't know about waves: how they come in and go out, some far, some near.

She didn't know what I knew, which was this: it isn't easy to throw something beyond the surf. For one thing, it's further than it looks and for another, if you time it wrong the thing gets caught in the waves and pushed back to shore again. I've seen an old bicycle picked up by a wave and driven into shore. So I knew that gun was not going to get very far unless Ma got it right, and of all the people on the shore that day the only person who could do it right was me.

'Ma . . .' I began. I wanted to say that because I could throw cricket balls I could probably throw a gun.

But her blood was up and she was not listening to anybody.

She reached the waves and pulled her arm back to throw the gun out to sea.

Girls are not as good as boys at throwing because of the way their arms are made, and that's proved by Olympic records. Also, if you're going to throw something into the surf off Stoning beach there's only one way to do it and it means getting your feet wet.

Here's what you do: be ready when a wave comes in to follow it out as far as you dare. Then, while it is gathering its force again to come back in and your feet are getting sopping wet in the stones, throw whatever it is out beyond the surf and turn round and run back to dry land for dear life. That's the only way I ever found that worked and I walked that shore for years.

Ma did not think about that and wasn't going to listen to me.

So, standing too far back, she threw at the wrong time and not far enough. The gun landed on the wet and shifting shingle above the broiling surf.

People shouted, 'It's not gone far enough!' and three of them including Ma ran in to get it and try again.

I wanted to tell them not to because another big wave was on its way in. But nobody ever listened to me anyway and they ran straight into the oncoming wave and they and the gun and their high heels were all caught up together and turned head over heels.

In all the fuss, and the rescues and the confusion, I watched as the waves went in and out and slowly the gun was sucked under the stones and lost to view.

They searched and searched but I knew they wouldn't find it, for the sea was cleverer than they were and the tide was coming in.

Ma would have done better dropping it off the Pier or giving it to the police. But, as it was, there was not a mother thereabouts who didn't know she had done her best, and what she thought of the Man Who Wasn't for leaving his gun and bullets in the drawer of his desk for boys who didn't know better to find.

I was sent to bed and had to pay back the money I made and forfeit two weeks' pocket money. But Ma learnt her lesson about throwing things in the sea and didn't try to do the same with the bullets. She handed them in to the Royal Marine arsenal, where they stayed.

A few days before the next Christmas, Ma said, 'Daddy's coming home; what do you want for a Christmas present?'

I told her about the Dinky car.

On Christmas Day I was really excited and woke up thinking about what I was going to get. But the box he gave me to unwrap was too big to be a Dinky car. It was nearly as big as a dressing gown.

When I opened it and saw what it was I was disappointed. It was not a car, small or large, but a balsawood model of a Wellington bomber in nearly one thousand pieces. According to Ma it read 'For experienced model makers' on the side of the box, so he should have known better. But the Man Who Wasn't always bought presents in a rush at the last minute, not getting what you wanted but the first thing he thought would do.

I said, 'Thank you,' and looked inside the box. I saw it would be as difficult for me to make as throwing a gun into the sea was for Ma. That night I put it on the top of the cupboard so that at least I could see the picture of the bomber.

I thought there were so many things I could have done with the money, or he could have done if he had asked what I wanted. But that was the Man Who Wasn't, bringing things I didn't want and then going back to his ancient university town to put on his silk dressing gown and drink gin with his friends.

Then the holidays were over and he left again and the house turned back to normal.

One day there was a gale and the waves drove high because the wind was westerly. I took the Wellington bomber down from its place and looked inside its box again. There was a knife and glue as well as the thousand pieces, but I left them where they were.

I knew there was another way to get things beyond the surf, but they had to be light and the wind had to be offshore.

I took the bomber in its coffin box down to the shore and waited a long time for the right moment. A great sea came in, up and up and up, and I stepped into it and placed the box and its contents carefully on the water at the moment it turned back.

It was taken from my hands and rushed back towards the surf. Away and on it went towards what seemed impending death as a new wave gathered force and started for the shore, its front mounting and mounting, higher and higher.

The Wellington bomber hit the wave good and true and rode up and up and reached the top in time to begin the long descent on the other side before the waves broke up.

The wave came in and I saw the box had reached the next incoming wave. Again it rose up, and again it survived, each time pushed out by the wind.

The last I saw the bomber it was beyond the dangerous surf and heading towards the Goodwin Sands. Seeing it go, I didn't feel sorry, I felt cleaner.

The Man Who Wasn't came every Christmas and it was always the same. I cannot remember a single present he ever gave me apart from the Wellington bomber. But I would give them all away to be able to remember a time when he stood on the shore and listened as I told him what I knew about the wind and waves. But he never did.

Or to see him take off his shoes and socks, and shirt, even if it meant showing his scabs, so that he could go swimming with me. But he didn't, and he never knew I would have washed his scabs just to have him hold my hand with love.

Or to know who he had been when he was young, and why he never told me then what he told Michael, which was the name of all the flowers on the verge, every single one, from knapweed to scabious, from sea poppies to alexanders, from fennel to bird's-foot trefoil. You could have knocked me down with a feather that he knew such things and never let on to me.

I would have asked him who had taught him the names, and where. But he never even got me to the starting line of asking. It must have been his dad.

The man who Ma called Howard Scupple and I called the Man Who Wasn't was a scholar and a teacher, who didn't know that a Dinky car bought with thought and love would have been worth more to me than a Wellington bomber bought in haste. As it was, I never had a Daddy and Howard Scupple was the nearest I ever got to having one.

# 6

# HOBNAIL BOOTS

There came a day that was memorable for three reasons.

First, Uncle Max came down to stay with his new fiancée, whose name this time was Aunt Fiona.

She wore red lipstick and rouge on her cheeks, morning, noon and night, and stood on tiptoe in high heels. The moment Granny saw her she pursed her lips and went back into her room and closed the door. She often said there were times when a headache could be a useful companion.

Ma liked Uncle Max's fiancées because she said there was no chance of him marrying any of them.

'I'll make you a nice cup of tea,' she said, sweeping her hair from her brow with the back of her hand because her fingers were covered in pastry.

Ma had no sharp, pointed shoes and only wore rouge and a clean frock when the Man Who Wasn't came visiting or when she went out alone. Ma looked funny when she dressed up, and got bad tempered, but Fiona looked beautiful and smelt of perfume like the ladies from Fitzroy Square Croquet and Lawn Tennis Club.

'Now,' said Ma when the kitchen table was set with the tea things, 'Jimmy can pour and remain silent. Listening to adult conversation is good for him and engaging in one is a rare treat for me.'

Then she asked Fiona a question in that quiet way she had when she intended to examine the answer: 'What *exactly* is it that you do?'

Uncle Max's previous fiancée was a City secretary; the one before that a clippie on a London bus who had tickets to prove it; the one before that was training to be a hairdresser and the one before that, who was the first I remember but not the first fiancée he ever had, was a hotel receptionist, or 'so she said', as Ma put it.

Fiona listened to Ma's difficult question about what she did and replied, 'I fly aeroplanes.'

I was so surprised I spilt the tea, but Ma didn't bat an eyelid.

She said, 'Your own or somebody else's?' As cool as a cucumber.

Fiona said, 'I am a pilot with the British Overseas Airways Corporation. I learnt flying in the war.'

Then she said with a smile, 'But don't let's talk about me, let's talk about you.'

Ma said, 'My life is filled with tedium and looking after Jimmy and my other children when they are home, which they usually are not, as I board them in cruel establishments designed to subdue their natural spirits. I work as a farm secretary in Wingham, which is a village ten miles away.'

'I will look out for it next time I fly over East Kent,' said Fiona calmly.

They all thought this so funny they couldn't stop laughing. For long years afterwards, whenever I saw an aeroplane fly over Stoning I thought it might be Fiona looking out for Ma's workplace.

The second reason that day was memorable was that the Queen was crowned in Westminster Abbey. We all went to a posh neighbour's with a television set and sat on a sofa watching and listening, right up until the anointment, when they put screens around the Queen so we couldn't see her chest. That's when Granny got up and said, 'It's all stuff and nonsense.'

When she saw no one but me was listening she added, 'And anyway, I am a republican. I do not believe in kings and queens, for all of them are knaves.'

Aunt Fiona said, 'I agree with you! Shall we leave these royalists to their autocratic ways and take the air upon the Promenade and show the world that life goes on, whatever may be happening in Westminster Abbey and Buckingham Palace?'

From that moment Granny and Auntie Fiona were the best of

friends. Which was why Granny allowed Uncle Max to take me to climb my first mountain – because Aunt Fiona was going to come too.

'I wouldn't trust Uncle Max with a dead cat,' said Granny, 'but I can see you are a sensible woman, Fiona, and one who will make sure that no harm comes to my Jimmy while you are away.'

'Why should harm come to me?' I asked. 'And anyway, why is a mountain dangerous?'

The subject had come up because of the third memorable thing that was announced that day, which was that Edmund Hillary from New Zealand and Sherpa Tensing from Tibet had climbed the highest mountain in the world. No one in the whole history of the world had stood on top of it before.

Uncle Max said, 'This is a great day for England and the monarchy.'

Granny said, 'It seems to me that it is a great day for New Zealand and for Tibet, and a bad day for Mount Everest. It is nothing to do with England at all, let alone the Queen.'

Uncle Max said, 'Well, anyway, it makes me think it would be very good if I took Jimmy to climb a mountain. He can come with Fiona and me to North Wales.'

I said, 'I would like to climb a mountain no one else has ever climbed.'

Granny said it was best to start modestly.

Ma declared, 'Much you know about it!'

To which Granny replied, 'You do not know all the details of my past. It happens that you are talking to a former Lady President of the Combined Universities Ladies Alpine Hiking Club . . .'

We were all very surprised at this and Ma fell silent as Granny's eyes misted over at her own memories of rock climbing in the Alps with other ladies, and also with Grandfather, who she said was as intrepid and agile as a mountain goat before they got married, when everything changed.

She added, 'And that was also before he joined the Temperance Movement, after which he never picked up an ice axe again.'

Uncle Max asked if she had ever been to North Wales, where he and Aunt Fiona now proposed to take me.

'Gustav took me to North Wales once,' said Granny, 'and it was the most fearful place I have ever been, more so than the Alps. The wind never stops blowing, it is always wet and the rocks are so slippery that it is nearly impossible to walk. Fiona, you will not be able to wear high heels, and your face powder will blow off your cheeks in seconds.'

'It is not my cheeks I shall worry about,' said Fiona, 'but my hair! I shall take a scarf.'

'Much good *that* will do you in the Welsh wind!' said Granny.

It was decided there and then that we would go in the autumn and that in the meantime the main thing to do was to get me something to put on my feet.

'I have no boots,' I explained, 'and mountain climbers wear boots.'

Uncle Max nodded: 'You're quite right, Jimmy. You'll need boots with hobnails. We'll have to get you some.'

I asked if there were many about and she said there were hundreds of thousands because they were left over after the War. There was a place called Army Surplus where they kept them in piles as high as mountains and sold them off to the public, but unfortunately there wasn't one in Stoning.

I remembered that the Royal Marines had been in the war and they wore black boots. I said that Granny and I knew them and they might help.

Fiona smiled and said, 'You had better go and ask them then.'

I went to Granny and said that I couldn't climb a mountain unless I had boots and I couldn't get boots unless I went to the Royal Marines. I asked if she would come with me.

'As far as the guardhouse at the main gate,' she said. 'There are times when you have to go on alone and I do believe this may be one of them.'

With a thumping heart I walked with Granny down Dover Road, all the way past the shops, past the Royal Marines' swimming pool and to the main gate. There was a guard standing to attention on either side. The gates were shiny black iron bars with spikes on top, higher than a lamp-post. There was a high brick wall that stretched away on either side for miles.

I said, 'Granny, I don't want to go in alone. I may not be able to get out again.'

Granny squeezed my hand and said, 'I'll wait for you in the guardhouse. I expect they'll brew me up a cup of tea; they usually do.'

The guard came out and talked to Granny and they seemed to know each other. They looked at me, grinning, so I knew it would be all right.

But then the guard came right up to me, left right, left right, left, and said, 'Hello! And what can Her Majesty's Royal Marines do for you?'

'Please, sir, I want some boots so I can climb a mountain.'

'Boots?'

'Boots with hobnails.'

'We issue the hobnails, son, which you put in yourself. But the only way you'll get boots is by joining the Royal Marines. Wait there. Meanwhile you can take those shoes off.'

'But . . .'

I looked round for Granny but she had gone. Then they closed the gates so I couldn't get out. My heart was thumping like a battering ram inside my chest and my breath was coming out in jerks faster than I could get it back inside again. So I took my shoes and socks off and waited on the tarmac.

The guard returned with another Royal Marine, who stood to attention.

'Private Horton,' he said, 'what do you see here?'

'A small boy, sir.'

'What else do you see, Private Horton? And please don't try my patience.'

'A boy with no shoes, sir!'

'Well observed: there is hope for you yet. Now, Private Horton, this small boy who has no shoes is no ordinary boy. For one thing he is the grandson of the lady who is at this moment partaking of a brew-up in the guardhouse with the duty watch, in consequence of which she cannot be disturbed and has therefore put me in charge of this boy.'

'I see, sir.'

'I am not so sure you do, yet, Private Horton, so I hope you washed your ears out especially well this morning and continue to listen carefully. This boy's grandmother is a special friend of our commanding officer, who is the nearest thing to God you are ever likely to meet on this earth.'

'Yes, SIR!!'

'And finally, and not to be forgotten, this boy with no shoes is also a friend of the regimental bugler, who will have your guts for garters if you do not guard him with your life.'

'Yes, sir,' said the private in a small voice.

'So, do you know what you are going to do, Private Horton . . . ?'

'Sir?'

'You are going to accompany this boy with no shoes to the stores where you will find and locate Quartermaster Treanor.'

'Yes, sir.'

'You will explain this boy's shoe situation to the quartermaster and apprise him of the fact that this boy has friends in high places. He will know what to do, and you, Private Horton, will give him every assistance. *Do you understand?*'

'Yes, sir.'

'*Do you appreciate the importance of this mission?*'

'I do, sir!'

'At the double!'

With that Private Horton told me to follow him and we set off so fast I had to run to keep up.

The buildings were of grey-red brick, with lots of shiny blue doors all the same except for white writing on them. In the spaces between the buildings there were Marines in lines, Marines in white shorts and plimsolls, Marines preparing Brussels sprouts, Marines standing on their heads and Marines standing to attention and staring fixedly at blank walls.

Sometimes there were officers in blue and red, and one of them stopped us. He squatted down and looked me in the eyes and grinned, and that was when I knew I was among friends.

'You're the boy who came to the concert.'

I said I was.

'You're the boy who was ill in Stoning Hospital.'

'I was. I'm better now.'

'You *look* better. Have you come to join the Royal Marines?'

I said, 'I don't think so. I asked if there were any hobnail boots because I need some to climb a mountain in North Wales.'

He said he had been to North Wales on a training exercise and was going again.

'Snowdon is where Edmund Hillary trained for the ascent of Mount Everest, which I expect you've heard of?'

I explained that was what made Uncle Max decide it would be good for me to learn mountain climbing.

'Is he trained in mountaineering?'

I said that Auntie Fiona knew something about it and that Uncle Max was very good at other things like motor cars.

'Private Horton?'

'Sir?'

'Ask the quartermaster to issue this boy who has no shoes the correct Ordnance Survey map or maps for his expedition and to mark them down to me.'

'I will, sir.'

With that the officer got up and saluted me.

'Your Aunt Fiona's trained in mountaineering, you say?'

'And flying aeroplanes.'

He did not spill any tea but he did bat his eyelid. Soon after that we reached the stores and found Quartermaster Treanor.

He was old and tubby and had a bald head.

He heard Private Horton out in silence and then said to me, 'Before you get your boots and your maps you've got to prove yourself worthy of the Royal Marines. Take this and follow me.'

With that, he gave me an enormous broom, with a handle as

tall as the main gate and a brush as long as the front of a bus.

'Fall in!' he cried and we all marched together to another door which opened up into the biggest and most echoing room I had ever seen. There were ropes hanging from the ceiling with leather on the end, and wooden bars, and huge big doormats, and all sorts of apparatus.

It was the Royal Marine gymnasium.

'Sonny, I want you to sweep this floor so shiny and clean you could eat your lunch off it and live to tell the tale. Do you think you could do that? Would that be worth a pair of boots and an Ordnance Survey map with Official Secrets printed in mauve on it?'

I looked up one way and down the other; then across from the near side to the far one. I had never seen a floor so big. The only good thing about it was I could not see a single speck of dust on it anywhere. It wasn't like Ma's kitchen floor, which was always dirty. I could see no congealed cabbage or grey hairs.

I thought of the boots and the map.

'I will, sir,' I said.

'The private here will help. Seeing as he did not distinguish himself in the Lord Nelson yesterday evening, which is why he is on punishment duty this morning, I do believe that a spot of brooming will do him good.'

With that he left us, and Private Horton and I swept out the gym. But it was already so clean from others who had done punishment duty that when we had finished we did not even have enough dust to fill a teaspoon.

'Do I get my boots now?' I asked.

'You never can tell with the quartermaster,' said Private Horton, 'but them's that ask in the Royal Marines often do not get.'

Sure enough, when we got back to the quartermaster he did not have my boots ready. Instead he put down the green telephone into which he had been speaking and said, 'I have been thinking that maybe our new recruit here needs some basic training if he is to get the very best out of his boots.'

'Yes, sir!' shouted Private Horton.

'What I want you to do, Private Horton, is to show him how the assault course works by having 'im watch you go round it at double speed five times.'

'Yes, sir!'

We set off back across the parade ground and I thought that the private did not seem quite his former cheerful self.

The course had a rope net up which he had to climb, a high bar between towers off which he was not to fall, camouflage netting under which he had to crawl, a wooden wall as high as two houses up which he had to clamber and some rubber tyres through which he had to crawl while holding on to heavy weights.

No wonder that by the time he finished he could hardly speak.

'Only four more times to go,' he panted, wincing in pain, 'and then you'll get your boots.'

I said, 'I don't think I want boots if you have to go round by yourself. Maybe if I come round with you I might be able to help.'

'You're a plucky kid,' he said, 'but . . .'

I was already off, because I was good at climbing netting; I had done it on the old war defences down at Southdown. And the tyres were easy because I was small enough to get through quickly.

But I got scared on the high bar and Private Horton had to stand underneath to encourage me across. As for the wall, he had to lift me over the highest part.

When I had finished my round and recovered my breath, I said, 'Let's try for a world record.'

He said doubtfully, 'We could, I suppose, but . . .'

So I was off like an arrow out of a bow, but before I got very far some Marines came over in white shorts and singlets lined in blue.

'What this then, Eric?' they said.

'It's a world record attempt,' he said.

'Let's get this straight,' said a Marine who looked bigger and stronger than the rest and had tattoos on his arms, 'this boy, who has no shoes, and hardly comes up to your kneecaps, is trying to break the world record for this assault course.'

'That's right,' said Private Horton, winking at me, 'with a little help from his friend, and always hoping that Quartermaster Treanor does not catch sight of what's going on.'

He explained about the five circuits he had to do as punishment.

'I don't think,' said the very big Marine, who had *Instructor* sewn in red on his white vest, 'that there is one gentleman here who has not already seen you do each and every one of those five circuits, eh lads?'

Every single Marine stood up and bellowed, 'No, *sir!*'

'World records, however, is a different matter, seeing as, so far as I know, there is not one officially recognized for this assault course.'

'No, sir!' bawled Private Horton.

'We will therefore proceed to establish one here and now. Your official timekeeper, referee, judge and arbiter will be myself, with this boy who has no shoes as official starter and judge's assistant. Is that understood, gentlemen?'

'Yes, sir,' they all shouted.

He pulled a silver stopwatch out of his pocket and told me to stay by him. His hand was steady at my shoulder, strong as a rock.

One by one the Marines went round the circuit. Some were slow, some fast, some very fast.

'Your turn, Private Horton.'

He went round faster than anyone else and I cheered him as loud as I ever shouted before. One or two of those Marines said 'Well done, Eric!' to him when he had finished. I could see they all liked him.

When they had all had their turn the gym instructor said, 'Well, it seems that Private Horton has established the Official World Record, which is three minutes twenty-six seconds, but don't go congratulating him too fast because there's a lad here who's not done his official timed circuit yet and he might beat Eric's record. Eh lads?'

'Yes, *sir!*'

They all looked at me and I felt my heart beginning to beat in my chest again. By now a good few other Marines had come over to watch what was going on, so I felt even more nervous.

'However, this boy here doesn't have the benefit of wearing boots, since he has none on his feet, and he is smaller than everyone else. So to make it fair we are all going to help him, gentlemen, *is that understood?*'

'Yes, *sir!*' they thundered.

Then they made up pairs, and each pair stood by a different part of the course ready to help me.

'Now, lad, listen to me. As far as I can see, there's three bits of this assault course you can do for yourself better than if our lads help you, that's the start to the first obstacle, across the high bar and the run in at the end. Can you do those by yourself?'

'I was a bit nervous before on the high bar,' I said, looking up at it. It was high and it was narrow and it was long and I didn't want to fall off it. 'But I'll have a go.'

They all cheered when I said this and I began to think I could really do it.

'Right, lads,' said the gym instructor, 'you heard what this boy with no shoes said, he said he would have a go. Shall I tell you something? He'll have a go and he will succeed, and do you know why?'

There was silence.

'Because this boy here has "Royal Marine" written in gold letters on his heart. That's why. Haven't you, lad?'

I said I wasn't sure but I thought that perhaps I did have.

'Let's get on with it then, lad, and remember – when you get to that bar run like a bat out of hell, because that's the bit that's going to win you the world record.'

I went to the start and as I was about to begin the officer who had talked to me earlier came by. Then I saw the regimental bugler, who was my friend. And then on the far side of the parade ground I saw Granny standing with the commanding officer. But they did not come near because ladies were not allowed where Royal Marines are training.

'One last word, gentlemen. If any harm comes to this boy with no shoes, who has the words "Royal Marine" written upon his heart, if he suffers a bruise or a cut, a knock or a jerk, if he loses one hair of his head, then that gentleman, or those gentlemen, responsible, will live to regret it for the rest of their lives. If, on the other hand, this boy survives to tell the tale, unharmed, then I will make history tonight in the Lord Nelson and buy every man here a round. Is that clearly understood?'

'YES, SIR!!!'

With that, he got his stopwatch out, raised his hand and with a 'Ready, steady, *go!*' I was off.

I ran for that great net as fast as I ever ran in my life. I was lifted up to the top, picked up by two Marines and lowered down the other side, and then I was off again towards the tyres. The lads cheered me on as they carried me, and they nearly threw me up the wall and more or less hurled me down the other side.

The ground raced past beneath me; the ropes burned my hands; the lads shouted, 'You can do it, you *can!*' And I'm sure I heard Granny shouting encouragement too from where she stood so far away.

Suddenly I was high up, at the beginning of the bar, and all the world was below me, and lots of faces were looking up, and that high bar seemed so narrow and so long, with everywhere to fall if I missed my footing – and there was no one to help me.

Then I saw Private Horton below grinning up at me and I knew as sure as eggs are eggs that even if I fell he would catch me all by himself. Then I didn't think of falling but of running, running as fast as I could, running for a world record, like a bat out of hell.

There were two Marines waiting at the far end of the bar and I went faster and faster towards them, for the gym instructor's silver stopwatch caught the sun and warned me that time was running out.

I dived into their arms, they threw me to waiting hands below, I was pushed and pulled under the camouflage netting until I was back out from under it and standing up, my lungs exploding.

I saw the end of the circuit and the lads waiting there.

'Come on, lad, come *on!*' they roared.

That was the first moment in my life I found I could run fast, really fast, even faster than a bat can fly.

I ran like there was no tomorrow.
I ran like I was flying through air.
I ran for a world record.

'Gentlemen,' said the gym instructor when I had recovered and been given two glasses of Tizer and everybody had gathered about, 'this is an historic occasion. I am happy to declare that a new world record has been set by our newest, youngest, smallest and most temporary recruit, the Boy With No Shoes. That record is two minutes fifty-eight seconds, which is faster than the speed of sound and nearly as fast as the speed of light.

'In recognition of this achievement I have been asked to present him with a pair of black boots and this map, which I now do.'

They all cheered as I came forward and took the prizes.

'We will erect a notice by the side of this course and challenge anyone who likes, be he a Royal Marine or a member of one of the lesser Armed Services such as the Army, Navy and Air Force, to beat this record. If he tries and fails, it's the Lord Nelson for him and a round for each one of us!'

They all cheered and carried me on their shoulders back to where Granny was waiting with the commanding officer.

The gym instructor was as good as his word.

A notice was set up by the assault course, and every time a team came to play a match against the Royal Marines from outside things ended up with everyone having a go at the circuit to beat the record set that day by 'Private BWNS of the Royal Marines'. People often asked what BWNS stood for, but the Royal Marines of Stoning never let on.

# 7

# THE HOUSE OF A
# THOUSAND ROOMS

One day I climbed the stairs and found my bedroom was no longer mine. It belonged to a lady from France. My Ma had decided she was going to earn money by taking in paying guests from abroad, so she had put my things in a suitcase and shoved it in the boxroom, and me along with it.

Things you collect look different jumbled up together by someone else. They lose a lot of what they were. Stones, coins, a yellow pencil with a rubber on the end, a Dinky car which had three good tyres, things in a line, things in a row, things I journeyed into and lost myself among.

She tore the special world of all my things apart and put it in the suitcase. I slept with my hand on the case but I never took them out, the things. I put more things in but never took them out. That brown cardboard suitcase was where I had been put and I dared not bring it out to be torn apart again.

One hot day everybody said let's play hide-and-seek. So I did. I knew a place and crept inside my lost bedroom and hid in the cupboard waiting to be found, waiting and waiting, hardly daring to breathe. I didn't often win anything but I waited so long that I knew I must have. Then I crept out and went downstairs to tell them I had won, but the house stretched away from me in silence. Room after room was empty, not a soul to be found, and I knew I was the only one left in the world.

It was summer, but I found myself standing in a freezing cold place that went for ever always everywhere and it was called loneliness. I stood knowing there was nowhere to turn. Even Granny had gone.

They had forgotten I was playing with them and had gone off picnicking for lunch and left me behind.

You can't win a game if you're so unimportant that no one notices you're playing.

I wandered from room to room that day, with flies my only friends. Around each hanging light they buzzed except in Granny's room, for she had a sticky spiral there on which they stuck, a leg or wing struggling until they got stuck as well, and then they quivered and died.

I wandered through room after room but felt scared only once, which was when the Coalman tapped on a pipe from the cellar far below, where he lived.

Those hours when they forgot I was alive, something in me died inside. I wandered about like a starling caught in a greenhouse, not knowing the way out and banging my head against glass, unheard.

There was a cupboard with Ma's clothes hanging like dead things. Beige and brown and horrible. I stared and didn't touch. That was the day I learnt I didn't like her.

Granny's things were neat and bright as dress pins, but her room wasn't the same without her. I didn't linger there or open her cupboard doors.

There was a settee I sat in for a time, listening to the house make its sounds: Granny's clock, the Coalman tapping, pipes bubbling, and the ivy scratching at the window pane. Sitting and thinking, 'There's one good thing: there's no one here to stop me doing nothing.'

There was another good moment.

One of the lady foreigners had a suitcase and I opened it. It smelt of woman and smelt of good. I reached inside and touched her things and sat on her bed with her petticoat in my face and closed my eyes and was safe, safe back in the time before Darktime. Back then the petticoat had had someone in it and she had held me close. I remembered it now as I curled up on that bed in the house of the thousand rooms. I cried to know her name, who loved me before Darktime. I cried for her to come back. I cried to find a way back to her. That was the first time I realized that once there had been someone who loved me as well as the Man Who Was, someone who had got lost along the way.

The kitchen was at the back of the house, with a scullery and other rooms, dark and dank. I was hungry now, so I got some bread and found some beef dripping in a little white bowl. I sat at the table where all of us sat, shouting and hurting and wondering why I was always wrong. I sat that day all by myself, and when I was done I cleaned and cleaned where I had been to leave no trace behind.

In all my long childhood that was the only time I ate at peace in my own home.

On the windowsill there was a bottle of pop that was open. I raised it to my mouth and drank. They were alive, the wasps inside, and they crawled in my mouth for only moments before I spat them out onto the table I had cleaned. They crawled about desperately, their wings bedraggled and dragging them round in arcs and circles.

I watched them until one fell onto the floor. Then I found a spoon and jiggered the wasp into it and took it to the kitchen door. I didn't go out, but that first wasp did, crawling into the sun towards freedom and dryness again. Then I went for the others and did the same. I watched them recover and suddenly work their wings, and one after the other they buzzed up into the blue blue sky and away. Those wasps that walked in my mouth flew further in ten seconds than I did in ten years.

Then Granny's big clock chimed.

*Ding dong, ding dong*, and I moved from one room to another that long day when I was left alone to discover how many rooms a house really has, which are rooms of memory.

*Ding, dong,* and I arrived at our drawing room where they used to dance, the Boy and the Girl, and all of us sometimes. Its wallpaper was a world of pointed leaves out of Mr Morris's head, intertwined and interlocked, green and brown, their veins white or green; decked out with flowers like ones I could draw, with five round petals and a star or a circle at their heart; all joined together by writhing stalks, green ones near your eyes and others of grey that seemed far away.

My Ma had put up the wallpaper with somebody's help and shouted for me to go away . . . *go away* . . . and I did. I only wanted to be part of things. Not part of nothing.

There was a fireplace that was empty and dead that day I wandered about. Once, in winter, when it was alive and dancing with flames, the boy had said, 'You can read my *Eagle* when I've finished it, if you sit there and are quiet and say nothing at all, not a word.'

This memory always made me want to scream my hurt and my not belonging.

I sat and watched him read Dan Dare, and then read it again slower still. I watched the pages turn and turn. I moved no arm or leg that I possessed on the settee where I sat. I watched the fire burn, and heard it creak and drop a little, easing itself as it wasted into ash.

'Shall I put on more coal?' I said.

'Don't speak, or else.'

His voice was so cold, as cold as the voice of the Man Who Wasn't.

I sat in silence awaiting my treat, in that room, with the boy and the *Eagle* I wanted to fly. Dan Dare and Digby waited with me, for my brother to read them through.

A page turned and then another, and finally the last one.

He looked at me sideways, his eyes in Darktime. Then he turned back to the front and began all over again, right from the start, laughing this time at the jokes I wouldn't have been able to understand. I couldn't read. But Dan Dare and Digby could read to me.

I couldn't read then, but I loved the pictures when I was allowed to look, and in them I could journey beyond any room.

So I waited to the sounds of the dying of the fire and the distant chimes of Granny's clock.

Finally he finished and turned to the front and folded the *Eagle* in half, and then again, back into the form it was folded when it was delivered each week with his name on.

He got up with it in his hand, and I leant forward for what was mine.

'Can I have it now?' I asked.

He went to the fire and put it straight on and turned and studied my face as I watched in horror. I couldn't get past his legs, I could only watch as Digby died and Dan Dare turned black and flew up the chimney, and the *Eagle* went up in flames.

'I said not to talk,' he said, and he walked out of that room while I stared at the ashes of what had been and heard their last sigh and creak. In that room, on that day, the *Eagle* died for me again and I knew Darktime wasn't dead. I went to the window and just stared at the sea and watched it move.

That day of remembering, the day of the wasps, when I got left behind, I went to that window again and this time I looked across the sea through a day light enough for the chalk cliffs of France to be shining white like newly washed handkerchiefs dancing on a clothesline in the wind. It seemed like a place of warm and light, and I wondered if a boy like me was over there across the sea looking back towards the window where I stood glad he wasn't where I was.

I moved to the middle of the drawing room and looked around. The fire was there, and the table, and the wallpaper too. But with no one's sound in the house but my own, the room was mine and nobody else's.

I know what I did then but not what it meant.

There was a tallboy of light oak. I went and opened the drawer to see the inside. I know I did that.

There was a gramophone and black 78s they played for the dances. I wound it up and put one on and stood in the place where everyone danced, round and round, twirling around.

Alone I stood and listened to the tune the Man Who Wasn't liked and sometimes hummed: *Now fiddlers ready let us all begin, to the merry music of the violin . . .*

I put my hand on the silver thing that holds the needle and I pulled it scratching to the end, scoring the record where it hurt and let it play again – *Now fid . . . Now fid . . . Now fid . . . Now fid . . .* – for ever more, if I'd let it play. But I put it back where I'd found it and watched the brown felt of the turntable turning and turning until it slowed and stopped.

There was a tiny silver drawer that came out of the corner of the gramophone which had the needles in, which were hard to get out. I opened and closed it for a time, listening to the soft sound of needles and staring into their thousand shines. Then I closed it finally, wound the gramophone up, turned it on with nothing playing and closed the lid.

I left it turning and turning all unseen in its box in the room, like me in each room in the house, and wandered on.

There was an attic in the house and the entry was through a hatch in the ceiling just outside the lavatory. If I stood on a chair I could just reach it and push it up an inch or two to hide things there against the day I grew tall enough to retrieve them.

Things I stole. A toy from Mr Newing's with which I never played.

Things I broke on purpose. A ping-pong ball I cracked.

Things I did not understand. That day I got forgotten I pushed the petticoat of the woman up through that crack that led to the attic, up to comfort the darkness. But even comfort has a consequence.

Days later, in the future I could not know during that day of wandering around the empty rooms, Michael shouted, 'Jimmy, Ma wants you; she's in Daddy's room.'

I dragged slowly upstairs to the room and saw Ma and at her side the French lady with hair as dark as soot. The man who wasn't my Daddy was away or else he would have been there as well.

On the desk was the toy and the ping-pong ball and the pale petticoat. My heart stopped and I looked down in shame at the dirty carpet. The carpets were always dirty in that house.

'Well?'

There was no one to save me.

'*Well?*' said Ma in the voice she sometimes used. It was like a sharp saw with poisoned teeth.

I stood in the room alone, so full of shame.

She beat my knuckles for the toy.

She crushed the ping-pong ball and put it in a basket where the man who wasn't put his spent poems.

But, worst of all, she said, 'Put it on,' holding up the petticoat and glancing at the stranger woman, who blinked and opened her mouth enough for me to see her yellow teeth.

'*Put it on!*'

I was dying of shame, and I heard a titter at the door and knew the Boy was there and the Girl as well: they who were tall enough to reach up to the attic and bring my secrets down to earth and tell on me.

I was dying in that room that afternoon, like a fly on the coiled sticky thing. The petticoat she held was not to blame if it gave comfort to me. I knew no way to explain or defend the moment when I sat on the bed and held it close and smelt the woman smell that was good. It took me back to before Darktime, when the Man Who Was may have been and a woman held me close.

'*Put it on!*'

I shook my head because I would rather die than have them see me dressed like that.

I watched a bird dying by the roadside once, and its wings fluttered softly and its beak opened into noiseless song. That was how I felt.

The tittering from behind the half-open door suddenly stopped. The door crashed open and an arm grabbed mine and I smelt mothballs.

'This is quite enough. *Quite* enough!'

It was Granny, saving me from shame.

She took me out of the room and into her own. I couldn't look her in the eyes but stood stock-still, dumb, staring at anywhere but her. I felt so ashamed I couldn't even cry. It was that day, that moment, that Granny cuddled me for one of her few and only times.

She got down onto her knees, which was not easy for her because she had arthritis, and she held me tight, with her papery cheek to mine. She gave me what the petticoat could not, which was a place to cry out my shame. I couldn't breathe for choking back my tears and trying to scream away my loneliness. I cried and cried in her arms.

A little later she toasted crumpets at her gas fire with her retractable brass toasting fork. I watched her and saw that it was true that Granny had a very long nose.

'Granny?'

'Yes, my dear?'

'Is it true that when no one's here you lock the door and toast crumpets by sticking them on the end of your nose and sitting by the fire?'

'Who told you that?'

'The Boy did. *Is* it?'

'As true as thinking that taking that underslip was something to be ashamed of, which it was not, though I do not advise it as a general rule. What would you think of your grandmother if she borrowed a pair of Mr Hammel's drawers?'

'That's silly,' I said.

'And that's *all* it is,' Granny replied, putting things in their proper place like she always did. 'Now, do you want just butter, or Marmite as well?'

That long day I wandered through the house of a thousand rooms hoping to find the room I never found, the one before Darktime where the Man Who Was and the woman were. Once it had been, but not in that house. It was warm and light and everything was in place but not too much. The counterpane on the bed was neatly folded back, and the pillows smelt of fresh sea-summer air, and on a table was some perfume, and on the floor there was a brown leather case with foreign labels.

I sat in that room a thousand times, but it always disappeared when I opened my eyes, and the woman I wanted to come, whose scent I sensed in a petticoat, who held me once, safe in the long ago before Darktime . . . oh, she never came back.

But *they* did. Suddenly, disturbing my peace, back from the picnic they forgot to take me on after hide-and-seek. I heard the Boy and the Girl and Ma and Granny and Uncle Max and the strangers as well, all coming in one by one: together they were invaders returning through the big front door.

I hid the lovely room back in my mind where it couldn't be hurt and crept across the corridor, through my room, past the Boy's bed, through the narrow door and raised the latch of the door that led down the green narrow stairs to the kitchen.

Down I went, silent as a ghost, and crept across the kitchen to the back door.

Then, as the old invaders conquered the rooms again, I went outside into the late afternoon air. I went on all fours to the back gate, so no one could see me if they came into the kitchen.

I opened the back gate and slammed it shut, not caring if they heard. For by then I was running, running, running so hard away from the house that was never my home.

Into Liverpool Road, past Bristol Street to Fitzroy Square: running, running, gulping down the fresh air and freedom.

On past the *thwack* and the soft *thud* of the tennis balls to the public recreation ground. To pause, catch breath and look back and imagine just for fun that it was the rooms themselves that were chasing me, all of them by their tens and hundreds, by their thousand.

Turning away and running, laughing, out of Markewood and left at Granville Road. Over the rickety metal fence, one, two and jump, and past the cowpats to the pond by the castle.

To sit there heaving, breathing, gasping and staring into the still waters, where I saw a newt roam free. Maybe its pond had a thousand rooms as well.

I watched the newt and prodded at it with a stick to make it move. It slid off into the murky depths and I turned away to the beach.

I got home at dusk, in time to hear Ma shout out, 'Where's Jimmy? Tell him it's on the table. Oh, *there* you are! Where have you been? It's getting cold.'

Where had I been? It was not a question she meant. No, she said it and then turned away before I replied, as she often did, and started talking Standard English to one of the strangers who was paying to learn the language we spoke and all about our customs and our way of life.

'I went on a hunt,' I said, *for a room I know I knew before Darktime that was never in this house* . . . but no one heard my words. Instead, they echoed and died out one by one in nine hundred and ninety-nine rooms of our house.

But in one alone they lived on, and I ached for the day when the petticoat woman would come back and have by her side the Man Who Was, who was my father. Because he it was who gave me the shoes, my special thing, which others stole; and he was the man who was loved by the woman who had a bottle of perfume and wore a petticoat when she held me close and for a moment gave me the meaning of being me.

'What were you hunting for?' said Ma, glancing at others as if to say, *What could Jimmy hunt for in this house and over the Green? Giraffes? Elephants? Crocodiles?*

'For a room,' I said, *which is only in a room in my mind whose door I can never really find, like I never found my shoes.*

'Humph!' said Ma.

I slid away. I went outside. Then I stood on the Green breathing salt air and watching how, as the sun fell down, the white cliffs of France began to die away to almost nothing at all.

# 8

# MR MEE

At last there came the day when I learnt to read.

Every boy and every girl in my class could read and some even read whole books when they didn't have to, but not me. When I looked at a page I saw only barbed wire in front of my eyes that made a cage from which I didn't know how to escape to the place where the words made sense.

I knew only my alphabet and that 'D' is for Dunce who stands in the corner.

Granny said I was the despair of Ma, who always had her nose in a book when she drank her tea, and had had that nose there since she was four.

Ma would say, 'Jimmy, if you read you would know why I do, and why clicking your tongue and waggling your feet like that drives me mad. Either be quiet or go away.'

But that wasn't why I decided to read.

Granny said, 'Reading improves the mind, Jimmy, always assuming someone has a mind to improve, of which I have not always been convinced, considering some of the things people do and say. Nevertheless, it's time you learnt, because you'll always be bottom of the class until you do.'

But that wasn't why I learnt.

'Reading's useful for lots of things,' said Uncle Max, who Granny told to talk to me about it, 'but especially for filling in time.'

'What time?'

'Waiting for trains to Cannon Street, for example.'

'Why's it called Cannon Street?'

'That's not the point,' said Uncle Max, sounding exasperated, 'not the point at *all*.'

'Where are *you* going?' asked Ma one day when I was trying to escape from the house.

'I've done all my jobs,' I said, sliding towards the door.

The sea had been rough all night and there would be things to find along the shore or herring gulls to watch.

'Well, you've still got to . . .'

But Ma was distracted by the smell of burning, which was Michael lighting a fire with crumpled newspaper in the kitchen sink.

'*You have only been home five minutes and already* . . .' I heard her shouting, and then going slap bang with that hand of hers.

I slipped away onto the Front and bent into the wind to zip up my windcheater as I went down to the beach. No one was there, just me, myself and my thoughts, and the tide-line to explore.

No one but me and the wet shingle, and the raging of the sea as it went out with the falling of the tide. No one to tell me I must read. I found cuttlefish shells and tangled twine, tar balls and nine green bottles.

Then the long, long walk along the beach towards Southdown, where the shore is out of sight of the houses. I stopped to watch a flock of herring gulls pecking on the beach before they rose wheeling and screaming at my approach from a heap that looked like clothes.

I went to see what it was and found a man lying there, with a face like a swollen ball. His eyes were staring, white as a codling's belly; his blue shirt was swollen out by grey flesh that showed between the buttons blue-grey; and it was hairy.

One of his hands was gently buried in wet shingle, the other rested near a broken orange box on which there was writing burnt in black.

And *that* was how I came to learn to read.

\* \* \*

I picked up the box and left the hand behind as I turned my back on the Deadman's eyes and let the wind blow me along the shore, down where the waves thundered in and out and washed the Deadman's eyes from my mind.

In and out came the waves on the beach, rasping and grinding, in out, in out, and in their endlessness was my comfort and forgetting of all things, like the Deadman on the beach.

The box was tugged out of my hand by the wind and driven on past me, rolling end to end, and then falling flat as I caught up with it. I crouched down to look at the words and I suddenly thought there was someone who might show me the way through the barbed wire that rose between me and the printed words.

Not Granny.

Not my Ma.

Not Uncle Max.

Long, long back along the shingly shore I walked, straight past the part of the Green where my house was, my anorak open to cool me down after that time of my trudging, crunching by the waves that came in and out, one two, in and out.

I raised my head and saw the mast of Stoning Castle.

Mr Boys was the Keeper and my friend. He let me help him paint the black rails round Castle Green. He let me count the tickets at the end of the day. He let me listen to his guided tour, which the Ministry of Works no longer allowed him to give because he was not qualified: the whole history of Stoning from when the Romans under Julius Caesar landed near where the Castle was built more than fifteen hundred years later.

Mr Boys said that, though I couldn't read, if only I could remember dates and things it would be a starting point.

'Reading's protected by a castle you've got to find a way to storm,' Mr Boys told me, 'and there's always a weak point in a castle that a persistent invader can find. One day you'll find the weak point, Jimmy, and then break through like the Roman army into the Land of Reading in your mind.'

He often said things like that and so, that day of the Deadman and the wooden box, he seemed the best person to teach me to read.

I climbed up the shingle and went to the Castle gate, which was where Mr Boys found me snivelling.

'Mr Boys . . .'

'Eh!? What is it, lad? What is it, boy . . . ?'

He let me cry and tell him how I had found the Deadman on the beach and hadn't dared look back all the way from Southdown in case his eyes blinked and he got up to follow me.

'I must telephone the police,' he says.

I cried some more, because it had been policemen in the long-ago time, before Granny took me by the hand, who led me back into Darktime.

I heard Mr Boys on the black telephone: 'It's all right . . . I've made him cocoa . . . so you know already . . . it's all right . . . tell his Granny that he's here. I'll bring him home when he wants to move. No, he's best with me for now.'

That day when I learnt to read, Mr Boys closed the Castle early especially for me and I never let go of the orange box.

'What's that box, lad?' he said when he'd drunk his tea and lit his pipe and thought for a bit.

'It's the Deadman's. It's got words on it,' I replied. 'What does it say?'

He looked at it and said two magic words, 'Search me.'

'But you can read,' I said.

'Anyone can read,' he says, 'provided it's in words you know, but they can't if they don't. I think these words are what the Spaniards speak, who were our mortal enemies once.'

'The Armada,' I said, remembering.

'Yes,' he said with a grin, 'did I tell you that?'

I nodded, because he had, many times, and I looked at the writing on the box in wonder.

'You can't read it?' I said.

'Not me,' he said.

He was the first adult I ever met who said he couldn't read like me.

Then he said the words which were a golden key to all my life to come.

'We could *try* reading it together,' he said. 'Would you like to?'

I nodded my head, thinking that if I followed him through the barbed wire I could learn the way and go through all by myself another day.

'I'll tell you what, lad,' he said, 'I'll telephone your Ma. Reading this box may take a little time and she might get worried.'

'Tell Granny,' I said. 'She's the one who worries.'

'I'll tell both,' said Mr Boys cautiously.

Then it was that Mr Boys took me to Stoning Public Library for the first time, to read.

'What we want, Mary,' he said to the Librarian, 'is a Spanish dictionary. Does the library run to that? And don't look so worried; I'll not let him drip that box all over the pages.'

We sat at a big table, Mr Boys and me, and he said, 'I do believe you know your letters.'

I nodded my head.

'J is for J, I is for I, M is for M, and M is M again, and Y is the last: JIMMY.'

'Now then, I'll point to the letters on the box and you tell me what they are.

'E,' I said.

'Here, lad, you can write it down as well . . .'

I wrote it down.

'S.'

I wrote that down.

'P.'

And that as well.

'Will the Deadman come alive?'

'No, lad, he'll not come alive.'

'And an "A" and an "N".'

'. . . and "A" again,' I said.

'*Espana*,' said Mr Boys, 'and what do you think *that* means?'

'I know what it means,' I said, 'because you told me when you told me the story of the Armada. That word means *Spain*, where Spaniards live. *Espana* for *Spain*!'

I remember looking at my finger, which smelt of sea and seaweed from the box, and at the letters that made the first word I ever learnt to read, and thinking it was clever that words were made to be written and spoken and read all at once. I felt surprise and that was good.

I'd thought words to be read were different from words to be written, and different again from the same words spoken, so no wonder it seemed like barbed wire to me.

'It's *very* clever,' I said.

'What is?'

'Reading and writing and speaking all in the same small word,' I said. 'Who invented it?'

'Mmm . . .' he wondered. 'Probably a woman.'

'Why?'

'Because they think cleverly, like Mary over there.'

Mr Boys was not married but I could see he liked Mary the Librarian.

'Now . . .' he began.

'Did the Deadman come from Spain?'

'Maybe, but he won't come alive again. Now . . .'

In fact, reading was not barbed wire after all: reading was a tree to climb to get a better view and you just had to be able to see the bits that would hold your feet.

'Can you see that word *Espana* somewhere else on this box?'

I nodded my head and pointed. I had seen it already. In two places the words on the box gave me places to climb.

'Let's try this one next,' he said, pointing to another word.

The second word was an

N and an

A and an

R and an

A again, and an

N again a

J like in James, my first name all over again, and an

A and an

S for sugar.

'Can you say that?' asked Mr Boys.

I couldn't.

'I'll try,' he said. '*Naranjas*. Hmm!'

'Say it again and I'll close my eyes,' I said.

'Naranjas,' he said quickly.

'Oranges,' I said, 'it sounds like that.'

It is not easy finding a word in a dictionary if the writing's small and you don't know the order they come in, but Mr Boys and I found it: *Naranja* for *orange*.

'How did you know?' he asked.

'Because it's an orange box,' I explained. 'I've found them before and chopped them up for kindling. I worked its meaning out when you said it aloud. It sounds the same.'

'*Spain* and *oranges*,' he said. 'We're doing well, you and I.'

I never learnt more Spanish words than those two, not for years, because Mr Boys suddenly got diverted. He looked over my shoulder and said, 'Well I never! It's Mr Mee!'

I turned but there was no one there, just shelves and shelves of books.

'That's right,' he said, reaching up to a row of ten blue ones, 'Arthur Mee's *Children's Encyclopedia*, if I am not very much mistaken. Jimmy, you're looking at one of the great works of the human mind. These books have an answer for everything.'

'Does it say why the tides come back in?' I asked.

'Yes, it certainly does.'

'Does it say why some pebbles are bigger than others?'

'In a manner of speaking, yes,' he said.

'Does it say what a fish can see?'

'Most certainly.'

'Does it tell if I can hear the Coalman coming in my sleep?'

'Humph! Not so sure of *that!*'

'Does it say about Spanish oranges?'

'Let's see,' he said, taking down a volume and opening a door on a whole new world for me.

'Page 5271!' he announced eventually. 'Here, you find it . . .'

Which took a bit of time, but when I did there were photographs of people picking oranges in Valencia and a horse and cart and . . .

'There's my box!' I said, and there it was, lots of times over, all waiting to be put on a ship with a funnel to set off across the world.

'Where's Valencia?' I asked and soon one thing led to another, from oranges to dates, from olives to red pepper, from esparto grass and nuts all the way to rice.

Nobody had shown me books were windows onto wonder until that day.

We sat together reading until the library had to shut and Mr Boys's friend Mary said she was sorry it was time to go and she had to make her mother tea. But if, perhaps, we would like . . .

I said, 'It's time I went home.'

Mr Boys said, 'Yes, it most probably is. Let's go by the shops and later, Mary . . .'

'Yes,' she said, putting on her coat with keys in her hands.

Mr Boys looked pleased.

'Can I come back tomorrow?' I asked.

They said I could.

On the way to my house he bought some oranges all the way from Spain.

'For your granny and you,' he said.

'Thank you, Mr Boys,' I said, as polite as can be.

He grinned and saw me home.

Ma said I should write to thank him right away for looking after me that day, but Granny said it might be best if she talked to me a little first.

She settled me down in her sitting room facing the sea. I saw the shingle shore and remembered the Deadman.

'I can read,' I said, showing her the orange box. '*Espana* for *Spain* and *naranjas* for *oranges*, and other things in Mr Mee's encyclopedia, like rices and nuts, and they grow only in the south.'

'Can you read, my dear?' she replied. Granny never ever doubted my word, so I always told her the truth and nothing but. 'Was that what happened today?'

'The best thing, yes . . .' I said, 'and I saw the Deadman's eyes.'

'Did you?' she said, pouring herself a cup of tea.

I told her all about my day from beginning to end.

'Are you going to chop up your box for firewood?' she said finally. I shook my head.

'I'm going to keep new things I get in it,' I said. I was thinking of those things I lost when Ma shoved them all in a suitcase and they died.

'I haven't got anything yet but when I have something I'll put it in.'

'You've got lots of things,' she said, trying to make me feel better, because I looked sad thinking of my old things.

Four days later Mr Boys came by.

'Got something for Jimmy,' he said.

It was Mr Mee's encyclopedia, each and every volume, all for me. He had bought them second-hand at Mrs Smith's junk shop down in the North End of our town where the fishermen lived.

For a long time after that, when I was not with Granny or Mr Boys or Uncle Max, or when I grew tired of the wind and the rain on the beach, or when I heard the Coalman tapping or thought I saw the Deadman's eyes opening again in the flap of a herring gull's wings, I would go to my room and lose myself in the wonders of the world with Mr Mee. In his great books I found more and more words to read, with Granny's help, until one by one, like mileposts on a road leading to a great wide plain that never ends whatever direction you go, the day came when I read a whole story from beginning to end and didn't even notice I was doing it.

That day I went all the way down to the Castle carrying the book so that I could see Mr Boys and read the story aloud for him. I sat in the Keep and he puffed his pipe and at the end he said, 'One day, Jimmy, you'll find there's a day comes along that seems to make all the others worth living for. Today you made such a day for me.'

Afterwards I carried that big book all the way back home and put it with its nine brothers. Mr Mee's ten blue books were the first of my new treasures I kept in the orange box that had floated across the sea, and which the Deadman gave me on the day I was ready to learn to read.

# 9

# MY FIRST MOUNTAIN

The biggest mountains I had seen were the white cliffs of Dover, and the steepest climb I had ever tried was Folkestone Warren, looking for fossils. So I was filled with excitement and hope when Uncle Max and his fiancée Auntie Fiona said the time had come for our long-planned expedition to climb mountains.

I asked if where we were going was higher than the Dover cliffs. Uncle Max laughed and said that compared to the mountains we were going to, the white cliffs and the Warren were like a bicycle to a ten-ton truck.

'Or a rice pudding to a paddy field,' said Ma, who was on her way out to the corner shop.

'Or Stoning Promenade to the farms of Rhodesia,' said Granny who was putting her smalls on the line.

I thought a bit and decided what they were trying to say was that the hills I knew were like a pouting to a great white shark compared to real mountains, but I said nothing in the end, as I was the only one who had caught a pouting and knew how small it was.

A week before we went, Uncle Max turned up with four pints of pink turpentine he had bought in the Dustpan Stores. He poured it into the washing-up bowl, put it on the kitchen floor and got me Granny's stool with the raffia seat.

'Jimmy, you're to sit here and put your feet in this bowl every day, morning and evening for quarter of an hour for the next four days.'

'Why?' I asked. The turpentine smelt very strong, like petrol only worse.

Uncle Max said, 'I read that it's what mountaineers do to harden the skin and prevent blisters from their boots. Fiona says she has heard of it and believes it may do the trick.'

'Is Fiona sitting in *her* kitchen with her feet in a bowl of turpentine every day this week morning and night?' asked Granny with that look in her eye which said she doubted Aunt Fiona was.

'She has known people in the past who have done it to great effect,' said Uncle Max, frowning.

I decided to try it out there and then, which was why Ma found strong-smelling wet footprints all through the kitchen, along the corridor and up the stairs to where she kept the towels when she came home.

Ma was not well that year and so she didn't hit me or shout, she just held her hand to her forehead and with a weary look said, 'The sooner you and Uncle Max get out of the house and on your way the better. And if you must do that with your feet, do it in the garden and wipe them with a rag, and don't play with Uncle Max's Swan Vestas while you're doing so, otherwise you'll have no feet on which to put your big black boots, only charred stumps.'

Later that day Uncle Max gave me a tin with soft slimy wax inside called dubbin.

'You must rub this into the boots the Royal Marines gave you every day for four days because it will make them supple, and by then your feet should be hard enough for you to practise in the boots.'

I said I would, and carefully rubbed in the dubbin, inside and out. The grease got under my nails and turned them black, and the taste didn't go away when I licked it, but it had a nice smell.

Four days seemed too long to wait and as my feet were already getting harder and harder I decided to try the boots out on an expedition of my own over the cliffs to Dover.

Granny said, 'Mr Baden-Powell advises Scouts and Cubs to be prepared, so you had better be. You will need a thermos flask and a map, and you will need a compass and a showerproof raincoat and warm combinations; you will . . .'

She went on like this for a long time and ended up saying I would need a haversack to put everything in and asking if I had one, because if not, then she was willing to go out and . . .

I went to her window and looked out at the beach. I could just see the cliffs where my practice expedition was to begin. I could also see that Granny was getting very excited about my trip.

Finally I said, 'Granny, I've walked and walked along the beach and up the cliffs ever since we moved to Stoning and I've never carried all those things. I bet I know as much about walking as you and Uncle Max put together.'

'Humph!' said Granny.

Then I went downstairs just as I was, as I always was, in my khaki shorts and shirt, and I found my boots and I put them on.

As I set off towards the Green I heard Granny open her window. She couldn't help herself.

'Jimmy!' she called after me. 'At least put on these socks which I knitted for you.'

But I didn't look round. I remembered that Granny once told me that sometimes it was convenient not to hear, and that morning I decided she was right.

The boots felt heavy, and some of the dubbin I'd put inside squidged between my toes. Ma had warned me that maybe the dubbin was only meant to be on the outside. By the time I got to the cliffs my feet were slipping all over the place in the squidge inside.

I sat on the sea defences by the water and took off the boots and left them there while I cleaned my feet with wet sand. Then I walked the tide-line, looking for something I had seen a few days before. It was an old bit of sail, all torn and stained, which had blown up beyond the sea and dried in the wind. I tore it up into smaller bits and cleaned out the boots inside. Then I tore some more and made a pad for each of my feet to go in the boots. Finally, I tied the leather laces tight and wiggled my feet and found they fitted as neat as a crab in its shell.

I looked back towards the South End and beyond to Stoning and then up the little path that leads to the top of the cliff and the start of the walk. I remember thinking, 'This is my first expedition in boots, so I'll make it a good one.'

All that summer day I walked over the cliffs, all the way to St Margaret's Bay and back, with lots to do in between. The boots did the walking more than me and when they decided to go one way and not another I followed them.

There were blue harebells in the grass, and the red ants' nests were getting big. Overhead was the high singing of skylarks. I could only see them against the bright sky by lying in the grass and screwing up my fists like binoculars and finding the skylarks in the curved hole of my little fingers.

When I was tired I sat looking out to sea, and as the day wore on and the tide went out I could see the Goodwins, dark islands on the sea, and off to the east, all the way over to the white cliffs of France, where one day I had decided I would stand.

A man came along the cliff path who looked strange, so I hid in a dugout left from the War and heard him go by, talking to himself.

'Bye, bye, bye, bye, bye,' he said again and again as he went past.

When I crept out to look at the back of him he had a bald head and I knew I could run faster than him so I wasn't afraid. I caught up with him and he was still saying, 'Bye, bye, bye . . .'

I said, 'Hello,' like Mr Boys did to everybody, because I wasn't scared of the man. Then he and I talked about things.

'The Germans never did invade, did they?' he said. 'But the skylarks are dying out all the same. Only a few years ago there were more than there are now.'

I said, 'Were there?'

He said, 'You're not a day-tripper then?'

'I'm a boy,' I explained.

He laughed himself nearly silly and said, 'I was one of them myself once long, long, long ago. Keep walking if you do nothing else; it's the only thing you've got to do to survive. *I* do and now it's the only thing I've got left. It's good to pass the time of day.'

Then he set off in a new direction, 'Bye, bye, bye, bye, bye . . .'

\* \* \*

That first day with my boots I walked so much that my legs grew tired and it was dusk by the time I got home.

'Your supper's on the sideboard,' said Ma without looking round or getting up, 'and you'll have to eat it cold as I've got work to do now.'

She was doing the accounts for the local National Savings Committee meeting, so off she went. Granny came down and found me eating cold shepherd's pie at the kitchen table.

'I had some socks for you,' she said; 'didn't you hear me?'

I said nothing and so didn't tell a lie.

'Well?' she said, sitting down. 'Tell me about your expedition.'

I told her what I had seen and done, and that I had got no blisters. The boots fitted like a glove. I told her about the bye-bye man.

'Let me look at your feet,' she said.

I showed them to her and she looked puzzled for a bit and then laughed and laughed and laughed. In all the long time I knew Granny I rarely heard her laugh so much.

'What's funny?' I said.

'The pads you made out of the sail on the beach,' she said, 'they're still sticking to your feet.'

I looked down and I saw they were. I pulled them off and the soles of my feet were squidgy with dubbin and sweat, and marked on them, like print on a page, were the warp and the weft of the sail cloth.

Granny said, 'Maybe socks would be better next time.'

I agreed to take the socks she had made when I went on the expedition to the mountain.

'When am I to go?' I asked, for Uncle Max was always vague about time.

'Tomorrow,' said Granny, 'at the crack of midday, if I know your uncle, or thereabouts.'

She was nearly right.

Uncle Max came down the day after that with Auntie Fiona and said we were off once we had had lunch and he had bought a few things.

'Lunch yes, things no,' said Auntie Fiona firmly. 'We're going at two sharp, so that we get there by ten. It's an eight-hour drive.'

I heard Granny say to Ma, 'There's someone to respect. She's just what Max needs. If he's got any sense he'll marry her.'

'And if she's got sense she won't marry *him*,' said Ma.

I didn't know what to think, but I liked Auntie Fiona.

When we left, Granny and Ma came out to wave us goodbye and wish us good luck. I noticed that Ma had a suitcase all packed and had had a hairdo. She was going off somewhere as well, so it was convenient I was going away just then.

That meant Granny would have the run of the house, which she once told me she quite liked from time to time.

'Your grandfather was a lifelong member of the Temperance Movement,' she explained, 'but on occasion he would allow himself to sin sufficiently, as he put it, to have a glass of bottled cider. Sometimes when I am alone in the house I pour him a glass of cider and put it on a table in the garden as if he was still here, and I sit and remember such few good times as we had.'

'What do you do with it when you go inside again?' I asked.

'Drink it!' said Granny.

As we turned onto the Dover Road towards Star Hill I heard the Royal Marine clock strike two, so we were very sharp indeed.

'Are you all right at the back there, Jimmy?' called out Uncle Max.

I said I was.

'And you?' he said more softly to Auntie Fiona.

She nodded and smiled. Then she turned round to me and said, 'These are for you, for the journey. My father always gave us toffees for long journeys and as you . . . Don't eat them all at once. And if you get cold there's a blanket on the seat next to you.'

The car was open-topped and the wind blew in my face when I leant my head on the door where the window was wound down. I stared and stared at the verge as it rushed past, trying at first to see it properly and then letting it become a blur.

I remember opening the first toffee slowly and smelling its delicious smell.

I remember putting the blanket around me and smelling the same scent as Fiona's perfume when she hugged me on arriving and departing. I liked her woman smell but it wasn't quite the same as the one I sometimes remembered from before Darktime.

But as Uncle Max's car zoomed along I remember thinking I had never felt like that before, with so far to go and so much to look forward to.

The next thing I remember was waking into twilight at a petrol station, with Fiona asleep in front.

'Is it far, Uncle Max?'

'Two more hours,' he said.

'Are there any mountains yet?'

'Not quite yet. You won't see them until the morning.'

I remember Uncle Max walking me in through a hotel door later and supper on trays served by a man in black who called me 'sir'.

I remember waking up at dawn in a room with another bed in which Uncle Max was asleep. I was desperate to go to the lavatory but didn't dare move. I listened to the birds outside, which were louder than at home and different. They didn't squeal and squawk like gulls. I was so desperate I counted the chimes of a clock in the corridor outside and then on and on until the next chimes. I listened to the creak of the pipes as the plumbing woke up. I squeezed my nails into the palms of my hands to stop myself going in the bed. I thought, 'If I wet the bed, Uncle Max will be disgraced and have to take me home.'

To make matters worse, there was the constant sound of a river running outside, *tinkle tinkle tinkle*. It made me want to go even more.

But when dawn came I suddenly remembered that this was an expedition and we had to fend for ourselves through thick and thin. That's what Granny had said.

So I got up, went into the corridor and tiptoed about until I found the lavatory. The funny thing was that not much came out after all that fuss. But on the way back to the room I saw a lace curtain blow in the breeze at a window.

I went to look out and that's when I saw it, my first mountain. It went up and up to clouds at the top, with valleys and forests between it and me, all shining in a misty light. It looked near and far at the same time: it looked like you could touch it just by opening the window; and also so far off you could take a lifetime walking to it. I stared and stared and forgot where I was until the sun rose higher and the mountain turned bright.

'Uncle Max!' I said when I got back in the room. 'There's a mountain down the corridor.'

He opened one eye and then another and looked at me.

'What time is it?' he mumbled. Then, 'There's a mountain, is there? Just the one?'

'One's big, many would be huge,' I said.

He grinned and sat up in bed.

'Stand by the window and close your eyes.'

I stood there and heard him pull the curtains open, and opened my eyes.

The window was a picture of mountains, peaks and valleys, shadowed cliffs and patches of green on which the sun was rising fast. They were so high I thought it would take a lifetime to reach the top of them. Stoning and the waves on the shingle beach seemed far away.

'Those mountains are where Edmund Hillary practised before he went to climb Everest,' said Uncle Max. 'That big one is called Snowdon and all together they're called Snowdonia.'

Auntie Fiona was down at breakfast before us but she gave up her place so I could look at the view.

'We'll set off at nine-thirty sharp,' she said. 'They're making us packed lunches and there's a drying room where we can put our walking things afterwards. Jimmy, you're not to wear your boots in the hotel.'

Uncle Max wore breeches for his walking, and Auntie Fiona had a divided skirt made of tweed. I just had my khaki shorts.

'They'll do for today, as it's warm and dry,' said Uncle Max, 'and we're only doing a short walk just to work in our boots. This afternoon we'll get you something warmer to wear.'

I had my haversack and a jersey, and I had decided to wear the socks Granny made. I carried my own packed lunch and the woman at the hotel gave me an extra bar of Cadbury's chocolate and a packet of Refreshers.

We walked by the roadside for a while towards the big mountains. The valley swept up smoothly on one side and steeply the other and there were sheep in the fields with black faces and black legs.

'Why are their legs black?' I asked.

'They're tidal sheep,' said Uncle Max, 'and the black bit is where the water has been.'

You never knew with Uncle Max, unless you caught him grinning. He was grinning now. He and Auntie Fiona kept looking at each other like two stars in a film poster. But I felt like a soldier from a war film and walked in silence like I did on the beach, one two, one two, one two, pretending there were Germans about. Then I forgot about that and just enjoyed the view.

We turned off the road and onto a path. Then over a bridge across a little river linking two lakes and up into an old wood whose trees were covered in moss. It was silent in there, dark and green, and the air was cool and sweet. I tripped just once and after that I looked where my feet went as we climbed the rocky path among the trees, one two, one two, one two.

'Jimmy, we're resting!'

I stopped and turned round and saw that Uncle Max and Fiona had paused to look back at the view shoulder to shoulder. I thought we had climbed only a little way but we seemed to have climbed far, and high. The little lakes were below us now, and looked tiny and we could hardly see the bridge we had crossed at all. I saw the road we had walked down and followed it back with my eyes to where there were trees in the distance and the smoking chimney of our hotel.

Rising behind it, above it, huge and dark like the wall of Stoning Castle on a winter's day when you're down in the moat, was Snowdon. Looking across the valleys and the mountains with the breeze in my face I felt like a tern fluttering on the wind. The breeze felt like it was trying to get into my head and blow the Darktime away. It was that good.

'I've never seen him look so well and happy,' I heard Auntie Fiona say.

'He's like a puppy, the way he runs ahead without seeming to get tired,' answered Uncle Max.

I knew they were talking about me but I didn't mind. They were saying good things. They were saying they didn't mind me being there. They were saying I was not a nuisance and in the way. I wanted to run and shout, I felt so good, so I did.

I heard Uncle Max laugh and when I looked round they were just standing, staring up at me, arm in arm. Auntie Fiona waved and I waved back and then I turned back up the slope.

'Don't go too far!' I heard Uncle Max call.

We climbed on and on, one two, one two, and I wasn't scared of the sheep when I found they always got up and out of the way, grumbling and calling warnings to each other like birds sheltering on the beach when you walk too close. You could never quite reach them.

We stopped and had something to eat.

Uncle Max asked if I was tired but I just shook my head and ate my chocolate. I wasn't used to talking out of doors because I was always alone. But I liked sitting in silence with them nearby.

'I want to go right to the top,' I said.

Auntie Fiona looked at the sky and the run of clouds and I said, 'It isn't going to rain.'

'How do you know?'

I learnt to read skies long before I ever learnt to read a book with Mr Boys; and to sniff the air for rain, and feel the run of the wind in my hair.

'I just do.'

'Come on then,' said Uncle Max, 'we'll climb to the top.'

The last bit was nearly all rock and my hobnailed boots made a clatter. I learnt to wedge them in the hollows and cracks and not to slip.

'Jimmy, you're like a mountain goat,' called Uncle Max from below. 'Wait for us and don't go out of sight.'

As we neared the top I saw a pile of stones ahead marking the top itself. The wind was suddenly strong and cold, and there were goose bumps on my legs. I stopped to put my jersey on.

Uncle Max said, 'On you go . . . you lead us up to the cairn.'

That last bit I felt like Edmund Hillary himself, and I went slow and breathed heavy, as if I was carrying oxygen like he did on Everest.

The very last bit was easy because a view opened up far beyond, hills and hills spread away below me as far as the eye could see. I had climbed out of Darktime for the day and my heart sang because I knew I had found a place I could come to in the days and years to come, again and again. Like Stoning Beach, it would always be there. Places to remember the good things and forget the bad.

We sat huddled together on the lee side of the stones, looking at Snowdon and eating our lunch. We didn't talk much and I felt Uncle Max's shoulder against mine, while his hand held Auntie Fiona's for a time.

'Are you tired?' they asked.

I wasn't. I knew about walking from the beach; and I knew about keeping going steadily.

'Mountains are dangerous places,' said Uncle Max, 'but only if you're stupid or very unlucky.'

'Like the sea,' I said, 'like the waves coming in.'

'What do you mean, Jimmy?' asked Auntie Fiona. When she asked me questions, she meant for me to answer them.

I explained about walking along the shore in a gale and how the waves came in suddenly sometimes and you had to learn to listen out for those.

'There's no one there to save you,' I said, 'so you have to watch out for yourself.'

'Were you ever caught by one?'

I nodded, and told them how it came in hard and pushed me right off balance and dragged me into the surf. I remembered the run of the sweeping waves against my legs and knowing I might drown if I didn't think. I said I was not afraid at all, just angry at myself. I remembered waiting and waiting while the waves roared and rose up and came back towards me. I was scared of that wave but not of the sea.

I told them how I rose up to meet it and turned to the shore, doggy-paddling with all my strength for moments that seemed for ever as the undertow tried to suck me down. Then I was pushed back to shore like old rags and pulled myself up onto the shingle and out of their reach; and then a bit further still.

Ma hit me for getting soaked through when I got back and gave me a nosebleed, but it was worth it to be alive. Michael said that for anyone to fall into the sea from dry land was about as stupid as could be but that it didn't surprise him as he knew I was stupid anyway. That night I took myself to bed early and lay shaking so much the bed rattled against the wall. But next day I went down to the shore and walked near the waves and I said again and again, 'I'm not, I'm not.' Stupid, that is.

Up there in the shelter of the pile of stones, eating our packed lunches, I told them all that. It was as easy as talking to Granny.

'Your legs are shaking now,' said Auntie Fiona, giving me a cardigan to put over them. 'We'd better get you down and buy those breeches we promised you. As for being stupid, Jimmy, well . . .' She looked cross. 'Well . . . you're not and that's all. You're just not.'

'What's this mountain's name?' I asked.

'Moel Siabod,' said Uncle Max, 'your first mountain.'

'Can I sit here just a bit longer, please?'

I was thinking that I didn't want to forget this moment and this day, not ever.

Uncle Max said I could and he and Auntie Fiona got up and walked a little way along the ridge from the top. Later I saw them stand together looking at the view like me. He put his arm over her shoulder, and she put her arm round his waist. They were two people, but standing close together like that they seemed more like one. They kissed and talked and kissed again, and when they came back they were smiling.

We walked down into sunshine, steadily, one after the other. I stumbled once or twice, and my boot went into a little stream.

When we reached the road we got a lift from a farmer back to the hotel and then went to a place called Llanberis. In a shop there they bought me some breeches made of tweed and I wore them all that week.

Up Ogwen I wore them, and up the steep way to Tryfan. On the Glyders I wore them, and up the Pyg track to Llyn Glas.

With each climb, with each walk, with each blast of fresh wind and with the driving rain as well, I felt something new growing inside me. Something was being made there which could not be taken away.

On the last day, the day we were going to climb Snowdon, the clouds came down and the rain fell, so we stayed in the valley. We found a ruined slate mine, and sheltered in the mouth of a tunnel made by men a hundred years before. We got lost for a time in the mist and were cold, tired and hungry by the time the hotel came back into view.

'You've never complained, Jimmy,' said Auntie Fiona on the last walk in, 'not once all week.'

I didn't know how. Darktime took all my complaining away. It takes no time to get warm again, and rested, and to eat; it takes for ever to cast off Darktime.

'It's all right,' I said, my boots squelching in the slatey mud. 'I liked everything.'

Next morning, the cloud was lower still and the air was cold. Uncle Max loaded the car and people in the hotel came out to say goodbye.

They lined up with Auntie Fiona and me so Uncle Max could take a photograph with his Kodak camera, not one but two.

Then I climbed onto the back seat and settled down and Uncle Max said, 'Time to go.'

Auntie Fiona had put out a blanket for me, and a bag of toffees for the journey home. I watched the mountains go by as we went, and I waved goodbye to the tidal sheep.

There were no words to say but plenty to think.

'You all right, Jimmy?' asked Auntie Fiona, turning around.

I nodded and said I was.

Then I said, 'We never went to the Devil's Kitchen.'

That was a great cleft in the rock near Ogwen.

She smiled and said, 'Next time!'

I just grinned.

After that, she and Uncle Max had talking to do. There was a bright shiny diamond ring on her left hand. That morning they had told me they were going to get wed and I was the first to know.

She had asked if I was all right. Yes, I was all right, but different now and I didn't know why. I tried to see Moel Siabod as we passed it but the cloud was too thick. It was my first mountain and it was so high that in climbing it I left Darktime behind for a time and saw a new light. I settled back in the seat, took the wrappers off a toffee, put it in my mouth and closed my eyes. I found I could remember every step of the way up the mountain, right to the top; and I could remember the view as well.

Then there was something else I remembered which I should have before. It was something Granny told me to say when people had good news. I leant forward and touched Auntie Fiona on the shoulder to make her turn round.

'Mmm?'

'Congratulations,' I said.

'Thank you,' she said with her warm voice.

That was a week to remember, when everything felt right and was right; the best week of my life. But life never stays the same. Not for a moment. Life's full of shocks.

A few months later, Ma told me that Uncle Max and Auntie Fiona had got married quietly without any fuss and were sailing away for ever to America on the *Queen Mary*.

As it was a school day I was not allowed to travel down to Southampton with Granny and Ma to wave goodbye. But after school, before they got back, I put on my boots and my breeches, not caring what people in Stoning might think, and I walked the long way to Southdown and then up onto the cliffs. That was my goodbye to them and my wedding gift. I looked across to France and the white cliffs there and I thought about the distant day when I too would escape across the sea.

I stood up there a long while, remembering the good times in Wales, and the laughter with Auntie Fiona, and Uncle Max opening that bedroom curtain onto a view I would never forget.

I stood until France became a black silhouette and I could see the lights of the ships.

Then I walked home and put my breeches and my boots in the back of my bedroom cupboard and I said goodbye to mountains for a time.

# 10

# THE BATTLE OF
# SAN ROMANO

One September I was sent to a boarding school where I couldn't hear or smell the sea. The headmaster of the school was called Mr Franks and in the geography room was a copy of a famous picture in the National Gallery in London Town called *The Battle of San Romano*. That picture, and Mr Franks, introduced me to the wonders of art. It also helped me achieve my first, only and final sporting triumph.

The school was called Nunnestone Preparatory School for Boys, and boys were sent there who were an inconvenience to their parents to have at home. Some had parents far away in foreign lands; others had parents like my Ma who thought they had better things to do than look after kids.

I wasn't unhappy, but I never knew why Ma sent me there. I wasn't forgotten, but I wasn't much remembered. I wasn't much bullied, but a teacher touched my willy.

When I thought about it afterwards, what I learnt at that strange place was never written on a blackboard, but I learnt quite a lot.

There was a maroon uniform that everyone had to wear: a cap with a dragon on it, a blazer with a dragon badge, grey shorts, grey shirt, a maroon tie, black shoes and grey woollen socks held up with garters Granny made for me with knicker elastic.

Everything had to have name tags on it made by a special firm in London. Mine had my surname on it followed by a comma and then 'James', even though everyone called me Jimmy. So all my school career I had a name on my clothes no one ever used because Ma forgot to say and she never thought those things important. Ma sewed the tags on herself, but as she always did things for me in too much of a hurry so that she could get on with what she wanted to do for herself, those tags were all crooked and puckered up, and I hid them if I could. They were not sewn on with care as some boys' were.

The only place in Stoning where you could buy the uniform was at Beaven and Lane's, a clothing shop in the High Street. My Ma got into a rage about the prices and said that the owner and the schools were conspiring to make money out of poverty-stricken middle-class parents like her.

She decided to make a stand on the rugby shirts, also maroon, which cost so much she said she couldn't afford them. Although she was not practical by nature, she came up with the idea of buying white ones from a store in Canterbury, where they cost next to nothing, and dying them maroon, which she did in a galvanized bucket on the stove.

Afterwards, she put my rugby shirts out in the sun to dry and was very pleased that she had saved so much money. Unfortunately, as a result of this she got the bit between her teeth where saving money was concerned and dug out her Singer sewing machine and bought some grey cloth to make me some school shirts. She measured my neck with her tape measure and said, 'That's funny, your neck is bigger than your brother's. The tape must be wrong.'

She was definitely not practical, because the wings of the collars ended up different lengths and wouldn't stay down properly when I tied my tie, and when I tried to do up my top button the collar was so tight I almost suffocated, which Ma blamed on me.

'Not so tight, not so tight,' she said impatiently on the first morning, getting irritated with me when I tied my tie and the collar rose up in all directions and I began to faint. As a result of the shirts, and Ma's scrimping on other things, in all the time I went to that school I never did feel smart. My jackets were hand-me-downs bought from other parents and the first was as tight under the armpits as the shorts were tight under my privates, making me walk like a duck.

'Oh, I think that will do,' Ma said in her sweet social voice when the other mother brought the uniform round for me to try on. 'How does the jacket feel, Jimmy?' She sounded like the cooing of a dove.

'A bit tight.'

Her eyes darkened. She hated being shown up in public even if it meant not telling the truth.

'You should be grateful you're going to such a good school,' she said, betraying me by thinking more of the other mother than my comfort. Ma had to scrimp on money, but she didn't have to scrimp on caring, which is free. She could have bothered a bit more and bought the uniform from someone more my size. It ended with my having to have the shorts and jacket and her giving the other woman money and talking in whispers at the front door.

When the woman was gone I asked, 'Will I know anyone at the school?'

'Your brother,' said Ma.

My heart sank.

So I was going to the same school as him.

He was a boarder but I started as a dayboy, because Ma said the Man Who Wasn't wouldn't pay for me. As there weren't any other dayboys from Stoning, I travelled there each day by myself on an East Kent Road Car Company double-decker from Lugger Street. I used to sit on the top deck at the front on the right-hand side because that had the best view, and going down the hill just past Moreton was so fast it was like flying in the air and made your stomach jump.

The school was a big building which had once been a country house. It was up a long private drive through woods. It had a grand entrance at the front that parents used, and a back entrance by dustbins and the bootroom that we boys used.

The main corridor was tessellated, meaning it had coloured Victorian tiles, and it smelt of polish and boiled vegetables, except we boys didn't say 'smelt' we said 'ponged', which is stronger and more accurate.

For the first two terms, I was in Miss Norbert's class. She wore blue tweed skirts and I used to flick ink on her fat bottom with the nib pens we had.

There was a lot about Miss Norbert I never liked. She was clumsy, and though I sat in her class so many times, I cannot remember a single thing she ever taught, not a single thing.

But I do know she liked me and would touch my cheek with her fat red hand, which made me squirm. I had a friend called George Kellerman and I think she touched him too. She was batty in the head.

There was a week or two when she decided I was not being well fed at home and she saved her breakfast and brought it into class for me to eat. She said she had gone without to feed me and I should be grateful. The plate of cold, congealed scrambled egg was put on her desk with a knife and fork and a glass of water and I had to go and sit in front of the class and eat it with everybody looking on. After a few days I threw it behind the radiator when she wasn't looking.

'You ate that fast,' she said when she turned round.

'Yes, miss,' I said, hoping nobody would say anything. They didn't. But Miss Norbert found me out from the smell that came from behind the hot radiator and after that she stopped doing it.

There was a boy who tried to bully me, and succeeded for a few days. I remember Miss Norbert watching and not stopping it, with a funny look in her eyes as if she was enjoying it. She definitely had bats in the belfry.

One morning that boy went too far when he was standing in the wrong place, which was between the door and the wall. I saw Miss Norbert watching as usual and something from Darktime came into my head. I grabbed the door handle and smashed the door as hard as I could into the boy so he was crushed into the wall and he fell to the floor when I let go.

Miss Norbert screamed out but I was never punished because Kellerman and other boys said the bully had it coming to him. After that nobody ever touched me again and Miss Norbert ignored me, except for one more time.

That was on November 6th, the day after Bonfire Night, when Kellerman and I went out to the dead bonfire at break. We got caught by the bell and came rushing back into class with dirty black hands.

Miss Norbert went mad, because she put cleanliness next to godliness, and gave the class silent work while she took us both upstairs to the bathrooms, which were named after famous rivers. I was put into Danube and George went into Ganges.

Miss Norbert ran the water into the huge bath and made me take off my clothes while she went next door to George. I didn't know what to do when I was naked so I stood there waiting, my willy shrivelling in the cold. When she came back she looked at me and told me I was a very filthy boy and to, 'Get in the bath.'

She was looking at my willy when she said *filthy* in the same hungry way that was in her eyes when she watched us boys fighting. There was a bristle scrubbing brush on the side of the bath and I remember her rubbing my willy in soap and saying it was dirty too, which was impossible as we had our clothes on when we played on the dead bonfire.

Then for some reason she took the scrubbing brush and tried to scrub my willy with it. I remember looking at her with such surprise that she stopped at once and went into the other bathroom. I washed my hands, the only bit of me that was dirty, I got out of the bath and dressed and was out and downstairs to the classroom in a flash.

Miss Norbert left the school in the middle of the next term and never came back.

The daily bus had two places it stopped to pick up dayboys going home. One was at the school entrance and the other across the fields. After five o'clock it only stopped over the fields, so when I stayed late at school for games or homework I had to walk the long way down the drive by myself and then right across the dark farm fields and scrubland to a bus stop in the middle of nowhere.

There was a bush that had died and looked like the head of Julius Caesar and in the evening, with the dusk falling, it always seemed to move. I was scared but by the time I reached it, going back was as bad as going forward so I tried not to look at the head and carried on.

It was about a mile to walk and all along the lane I wondered if there was anyone on the far side of the hedge who was going to come through a gap and get me, or if there would be cows with horns in the fields I had to cross later. There were big beech trees in one place with shadows underneath that might hold bad people; and over to the left, in the gap in the hedge, was a cottage with a chimney that smoked and a dog that barked. Then past all that, along the muddy lane and out through the hedge onto the road.

That first time I walked in the evening I stood for ages by the side of the deserted road and began to think the bus would never come. Then eventually I saw it coming very fast with its lights on because it was nearly dark and it went straight by without seeing me and I started running after it because it was five miles to walk home. The conductor must have seen me running, because the driver stopped and I got on. After that I used to jump into the road and wave my arms to make him see me better.

Only once did it pass me again without stopping, and after hanging about a bit I decided I would walk the five miles home. I remember the old windmill near Coldharbour Farm all spooky in the dusk. I remember the wheels of the shaft of Nunnestone Colliery turning slowly against the darkening sky and occasional cars coming by with their yellow lights. I remember looking in the windows of homes I passed and a family sitting having tea with a man at the head of the table, like in Doris Day films.

I wasn't scared once I got onto the Stoning road where there was a cycle track for the miners who lived in Upper Stoning. I knew the way.

Walking along that was the longest part, but I could see the lights of Stoning, and across the sea to Ramsgate and Cliftonville and the Isle of Thanet, and it looked different from the place I remembered, a different world. Seeing Stoning that evening from afar, with other towns in the distance, a little door opened in my mind about my home town that showed that it was just a place with a huge world beyond, not a huge place in itself. That door never quite closed up again and ever afterwards I knew there was a life beyond Stoning, which was a comfort.

There was one place I was scared and that was near the house in the hollow where my brother once said murderers lived. I hurried past that bit with my eyes turned to the shadows in the wheat field on my right, which was less scary. Once in a while a car passed in the opposite direction, its light yellow in the night. I soon learnt to avert my eyes when that happened because otherwise I couldn't see so well afterwards.

That was the first time I watched nightfall in the open countryside, starting out in twilight and arriving at my destination in darkness. Ma asked why I was late and I said I had been kept back. I never told her about that night walk because my family always spoilt things in my head with words. That was why I learnt to keep things to myself.

I was glad I had my school cap on my head because the wind got up towards the end when I was very tired and I began to get cold. That taught me that journeys are not so much about getting from the start to the finish as starting them and then learning on the way.

It was soon after my long walk that I became a boarder. The dormitory was next to the bathroom and had a prefect who kept control. People say there's bullying and things you shouldn't do but there wasn't in my dormitory. I heard boys saying they sucked each other's willies in the dormitory next to Ganges. I never saw it, though, and after Miss Norbert left nothing like that ever happened to me. Because I had bashed that boy with a door I was left alone and never touched by others. But bad things happened to some.

There were two brothers called Singh with dark skin who went away one holiday and never came back. Their mother went mad and killed them with an axe. My Ma told me later that their mum chased one of them into the garage before killing him. I only remember the sad feeling of hearing they had died and wondering what it felt like to be killed by someone who was meant to look after you. Then I realized I knew about that. I had only to think of Ma to imagine it.

They put up a plaque in their memory but nobody remembered to talk to us other boys who had to live with that loss and grief. All the parents who had sent their children away never heard the cries of their children grieving for boys who were no more, wondering if the same might happen to them.

On the first day I was a boarder there was another boy whose name began with L, a name like Lupert or Lupin. He had a big head and was shy and weak. I was next to him when he had to undress for games for the first time and he was crying with the shame of it. His parents would never have known that no one cared for him.

I said, 'It's all right. I feel the same. It's all right . . .' I only said it to comfort him, because I didn't actually mind undressing in front of others. I said it because there was nobody else to comfort him. He was no good at games and I looked after him, but after a while I knew I couldn't save him from the bullies. If he had bashed a door into someone he would have been all right.

I remember him just standing there crying, and seeing him like that made me think I wasn't the only one in Darktime and there must be many more. But mostly when you're there you're all alone.

My peg was number 63 and ever since that day I comforted the 'L' boy and realized I had something to give another, I have regarded that as my lucky number.

I remember the teachers more than what they taught. Like Mr Bell, who used to joke with words all the time. He asked us, 'What's the difference between a mad Dutchman and a drainpipe?'

We didn't know, so he told us: 'One's a silly Hollander and the other's a hollow cylinder.' I thought it was funny but others didn't. That was because I liked words.

I made a joke myself once with Miss Leavis, who was old and grey. She taught religious knowledge and once we were reading about the sons of Levi and I put up my hand and said I didn't know she was married. She didn't think my joke was funny.

The School Secretary was Johnny Joyce, who had an office near the main door and only one eye as a result of an accident on his bicycle. Other boys said he hit something on a country road and had to cycle eighteen miles holding the eye that had fallen out between his teeth. They said that he could still see with that eye and was the only person in the world who had ever seen the back of his head, which he did by holding his fallen-out eye behind him. Someone asked if that meant he was the only person in the world who had ever looked right up his bum and we had a laugh so big that it was the biggest ever and we were still laughing when break was over and geography started. We would have stopped but one of the boys was laughing so much he made a rude noise from his bum by mistake and then we laughed until it hurt. We all got detentions, but that didn't stop it being funny.

Mr Franks the headmaster wore thick woolly socks when he took us for football. He had skinny legs and blue veins and his head looked like a skull wearing gold-framed spectacles. His passion was billiards and in his room he had a big table and a special Joe Davis cue. Favoured boys were allowed to play billiards and touch the cue.

The school against which we played games most seriously was Menmore School in South Stoning. We played football, rugby and cricket against them and if we lost, which we often did, Mr Franks got very upset and angry. Games to him were war, and Menmore were a worse enemy to us than the Germans were to Great Britain in the First and Second World Wars.

Woe betide the goalie who let in a goal from a Menmore boy; or the batsman out for a duck against a Menmore bowler; or the fullback who dodged a tackle against a Menmore forward and let a try through.

Mr Franks played football with us sometimes but he was so old that his legs and arms seemed to go all over the place when he tried to run. He looked as if he was about to fall to bits.

Once a ball hit him and he fell flat on his back.

'Never give up!' he said as everybody helped him to his feet.

I once scored a hat-trick of goals against Menmore Under-9s

which was a great achievement because Mr Franks strongly believed that the Menmoreans had sneaked some under-10s in their side, like we had done. That's war.

But really we had a good team and they didn't and that game we got seven goals including my three, which was surprising since I was goalkeeper. What happened was it got so frustrating me seeing the others boys score easy goals that I got someone else put in goal so I could have a go.

When I scored my third I noticed that the Menmore goalie was snivelling tears because he felt he was letting his side down. Maybe the Menmore teacher on the sidelines who was shouting at him was like Mr Franks about losing. But as I was a goalie too I knew how he felt and went over to him and said, 'It's not your fault; it's your team's.' That cheered him up and he waved at me when I was chaired off the field for my hat-trick.

But that was not my greatest sporting triumph.

That happened in the winter term, when we played rugby. I was good at running, catching, dodging and seeing what was going to happen in the game and so being in the right place at the right time and how to avoid trouble. But I spoilt it all by being afraid of tackling. When boys came running at me with the ball, especially big boys with hard knees and muscled legs, something cowardly in me said, 'Jimmy Rova, run for your life in the opposite direction.'

This was not what Mr Franks wanted from his boys, especially as, when we got older and bigger, we might be selected for the Senior match against Menmore, which was the most important fixture of the year, when wives of the teachers came, and even some of the Governors, to watch and give support.

Fortunately that was a long way off for me and I had plenty of time to find my courage for tackling. As it was, and as I couldn't run away, when I had to tackle I pretended to by sliding to the ground in front of the boy with the ball and putting out my hands and arms in a half-hearted way while closing my eyes and averting my head. I hoped nobody would notice and I wouldn't get hurt.

We all knew that cowardice in the face of the enemy, especially the Menmoreans, was the worst possible crime where Mr Franks was concerned. The law said it was not permitted to put small boys up against a wall and shoot them for cowardice, which it is possible to do with soldiers. My Ma said that if it had been permitted, Mr Franks would have shot several boys for shirking tackles, including me if he had caught me, even if it meant losing school fees from their parents.

Instead, he did the next best thing, which was to make those boys who showed cowardice write out lines in Latin. The only one of his punishments I remember had nothing to do with bunking tackles but was given to me when I was accused of stealing someone's ruler, which I did not do as I had one of my own. Who wants two rulers?

I was made to write out one hundred times: *Radix malorum est cupiditas,* which means 'Money is the root of all evil.' As a result, that is the only Latin I learnt at Nunnestone School, except for *Amo, amas, amat,* which everybody knows means 'I love, you love, he loves'.

I knew I was not the only boy who shirked tackling, either in my Junior team or in the Senior team, but I was never caught, so I kept my fingers crossed that I would learn the trick of tackling before Mr Franks found me out. If I did then one day I might earn the honour of being selected to represent the school against Menmore in the Seniors.

The tradition at Nunnestone was that the Senior selection was announced by Mr Franks to the whole school the evening before the match, at a special pep talk he gave entitled 'Heroism, Cowardice and Winning the Game'.

In the year I remember best, to make it memorable and inspire us, he did it by candlelight while wearing his rugby kit, in front of the picture of *The Battle of San Romano.*

'Boys,' he said, 'tomorrow our school takes up arms once more against Menmore. The rules of engagement are those of the Rugby Football Union, the field of battle is the rugby pitch. But let us understand that this game of rugby is really the Game of Life in which there are winners and losers, which is to say heroes and cowards. Each one of you will in time have to stand before the Umpire of Life and be judged a hero or a coward. Which shall it be?'

While we thought about this Mr Franks took up a candle and began examining the painting behind him, the candle flickering its light among the lances and the fallen horses and the fighting, dying men.

Silence fell and when he turned round, the candle still in his hand, the silhouette of his skull-head, huge and horrible, was dancing about on the painting behind him as his hand and the flame moved around.

'Look upon this picture, boys,' cried Mr Franks, 'which was copied from one by Mr Uccello, who was Italian in the days when Italians were still men and not allies of the Hun. You will see he has depicted the victors and the vanquished in the Game of Life. You have a choice. You can be a knight upon a horse carrying a bloodied lance in the name of right and justice for your cause . . .' Here Mr Franks turned back to the picture and brought the candlelight to play upon a knight on a great white horse. 'Or you can be this snivelling coward who lies on the muddied, bloodied field unable to do more for himself or those unfortunates he so dismally sought to represent!'

Mr Franks had no need to point at the person he was referring to. It was a knight face-down on the ground with funny pointed feet who looked very dead indeed. I decided there and then that I did not ever want to be that knight, but it was hard to imagine myself upon a horse in armour with a lance in my hand and a red hat on my head killing other people.

Then he turned and faced us once again.

'Tomorrow afternoon at 1430 hours our team will fight the Menmoreans. The fifteen boys who are our army will fight for all of us, their chargers will be their legs, their armour the rugby shirts that carry the brave colours and emblem of Nunnestone School, and their lances will be their strength and their intelligence in battle.'

Mr Franks put down his candle at this point and pulled from the pocket of his baggy shorts a silver whistle and blew it long and hard three times. It rang long afterwards in my ears.

'What is courage?' he cried out. 'It is tackling hard and not count-ing the cost! It is standing alone in the field of battle when your comrades have fallen about you and fighting on!

'What is cowardice? It is shirking the tackle; it is fleeing the enemy; it is failing in your duty to us all; it is a disgrace that is personal and public.

'Why seek to win the Game? Because then you win the power to impose your will on others for their benefit and the betterment of all. As did the Florentines at the Battle of San Romano against the Sienese, under the redoubtable leadership of Niccolo da Tolentino! As have we Britons on our lucky colonies . . .'

Mr Franks got rather carried away after this and said a lot more, so much, in fact, that Mrs Franks stepped forward and reminded him it was time for the younger boys' bedtime cocoa.

'Now it is my privilege to announce the team for tomorrow and name the boys who shall be our champions. Let their names be in our prayers tonight and liveth for ever more upon the vellum of our hearts . . .'

Unfortunately, I can remember only a few of them.

'Burton, R, Captain; Freeman, M, Vice Captain; Cowper, M . . .'

I was sitting next to Kellerman as Mr Franks went through the list and we were agreeing that the best place to stand on the touchline was at the end by the wood because then we could slip away and climb some trees if it got cold. Standing and cheering is not much fun, especially if yours is the losing side, which it always was against Menmore in the Seniors.

'. . . and the reserves,' continued Mr Franks as he reached the end, 'are two boys who have done exceptionally well in the Junior team, Collins, R B, and . . .'

When you hear your name read out in public at school, a shiver goes down your spine as you realize what you've heard. Names are read out either for praise or for punishment and for me it had always been punishment. This felt no different.

'. . . Rova, J.'

I saw George's eyes widen. 'Er, that's *you*, I think . . .' he said with awe in his voice. It was then that I felt the cold run of terror down my spine.

*Rova, J.* My own name became a dagger of terror stabbed into my heart.

'Well done, team,' said Mr Franks. 'Good luck each and every one of you, including the reserves!'

If it had not been for the candlelight, everybody would have seen that my face had gone pale. Me, the tackle shirker, had been selected as reserve against Menmore School Seniors. It was a terrible mistake; except it wasn't: it had happened.

'Bad luck,' said Kellerman. 'It'll be your job to put the flagposts out.'

That was the job of reserves, along with sweeping out the changing rooms after the game, and cleaning the rugby ball if it got muddy. Reserves didn't get to play, but they had to be there.

'It means we won't be able to go into the wood, worse luck,' said Kellerman, 'but at least you'll get your name in the school magazine.'

That night the wind blew hard enough for the dead ivy to scratch at our dormitory windows like witches trying to get in, and I had nightmares. I dreamt I was playing against the Menmore team and all my team had died and I was left to fight for Nunnestone's honour all alone, with Mr Franks and hundreds of his twins on the touchline urging me on. I dreamt all their forwards were on white chargers galloping towards me, carrying a ball with a lance sticking out of it.

I woke up sweating and my heart thumping.

It was only after a while that a cheerful thought came to me: I was second reserve after Collins and as in the whole history of the game no reserves had ever been used, and certainly never a second reserve, I was safe.

I went back to sleep and didn't wake up until the bell.

I was told to get my kit ready in the changing room by lunchtime so that I would be able to help with the flagposts. Some boys in my form congratulated me on being a reserve so I swaggered about a bit. But the boys in the proper team, who were all older, ignored me completely and when I got to the changing room I found my kit had been pushed into a corner and trodden into the dirt there. But I cheered up when I met Mr Bell on the way to the pavilion.

'Today history will be made,' he said, 'or not, as the case may be. I am a cricketer myself.'

'Yes, sir.'

'Rova?'

'Yes, sir?'

'I never even got as far as being a reserve for the Junior team, let alone the Senior one. Well done!'

Mr Bell's eyes twinkled and he grinned. I felt better after that.

I put out the flags with Collins, and we checked that the linesman's flags were ready and waiting. The groundsman had marked out new white lines on the pitch and there was tea being laid on trestle tables in the pavilion, as rain was forecast.

It was the first time I had ever seen how a Senior match was organized and never knew so much was involved. I began to feel nervous again. That grew even worse when the Menmore boys arrived in a coach.

They were big, very big, and one of them looked as if he shaved. Their rugby shirts were black and their shorts white and they looked much stronger, bigger and nastier than we did in our blue shorts and maroon shirts. Even though I was not playing I felt nervous.

It was a cold grey day with dark clouds building up over the woods at the end of the pitch, from where the wind usually came, and as Menmore won the toss they chose to play from that end. The Menmoreans had brought an extra coachload of boys to encourage their team and they started shouting right from the start '2–4–6–8, who do we appreciate? M–E–N–M–O–R–E! *MENMORE!*'

Right from that first thunderous shout it was obvious they were going to win and we were all going to end up lying in the mud like that knight with pointed feet, dead.

Nunnestone held out for about ten minutes before Menmore scored their first try and after that they scored three more so that by half-time, when it was my job to give our team their quarters of oranges, the score was sixteen-nil and would have been higher if they had been able to convert more of them, but their kicker wasn't much good.

Our team was not very happy and Mr Franks's half-time pep talk about cowardice and shame didn't seem to do much good.

When he was gone I heard Freeman say, 'We'll have the wind behind us next half and that should help!' which cheered some boys up.

Burton said, 'If we can get one try early on we might still have a chance.'

I could see they still wanted to win and when I heard them talk like that I felt proud to be a member of the Senior team.

Freeman said, 'Anyone got any fresh ideas?' but no one had.

Then Burton said, 'I'll put myself on the right wing from now on, because that's where we're weakest . . .'

That was the side the big Menmore boy who shaved was playing as a winger.

For the first bit of the second half the wind advantage helped us do a lot better and we scored a try and a conversion, giving us five points. Then our kicker Freeman, who was very good, got a drop goal, so we were halfway there.

Menmore began to look tired, especially when the wind grew stronger and the clouds turned darker still and it began to spit with rain.

But then total and complete disaster struck. Freeman tried to catch a ball with his back to where we were all standing on the touchline and lost his balance and fell backwards straight into, or rather onto, Collins, their heads cracking together like conkers, *crack!*

Everyone gathered around and it was obvious that neither of them was going to get up in a hurry.

'I'll get some oranges,' I said.

'No you won't, boy,' said Mr Franks; *'you're on.'*

'Sorry, sir?' I said.

It was as if the world was full of thundering silence.

Blood drained from my face.

My heart stopped beating.

'Get your jumper off and get on that pitch and show the Menmoreans what our reserves are made of!'

I did it as if I was in a dream, but my hands were shaking so much that I could hardly get my jumper off. When I eventually did I was in a state of terror and as I crossed the line onto the muddy pitch I could feel my legs shaking. Seeing the huge Menmorean forwards glowering at me, I felt like a sandhopper stranded at the high-tide mark in the middle of a flock of feeding herring gull.

Worse followed.

'Go on the right wing, Rova,' I heard Burton say, 'I've got to take Freeman's position.'

As the whistle went to resume play three things happened.

First, the rain started thundering down from behind and it was like a cold shower on my back and it quadrupled my fear.

Second, I found myself looking into the dark and evil eyes of the boy who shaved. He was about ten feet taller than me, and four feet wider, and his boots were size fives or bigger. He must have been at least twelve years old.

The third thing that happened was that the ball came flying through the air straight into his hands and he started charging at me like a galloping carthorse, *thumpety, thumpety, thumpety THUMP!*

The rain froze me up so much that I couldn't even pretend I was tackling. I stood in his path and he knocked me flying as his great feet and ankles and calves and shins and horrible fat hairy thighs went all over me and then on past.

If Burton hadn't run across and stopped him he would have scored a try. The rain continued and when the big boy ran through me a second time and I heard the groans of disappointment from the Nunnestone boys, I knew I would be shamed for ever.

'Tackle harder, Rova!' Mr Franks yelled at me, his tongue and eyes almost bursting out of his head, he was so angry and shouting so loud.

The third time the boy who shaved came at me, which was about four minutes later and no further score, with the rain still driving down, I just managed to move a bit and put up my hands to defend myself, so that when his white shorts came at me like a Churchill tank and he bashed straight into me, instead of flattening me into the ground he sent me flying over the touchline into a crowd of jeering Menmore boys who knew the truth.

'Coward! Tackle shirker! Mumsie's boy!'

That was what they hissed at me as I lay on the ground amongst their neatly trousered legs and black shiny shoes.

Then something unexpected happened, very unexpected.

The rain eased as I lay on the ground and that made me feel better. It wasn't such a cage any more. One of the Menmoreans could see I was winded and knelt down and held my head. Before he said anything else I heard him call out, 'He's all right, sir, just winded a bit. I'll help him up!'

That took the attention off me and put it back on the game.

The boy said to me, 'It's not your fault; it's your team's. You're doing your best.'

I saw it was the goalie I had scored three goals against the previous term. He was grinning at me as if he was my friend. He said to me what I had said to him in the soccer game.

But then he said a few more words that helped change my life: 'That winger Watts bullies me, but he's a coward when he's hit.'

'You mean the boy who shaves?'

He nodded.

My head was still ringing as I got up but I was thinking straight. When Burton came over and said, 'Are you all right? Do you want to move from the wing?' I shook my head.

When he added, 'Well done, Rova. You nearly got him over that time. Keep it up!' I felt even straighter in the head.

They didn't think I was shirking, just that I wasn't much good and maybe not big enough. That didn't seem so bad.

The Menmorean boy on the line grinned and made a tackle movement and that put heart into me. So did the rain having stopped. I knew what to do with bullies: smash doors into them and they don't get up because they're cowards at heart. I went back to my position and I didn't have to wait very long.

Watts, the boy who shaved, got the ball again and came charging at me just as he had before. This time he was even more confident and was yelling as he ran, with a horrible expression on his face.

I wasn't scared this time but very calm. It was as if I was there not for me but for someone else, for lots of people: for all the people who had ever been bullied by boys like Watts. So I stood still, knowing exactly what he was going to do, which was to charge straight at me. I felt exultant, I felt in command, I felt better than I ever had on a rugby field, and maybe better than I ever had off it.

I saw his white shorts coming, and his big fat legs, and I moved forward a little. I felt my heart thump with excitement and as he reached me I shifted to one side and put my arms right round his knees and thighs and, tightening my grip more and more and *more,* held on for dear life.

He came crashing down with a thump and I heard the breath come out of him in a gasp. Even better, I found myself getting up unhurt and there on the ground right in front of me, loosened from his grasp, was the ball. I grabbed it and began running like the Royal Marine gym instructor once told me to run, like a bat out of hell.

I knew nothing much about rugby but I did know about running. I ran straight ahead into the huge gap and vast area of empty pitch that lay behind Watts because nobody on his side thought anybody could get past him. I felt that ball in my hands and against my chest like a piece of driftwood I was carrying against the wind on Stoning beach.

I felt my legs running hard but easy, and my body balancing as it went. I heard the cries from the onlookers like the fading squeals of gulls in the shadows of far-off cliffs. And I remembered that fallen knight with the pointed feet who Mr Franks had told us about the night before.

But I suddenly knew he wasn't a coward, not deep inside. He had been winded, and now he had got up and he was running,

running against all the boys who ever shaved and were too big for their boots, against all the knights who gloated over others with bloody lances in their hands. He was running and his armour was impregnable.

I saw the Menmore fullback in front of me and I recognized in the shifting of his feet, in the dither of his hands and in the hunching of his shoulders, the coward and the tackle shirker I had been.

I knew exactly what he would do and when he did it, I jumped over his sliding legs as if they were one of the broken groynes that run into the sea near Southdown, which I had been jumping over for years.

I pushed the last of him out of the way with my right hand and held the ball tight with my left as my legs took me safely over his and I ran the last steps to the try line.

Sometimes everything happens at once as if it was arranged that way thousands of years ago. As I touched the ball down on the grass beyond the line there was a crack of thunder and the heavens opened with a downpour of rain. I stood up and felt that rain on my face and I wasn't scared, not scared at all, as if I had broken out of the cage I had been in.

People were cheering and Burton came and clapped me on the shoulder and the rain was everywhere and I didn't mind, I just didn't mind.

That was when I saw that the ball was running with blood. Bright fresh blood.

As I turned back towards the pitch with the ball in my hands, and Burton at my side as if I was his equal, my heart leaping at the sounds of the cheers for my successful run, I was thinking, 'Why is the ball bleeding . . . ?'

Then . . . 'The ball can't be bleeding; it must be me.'

And then . . . 'It can't be me, because I don't hurt.'

I looked at it before giving it to Burton for the conversion and saw where the blood was coming from. My wrists and my hands were streaming with blood, maroon blood: the blood of the Nunnestone School colours.

It was my rugby shirt, the one my mother had dyed to save money; the teeming rain had made it bleed. The dye was coming out in streams and rivulets. But I didn't care because I knew that the fallen knight was only wounded after all; it was just that the picture was painted before he got up again to fight the good fight. My blood was up, or down, depending on your point of view.

I stood once more near the touchline, I saw that the face of the goalie who had encouraged me was now alight with pleasure, and I saw that the boy who shaved was wearing white shorts that were now stained pink where my arms and hands had clung on; and that he was limping and holding his thigh in pain.

'Well done!' I heard Mr Bell call out, and 'Oh, *very* well done, Rova!' from Mr Franks.

At the next kick-off, we rushed forward in a surge of new life, rampant, eager, brutal, terrible, berserkers in our rage.

None more so than me.

As the minutes passed our score went up and up and overtook that of the demoralized Menmoreans. While my tally of stained and dye-ruined Menmorean white shorts went up as steadily, one by one, I marked the opposing team with my tackles.

I didn't get any more tries, but that one was enough to banish for ever my fear of tackling, and to promote me for good into the Senior team.

Of all the fearless tackles I made that day there is only one encounter I clearly remember after the one with Watts. It was a boy on the far wing with still-virgin white shorts. I charged at him and he saw me coming just as the final whistle went.

'No!' he shouted, before throwing down the ball and running away.

Cowardice?

Courage?

Winning the game?

I do not know. As the final whistle blew again I ignored the ball and chased him right off the field to tackle him anyway and make sure his shorts were pink.

* * *

A week after that term ended Ma had a letter from Beaven and Lane's, the school outfitters in the High Street. It was from Mr Beaven himself. She read it out to Granny and Uncle Max and especially to me.

*Dear Madam,* it said, *I have been asked to inform you on behalf of the management of Menmore School that for the duration of your son's sojourn at Nunnestone School the cost of his games kit, including and especially his rugby shirts as and when his requirements necessitate a successive size, will be borne by them in recognition of his valour upon the games field last week. Yours faithfully . . .*

Mr Beaven had added in his own handwriting, *Dear Madam, I have known some peculiar requests from customers, but this takes the biscuit! In view of what I understand to be the circumstances, please pass on my congratulations to Jimmy.*

Ma said, 'Well, I think we shall put this letter in a scrapbook. Well done, Jimmy!'

Of all the many things I learnt at that school the best was this: fallen knights can get up, and they can hit you, so beware. Mr Franks taught me that from a painting that was five hundred years old. *The Battle of San Romano* showed me I could make things change.

But it was the one and only time I did not fear rain. After that the fear crept back and the unease at darkening skies returned. But I didn't forget the taste of freedom or stop hoping I would one day know it again.

# 11

# GRANNY AND THE
# AFRICAN GENTLEMAN

Granny sometimes talked about who it was who gave her the ornaments she kept on her writing desk, like the giraffe made of dried skin that was yellow except where it was burnt, which was the spots.

She said, 'An African Gentleman gave that to me.'

There was a tall, shiny, heavy man made of ebony, as big as my two hands, his head enormous and his legs carved bent and his arms up in the air. He was naked except for a beard around his wide mouth.

'The African Gentleman gave me that as well,' said Granny.

'What was his name?' I asked.

'His name doesn't matter; it was what was in his heart and mind that counts.'

When Granny spoke like that I never dared ask any more questions because I knew she had said all she wanted to say on the subject.

'Did the African Gentleman give you that as well?' I asked one autumn morning when I found her stirring her chutney with a great big wooden spoon with lined and dotted patterns burnt into it.

'He did,' she replied. 'He said I was not just to look at it and dwell on the past, but to use it and enjoy the present. He said spoons aren't made only to be looked at like objects behind glass in a museum. A spoon is not a spoon if it can't scoop and stir. He liked my chutney as his people never made it for him, so now I always make chutney with this spoon.'

'Will you ever see him again?' I asked Granny.

'He said that one day he would come to England to see the Queen and meet the Prime Minister and that when he did it would be a great day for his people. He promised me that on that day he would come and see me too. That day will come to pass.'

'Will *I* see him, Granny?' I asked.

'Oh yes,' she said, and she reached out her hand to touch my cheek, which she did not often do.

So it was that day *did* come.

When I saw Granny that morning she said, 'You must be available today.'

'Why?'

'You're not to go to Fitzroy Square and watch tennis through the hedge.'

'Why?'

'You're not to go beachcombing and chasing seagulls.'

'Why?'

'You're not to visit the Castle and start helping Mr Boys.'

'Why?'

'Because today is the day when the African Gentleman is coming and I want you to be here to meet him so you can tell your grandchildren that you shook his hand.'

'Does Ma know?'

'She knows enough that she's decided to tidy up her part of the house for once and make some scones for the gentlemen who will be accompanying him and will stay downstairs while he talks to me.'

'And me as well.'

'Later perhaps,' said Granny with one of her rare smiles.

He arrived in the afternoon in a great black shiny car with mirrors on, which I watched come along the Seafront and finally stop by our house for a moment, then move on a bit and park. I watched the doors open from the sycamore tree I had climbed.

The driver got out and looked up at me. He had a peaked cap on and a grey suit and I knew he wasn't the African Gentleman because he had a white face. He opened the door of the car and the African Gentleman got out. He had a funny hat on his grey and grizzled hair, and he wore clothes I remember for their black and yellow stripes and strange designs. He carried a wand in his hand like a magician.

He looked up and saw me and he laughed a deep laugh.

'Are you Master Jimmy?' he asked in a voice like rough waves in the shingle on the beach.

I nodded.

'Your grandmother has written to me about you. You and I will meet officially later. Now . . .'

Two other men got out of the car, younger and bigger than him, and they went with him up to our house and then stood like stone lions on either side of our front door.

There were two motorcycle policemen on the road by our gate.

I stayed where I was and watched.

Granny came to the front door and shook hands with the African Gentleman. She was dressed in her very best clothes, which were blue and white, and she had her best shoes on too. Her hair was done up. She looked ten years younger than she usually did, about the same age as the African Gentleman.

She waved to me and called, 'Don't stray too far, Jimmy, don't go too far.' She sounded happy, like a girl in the sun. But I would not have strayed a single inch that day for fear of missing Granny's call. There was history in the air, and more.

It was a windy October day and the sea was made grey and rough by the north-easterly that blew against the current. There were boats out fishing, and you could see the surf on the Goodwin Sands.

Across the Green on the Promenade the ladies out walking had to hold on to their hats to stop them blowing away; while down by the lifeboat the wires on the masts of the dinghies on the beach made a noise like tent flaps in the wind.

But I couldn't hear them because I didn't venture that far. I just imagined the sound.

That afternoon time moved so slowly that I thought the clocks had stopped and high overhead I saw birds migrating south towards the Seven Seas.

'Jimmy! You can come up now!'

It was Granny at her window, and behind her in the shadows looking down at me the dark face and smiling white teeth of the African Gentleman.

I ran into the house and up the stairs two at a time, and Granny's door was waiting open for me.

'Close the door, Jimmy, there's a good boy,' said Granny. She had all her best tea things out and had just brewed a fresh pot of tea.

She introduced me to the African Gentleman who was sitting in her best chair and remained just where he was. I went up to him and he held my hand in both of his and he looked at my face as if he was studying it.

'Laura says you are a good grandson to her,' he said eventually.

That day was the first time I ever heard anyone call Granny by her Christian name and it suited her, the way she looked that day. I had seen her young in black-and-white photographs but that day, though she was old now, she looked beautiful as well. She poured his tea like it was red wine in Church communion. She poured me a glass of ginger beer. When she sat down near him it seemed that together they were much more than two; they were a whole world, something like Uncle Max and Auntie Fiona on the mountain.

'Granny said you'd come one day and that you'd see the Queen and Mr Churchill the Prime Minister.'

'I have done so,' said the African Gentleman, 'except that Mr Churchill is not Prime Minister any more. Still, I saw him all the same. The only person left for me to see in Britain before I go back to my people is you.'

I asked him why.

He told me that one day in Africa Granny had told him about me being born. He said she had hoped it was a sign that there was more to life than war.

'Laura told me that the day you were born was May 12th, 1944 and it was on that same day that I dreamed my people would be free. So I said to your grandmother that when I came to see the Queen and the Prime Minister I would come and see her and you as well.'

I looked at his wand and asked if he was a magician.

He laughed his deep, deep laugh and said that some people said he must be, but others thought not. He himself did not know.

'Is that a wand?' I asked, looking at the thing I had seen him carrying when he got out of the car.

'It is a ceremonial fly swat,' he said.

'Can I try it out? There's always flies circling the light that hangs from Granny's ceiling unless she's got a sticky spiral out.'

He said that to his knowledge it had never been used as a fly swat for real but since I had asked I should try it out. Its handle was made of leather with a silver bobble at one end and the swat bits were animal hairs. I took it and I went and bashed a fly on the window. The fly fell stunned to the floor and then woke up and started crawling about.

'It's not as good as a plastic fly swat like the red one Ma bought in the Dustpan Stores.'

'It's good enough for my purposes,' he said.

I noticed that Granny's hand was holding his and she was smiling. That was like a window opening on Granny's life through which I could see something bigger than before, but back in a place and time to which I could never go.

'When's *your* birthday?' I asked the African Gentleman.

He said he was not sure because his mother never wrote it down, but he was born on a lucky night when the crocodile was caught among the stars right across the night sky.

'Which crocodile?'

He said that in the long-ago time before the sun there was just the River and the Dark, and nothing else until the Crocodile rose up from the deep and its eyes poked out of the River and looked about . . .

The African Gentleman told me about how the Crocodile tricked the sun into coming, and the moon into going, and how he or she – for no one knew which it was, but boys said it was he and girls said it was she – made all the other animals and all the people by swishing its tail first one way and then another. The swishing made the waves and the waves ran up onto the land and made every living thing out of the mud that formed.

'Was the Crocodile good?'

'He made us,' said the African Gentleman, 'so if you think we're good he's good, if not he's bad.'

'Granny says there's good in everyone, including me.'

'Your grandmother is right about nearly everything,' he said. 'Now . . .'

He continued the story, which became more than one and then turned into a whole world in which I travelled with him as my friend. It was like being round a fire with a group of natives photographed in Mr Mee's encyclopedia and all of us being talked to by a tribal storyteller. His voice was like the distant roar of a waterfall.

I remember him telling me that among other things the River is what divides the peoples and animals of the earth but because the Crocodile lives in it people are afraid to go into the River to see what's on the other side.

I remember him saying that people have to find the courage to go into it if they are to live properly.

I remember that because he was born on that lucky day when the Crocodile was caught in the stars he knew without being told how he must go into the River.

'It was on your birthday, May 12th, 1944, that I went in the River and dreamed a dream of freedom.'

'Did the Crocodile attack you?' I asked him.

'Have I scars on my hands?'

'You've got scars on your face, three on each side.'

'That was when I became a man and long before I went into the River to see what was on the other side. No, the Crocodile helped me get there. He will help you if you ask him. Here . . .'

That was when the African Gentleman let go of Granny's hand and dug deep into the folds of his black and yellow clothes and brought out a crocodile. It was made of wood, with bulgy eyes and an open mouth with teeth. It was burnt black like the giraffe on Granny's dressing table, and where the carving was, was not burnt.

'This is for you,' said the African Gentleman.

At first I was afraid to touch it because I thought it might be the Crocodile himself. But when I took it, it did not bite, or even swish its tail.

'But it's real,' he said, 'if you think it so. It will protect you and it will remind you that in the time long ago there was a boy like you who sat by a fire on the night before he began his journey into manhood and he made this to protect himself on the way.'

I knew then that it was he himself who had made it and it was an object from his treasure chest like one of the things I kept in my orange box.

'Now my journey is nearly done,' he said, reaching out his hand to hold Granny's again, 'but yours is just beginning.'

'What shall I do with it?' I asked

'You'll know when the time comes. I bought it with me to Great Britain because I knew that in all the world you would be the one to know. Also, you will work out when the time comes to make your own.'

The African Gentleman talked so long to me that night came.

'Before I go I want you to show me the sea, for where I live, there is only the River.'

Granny and I took him down to the sea, one on either side, and she held his hand. The men by the house stayed where they were. I wanted him to hold my hand but I never dared ask.

We looked up at the sky and there were some stars now above the Southdown cliffs.

'The sky here is different from the one on the other side of the River, but you can still see a bit of the Crocodile's tail where it is caught in the stars.'

He showed me where to look and knelt down by my side to point out how to find the Crocodile's tail. Like riding a bicycle, once you can see it, you can see it for ever.

'Now,' he said, 'Laura and I have a few things to say to each other before I go. In my country young people look after the old and do not let them wander alone through the last years of their life. Laura says you are a comfort to her and are learning to watch out for her. That is good. We are both old now and in need of younger ones like you. When the time comes, you'll know what to do for her.'

I said I would do my best. Granny had looked younger when he first arrived, but now she looked old and frail and a little afraid. But I knew she would be safe with him.

I left them where they stood side by side looking at the stars and walked back over the shingle towards the lights of our house on the far side of the Green. I was not afraid because in my hand I had the crocodile he had made for himself and which would now protect me on my way and help me do the right things when I had to, whatever that was.

I looked back one last time.

Granny and the African Gentleman were standing hand in hand, looking east across the night-time sea. There were stars above their heads, and all the world and all of time beyond. Granny taught me many things and that day she taught me that love and devotion can reach right across the world, past every obstacle, and last for ever. As I held the crocodile in my hand for comfort I glimpsed in the stars that love is the healer of all things, including even me.

Then the African Gentleman said his last farewell to Granny and to me and climbed into his car and disappeared into the dark. Granny went to her room and closed the door without a word. I went to my bed and put the crocodile on my pillow by my head so it could watch over me through the night and speak to me if it had something to say.

I think it spoke because in the morning there were words in my head which said, 'Stay close to Granny today, just stay close.'

So I did, and for some days more.

Until I knew she was all right.

# 12

# MR COALMAN MOVES ON

There came an ending to the time in our house in the South End and my walks along that part of the shore. An ending to Granny's room with a view and the House of a Thousand Rooms.

For Ma it was an ending that was the beginning of her liberty; for me it was a forgetting of the time that had been Darktime that was convenient to all concerned. A forgetting but not an extinction.

Darktime was still there, unseen, a volcano waiting to erupt, and that can take a long time.

The ending came when Ma decided to move and put her own name and nobody else's – *especially* that of the Man Who Wasn't – to the deeds of a house she could call her home.

After her long years and decades of struggle, when Adolf Hitler rose and fell, when Britain lost its empire, when radios gave way to television sets, when menfolk weakened and women began to find their strength, Ma decided to stand up and be counted alongside the women.

One day she said, 'I have been to look at a house in Compass Street and I like it very much. Our needs are changing, the big ones are never here now and we don't need the rooms we used to. Therefore, Mother, I think . . .'

Granny was not pleased.

You can stand on Stoning Pier when the tide turns, as it does twice a day, and you can see the flotsam and jetsam hesitating. For a long long time it goes one way, often so fast you can't swim against it for more than a minute or two, but then it falters and weakens, which is the tide turning, and then it goes the other way. In those moments of doubt the flotsam doesn't know which way to turn and floats about aimlessly by the legs of the Pier.

That flotsam was me, and my brother Michael, the hangers-on to my Ma's world. The tide now was Ma herself, and it had turned and it wasn't going to be stopped from coming in.

After the announcement, Granny sat in the room she had left Africa to live in, and which she had come to love, and Granny was silent and angry; and Granny cried. Many times in those months she opened her door and came down the stairs, her hand on the shiny mahogany banister, with arguments to present.

*It's unnecessary.*

*It's expensive.*

*It's unkind.*

*It's ungrateful.*

'It's so hurtful of you, *so* . . .'

Many times.

But in the end Granny's argument was this: 'I cannot move, I am too old and it will kill me.'

And in the end Ma's answer was simple: 'If it kills you, Mother, so be it. I have served others long enough and nearly killed myself doing so. It is my time now.'

My Ma convinced many otherwise over the years, but as far as I was concerned she always thought and acted as if she was the only one in the world and did not have to think of anyone else.

Ma was the woman who shut the gate and left me to the mercy of the man with the shears; the Ma with the hitting hand; the Ma who liked her men so much she would put her children to one side from time to time, and even lock them out, for the chance of male company and a man's caress.

But maybe she was someone else as well, someone I didn't know then. Maybe history was on her side at last after years of being against. History was saying to many a ma like Ma, 'Think of yourself at last. Your time has come, so step forward and grasp it.'

That was no help to those of us who were the flotsam in her life, of course, like Granny and me, there by a change of circumstance or maybe by accident – in my case the accident being who she was with for a night in 1943 – not the Man Who Wasn't, that was certain.

She never said as much and I didn't ask, but maybe Ma only thought of herself because she too was lost in Darktime. She too was seeking a way out.

I wouldn't have needed to ask what was responsible for her Darktime because she'd answered the question without being asked, a thousand times. Us two there in the parlour by our fire, with Granny sitting alone upstairs, Ma made and drank endless cups of tea and talked and talked and talked about who she was running from. Except to me it wasn't a who so much as a thing, huge, dark and nearly unimaginable, because it didn't look anything like the photograph on Granny's writing desk. That thing was Grandfather.

'Did I tell you, Jimmy . . .'

*Yes, Ma, yes you did, many times,* but there was no escape and none wanted. She could tell a tale, could Ma.

The move to a house in her own name was part of her running, part of her escape, and though we didn't like it, her seeking after liberty infected all of us. It infected Granny with new loneliness and sadness; but it infected me with new life and showed me that change only happens when you get up and open the door and walk straight out of it.

Ma found our new home one day when she got up, opened a new door on her life and took a walk to the North End.

Across the green and onto the Promenade, down past the lifeboat house and the lifeboat forever poised for action on the shore past the Royal Marines' swimming bath, past the Southern Railway Hotel, past the Apollo Cinema, to Lugger Street, which was the terminus in Stoning for the East Kent Road Car Company buses.

Maybe Ma's heart was beating with anticipation, but more likely she made that appointment to view, on a Thursday, having seen an advertisement for a house in the *East Kent Mercury*: the house in Compass Street.

Lugger Street was the start of the North End, a world apart from South Stoning, which revolved round Fitzroy Square and the Lawn Tennis and Croquet Club into which I was not allowed.

From Lugger Street three streets ran parallel with the shore: Prow Street, which faced the sea and beyond which was the Promenade and the sea wall; Chandler Street, which ran in the middle the whole length of the North End; and Nore Street, which ran inland of Chandler Street by fifty yards, and a few feet lower down, so it was liable to flooding if the tide ran high and the rain didn't stop.

These three streets each found their end at the top, the middle and the bottom of Printer's Square.

Fitzroy Square, near where we lived, had lawn tennis courts on top; Printer's Square had smugglers' tunnels running underneath. Fitzroy Square had posh houses all round it, not a pub in sight, and the high road to Dover; Printer's Square had two-up-two-downs, terraced slums at the back and pubs galore.

Children in Fitzroy Square went to private schools, or came down to stay only in holidays; children in Printer's Square went to the Union Street state school and did newspaper rounds or helped their dads with the boats.

Women in Fitzroy Square bought their frocks in Town, and wore silk stockings and had men friends; women in Printer's Square and thereabouts raised large families, and never called what they had affairs; they had grey faces before their time and greasy hair and the food they ate made them fat.

Men in one drank sherry and gin and tonics sitting on verandahs, and in the other they went to the pubs and drank beer.

At least they did in the long-ago time of 1954, when Ma made her historic walk from one world and way of life to another – and everything in our lives changed. She'd had her fill of being made to feel small in Fitzroy Square. Now she just wanted to be herself and that was easier in the North End.

One more thing.

Houses in South Stoning were expensive, which was why the Man

Who Wasn't paid for ours, but in the North End they were cheap and Ma could just afford to pay for one out of her savings.

One last thing.

To my Ma the houses in the North End, slums though they were, narrow and dark and damp and liable to flooding with the spring tides, these houses had a beauty that was not just outer but inner as well. For Ma there was no beauty in endless repairs to a house that was too big and no comfort in pretence. Ma was tired of it all and she just wanted something she knew she could afford.

So it was she found an old house that was for sale in the North End, a house that no one but her seemed to want.

'Jimmy,' she said that day the house in Compass Street became hers, 'you're coming with me.'

Lacking male support, not wishing the Man Who Wasn't to know or be involved, though he was away anyway, it was me she took along for company. To help her escape the world of men she took along a boy.

First we went to the estate agent in Stoning High Street to pick up the keys, which were kept in a cupboard with lots of others.

'There you are,' said the agent in his dark suit. 'Don't forget to return them when you've looked round.'

As if she would forget. That man didn't know my Ma.

It is at such small moments that the tide of history becomes visible and is seen to move. 'Come on, Jimmy,' she said, putting the keys into her tatty handbag as I lingered because I hated being seen out with Ma, who looked a fright compared to the ladies of Fitzroy Square. 'Come *on*.'

She bought me a cornet at Gelato's and told me to wait on the Front in the big yellow sea shelter at the top of Coster Street. I sat looking at the sea, and when she was gone I stood up and watched where she went, which was towards a gap in the buildings so narrow you wouldn't think a coffin could be taken down it.

That was my first sight of the top end of Compass Street. To one side was a pub, the Albatross, with a great squeaking sign over its front showing a bird that looked more like a Dodo than anything else. To the other, painted yellow, its corner curved with a window inside, was a private house in which lived people I did not yet know.

Out on the Front, where I stood eating my ice cream, there were fishing boats and men in blue jerseys, and Freddie Hammel's white clapboard hut from which, in summer, he hired his little fleet of skiffs and fishing boats.

I stood by his pitch but his boat was out.

'Hello, young Jimmy,' someone said, and I waved. It was Freddie's nephew greasing up some runners. 'Freddie's mac'relling.'

The air was heavy with the scent of tar and old ropes, of petrol-driven capstans, and the shouts and jibes, taunts and laughter, teasing and jollity of fishermen and hovellers.

I stood there for a time and then began to explore the Front, up one way and down the other, not too far. When Ma came back I wanted her to find me easily.

'Jimmy! There you are!' she said. 'It looks all right on the outside, and the street seems all right too, so we'll go inside. Come with me . . .'

For once Ma had colour in her cheeks that had nothing to do with rouge, and a light in her eyes that had nothing to do with men. It came from the heady scent of independence.

'Come *on*!' she said and we crossed from the Front to the Albatross so fast it was as if we were hurrying for the bus; and then it was like going through a door into dusk as we entered Compass Street.

'It's here, just here,' she said, fumbling with the key outside a door whose two steps were white marble.

She was eager to get in because she didn't want to be seen through the neighbours' windows. Up the steps she went, and I followed as she opened the door.

It was even darker than the shadowed street, its narrow corridor lined with sagging American cloth painted dark cream which was tacked on to pine panelling from floor to ceiling. There was an arch halfway along this corridor and beyond that I saw a door with a window in it whose glass was so old and bottled that it contorted whatever was on the other side, and turned it pale green.

Ma opened the door, which was wide, onto a narrow parlour with an ugly tiled fireplace. Beyond that was another door leading into the kitchen, which was no more than a damp scullery. Beyond that was another door, which led to a lavatory that smelt of damp, and had mould growing up its walls near where you sat to do your Number Twos.

But then, hurrying no more, as if she had come home after those two thousand years, she opened the parlour door onto the walled garden, and from that moment our life in Compass Street really began.

There was a battered old chair against a whitewashed wall and I watched her sit down in the sun. She leant her head against the wall and she seemed to let the fight go out of her. She sat there, pale and tired, the sun catching the lines and pockets of her face and the straggles of her unkempt hair.

There was yellow ragwort in the flagstones at her feet, and white-pink saxifrage growing along the wall. There was no one to see and I didn't count, so Ma let herself droop. It was as if she was the last one in a marching army who had fought through the years to get home and now that she had finally done it she didn't know what to do or say.

As often with my Ma, it was as if I wasn't there. I got bored and went up into the house and explored by myself right up to the top. Wherever I went it was filthy, and there was the smell of old cooking and unflushed lavatories, and the windows were clogged with dead flies.

The bathroom had a great white cylinder on the wall like a steam engine and a name in a blue triangle: 'Geyser'. The stairs were spiral and if you missed your step you fell right down. The woman before fell down those stairs and broke her hip and lay there for four days before she was found.

There was a cellar door, which I opened to peer down into dank darkness and the smell of mould. I heard a sound and didn't go down. The Coalman had already taken up residence ahead of us but he didn't seem as fierce as he had before.

I went back past the bottled glass in the kitchen door and outside to the garden again. Ma was still there in the same position with her eyes closed. She looked like a dead body propped up in an old chair. She looked like Granny but larger all round.

There was an outhouse door which I opened. It was an old boathouse, built between No 10 and No 11, and had rafters and ropes and a rusted kedge anchor hanging from a nail. It had the boatmen's smells of tar and oil and rotting canvas. In one corner, on the floor, was a stick with two notches cut in it round which was wound a hand-line of old fishing twine. It had a trace of mackerel feathers at the end.

There was a low double swing door down into the cellar, which swung open when I pushed it. One of the doors was hanging from only one hinge. It had been painted brown long, long ago. Below, in the dark, I could smell coal, and mould. I heard the Coalman stir but out there in the open, with the sound of the sea nearby, I wasn't so scared. It wasn't just Ma who was changing.

'Ma . . .'

I went back but she had finally got up and gone inside to look round the house.

I listened to her going where I had gone, a tired woman shifting from room to room, sunny on the south side facing the garden, dark on the north side facing the houses on the other side of the narrow street. That was that house: light and dark and a spiral staircase, and a victim of the wind nagging at the tiles on the roof and getting its fingers into the warped old casement windows.

'Ma . . .'

But she was lost in her world of dreaming and scheming and thinking of who would have what room if she dared to buy the house.

I went and sat in the garden and waited. There was a lizard sunning itself on the wall, and rubbish, and hardly any room at all. One tree and the place would have seemed crowded; a flowerbed more than two feet deep and there wouldn't be room enough for a chair and a cup of tea. Except at the end where the rubbish was.

'Jimmy . . .'

I heard Ma calling and slunk away into the shadows. The house was older than the House of the Thousand Rooms and its walls were mellow brick and not pebbledash.

'Oh, there you are. Do you like it?'

I didn't know. I only knew we were going to move there because Ma had the light in her eyes that said we would.

'We'll have to think carefully about where Mother will go, but I think . . .'

'She'll like that room there,' I said, pointing to the sunny room above the garden.

'Yes . . .' said Ma, but she didn't sound convincing.

'Can I go up to the Front?' I said.

Ma nodded and I escaped, leaving her behind to do her calculations and make her plans.

Ma got the money, which was £750, and another £200 for the roof and a bit more for solicitors' fees, by borrowing some from Stoning Building Society, some from the Man Who Wasn't and the rest from Uncle Max, who was getting rich in America.

In the weeks that followed, which became the months of buying No 10, Ma was not herself at all. She had things on her mind and jobs to do. But most of all she had Granny to cope with.

'I refuse,' was an expression Granny used lots of times, but Ma stayed firm. The tide had turned and now was running Ma's way, sweeping Granny to a new shore onto which she had no wish to go to but no power to escape from. It was sweeping me as well, but I didn't mind because one day I would leave, one way or another.

As the tide got higher and the day we were to move drew nearer, Granny just grew sadder and more defeated. Often she stood by the window of her lovely room which looked out across the Green to the sea; she just stood.

In those tense days Ma seemed to get younger and Granny much older.

'I'm going back to Africa,' Granny announced one day.

I felt my heart jolt.

I thought of that house in the North End, with its dark side and light side, and I thought of me in it, alone with Ma. I thought of the spiral staircase with me at the top and Ma at the bottom. I thought of the clutter and the mess there would be, and no room like Granny's to escape to.

I felt Darktime coming back into my mind, and I felt a chill and a cold I had forgotten that I knew.

I said to Granny, 'Please don't go. *Please.*'

'But I must,' she said, 'or I shall die.'


The day she said that my mind went nearly blank. Darkness was there and I could not wander inside or out because of it.

'I'm so sorry, Jimmy, but I *must.*'

I was going to be left alone with Ma again and this time it would be for ever.

I must have wanted to die because that day I did what I had never done before. I opened the cellar door and went down the wooden steps into the dark depths below to meet the Coalman face to face. All those years I avoided him but that day I wanted him to take me into death. Outside was the sun, but down there, where my heart beat painfully with fear and finally slow with despair, I tried to return to Darktime of my own free will.

I went down and closed the door behind me and heard the sound of sobbing women above my head. I heard their arguments and their cries and I ventured on into the darkness of those fearful cellar rooms.

Into the first I went and stood in the gloom, smelling the damp, my fear subsiding.

Then to where the coal came down, with the slab of glass above to let in the light, my fear growing less.

Then on away from their arguments above, and the tide of history, into the cellar room under the drawing room where once an *Eagle* was burnt, where once I ruined that dance record secretly. The cellar room had a half-window that came out under the stairs from the drawing room down into the garden. It was blocked with dirt and leaves and ancient cobwebs. On the floor was a dead rotted bird with feathers the colour of Granny's hair.

Then into the side room where the Coalman lived and who I had only ever heard. In all the houses I had been in with cellars the Coalman had lived, tap-tap-tapping one way or another to tell me he'd get me one night. He was in this one and he was definitely in the first of the houses I remembered, which was No 15 in Ramsgate. The one with the gate whose latch I couldn't reach.

Now I was there before him and I wanted him to take me. Granny was going and my life would end the day she went. Tap-tap-tap . . . and there he was, there, there . . .

And he was, right there where I could see him, right there. He was along the corner of the ceiling by a grille to the outside through which the wind came as it came now, making the end of an old electric wire go tap-tap-tap – as he had tapped darkly all down my childhood years. The Coalman was just a loose electric wire.

That was all the Coalman was, a piece of wire, something that tapped when the wind blew. He wasn't real.

The room was dusty but empty, but the light from the grille was as grey as that Deadman's chest where it came out between the buttons of his shirt. The Coalman tapped and I wanted him to take me, but now that I'd seen what he really was, which was nothing much at all, he had lost his power over me and he couldn't show me the way back to Darktime.

I stood in the murky darkness and looked at that wire and found I was afraid of him more.

The tide of time covering up my childhood was coming in so fast now, as fast as galloping horses, that as I stood free of fear I nearly missed what was as plain to see as the silly piece of wire: something more horrible than anything I had ever seen or heard or known.

Then all of a sudden when I realized, when I knew something for sure, my eyes were blinded by tears as the women sobbed through the thousand rooms above.

Because what I suddenly understood was exactly where in the

house of my childhood, in the long ago, in Number 15, where my Darktime began . . . I knew where my shoes had got lost.

And how they got lost, I knew that too.

So I stood there as Ma and Granny fought and wept, crying too. Because I had not had the courage to find my shoes in the time long ago and I was wrong to abandon them.

I went back upstairs, not bothering to close the door to keep the Coalman in. I went to Granny where she was angry and drying her old eyes and asked for three shillings. Bobby had a shilling but I needed three to get to our old house over in Ramsgate at No 15 and back again.

I had never ever asked Granny for money and she gave it to me now without asking why.

'Jimmy . . .'

'Don't go to Africa till I come back,' I said.

'I'm not going, my dear, there or anywhere. No one needs me now.'

'I do,' I said. '*I* do.'

Her old face was wrinkled towards a smile, and the shillings jingled in my pocket as I ran down the stairs and out of the house.

I ran and ran and ran as hard as I could to Lugger Street and the bus, to forget the grief of realizing how and where I lost my shoes. The journey there passed Nunnestone Colliery, and then all along that long long way we had once journeyed in a pantechnicon, back to the Isle of Thanet, which isn't an isle now but once was.

I got out and looked around. Nothing was familiar at all.

'Mister, do you know where . . . ?'

'It's along by Dumpton Park . . .'

Then I was there.

Oh, I remembered the Park, and the grass I should never have walked on and the man with the shears who was going to cut off my ears.

Then out through the black iron gates that have spikes and shadows and spiders on top . . . Down, and up, and across the streets, away from the shears that cut when they shut . . . Past a black car that squealed and shouted . . . Past a black dog that rose and growled, and snarled as I passed, so I ran faster still . . . Into a street I once knew, past the old woman's house at the end, with its wall still there. Fast as I could, I ran back towards the darkness I had never before found the courage to enter.

I knew what I was looking for and it was called No 15. But I wasn't afraid because nobody could do worse than what happened before.

I reached No 15 and went to the gate and discovered I was tall enough to look over it and to raise its latch and open it myself.

I knocked on the back door and a man came and said, 'He's out, he's out, he's gone to Dumpton Park.'

I said, 'I know, he's left something of mine in the cellar.'

I had learnt many things in the long years since, and one of them was how to think quickly on my feet. The man must have thought I was one of his son's friends.

'He shouldn't have, he shouldn't have been down there. It's dangerous. No one goes there because the ceiling's falling down. What's he left?'

'A pair of my shoes.'

The man looked at me and I looked at him.

'Go *on* then,' he said impatiently, 'whoever you are.'

The house felt no more happy that day than it had in the days when we lived there.

I opened the cellar door and went on down to where the Coalman once lived.

All that time and it was as easy as that.

'Close the kitchen door behind you, lad, when you come out,' the man shouted down. 'And don't touch the ceiling plaster, it's like to fall down.'

'All right,' I said.

I went to where the Coalman had once tapped in the night, but his tapping had stopped because I wasn't afraid any more. Just pipes and the wind at gutters, that's all he was, all he ever was.

I went to the darkest place: the shadows beyond where the coal came down, which my brother and cousin knew was the one place I would never ever *ever* dare look for my shoes. Knew that little Jimmy would not even *think* to look.

It's your closest family that knows how to hurt you worst.

Now I went to that dark place and what I found in the ancient gloom was where my poor shoes died alone.

I had called their name and they had been so near and must have heard my call. But shoes have no voice to reply.

There they were in the gloom, as grey-black now as the coal and plaster dust that covered them.

'Oh, oh, oh,' I said, and I stood crying to see them like that. 'Oh . . .'

There was a mangle, grey in the grey gloom, its rubber rollers perished with age, but I knew exactly when it had last been used. The Boy and the Girl, combining their strengths, had put my shoes toe-first between the rollers and rolled them in as hard as they would go. Not far, an inch or two, at the front, and the laces trailing in the dark and the heels all worn with my wearing, my shoes bent now with old age.

'Oh,' I said and reached for them as if they were a hurt, tarred-up bird, huddling hopeless on the shore against a gale it will not survive.

'Oh . . .' I said, and then I turned the handle of the mangle back to set them free, for I had the strength to do it alone now.

They had known I would never go where the Coalman was; but the worst of it was that they had thought what to do in case I did, which was to squeeze my shoes between the rollers, from which I would not have had the strength to set them free.

I held them gently, too upset to look at them closely.

Then I put my poor shoes upon the ground and in the gloomy light I saw that my feet were now too big for them. The tide of history had come in and my shoes had been left behind, and with them something I could never replace. I don't know its name but it begins with trust and continues with hope and ends in the joy of believing the world is right not wrong. That's what they stole when they hid my shoes.

\* \* \*

I left the cellar, climbed up the steps and went out of No 15. I closed the back door like the man said, and the gate with its latch as well. I walked the long way down to Ramsgate Harbour to the jetty wall I once slipped on. The tide was not yet fully in so I had to wait. I sat at the high-tide mark for a time and then I found a cuttlefish bone all stained with tar, and in it I saw the grinning face of my friend the Crocodile, which gave me an idea. So I got a flint and a piece of slate and carved out its protruding eyes, its teeth, its clawed arms and its tail.

Then I waited on the beach for the tide to come in, my old shoes basking in a warmth they had not known through the centuries of their loss. When the tide was right, and the waves surging at the wall, I went back to where once I had fallen in and wished that I might die, on the same day I learnt to swim.

I placed one dry shoe and then another upon the rising waters, and then I put the crocodile in after them, to guard them on their journey across the River and on to the stars.

I watched them drift away until I could see them no more. By then my tears were dry.

Had I said goodbye to the shoes that I lost?

I thought I had, and wished them well, and had no need of a policeman now to lead me back towards Darktime: I could go home by myself. So I turned my back on the ocean blue and climbed the hill from the harbour to where the buses were.

The great shaft wheels of Nunnestone Colliery were turning against the darkening sky when my bus hurried me past and back to Stoning. Back to the bus terminus, and then up the Front and along the Promenade to the House of a Thousand Rooms. The Coalman had moved out ahead of us, like a rat from a sinking ship. He stayed behind only as a memory in my head, where he would tap-tap-tap so long as any Darktime lingered there.

Granny was waiting for me to come back, fretting.

'Where have you been?' she asked suspiciously.

I didn't tell her then, nor ever.

This is the first time I've ever told.

It takes a long time to find the courage to talk of shame.

* * *

My Granny didn't go to back to Africa because Auntie Ellie didn't want her. It was Compass Street and be grateful, or an old people's home for you.

But a long time before that Granny had reached out a hand to help me, and now it was the beginning of my time to help her.

On the day the removal men came, and everywhere but Granny's room was packed up ready to go, I knew what to do. The deep voice of the African Gentleman echoed in my mind and I had to help Granny as he would have done had he been there. You can't keep the tide from coming in so you need to know how to swim.

'What shall I do?' Ma was saying.

'Leave it to me,' I said.

I went to Granny's room and got her hat and coat and stick and said, 'Granny, we're going for a walk.'

'I don't want to,' she said.

'Well, I do,' I said in the way she sometimes did.

'Oh!' she said, surprised.

Then, putting on her hat and coat taking up her stick, she said, 'Where to?'

'The North End, where our new house is. We're walking down there to look. You've got to some time.'

'There's nothing to see,' she said, 'and I'm not leaving.'

'You once told me there's everything to see if you bother to look. You *told* me that, Granny.'

'Well!' she said. 'Well, maybe I did.'

'You *did*.'

'Where are you two going?' asked Ma.

'We're going out to tea, as a matter of fact,' said Granny. 'To the Monarch Hotel. I shall expect . . . I shall expect . . . I shall not do the packing myself. That I shall *not* do!'

'No, Mother,' said Ma quietly, looking gratefully at me.

'And these packing men had better be careful, very careful of my china. It's travelled the world without a single piece getting broken and I shall not be pleased if it gets broken on the short journey between South Stoning and the North End!'

'Yes, Mother; we'll do our very best,' said Ma, even softer now. Even so, in victory the eyes of my Ma were cold.

Granny walked slower than she used to do, and she needed her stick more. When we got past the Lifeboat Station she stopped and said, 'Jimmy, I hope you know the way because I'm not so sure I do.'

I said I did.

We walked past the Southern Railway Hotel and then past the top end of Lugger Street towards the Monarch Hotel.

But when Granny saw the ice cream parlour by the Pier she stopped and said, 'Do you know, it is a very long time since I had an ice cream cornet. I think I shall sit on this bench and look at the sea while you fetch me one.'

She gave me no money but I had some change from the three shillings she had given me for the bus. I walked on a bit to Mr Gelato's because his ice cream was softest and the Best in Britain. I bought us both a large one, with chocolate wafers.

'Granny, you better eat it before it starts to drip.'

We sat and ate our cornets side by side on the bench, Granny getting ice cream on her nose because it was so long.

'Delicious,' she said. 'Very good. Better than you get in Africa. Now . . .'

She stood up slowly with a look of determination on her face.

'. . . perhaps you would be kind enough to show me this house about which there has been so very much fuss.'

'All right, Granny,' I said. 'Which way do you want to go?'

'Whichever way you judge to be the best, my dear,' she said.

So I took her along the Promenade and we walked in the sun.

'How much further?' she asked as we passed Freddie Hammel's pitch. She was getting tired.

'Not far now,' I said.

'It was time for a change,' she said, and took my arm.

# 13

# NEWFOUNDLAND

This is how my Ma decided which rooms to give us in the house in Compass Street.

Granny had the darkest, on the north side of the first floor, with her own kitchen off it, and facing a house twelve feet away. There was no view except for bricks. You couldn't see the sea but you could hear it, except that Granny couldn't any more because she was going deaf.

Granny's was a room for growing old and lonely in, and slowly dying.

My Ma was across from Granny on the south side, looking at the sunshine and the peg-tiled roofs.

Ma's was a room to sleep in after her years of austerity and being put upon, a place to find her liberty.

Howard Scupple, the Man Who Wasn't, had the best room, above Ma's, which he very rarely used because he very rarely stayed.

His was a room to mark examination papers in, and drink, and drop his psoriasis skin in scaly pieces on the brown carpet round his desk.

My brother had the room above Granny's kitchen, which was north-facing but had a view owing to a gap in the houses.

His was a room to have a breakdown in.

I had the room above Granny's sitting room, also north-facing, and looking onto a window and the roof above it, twelve feet away. When the wind blew, which it did for most of the year, everything in the room, from door to window, from fireguards to floorboards, creaked and rattled.

Mine was a room with a secret door I made that opened onto new worlds and was the beginning of the search for the world where

Darktime was no more, where the Man Who Was had once lived and might yet be found again.

At the bottom of Compass Street where it met Chandler Street, was Fender's the Corner Shop, which was up little steps into a front room and sold sliced bread and milk and baked beans, soap powder and Wagon Wheels.

On the Seafront were the boats and the fishermen and a sea wall that sent the surf shooting high in the air on stormy days; and a promenade dogs liked.

All about were public houses, remnants of the old days when the North End was alive with fishermen and hovellers, who were now a dying breed: the Albatross, the Star and Garter, the Rose and Crown, the Three Compasses, the Albion, and the Port Arms. In their names was half the history of our nation, and of Stoning.

There was a boat-builders nearby called North Stoning Marine Craft Ltd, and Goldfinch's Bakery in Dragon Street and the Tackle Shop on the corner of Budd and Chandler Streets, which had an advertising board that blew off in a gale and injured the milkman.

There was a poor woman with tatty clothes and unhappy children; a famous artist called Edward Fiortino opposite; and Mrs Simms next door, whose husband died in bed next to her; and her daughter Peggy, who was a fan of Frank Sinatra; and living at the top end of Compass Street was Mr and Mrs Mulliken, who once had a fishmonger's in South Street and now looked at the sea while they waited to die.

But all these people and places, the back alleys and the fishing at night on the shore and the Ramparts and Printer's Square and Noel Coward walking on the Front, all these I had not yet found the courage to discover and explore.

All I had was the spiral stairs of our house to go up and down, and the unhappiness of Granny in her dark room and her draughty narrow kitchen, and the rattling doors and windows in my room when the wind blew hard: that was all I had for now.

'Go out and about, Jimmy, like you used to do,' said Granny sometimes, but her heart wasn't in it. Without a view she was beginning to die, so she couldn't find the strength to make me want to live.

I just scurried here and there with downcast eyes, and escaped sometimes along the Promenade back past Stoning Castle and Mr Boys to the shore I once knew, and on up Southdown way. But it wasn't the same with no house nearby to go to, and I had never had any friends to visit, and the walk home was now too long to carry driftwood all the way. The centre of my world had been ripped right out and I had to make a new map for myself.

But I was not yet ready to give up what I had left behind and enter into the North End with an open heart. I felt a stranger there, learning English in a foreign land, with new customs and different ways.

. . . And from my bedroom window, even when the wind was from the south, I could no longer hear the bugler's call.

One day I left for school but my feet took me the wrong way. I walked past the bus stop and then turned down a lane in case I was seen. I didn't know where I was going but my feet seemed to. They took me along the Seafront and when my satchel grew too heavy I hid it under an upturned boat, shifting the shingle and squeezing it in.

I heard the Royal Marine clock strike nine so I knew I was late for school, but my feet carried on. I sat for a long time by the Sea Scouts' boat-shed, hidden from view, staring out across the sea and trying to see France, which I couldn't because it was lost in sea mist. My legs were so weak when I got up again that I could hardly stand. My brain felt funny.

I walked along by the shops in South Stoning looking at window after window of all sorts of things, as if I was trying to find something I had lost but couldn't remember what. There was a greengrocer and the butcher and the little shop with steps up to an old door in which they sold pipes and tobacco. There was the toyshop I stole from once and a shop with pictures of houses for sale and Clark's the shoe shop.

That's where I stopped to look at the shoes, black and brown and some blue ones for women and sandals for children and black canvas ones with rubber round the edges for sports. But not my shoes; there weren't any like them, though I looked at every pair they had in their big window.

I felt myself snivelling and I wanted to cry but I didn't. I turned the next corner and as I walked I felt pooh come in my pants and I didn't know why or what to do.

So I walked some more, here and there, turning corners until I didn't know where I was, I felt so strange, and my bum sticky and sore and soreness in my throat, and my eyes wanted to cry tears they couldn't find. I knew I was walking towards Darktime that day; I knew that much.

Then I felt rain on my face and I couldn't find the strength to run, not even to shelter. The rain came drumming down and stopped me in my tracks, a shaft of misery coming right down from the sky and I found myself in a cage of rain.

When it stopped I walked on and passed the Library and that gave me a clue where I was. They had Mr Mee in there and he would have been a friend. He would have answered my question if I had known what it was. My bum was so uncomfortable and sore and I didn't know what to do or . . .

'Jimmy? It's Jimmy Rova, isn't it?'

It was Mary the Librarian, Mr Boys's good friend.

I looked at her but I felt so weak I couldn't speak. I could hardly raise my head. My eyes hurt.

'What's wrong?' she said, kneeling down onto the pavement and her arms coming out towards me on either side of me. 'What's wrong, my dear?'

'I . . . I . . .'

I went into her arms and she held me and as I cried and cried and cried I said, 'I don't know, I don't know . . .'

Because that was the worst thing, I didn't.

Except for one thing: as I said it all I could see was my shoes in the mangle covered in dust and bent down with age. They must have been so lonely down there all that time and in such pain.

I cried into her as she held me close and the holding made me cry even more because it reminded me of something else I had lost.

'I can't go home: I've got pooh in my pants.'

'Then will you let me take you to Mr Boys, dear? He'll sort you out and then we'll take you home together and explain.'

I nodded.

'It hurts to walk. I hurt all over.'

'I don't think you're very well, Jimmy,' she said, holding my hand. 'You're just not well. You're hot. Come on.'

So she took me to Stoning Castle and banged on the gates and Mr Boys came and took one look at her and then at me and she explained about me not being well and wet with the rain and the pooh in the pants.

'Come on, lad,' he said; 'there's worse things than that. Come on.'

I felt safe with them there and didn't mind him and her cleaning me up in the Castle Toilets.

'Ladies aren't normally allowed in the Gents,' said Mr Boys to Mary, 'but seeing as the Castle's closed, well . . .'

'I've seen more exciting things than these WCs, you know,' she said. 'Now get your shorts off, Jimmy . . .'

I pulled them down and then my smelly pants and Mr Boys said 'Dear me!' so suddenly and with such surprise that I grinned.

'Well, have you hot water?' said Mary.

'It's for me tea,' said Mr Boys.

'Get it then . . .' she said, grinning as well.

I don't know why we laughed but we did and I got cleaned up and as my shorts weren't dirtied, just my pants, I put them back on once I was clean and dry, for decency's sake.

Mr Boys tried ringing Ma but there was no reply because she was at work.

I started to shiver and ache.

Mary said, 'I'm not having Jimmy shivering in this place all day, he's coming home with me. I think he's got the 'flu. You can leave a note for his mother and she can fetch . . .'

I don't remember much more. Just a house near the barracks and hearing band practice and a hot-water bottle and a radio downstairs and me drifting into sleep and out of it and Mr Boys's voice and the telephone ringing and me thinking I never wanted to move from the big wide bed whose sheets smelt of lavender, I never wanted to go back to Compass Street; I remember thinking that.

Then Ma came and I was taken home in a shiny car and the dank grubby walls of our house in the North End were all around me and the Coalman tapping but me no longer scared, just ill and my mind lost somewhere.

Mr Boys came once or twice and Mary and one day I remembered something.

'Get Mr Boys, Ma,' I said.

'I will not. He's done enough, more than enough, already.'

'Please.'

She shook her head and pursed her lips like Granny.

When Granny came to see me, which she did every day, she was different from before and she couldn't help me now. It was she who needed me by then. She who was reaching out her hand and asking me the way. It was for her I wanted to get better.

One day Mr Boys came and I asked him what I had wanted to ask before.

'Don't tell Ma; she thinks you've done enough for me already.'

'Your Ma can think and say what she likes, but on that score she's wrong, lad, as well you know.'

I did know it. That's why I told Mr Boys where I had hidden my satchel and asked if he would go and get it for me.

'Course I will,' he said.

He found the satchel and it was as dry as a bone. I got better soon after that.

But there was one thing I didn't dare ask him, which was what happened to my pants.

I never did ask him and he never did say. Except one day there they were in my drawer again – and they were folded and ironed for once, neat as anything.

When I was better, or getting better anyway, because something still wasn't right, I started going into Granny's room again. I knew she needed me, not from words she spoke, nor from looks she gave, but from the way I found her sitting staring out at bricks, and from the soft murmur of her voice as she began to talk to herself without being able to hear that she did it. But I was too weak yet to know how to show her the way as once she had shown me. I had to find my strength.

In those dark first months in Compass Street Ma thrived, so that was one good thing, with her Cyclemaster, a motorized bicycle, and a pay rise for her farm work, and voluntary work for the National Savings Committee (Stoning Branch).

A dark winter came, and then a bitter spring, and the illness lingered with me, and Darktime re-entered my mind. It was worse when Michael came back from school, and when Hilary sometimes came back in the holidays.

'Jimmy . . . *Jimmy . . .*'

I heard their voices spiral up the stairs, and the creak and groan of the wind at my window. I couldn't look them in the eyes for what they had done to my shoes.

'Jimmy . . .'

I couldn't get it out of my head.

I had no friend in those dark days, and the North End was a labyrinth into which I dared not go; Jimmy Rova was beginning to lose his identity again.

'Jimmy, where are you?'

I was up on the Front huddling out of the wind in the yellow sea shelter at the top of Smithy Street, looking at the seahorses coming in.

'Supper's on the table.'

I could have fished from the shore, but I didn't.

I could have helped with Freddie Hammel's boats, but I didn't.

I could have walked over the Southdown cliffs, but it seemed so far and I was so tired.

I was drifting nearer and nearer to Darktime.

Then, just for once, Ma and the Man Who Wasn't did something right for me, though for the wrong reasons. They saw I was ill and decided a change might be as good as a rest. I was to go away for the summer term to yet another school, this one in Germany. It was to widen my horizons, to improve my mind, to educate me further, to see the wide world; to get me away, that's what it was.

It did something else: it gave me room to breathe for a time, just breathe.

I went by aeroplane to a farm in Rinteln near Hannover with Frau Kersting and ate black bread and bratwurst, and fished for trout in the River Weser and got told off for using worms.

Away from the house in Compass Street, and the shadows and silences of my family and Ma's past, I began to get better. I discovered that Germany was not all black and white like in the films, and not all the men wore shiny peaked helmets and boots, and shouted orders before they killed people. Not at all.

The first home I found myself welcomed to day in and day out was there waiting in Germany as if there had never been a war: it was the farm pigman's, whose door was always open and whose wife would sit me at the kitchen table and make me omelettes with real butter, and give me glasses of buttermilk.

If she had said, 'Stay,' I would have stayed all my life. Frau Kersting said that the pigman and his wife could have no children and so they could never have a son. I didn't know enough German then to tell them that a part of me would be their son for evermore. When Mrs Pigman hugged me once I caught again the woman smell I discovered once when I'd found the petticoat, which reminded me of a time of happiness before Darktime and a woman whose name I probably never knew. Someone I had lost and couldn't find, however hard I searched.

So when I sat in their little home and looked about, it seemed to me that the sun always shone, and theirs was on the way to being the room I could only find in the House of a Thousand Rooms if I shut my eyes. I discovered in those days that the insides of houses could be clean and bright and people who lived in them happy. And I discovered something else for which Ma had never prepared me: something the Germans called *gemütlich*, which means cosy, comfortable, filled with love and safety, all at once. It wasn't something the people who lived in Fitzroy Square, or Printer's Square, even had a word for.

I was taken for the family summer holiday to the Tyrol and shown mountains higher by far than Moel Siabod, but as I wasn't allowed to climb them Siabod remained the highest I knew.

I wore lederhosen, shorts made of leather with braces attached and green oakleaf decorations. I learnt to speak a little German. I got attacked by a dog.

I was only lonely the first night, when I cried, after which my training in Darktime, and all the years after, got me through.

I met a girl my age with red hair who said, 'The sun is high in the sky,' which seemed a strange thing to say, but she didn't speak good English.

I said slowly in English like Ma taught us to, to foreigners, 'The sea is big in winter,' and 'My mother works on a farm.'

She said, *'Das ist gut!'* and I said I was glad in English.

Of all my conversations big and small in Germany in those long months alone recovering, that is the one I remember most clearly, with that girl from the big house who dared to come and speak English to me.

She had pigtails and freckles and I didn't know how to say 'Please don't go back to the big house,' nor did I guess that she was the first girl for whom I felt the sweet pang of love. So I said nothing and she went back to her house, and all that remained was the sun high in the sky.

Suddenly one day the pigman came with his wife and said goodbye. They gave me a pair of new lederhosen as a present, but it was his quiet tears I treasured most. He was the first person, man or woman, to cry for me and I felt his strong hand on my shoulder, never wanting him to let me go.

Long, long the years I had known the Man Who Wasn't and he never touched me like that. But the Pigman touched me once and for ever and maybe if I had stayed his touch would have come to feel nearly as good as the touch of the Man Who Was.

* * *

I returned to England for the start of the autumn term stronger than when I left. But not quite so strong I dared explore the North End yet, so I still walked through it with my head down and dreamt of the beach down South Stoning way.

There was a week to go before the start of school and my brother Michael was living in the house again. He had put some of his things in my room and I said I didn't want them there.

He shrugged and closed his door on me. My hand was shaking when I opened his door. I went in and said more words and before I knew it I was fighting him. I wrestled him to the ground and as I did I knew it was a fight for real, for life, and that I was opening that secret door on new worlds.

I wrestled with the strength of all my Darktime and Michael never stood a chance. But at the end, when he weakened, and he fell back beneath me, pushing at me in one last struggle, and I saw his mouth quiver towards tears as I raised my fist to hit him, I showed him something I do not remember him ever showing to me.

I showed it to him because, without intending to, he and my cousin Hilary had taught me how much it can sometimes be needed.

I showed him compassion.

I had lost so much that losing was less important to me than winning was to him. I rolled over and let him win and in that moment discovered that deciding to lose, to give up, often leads to winning what was given up. It's the act of choice that gives the victory.

He stayed on top for only a second or two before he was off me without a word and gone. That same day he removed his things from my room and never touched me again with his fists, never; but it wasn't so easy to leave behind the dark blows that his clever mind inflicted on me.

That same day I thought maybe I could kill two birds with one stone and get Granny out of her dark room to help me explore the North End.

As I set off to find her I heard my mother cry, 'Jimmy, is that you?'

I ignored her and went up the spiral stairs to Granny's room and knocked loud so she could hear. I told her what I had in mind. She would enjoy the walk and I . . .

Granny shook her head and stayed in her chair.

'You can use this to fetch us some crumpets for later, and if not today then tomorrow,' she said, giving me some coppers. 'You just run along and explore the North End by yourself, which is the best way anyway. Come back at teatime and tell me all you saw and heard. I can't walk so far now, nor can I see or hear very well. But, my dear, you can do all three.'

But it wasn't as easy as that and instead, and as usual, I lingered on the Seafront, unable to find the will and the courage to enter the North End world.

Next day Hilary came from Oxford for the last weekend of the summer holidays and Ma sent me off to meet her, with Michael.

When she got off the train at Stoning Station she was wearing a new coat and looked very grown-up. She told me to carry her case, and that I had to walk behind them both like in the old days in the South End. It was not thirteen paces these days, or fourteen, or twelve, because now behind was enough. I was that well trained.

She and he walked ahead, singing and dancing in their secret laughter. As they turned down Macaulay Road without even looking back at me I remembered suddenly how together they'd stolen my shoes and left them to die in the mangle guarded by the Coalman.

Something broke in me then and it made me feel scared but good. I watched them go ahead, and slowly, very slowly, I came to a halt and put her case down, right on the pavement.

I came to a halt and put her case down.

I came to a halt.

That was the moment I stopped running to get away and instead just stopped to see where I had got to. When I saw where I was and I liked what I saw, I left the case right there and took a different route from them, through St Andrew's Churchyard. I took it fast enough that when I emerged into Lower Street I did so ahead of them. I turned and watched them come towards me.

Hilary's face was fat and went angry and red the moment she saw me standing there without her case: and in *that* moment I knew I had been right about who it was who stole my shoes and who knew just the place to hide them where I would never look.

'Where's my case?'

'I left it on the pavement by the chapel of the Salvation Army.'

I don't think she even knew where that was. She didn't know our town like I did. She was the one who didn't belong, not me.

I remember she screwed up her fists and her face all at the same time and her mouth grew ugly like the mouth of her uncle Howard Scupple, who was the Man Who Wasn't, when he had drunk too much gin. As she shouted she came to hit me.

What was she then?

She was the teeth of the Great White Shark.

She was mockery in Darktime.

She was Watts the Menmore boy who shaved but who I found the courage to tackle to the ground.

She was the knight on the white charger who despises the fallen knight with pointed feet and makes the mistake of thinking he'll never get up.

She was a conker in a conker fight that had had all its goes and left me with the last strike.

I wished there was a door in the middle of Stoning's Lower Street to smash bullies down to the ground, but there wasn't.

So I hit her. I hit her.

I hit her as hard as I possibly could.

As she fell back I saw surprise in her face, and then the rage and ancient mockery replaced by hurt and fear; while Michael just watched with a dead man's eyes, so I just looked at him and raised my fist, and he backed away like the coward he was.

When she got up I did something I don't regret, though I knew it was wrong. I hit her again.

The first hit was for the left shoe, the second for the right.

'You stole my shoes,' I said.

'W . . . what shoes?' wavered Hilary, looking at Michael.

I think he remembered but I don't think she did and that felt like the worst thing of all. She didn't even remember.

'My shoes,' I said.

'I don't know what you're talking about,' she said.

I stared at her and felt my hand turning into a red raw hitting hand again. I didn't like her forgetting. Maybe she saw our Ma in my face or maybe she didn't want to be hit again. Maybe she didn't want me to see that she was beginning to cry. Whatever the maybe was, I just didn't care. But I stood there not moving because they were in my territory now and I didn't want them there.

'Go away,' I said and she looked at me like that boy did who I hit with the door, who I knew would never trouble me again. He never did and she wasn't going to.

'Go away.'

Then, as they scurried away whining and crying back up Macaulay Road to see if her case was still there, I turned and crossed the street to Cox the Chemist's and the long mirror in its outside wall.

I felt as if I had won a war, but it was only a battle. You cannot win a war against your own flesh and blood in two quick blows. But it felt good to try. Even if it was only a battle I had won, it gave me something I could call my own.

I stood and looked at myself in that mirror and saw a boy who was no longer small, and who no longer shooted at bumble bees.

I saw a boy with tousled hair and khaki shorts and a shirt, and bigger shoes now to call his own. A boy with tired eyes, tired from running through Darktime all alone, who had finally stopped to see if there was another way out, and had discovered there might be.

I reached out a hand and touched the outstretched hand of the boy in the mirror and took it. Then I led him down St Andrew's Alley into the shadowed world of history and memory, of the dead and the living, that was and is the North End. It was *my* territory and not theirs: mine to discover, mine to explore, mine to call my own. They would go away but I could stay and become its conqueror.

From that great day I did as Granny had said I should and made the North End all my own. I had discovered my Newfoundland. I walked and I saw and I heard, and I began to learn who Jimmy was, the boy who had had no shoes.

There was so much to see I hardly went home, except to eat and sleep. Apart from one other thing. Often, when I was done with exploring, or the rain came down, or darkness fell, I would go back to the house and climb the spiral stairs to Granny's room.

She would close her curtains against the night, and put on the kettle to make a pot of tea, and she would toast crumpets with her brass toasting fork. Then, unless she was tired, she would make me tell her all I had seen and done. She listened so well she seemed to make time stand still, even though her clock, which had once been Grandfather's, ticked on.

Sometimes she would talk about her own life, and sometimes give me good advice.

'Jimmy,' she said once, 'the ticking of a watch or clock gives you a sense of security and also teaches you discipline; don't you forget that. When I'm gone, which one day I will be, you have Grandfather's clock. It'll see you though hard times and keep you steady.'

Other times, most times, she asked me questions.

'What did you learn about today?'

'About greasing runners for the boats from Freddie Hammel.'

'I meant at school . . .' said Granny, smiling.

'The eight-times table.'

'What will you do this weekend?'

'Try and find a stone with a hole in it on the beach.'

'Humph! What will you be when you grow up, that's what I'd like to know but probably never will.'

'Rich enough to buy a split cane casting rod,' I said. 'But . . .'

'But what, my dear?' said Granny, buttering another crumpet the way I liked.

'I'd have to be *very* rich for that. The Pier Master said they cost a lot.'

'Nothing's impossible if you put your mind to it,' said Granny as she often did, 'and don't you forget it!'

I never did. Of all the many things she told me that was the most true. You can do anything you want, even become rich enough to buy a split cane rod and have enough left over to buy some bait as well. The problem isn't the money but knowing what you really want.

Many an evening Granny listened to me answering her questions and it was her listening that helped me begin to find who Jimmy was, and help him start looking for the way out of Darktime and into the light.

But if she was tired when I came up to her room and the effort of listening grew too much, we would just sit by the firelight and I would watch her fall asleep. Then I would sit some more, and listen to the ticking of the clock, and the wind outside, and I would tell myself the stories that I would tell her next time, when tomorrow came.

PART TWO

# NORTH END

# 14

# TREASURES OF THE SEA

Granny said, 'There's a storm brewing, and a big one. Jimmy, you can take me up to the Front and hold on to my arm so I don't blow away.'

This was in 1954, a year after we moved to Compass Street and just before I started at big school. I was still young enough not to worry about being seen out with Granny; the dark cloud of teenage self-consciousness had not yet settled over my head. Granny had dealt with the gloomy view out of her window as she dealt with everything she did not like: firmly. When Aunt Ellie sent her a poster of Victoria Falls in Northern Rhodesia, Granny stuck it over her window with Sellotape so that the light shone through it and made it look alive.

One day she took this down and put it in her cupboard. She got Ma and me to put up a hook for a mirror that reflected the light back into the room. Then she found something the African gentleman gave her, which was a picture of the Zimbabwe Ruins, built by the Bantu over 400 years ago and stuck it back over her window, where the ruins glowed red from the light outside.

'There, that's better!' said Granny. 'Nothing like an African sunset to take me to the end of my days!'

I knew that from that day she had accepted her lot in her dark room and would fight her fate as best she could.

Our front door had two marble steps, slippery and steep, so on the day of the storm I had to help Granny down them. It was only thirty yards up to the Front, but when the wind was blowing even that short walk could be a struggle. That day the wind was loud and grasping and Granny held my arm with one hand and had her stick in the other as we battled up our street, then over onto the Promenade and across to the edge of the sea wall itself. There before us lay the pebble beach, and then the grey, stretching sea, and beyond that the whole world.

This was before the new sea wall, so there was no concrete wave barrier to clamber across, and the boats were still there, and Freddie Hammel's white clapboard hut, down by the Monarch Hotel, and the yellow bricks of Seagirt, a house turned into a gun turret in 1939 in case the Germans came. There were rusting capstans from the good old days, and flagpoles to mark each fisherman's pitch, against which the ropes and wires rattled with the wind.

We didn't stand too near the edge of the sea wall because of the wind. The sea was raging up the beach in great ugly waves of danger-ous water, which roared in and thumped down – *thump! thump!* – and then sent broken water racing in, shifting more pebbles in five seconds than a man could have shifted in five days.

The boats had been hauled up to the edge of Prow Street the day before to get them out of the way of the coming storm. There was shingle on the Promenade from the high tide the night before, and now the sea was coming in again and getting rougher and heavier by the moment.

There wasn't much life about.

Freddie down by his cabin raised an arm to say hello. He knew Granny and me from when we lived in South Stoning because, being the lifeboat coxswain, he was often up that way. Granny said he had retired now but still liked a chat. He waved again and Granny half raised her stick before he disappeared inside to sit by his stove.

A dog shivered as it sniffed at some discarded newspaper and chips and then bounded away down an alley to find warmth. A few gulls huddled up on the Promenade out of the way of the waves, eyes closing and opening, wings tight to their bodies, shifting uneasily when the dog went past before huddling down again.

Granny said, 'It's different from storms in Rhodesia. They're more sudden, wetter, hotter, more dangerous, and they drive grown men mad, and some women too, I've no doubt. The storms in those latitudes are enough to make you believe in the Devil. But here, *here . . .*'

With the wind tugging at her hairnet she gazed out at the sea, her big nose like a promontory of rock no waves could ever destroy. She was old now and knew it, but being in the storm made her younger and happier for a while. It was life to her, and brought happy memories.

Her days in Africa were the best of her life. She fell in love out there with a love that transformed her life and brought her peace. The storm that day was an excuse to get out of her dark room, to let the wind clear her head so that she could remember good things, like the day she and the African Gentleman met in the shade of some ruins in Rhodesia. She never told me their name but it wasn't hard to work it out.

For all her courage in facing life and though her gaze seemed as intense as ever, what Granny saw most clearly was now in her mind. Our house was just a place to die in.

'Look!' I shouted against the wind. '*Look!*'

I had seen my first treasure of the sea nestling down in the sand and shingle at the base of the sea wall. It was the green-silver half-moon of a coin uncovered by the waves of the previous tide and now sticking out of the sand. But Granny couldn't see it. Her eyes were too weak and her spectacles were mucky with salt from the spray. Granny had had her chances with the treasures of life; now it was my turn.

I wanted to run down the steep steps in the wall and get the coin but Granny's bony hand tightened on my arm.

'You're not to go down there, Jimmy. The sea doesn't mean to be unkind but it'll get you if it can. It's like a hungry lion: it will eat whatever's vulnerable. It'll gobble you up in no time and you'll be gone. You stay up on the wall when the weather's like this.'

Granny grew suddenly tired and her face went from pale pink to tired grey.

'You'd better get me home,' she said suddenly.

It was sad to see Granny losing the battle against age, and how she was forced to retreat before its advance, even if she battled all the way.

She knew she wasn't young any more and that the world and I were leaving her behind. She was just skin and bone and a big nose with a drop on the end of it, and already my arms were thicker than her shins.

I led her back to our house, keeping tight hold of her so she stayed upright when the wind tried to blow her away, and then supporting her from behind as she struggled up our steps.

At the top she turned to me and said, 'Off you go now, Jimmy. Go and learn about storms. But watch the sea because if it's not a lion it's a rhinoceros and it will charge you down so hard you'll never get up again.'

She smiled at me but I knew she was serious.

My Granny saved my life once, back in Darktime, and I knew she always had my interests at heart.

These were the days when I had only just started to explore the North End and discover its secrets and so make them my own. But I still felt scared of it and there was much yet to find. Getting me to take her up to the Front that morning was not just Granny's way of getting out of her room, it was also her way of getting me going, helping me move on.

I had no dad to encourage me, so that day she took it on herself to do his work instead, and it paid dividends.

I raced back to the Front and went back to where I had seen the treasure. The waves had come in a bit and were closer to the wall, but where it had been was not yet covered by water, so Granny's warning words flew out of my head with the wind and I scampered down the steps and onto the beach.

The wall rose behind and above me, vertical and dark. The sea raged in front, massive, grey-white and threatening. I watched it warily, unsure of myself, glancing back at the steps, ready at any moment to run back up them to the safety above. I had not yet learnt that on a shingle beach my ears were a better guide to what the waves were doing than my eyes.

Treasure is alluring and blinds you to danger. It says, 'I'm here, just here, but to get me you'll have to come a little further and leave your safe place behind.' The search for treasure is the journey of life, but its pursuit puts you in the way of risk and danger, and brings death to some along the way.

I stared down at the sandy shingle at my feet and it was like seeing the pink skin beneath the fur of an animal. The waves in the night had stripped the beach bare of its normal shingle cover and what was left behind were hard deposits of mud and sand into which old pebbles and bits of glass and corroded metal had set. It was some-where in there that I'd seen the treasure.

Here and there, like little bays on the beach, were spits of small-stoned shingle, orange-brown and shiny with salt sea that had just washed back down the treasure layer. These held no treasure at all, apart from the black hunks of scaffold ties from the war defences, rusting and encrusted with dead limpet shells.

What was I looking for?

As the waves pulled back and gave me moments of safety, I bent forward for a better view of the shingle-sand to try to catch again a glimpse of that magical silver and green treasure.

*Thump! Thump!*

The sea crashed to my right and a wall of water began to surge towards me. The wind roared at my back and chilled my neck, the sound of grating shingle mounted in my ears, but all I could do was search at my feet, my eyes racing to find . . . to find . . .

The only thing I saw was a spike of metal, black-red, which when I pushed at it with my boot turned out to be no more than a shred of old copper wire. Yet I bent to pick it up, something being better than nothing to the treasure hunter. Straightening up with the wall of water almost on me, I ran. And *ran*.

But it came roaring up the beach so fast it caught my legs and feet and made me fall, my hands plunging through its green-white depth to the shingle beneath, water forcing its way up my sleeves. I pushed myself upright and the water paused, turned and suddenly began to drag me back in the opposite direction, this time so powerful at my legs that it nearly toppled me backwards into the path of the next wave. It was in my boots, up my legs, pulling, pulling like a thousand watery hands, and its roar in my ears was the beginning of a vast silence I would hear for ever if I gave up.

I stumbled again, fell back into the water, heaved myself up as it tried to drag me back down, and blindly staggered up the shingle until *bang!* I hit the sea wall and there was blood on my hand from a graze on my forehead.

The steps were too far away to reach had another great wave come. But instead the water weakened below me and retreated. It petered out into yellow foam that died down into the shingle below where I stood. The next wave was nowhere near as powerful as the last, nor was the one after it, and sopping and sodden though I was, my eyes soon returned to their search of the shingle, as my greed for treasure took over.

I ventured back down the beach to where I had been, one eye on the waves, watching for another big one, the other unable to let the shingle go. That was when I saw again the crescent of green and silver I had first glimpsed, the fallen moon of a coin peeking from the shingle-sand that had long since accepted and held on to it, until the day came when it was uncovered for eyes to see if, in that rage of water, they dared to go and look.

I bent down as yet another great wave mounted up behind me and I picked up my first treasure of the sea.

It was encrusted with green and black, except for where the silver showed through. And the date: 1937.

> *Bobby had a shilling*
> *All his very own*
> *Should he . . . ?*

But I left that poem to itself as I thought that if there was one shilling, there might well be more and started looking again, heart beating, boots scrunching into sodden shingle, desperate not to lose what I hoped I might find before the next big wave came in.

I heard its roar and this time ran for the steps without hesitation, not looking back. I jumped up on the first step and then climbed a few more as the wave reached me.

As I waited for the water to retreat I looked at my coin and rubbed it with my sandy thumb to make it brighter. I saw the head of the King and some Latin words before I turned back to the sea, jumped down onto the shingle and followed the retreating surf back to the treasure line, my coin tight safe in my hand. Then I began searching again, not a moment to lose, seeking, bent nearly double with my craving to find another, something more, another one, something better still . . . though I was sopping wet and my head ached from its bang on the sea wall.

There is no cure for the beachcomber's obsession. It is revived in a moment by the stirring of the wind, by the sound of the sea, by the tang of salty spray at your nose. It can be fed by the distant sound in a shell, or the scent of dried seaweed; even the cry of a seagull over an inland rubbish dump will bring on the craving.

From that day, my eyes had the look of someone searching, looking, seeking: someone hoping to find.

I was a boy called Jimmy when I became hooked on the beach.

What is the cure?

It is something on the shore waiting to be found.

It is there, somewhere at our feet, waiting for a wave bigger than the others to come in and strip things away, leaving just the treasure for us to see.

The cure is the treasure that we never quite find. For me the cure would have been something I could *never* find. My own dad, a real one. By blood. The only one. Maybe that was what, beyond the coins and other treasure washed up on the beach, I really hoped to find.

That morning I began to learn to read the waves by sight and sound, and feel in my body the shape of the tide's advance. But the wildness of the storm that day turned me mad. Even as the tide approached its highest point, and every other wave was surging right up to the wall, I continued to search, though I tried to keep close to the safety of the steps. Standing there, soaking wet, a coin and bits of old metal in my hand, I would jump back down as the waves began to retreat, look about, find what I could, pick it up and then run back up with the next waves just behind, mounting the steps behind me now – *Pfft! Pfft! Pfft!* – and the spray on the wind blowing straight into my face when I turned round.

I didn't know the danger then, but I sensed it, deliciously. My treasure was not a gift given by gods but a prize won from one of them: the sea itself. As the waves surged and broke before me I stared into them and stared at death with fear and fascination. I wanted to know what lay waiting within the surf. If I could not find the greatest treasure, the one to end all treasures, I could find oblivion.

North of the steps, further along the wall, where the old groynes were, the sea had long since come in too far to allow safe passage. Occasionally it retreated, but when it did there was still a foot or more of water between the wall and the next advance of waves. This constant swill of water spread ever closer to the steps themselves as, increasingly, the bigger waves, like the one that first caught me, crashed straight into the wall with enough power to half crush a man, or knock him down, drag him out and drown him.

Then the moment would pass, the waves would retreat and I would turn my gaze from the wall to the decreasing area of the shingle-sand still left for me to search. I would grab what felt like one last chance to find something, anything, however small, to satisfy the hunger that I felt and jump back down to the shingle again. By now the water was surging almost continuously at the bottom step, reluctant to go back, and my forays onto the shingle-sand grew briefer and briefer, yet still I waited, hoping . . .

A sudden retreat, an exposure of shingle running with water, and amidst a disintegration of shingle-sand the glint of a second coin.

I jumped down, took two steps towards it and fell forward into the slushy weak shingle heavy seas can create to trap you. I put out my hands to break my fall and saw all the treasure I had found tumble from my right hand onto the shingle beneath me. Every piece of it, including the coin I had first picked up. The second one had disappeared as if it had never been.

I gouged frantically at the slushy pebbles for the fallen treasure and then began to get to my feet as a wall of water roared towards me. I turned, tried to run and felt the hammer blow of the water against my legs and then against my back. *Bang!* And I was down and flat and the water was surging over and past me, my hands scrabbling at the shifting shingle and sand beneath to find something solid to push against.

I tried to rise through rushing water but knew as I pushed and pushed at my legs and my boots filled with water that it would be hard to reach the bottom step because the water was already hitting the wall ahead of me, mounting up and crashing back down towards me to push me back out again into the path of the next vast wave whose roar I could already hear.

In that brief lull I saw that I had been swept so far to one side of the steps that however hard I tried I could never reach them. I stood paralysed and stared helplessly at the blank wall as the water powered up it, and then I lifted my gaze above it towards the sky. Not in hope but despair.

It was there that I saw him, vaster, blacker, wilder than any wave could be. He stood there, staring down at me.

Then, as the wave fell back over me, he jumped down and I saw two boots, black as night, waders as big as a wall, and I felt a hand at my back steadying me against the murderous sea; and another grasping my windcheater. My head lolled forward into the chest of his sodden black coat as he picked me up and heaved me through the waves and took me to the steps and threw me halfway up them.

Banged, hurt, crouching, I looked back. I saw a great man reaching to hold on to the rusty remnants of some rails as the sea that would have taken me crashed over him. A man who was a rock as the waters surged back past him, down his neck, through his fingers, between his legs, over the feet of his great black waders, until finally it was gone.

Then, slowly, he straightened up and stared at where I crouched, sodden, on the steps above. His dark eyes were deep brown, his chin black stubble, his coat hung flapping about his boots. He looked at me not in fear that I might have drowned, or triumph that he had saved me, but in surprise, astonishment, that I was there at all.

I stared at him: at his long legs, at his vastness, at his face, which seemed all black hairs. I stared at the dark hairs on the back of his powerful hands and fingers and thumbs, and suddenly saw that, even as he climbed the steps to where I was, his right hand, so much vaster than my own, was clutching its own fistful of treasures of the sea.

I had never seen so large, so strong, so rough a man in my life, nor a man whose eyes held such tenderness, and such puzzled surprise.

As he climbed on up the steps to the Promenade and I followed him, he said in his gravelly voice, 'Let's see what you've got, lad; let's see what you've found.'

I looked down at my tight-clenched fist and slowly opened it. It held a fistful of shingle and sand, and that solitary shilling piece, retrieved a second time.

He crouched down by my side, a fellow conspirator. He slowly opened his great hand and there was a half-crown, some battered pennies and a round lead fishing weight. Then I saw more: amongst the gritty sand was green copper wire, lead trading tokens, a huge hammered fishing hook and a roofing nail oxidized a beautiful green.

'You're Jimmy Rova,' he said, and his voice was deep and rough and soft all at once. 'Freddie Hammel said who you were.'

Behind us, at the bottom of the sea wall, the sea crashed about, angry and frustrated.

'By nightfall the sand'll be covered with shingle again,' he said. 'The wind's shifting. It's only the easterlies lay bare its treasures like this.'

His face was so dark and hairy I didn't know where it began and ended, and his eyes were dark brown with reflections of grey waves and the far horizon.

Briefly his hand touched my shoulder.

'You better run along home, lad, and dry yourself off. Next time you want to 'comb you come along and get me in Budd Street. Number 7. It's not a thing a lad like you should be doing alone. But you made a good start.'

He looked from me to the sea and stood up, towering over me.

I looked at the sea and at my first treasure.

'You're Mr Bubbles,' I said, 'Mr Hammel's friend.'

He nodded, looking down at me, and grunted to say that maybe he was.

I had seen him along our shore, usually in the distance, or cycling along Prow Street on his big old black bicycle.

I had seen him in Freddie Hammel's hut, talking.

He was so big, so dark, so strange that I never went near him because he had made me feel afraid. But not any more, not now he had saved my life and I could look up at him and see something beyond the fear I felt.

I had no name for it. But I had no name for many things that others thought I couldn't see.

So I could not have said that what I saw in his dark deep eyes was that in me he had found the one thing he had never been able to find until then: he had found his treasure from the sea.

I sensed what he was thinking as a warm good thing, though maybe he too could not have given it a name: that at his feet, soaking wet, battered and bruised, beginning to shiver, was the lad from nowhere he had looked everywhere to find. A lad with whom in the months and years ahead, to the last days of his life, he could finally share the things he knew about the sea as he was never able to share with anyone else; and share as well, roughly, gruffly and with passion, his pleasure in the elements and his rarely spoken dreams.

That was the nameless thing I saw.

I looked round at the sea and then felt a touch on my shoulder and a gruff 'Off you go, lad.' So I set off for home and the last thing I saw was not him but his good friend Freddie Hammel, Stoning's great lifeboatman, raising his hand to Mr Bubbles in acknowledgement, which made me think it was Freddie who had sent Mr Bubbles to watch out for me that day.

Freddie and he were the last of the longshoremen in the North End and if they had been younger, and things different, and me not a boy from a different class, they would have taught me their trade more formally. As it was, Freddie's boys weren't interested in that way of life, and Mr Bubbles and his wife had never had children, and so never a son.

That was their sadness, but it was my gain.

Mr Bubbles assumed the responsibility of being my dad along the shore, and Freddie was my uncle and my friend, and though I was never their apprentice, nor bound to them by articles, they were the ones who showed me the nature of treasure and how to harvest it.

But it was Mr Bubbles who taught me that one day our last tide comes in and takes all our treasure back for someone else to find, every last shilling and piece of sea-worn copper wire.

Later, telling no one what had happened, dried off and warmed but with my underpants still damp, I went to Granny's room.

Granny asked, 'Jimmy, where have you been?'

'I found a shilling.'

I showed it to her, all silver-green and encrusted, and she said, 'That's one for your treasure box.'

I said, 'My treasure box is from before, in the old house, when I believed in the Coalman. I'm going to polish up this shilling and spend it.'

'Don't spend all your treasure,' Granny said, 'or you'll have none to give away.'

'I met a man. He lives in a street called Budd Street. Nearby.'

'Tell me about him, my dear,' said Granny.

I told her everything, except how he had had to save me from the water. Granny listened right through into the dark until she fell asleep.

I sat by the warm light of her gas fire and I thought, 'The North End is a lot of houses and now I know two people who live in them. One is Freddie and one is Mr Bubbles. Four, counting Granny and Ma. Five, including myself.'

It was a start.

# 15

# ELEVEN PLUS

We moved to the North End when I was ten, and Michael twelve, Ma menopausal and Granny growing old.

Those were the days before the North End was elevated into being the Conservation Area. It was just a slum, a run-down place, with old terraced eighteenth-century cottages that were ripe for demolition, and a few failing shops left among the boarded-up ones, and damp houses with rotten front doors and sagging side gates, and cracked window panes encrusted with soot from long-dead coal fires and salt from the sea.

The three streets running parallel with the Seafront – Prow, Nore and Lower – were each cut through by smaller streets and alleyways with names that had a history or a meaning: Compass Street and Budd Street, Nelson, George and Cowper Streets . . . Customs House Lane and Anchor Field. These and all the others became my streets, their memories became my imagined life: who I was and part of what I was to become.

There were no detached houses, or hardly any. Ours was a community of terraces, but old ones from the eighteenth century, twisting and turning, each with different doors and gables, small, narrow, dark, built slowly through the years into a thing of complex beauty where the sun glanced this way and that and the wind found nooks and crannies in which to pile up litter and seaweed; a place built before there were planners to stop it happening.

A place that survived only because Stoning was so unimportant that after the War it was at the bottom of the list for redevelopment. When, finally, developers came knocking at the Town Council's doors with their silken words and pound signs for eyes, there were enough people like Ma who knew beauty when they saw it to stand up and shout, 'No!'

There were very few shops remaining from the North End's nineteenth-century heyday, when the Royal Navy had a dockyard nearby and the fishermen still found fish to catch and the hovellers, often the same men, had ships to service out on the Downs opposite our shore.

By the time we moved there that past was all but gone, but it was still present in the air, and in people's memories. The children had disappeared from the streets because young people looking for jobs when they finished at the local school moved out of the area, leaving behind only the old and the poor. But Ma, with her instinct for decline and faded glory, felt at home in the North End and could afford the price of its houses.

Among the cottages there were a few bigger, taller houses, three storeys high, built for captains, master bakers, brewery owners and customs officials, and these were two-a-penny when we moved in because of the cost of doing them up. That did not worry Ma, who was moving from something bigger. It was space she liked and needed, space to get away from other people, especially her own kith and kin. She didn't mind old rooms, rotten wood and cracked ceilings with damp in the corners; all she wanted was to close her bedroom door and leave the world and her family outside, as far away as possible.

But by then her family was a thing of tatters. Her husband, the Man Who Wasn't, lived in Oxford and only came down sometimes in vacations; Granny stayed mostly in her two rooms; and Michael was already strange. He was out more than he was in, nights as well, which was strange for a boy of twelve, but Ma did not care or seem to ask the reason why.

Ma had scented her liberty after the thirty-year jail sentence she saw her marriage as and taken it. Not that she was free quite yet: Granny would have to leave or die; Michael and I would have to go as well. She often said that, me being the youngest, the day I left she would be free. Like a prisoner whose sentence is more than two-thirds of the way through, she was beginning to count the years, and months, and maybe the days as well.

So to be in No 10 Compass Street was to be in a house in which a boy or two and an ageing grandmother just rattled around; and to be in the North End was to be in a place that had hardly a child. So few were the children in the streets that people's eyes lit up when they saw a boy like me, remembering their own children who had grown up thereabouts, skipping, playing tag, chalking out their hopscotch on the pavements, running their hoops and avoiding the cracks between the paving stones for fear of the dragons. That generation had gone now and their parents, left behind, grieved not to have their grand-children nearby.

So it was that for a long time adults were my only friends, and it was through them and through their eyes, not other children's, that bit by bit I grew to know the North End, and its soul entered my own.

Within months of our arrival, the question arose as to which of two senior schools I would go to when I was eleven. Michael had gone on to the grammar school in Stannick, a seven-mile train ride away.

'A brilliant boy', people said of him, and it was true, except they did not know him for the bully he had been, and the sadistic streak he still showed if he could get away with it.

Once I woke to find a pillow on my face and I'm sure that pillow was from Michael's room; another time I dreamt of a bang, a bang that hurt my face and nose, and in the slanting, swirling darkness of my room in the deep of night, waking suddenly to its glimmers of light from the stairs, from behind my eyes, I'm sure I heard footsteps on linoleum and Michael's door creak shut. I'm sure I did. In the morning my nose hurt but there was no mark.

It takes time to work out two and two makes four. One day, at Easter time, with everybody there round the table, Ma said that the Man Who Wasn't snored and that was why they slept in separate bedrooms. Michael said, 'Jimmy snores like a train, like a drain and it's a strain . . .' and, looking in his eyes, I knew it was him who'd hit me when I was asleep.

In our house, Ma's praise for my two siblings, one sometimes present and the other usually absent, was spoken carefully, to protect my feelings.

'Of course, Michael is bright, there's no getting away from that. Hilary too, I think, very. Jimmy . . . well . . . no . . . I'm afraid he . . .'

In that old house with its thin panelled walls and quirky corners, I heard enough to know I was not as bright as some.

It was then that from somewhere out of the past came the feeling that I was separate and different, really different, and that, unfortunately, like a handicap, 'different' meant lesser.

I felt like the orphan children I read about in stories: creeping about, for ever less than I could be. There was a sense, subtle and silent as morning mist hovering over a meadow, that the rightful due of Hilary and Michael was not likely to be *my* rightful due. This seemed to be because of something in the past, something I had done before I was old enough to know any words, perhaps even before I was born. Whatever it was, that something made me lesser, and made Ma and Howard Scupple, Michael and cousin Hilary, expect less of me.

But now, for good or ill, it was my turn to try to gain entry to the grammar school in Stannick and that prestigious daily train ride away.

*Ha, ha, ha!* said Michael, grinning with the triumph of someone who has already reached the greener shore in safety and takes malicious pleasure in the fact that someone else – me – is unlikely ever to get there too.

Ma and the Law said that I had to sit the Eleven Plus examination whatever happened. If I passed I would follow Michael and my future might yet be as golden as his looked set to be, despite my poor start. But if I failed I would go to the secondary modern school in Upper Stoning and my fate and my future would be worse than death. I would sit in classes with the sons of miners and the daughters of butchers and be taught metalwork instead of mathematics, woodwork instead of English literature.

Michael twisted the knife. He said I would be made to wear a flowery apron and bake cakes. *Ha, ha, ha.*

'And that's "flowery" as in petals and stamens,' he said, 'not "floury" as in cupcakes and buns.'

Everybody laughed, especially Ma, who liked Michael's witticisms. But they were a death by cuts to me.

'What did you mean?' I asked Michael later.

'In the school you're going to they work with their hands; in mine we use our brains. Not having any, Jimmy, you wouldn't understand that, so I wouldn't worry about it if I were you.'

*Ha, ha, ha*, he laughed and I felt like bashing his crooked yellow teeth right out of his mouth.

But I did worry about it because I didn't know what he meant. On the day before the Eleven Plus I said to Ma, 'What did Michael mean about brains?'

'I have no idea what he meant.'

'About his school using brains and mine using hands. What school will I have to go to?'

Over her face came a look I only ever saw a few times, but I knew it meant trouble. It was the same look as when she'd set off to try to throw the gun into the sea. It combined impatience with determination.

She said softly, 'What's the time?'

I had just come back from school so it wasn't late.

'Come with me,' she said, not even bothering to put on her overcoat.

She set off at a fast pace along Prow Street to Lugger Street, where the buses were. We got on one.

We went past the hospital and then down Bradford Road, where Ma said the working classes lived. We got off and then walked towards a school.

'This is Bradford Road Secondary Modern,' said Ma, taking up a position near the gates. There were other mothers there waiting for end of school.

'How do you know?' I asked.

'I applied for a job as school secretary here,' she said.

Full of surprises, was Ma.

'Now you just watch the children who come out at five past three and ask yourself if you want to be one of them.'

Ma wasn't generally much interested in my education, not in a practical way, but that was one lesson she gave me. The children who came out were like a horde of vandals from Mr Mee's encyclopedia. They shouted, they fought, they wore rough clothes and the boys had black boots and dirty hair. Worst of all, they were big and they stared at me and Ma and what lay behind their eyes was frightening.

'This is where you'll go if you don't get into Stannick Grammar,' said Ma.

She held my hand tight and it started to rain and I got scared.

'I want to leave,' I said, trying to pull away from her.

I was bigger and stronger by then, but Ma was bigger still and she had a man's hand.

'Just look,' she said.

'It's raining,' I said and the drumming on my head and the way she held my hand spun me around so that all the big children coming out seemed to circle me, staring; run at me, staring; shout at me, around and around and around.

'Please,' I said, 'I want to go . . .'

But my limbs were frozen and my head was drumming and when I looked up at Ma, her glasses covered in drops of rain, she wasn't looking at me but straight ahead, her eyes cold, her hand crushing mine and me in a cage of rain.

'This is where you'll go,' she said.

Then there was a rush and a push and to the drumming was added the terrible hooting and thunder of a train going past the houses behind us.

'Ma, *Ma* . . .' I shouted and I broke free of her hand and started running and found myself caught up with big boys who I never wanted to run with at all.

Then Ma came after me and we got the bus and went back to Lugger Street.

That was Ma's way of teaching me something, and it wasn't something she ever needed to teach me again.

Ma was always full of surprises. She could frighten you in a thousand ways.

That night I had a nightmare like in the old days, a nightmare set in Darktime. I was running, running and then I was falling, falling and my hands could not get a grip and a grasp to stop me falling into the dark place below, which was a torture place.

I woke up and ran from my room to try to escape my fear. It was not to Ma I ran but to Granny, right into her room. I stood crying in the dark next to where she lay asleep. The pee of terror trickled down my leg and wet my pyjamas. I was crying and shaking, back in Darktime, so lonely, a boy of five again, with my old screams of loneliness and breakdown beginning to return.

Granny woke up and turned on her bedside light and stared at me. She had her hairnet on and her face was white as chalk.

She looked like a skeleton.

'Jimmy!' she said.

Then I was in her arms, my nose and snot and tears on her shoulder and my wet front and legs on her coverlet.

'Jimmy, what is it?' she said at last.

But I could only cry and shake and I would have held her tighter but she was so thin I thought she might break.

She got out of bed and put on her gas fire with me right next to it and then went and made some cocoa and toasted some crumpets.

She told me to take off my pyjama bottoms and got a towel to cover me and keep me warm.

I only did so when I went into her kitchen where she couldn't see.

'Humph!' she said.

I told her about the nightmare and then about how I couldn't pass the Eleven Plus.

'Humph!' she exclaimed again. 'Not pass? Who said you wouldn't pass?'

'Ma and Michael and everybody,' I said. 'I'll have to go to the rough school where they bash you up. I'll have to wear an apron and cook cakes.'

'That's stuff and nonsense,' she said, adding darkly, 'and anyway, Michael's got his own problems. We'll talk before you go to school tomorrow . . . *this* . . . morning and I'll tell you how you're going to pass. But not now: I need my sleep and so do you. I shall wake you like you often wake me when an important day has come. Then we shall talk.'

'It's not stuff and nonsense.'

'Yes it is,' she said very sharply. 'Now, what about another crumpet before you go?'

I nodded my head and settled happily by her fire while she toasted and buttered it.

'Your grandfather liked crumpets,' she said suddenly. 'In that respect at least he was human. Sometimes, Jimmy, you look quite like him, you really do. I trust that looks is as far as it goes.'

I went back to bed and was woken by Granny's bony hand on my shoulder.

'Time to get up, Jimmy. Get washed and dressed, have your break-fast and then come and see me. I intend to talk to you.'

When we got to school that morning there was no lesson. We had to sit at shiny desks in rows specially set out in the gym. There was clean paper and a printed question sheet we were not allowed to turn over until we were told to. The clock with big hands on the wall of the gym, above the door, clicked and ticked in the silence before we began the examination.

Ringing in my ears were the words Granny had said to me before I left for school: 'Jimmy, my dear, in the past when I've needed you to, you've come up trumps. This morning you're taking your Eleven Plus and that's important. So listen, because I want you to come up trumps again.

'You've got brains in your head which you need to use today, and tomorrow as well, for the other exam which I understand from your Mother you will also have to sit, though she could have done me the courtesy of telling me before and not keeping me in the dark until it's almost too late to be able to help you. Your mother is not always . . .

sensible. So . . . kindly have your pen and pencil and everything ready, and be ready and waiting at the exam room door.

'Read what the exam paper tells you to do and do what it says. You don't get marks for questions unanswered, so you be sure to finish them all but not waste time on any you can't do. And another thing: trust your brain to find the answer for you; it'll find it.'

'Like coming home in the dark with your eyes shut?'

That was a game Granny and I did from church one Christmas Eve.

'You know a lot about finding your way in the dark, Jimmy, far more than most. More than should be the case in one of your age. But we must build on our strengths, and that is one of yours, however unfortunate its cause, so *use* it.'

'I climbed the mountain with Uncle Max and got right to the top.'

Granny nodded, she knew I had.

'Maybe the Eleven Plus is like that,' I said, 'or maybe it's like climbing the sycamore outside the front door of our old house. You've got to work out the right branches to get to the top the best way possible?'

Granny liked this idea better.

'Yes, Jimmy,' she said, 'it's like that. Especially maths, I think. I was good at it, your grandfather was good at it, your mother's good at it and Michael's good at it. So I shall be very vexed if I find you are not good at it. However, you have not been blessed with clever teaching and you have had a troubled mind. But fortunately your maths teacher will not be in the examination room with you today to confuse you, because that is against the rules. So you can forget everything that has ever been said about what you can and can't do and when each question comes you seek out the right branches of the sycamore and climb up to the top, where I have no doubt you will find the correct answer.

'Grandfather, who was himself an examiner, always used to say that too many teachers like to find out what their pupils *cannot* do, and then point it out, again and again, which helps nobody's sense of confidence; examination boards, on the other hand, are more interested in what you *can* do, so there is hope for you today. Do you understand?'

'Yes, Granny, I think so.'

So that's what I did on the maths day of Eleven Plus and it was the first time I enjoyed maths inside a school building. I finished the paper early, and that included checking it through like Granny said.

I put my ruler and my pencil and pen and rubber in my pencil box before anyone else and I looked at the clock. *Tick tock* it went, and the examination was over.

Next day was to be English and Granny said, 'One is over, one is left to come. I am wondering, Jimmy, that if maths was climbing the sycamore what will English be?'

I shrugged and said I didn't know.

She grinned and said she didn't know either, which was unusual for Granny. We sat frowning and thinking.

I said, 'If you were in the English class, Granny, I could explain it to you. I could get it right more often than wrong, but . . . I can't seem to do it for Mr Welch. He says I'm wrong all the time.'

'Then I had better be in the exam room with you.'

'It's not allowed.'

'Then . . . I'll tell you what I'll do. What time does your examination start?'

'At ten o'clock exactly,' I said.

'Then at ten a.m. precisely I shall put my mind to thinking about you in the exam. Every time I see you beginning to make a mistake I will bang my white stick on the floor as if a car has not seen me and I am about to get run over. Your coming mistakes will be cars about to knock me down. On the other hand, every time you are doing something right I'll smile because I know I shall not be knocked down.'

'You won't know.'

'I will.'

'*I* won't then.'

'I'll do it anyway.'

'Well . . .' I said, 'it would be better if you sat on the bench up on the Front in the yellow shelter facing the sea. Then I'll know where you are. I think better with the sea breeze in my face.'

'I'll go there then,' said Granny.

'From ten o'clock for two whole hours.'

She nodded.

'I shall catch my death,' she said.

'Then wrap up against the wind like I do when I go on the beach, and don't let anyone talk to you,' I said, 'it'll get in the way of my thinking.'

'I won't.'

So it was that I did the English bit of the Eleven Plus with Granny willing me on from miles away as she looked at the sea and got cold. Every time my mind wandered, or I got bored, or I wasn't sure of something, I could see her stick banging away and a car coming dangerously near and I looked at the paper and my pen and thought and thought and made it right, so I could make her smile.

When time was up I couldn't believe I had written so neatly, or found so many words that came out right, or answered questions with answers that didn't seem wrong.

Sitting there as the teacher collected the papers, I knew I had passed. It felt good and not like school at all.

When the day came to learn the results Ma made a phone call in the sitting room while Granny and I sat waiting at the kitchen table. Ma came back into the room and if she looked anything at all she looked surprised.

'Goodness me,' she said, 'you passed.'

She gave me money to buy a Wagon Wheel and some Refreshers from Fender's, the shop on the corner of our street. When I got back Granny said, 'Humph! There's no need to give the boy a treat for doing something he's perfectly capable of doing. Didn't I tell you he would pass? Jimmy's got brains in his head, they just don't always let themselves be heard. And I am not sure that you help much in that regard!'

Ma and Granny were always frowning at each other and

exchanging words and leaving rooms in a huff, but I didn't mind. Especially that day, because I had done something right which no one, not even Michael or Hilary, could ever steal from me.

On my first day at grammar school it was Granny who saw me off in my dark blue uniform with a badge woven in gold on my cap and blazer, as Ma had the 'flu. Granny's eyes were full of tears, but mine were full of hope.

Granny said, 'There's tears in my eyes because this is the day you go out into the wide world and never come back the same. Soon you'll forget your old Granny and that's as it should be. But who knows what's in store for you? It's never what you expect. But whatever happens, remember this. There's always some hope left even when it seems all your hopes have been dashed. Take a positive view and remember what I've said.'

'Okay, Granny.'

She smiled that smile she smiled when she thought of the African Gentleman. Then she hugged me in her bony way and sent me off down Compass Street to school.

I was wearing my new uniform and had a second-hand satchel over my shoulder that Ma bought from a friend whose children had left school.

I looked back once and Granny was there, watching from the steps of our house, but not seeing much any more. I waved awkwardly and so did she because she was not sure if I had waved at all.

Then I turned into Nore Street, thinking who were the spirits at my side?

Not Ma, nor Michael.

Ma was ill and strange these days.

Michael had refused to go with me to the station, though I wished he had. I was nervous and could have done with him there, despite everything. But he refused and went earlier or some other way.

Hilary was a stranger who I only saw sometimes in the holidays. She didn't count.

So it was Granny and . . .

'Hello, Jimmy!'

It was Mr Bubbles, leaning on his big black bike at the top of Pilot Lane. His bait fork was lashed to his crossbar because he was off bait-digging.

'Hello, Mr Bubbles.'

'It's your first day at school so I thought I'd stop by and wish you luck. You'll get an education good enough to help you leave our town one day.'

'Yes,' I said.

Mr Bubbles raised his great right hand.

'I don't know much about academics and certificates but I do know about survival. You can't learn if you don't survive.'

He clenched his hairy fist.

'If someone comes to hit you, you hit 'im first, and hard, hard as you can. It's the kindest thing all round. And if 'e's that much bigger than you and there's no hope, then send for me. Tell 'im Mr Bubbles will sort 'im out. Now, off you go, lad, and *learn*.'

He put his great hand on my shoulder and sent me on my way, watching me all the way down the lane.

I didn't see the tears that coursed down his great dark creased face and nestled in the stubble on his chin. I didn't know then that he had asked Granny when I would be setting off so he could be right there and ready to wish me well. It was what a father would do. I didn't know then that I was the closest to a son he and Mrs Bubbles ever had.

But I did know it was them and Granny who were the good spirits that went off with me to school.

# 16

# FAILING CHILDREN

My morning walk to the station took me through St Andrew's Churchyard. The eighteenth-century church was tall and rectangular and built of dark red bricks with a white-painted wood cupola on top of the tiled roof. There was a brick wall round the huge churchyard to whose sides most of the gravestones had been cleared from the centre to make a park with trees and benches.

Granny said, 'Jimmy, it is not right to separate bodies and their stones, not right at all. In any case, no one much sits in there; it's far too gloomy.'

Ma added, 'And they say queer men lurk in the shadows, so don't go there after dark.'

'Be that as it may,' Granny said, 'when I die you see to it that my headstone is not removed to make way for a park bench. I am not snobbish but I do not wish any Tom, Dick or Harry to be sitting above my head eating sandwiches and drinking beer on a Sunday afternoon. Are you paying attention, Jimmy?'

'Yes, Granny.'

'What will you see to?'

'That you are not buried under a park bench.'

'Quite so. And please also see to it that I am not cremated. It may be scientific but it is not humane.'

'Don't be so absurd, Mother,' said Ma; 'you won't be able to feel anything.'

'No, but the living will. They are the ones who suffer. You cannot grieve over a pot of ashes and ground-up bone, and grieving is important. It paves the way to a continuance of living for those who might otherwise let their spirits die.'

Ma frowned the irritated, impotent frown of a middle-aged daughter stuck for words.

'Nor can you be angry with ashes,' continued Granny, 'as is sometimes the right of the living with respect to the dead.'

She was thinking of Grandfather, who had been cremated.

'Oh, Mother . . . !' said Ma.

'Humph!' said Granny, going to her room.

There was a master at our school, a Deputy Headmaster, whose name, if we did not know it before we arrived at the school through hushed, awed, frightened mentions of it from siblings or older friends, we learnt within seconds of our arrival; and learnt again at our first assembly, when, though only the Deputy, he dominated proceedings, chilling them to a state of ice and menace.

His name was Captain Leonard Flax MC DSO and he was Head of the Boarding Houses and Head of Languages. He was also School Administrator, and as such included among his duties the administration of punishments.

The honours he had won in the War conferred upon him an unassailable moral ascendancy at our school; and among the boys, the knowledge that his speciality was German, and the belief that his wartime duties included the interrogation and torture of German prisoners, gave him a grim and terrifying aura.

Nor was this imaginary. When he was in the presence of other masters, including our Headmaster, the Reverend Bernard Smiles MA, it was all too clear that, to a man, they were frightened of him. Flax looked sharper, sparer, more formidable than all of them together and they quailed in his presence. They stood in obedience like junior officers before a general; and we followed suit.

Such was the fearful and malevolent potency of his character that he needed only to approach a class, usually from some unseen shadow or corner of the corridor outside, and us boys would fall instantly silent, frightened, restive, uncertain, like sheep catching the odour of a vicious dog. A dog, I discovered, who seemed to have a special hatred of me, but I didn't know why.

A few days after the start of that first term the door opened at the start of our first French lesson and our chattering died away as the man who was to teach us French for five long, appalling years came in: Mr Job.

'Hem!' he said in guttural announcement of his arrival, but by then our silence had given way to fear, for behind him loomed a shadow, ice-grey and cold, from which light-blue eyes stared, the shadow of Captain Flax.

Mr Job went to his desk while Captain Flax took up his place a yard or two inside the room, and stood.

Just stood.

'Carry on, Job,' he said, but his eyes were on us. His voice hard as quartz, his gaze as expressionless as a dead man's. His ice-blue eyes cast such a chill they would have taken joy out of sunshine.

Mr Job read the register and one by one we replied 'Here, sir!' and then sat down.

He reached my name.

'Rova?'

'Here, sir,' I said.

Captain Flax let out a little sigh, a horrible sigh, and his eyes searched the room and found me. I knew with a terrible certainty that he had come to the class that morning for only one purpose: to find out what I looked like.

As I sat down, I was caught in his gaze like a rabbit in head-lights.

It was not a lack of expression that I saw now but something far more chilling, and it marked the beginning of the opening of a great iron door onto Failure. It was a look that was as unexpected as it was inexplicable. It was filled with a dislike that bordered on hatred. Of me. It was vindictive, and it promised punishment.

Mr Job said, 'Has any boy in this room studied French before?'

My eyes dragged themselves from Captain Flax's to Mr Job and his sharp shiny jaws opening and closing around his thin mouth.

*Has any boy in this class studied French before?*

My heart was pounding in shock at Captain Flax's animosity,

but in Mr Job's question I saw a kind of hope and a chance of redemption.

Three of us raised our hands. We were the ones who had been to preparatory schools and so had had a term or two of French.

'Stand up the three of you,' said Mr Job.

We did so, but uncertainly. His tone did not augur praise. It felt like a trap. It was.

Mr Job's eyes narrowed and his tight, thin smile turned into a scowl, a kind of sneer. He glanced across at the silent, eerily still Captain Flax. There was unpleasant complicity between them.

'Good,' he said acidly, 'you three boys are the only three problems I have in *this* class.'

With the sniggering that followed, as we stood before the class and Captain Flax, exposed, fooled, betrayed, without support, I felt a death of faith in Mr Job as well as something worse. I felt the sudden waning of the desire to learn what moments before I had been so eager to learn; and I felt entrapped with a teacher who had lost my trust.

'You can sit down,' said Mr Job.

We slowly sat down, unutterably deflated.

But for me there was to be more, and though it seems scarcely possible, it was even worse.

Captain Flax suddenly moved.

He had short, grey crinkly hair, a pencil moustache and a tweed suit that fitted his lean, spare form perfectly. His tie was khaki, his shoes shiny brown, his gown hung straight, and he carried a clipboard under his arm like a swagger stick. He exuded effortless control, command and purpose.

He moved almost imperceptibly, yet it had the whole class at fearful attention. If we had stood up we could not have been more upright.

The direction in which he moved was towards me and he achieved his effect with the merest inclination of his head.

'Thank you, Job,' he said, his icy eyes remaining on me.

Then, astonishingly, he smiled, but it was the smile of a sadist before he inflicts pain and to me it was paralysing: it was Michael's smile.

'Does anyone speak *German?*' he asked.

He was staring at me.

I wanted to retreat, to escape, to get away as fast as I could, because after Mr Job's betrayal I sensed the question was another trick, but this time one that preceded attack. But then I had known people like him all my life, though never so starkly terrifying.

I had long since learnt that prevention was better than cure, because the weak can find no easy cure from personal demolishment. I had learnt to stay silent, to slip away, to hide. Against such odds there can be no victory.

But there, in that so-still classroom, with two masters gazing at me and a roomful of boys enjoying the frisson of someone else's suffering, there was no escape. To say publicly that I spoke German was to brag, to isolate myself from my classmates, and to risk challenge from a man who spoke it fluently – a challenge I could not win. But to say I did not speak it was to enter uncharted territory, for I didn't know how much he already knew about me. Something, evidently.

Nor did I know why he was singling me out.

Without knowledge I was defenceless.

'Well, Rova?'

'A little, sir,' I said.

'*Captain Flax*, sir,' he said, his voice rising very slightly, and continuing to rise, 'and stand *up* to attention when a master speaks to you.'

I rose back into the world of exposure.

'Just a little, Captain Flax, sir,' I said.

'*Wieviel?*' he asked.

How much?

For an instant six months of German memories passed through me: of fishing for trout in the Weser, of scrambled egg as yellow as buttercups, of sliding down a grassy slope in the Tyrol in my lederhosen, and of the pigman and his wife who had no children of their own, who wanted to adopt me and give me love that would have lasted a lifetime and more.

*How much?*

The question was the measure of the man.

There is no quantity that can measure the love its speakers feel for a language, or for the people and the country that gave the language birth and still sustains its life.

*Wieviel, Herr Kapitän Flax?*

I understood what he had asked and I knew how to reply, but every single word in my German vocabulary deserted me, fleeing before his voice and gaze like cowardly deserters before a superior force.

My throat dried, and inside me, deep inside, where my eagerness to learn languages and enjoy the excitement and richness of their sound abided, something important withered, and shrivelled, and began to die. Not trust, that had been lost in the trickery surrounding Mr Job's initial question, nor hunger, which stayed intact. It was joy that was destroyed.

I felt the death of joy as the sudden death of a friend who I had only just discovered.

I stared back at Captain Flax, so frightened that my legs knocked against my chair, while my mouth stayed open but silent; and where my pants were pee began to leak, evidence of the depth of my fear.

Had I stood a few moments longer, it would have been uncontrollable and coursed down my leg over my ankle into a shoe and finally to the floor below my desk.

As it surely did with those poor Germans he interrogated.

As it was, he moved again, half turning away dismissively, and said contemptuously, 'Sit down, Rova.'

But he had not quite finished.

He exchanged another chilling smile with Mr Job and sent off a final, appalling, gratuitous missile in my direction.

'*So . . .*' he said, and he said it in the sharp German manner, '. . . this is the second little Rova we'll have to deal with, I think, but hopefully the last!'

He spoke my surname with such dismissive venom that there had to be a reason for it. I did not – could not – know what it was, but the message that he saw me as the second unwelcome representative of a family he had reason to dislike was loud and clear.

In those moments I sensed that there was a kind of madness in his hate and that his war against me would be unremitting, and brutal, and in some appalling way, would be fought to the death.

My fear left me as suddenly as it had come, but not my sadness and despair. I was in a war for reasons I did not understand, but I had experienced that already, with my siblings. I felt the weary sadness of one who has fought and survived, only to be surrounded by the enemy again. I had climbed the hill to find that beyond it I faced a mountain.

It was in those chilling, isolating moments of my first French lesson, within a few days of the start of the new school career in which I had had so much hope, that my retreat into myself and decline into failure began.

With a curt nod to Mr Job, Captain Flax left the room and the first of our French lessons finally started. But I was already down there on the steps beyond the iron door and could only hear the lesson as if it was muffled and half-lost somewhere above my head.

*Ehh!*

*Ihh!*

*Aaa!*

*Ohh!*

*Uuoo!*

The five ingredients of French vowel pronunciation were uttered by Mr Job plosively, with strange aggression. As a lesson for learning sound that one was the most successful of my life. I never forgot it. But if learning is about trust, and needs the trust of a pupil in his teacher if it is to advance joyfully, it was lost at the start, and never found again.

As Mr Job began to teach French pronunciation, I did what I had long since learnt to do, I slipped into the comfort of my own thoughts. I hid in the shadows of my mind, seeming not to hear what he said or the instructions he gave, then or in the years of lessons with him that lay ahead.

That first term was my only time in an upper form in my school career. Because of the level of my eleven-plus pass, and because

Michael was clever, they had put me among the top thirty boys of the intake of sixty-three.

But soon they concluded that I was not bright.

Lost in confusion and despair as I was, my writing was bad, my spelling no good, the pages of my schoolbooks all blotted blue with the dip-pen ink we had to use. So the thoughts behind the words I struggled to write were never shared with the masters who marked them in their black academic gowns with their black academic frowns. They were not Granny or Mr Bubbles, nor even Freddie Hammel, who judged a man by whether or not he could read the waves and steer his boat, not by the blots in his copybook.

My thoughts and ideas became caged behind the angry lines of the masters' red ink pens and phrases like 'Poor work' and 'Do it again – neatly'. And from some 'Idiot!'. My eagerness to learn fell away from me so fast it felt like it might never come back again.

We had form orders at half term, read out aloud. When they came I was near the bottom of every subject, sinking into shame as the wait for my name to be read out became longer and longer. Failure over-took me faster than a rising tide.

We had to take the form-order paper home but there was a gale blowing up that evening and in the churchyard it caught the paper and tore it into a thousand tiny pieces and sent it scattering with the leaves, down among the gravestones. Ma and Granny never asked for it and in the days following I watched as the bits of paper rotted with the leaves, and the red ink of my positions ran into the soil like blood.

It was enough for Granny that I had got into the school, she did not ask and I did not volunteer about how I was doing. Ma had been through it with Michael, who always did well, and she had other things on her mind. She didn't encourage me to talk and I didn't encourage her to ask: it was grunts and silences all round.

When I got back to school after half term all the things in my desk were gone, and a bright boy from Lower One was sitting in my chair. There was the smug glow of triumph in his eyes.

'Rova, you're in Lower One now,' he said. 'Didn't they tell you?'

Sniggers.

Eyes looking, and the breathless pain of misery in my chest; eyes looking away.

I crept out of my class and left my old classmates behind, walked down a deserted corridor and into a class where the passing of half a term made me a stranger. No friendly eyes to greet me there.

'Rova II?'

I nodded, shocked yet further.

Of course he knew my name. The form master of Lower One, the man responsible for our welfare in everything, was Mr Job. I shrivelled inside and went to the desk he was directing me to. Defeat, personal shame, unutterable misery enveloped me.

'Rova II?'

The class froze.

It was the voice of Captain Flax, making his half-termly visit at the start of things. But I barely heard him. The first sob of despair was already in my throat.

'*Rova II,* I believe I said.'

Perhaps only *his* voice could have been enough at that moment to replace my coming tears with another, more powerful, more permanent emotion.

I looked up and saw him and his clipboard and his icy blue gaze on me, clearly taking pleasure at my situation. Suddenly it felt like a beginning and not an end. Cornered now, a new and unpleasant strength overtook me. It came with having been brought so low that I realized that I could go no lower. It came with simply knowing I was still alive and that whatever else I did could hardly make things worse.

'Captain Flax, *sir!*' I cried out, a shade too loudly, and leapt to my feet rather too confidently for his liking.

He stared at me and I at him and I felt no fear. I saw that there was something in my gaze that angered him almost beyond words. A slight flush came to his lean, well-shaven face.

'Detention,' he said coolly.

I blinked, surprised, knowing now there was a flaw in him, but not yet knowing exactly what it was.

I had been in worse places than this. They could hurt me no more.
He began to turn away.

'For *what*, sir?' I asked in as cool a voice as his own.

A shocked murmur ran through the class. Even Mr Job stilled in surprise. Boys did not ask questions of the Captain.

Captain Flax turned, evidently discomforted.

'Dumb insolence, Rova,' he snapped.

Whatever it meant, it sounded good.

'Yes, *sir*!' I nearly shouted, and the class titter was on my side.

It cast me dangerously into the role of class rebel, class fool. From being an object of pity for my rejection from the upper form I became the boy who stood up to Captain Flax in the lower one. It felt good, but it also set a pattern that helped seal my fate as one of the bottom-of-the-class failures.

Yet I *knew* that it meant something else as well. That meaning lay in the gaze that ran between us, Captain Flax and I.

I knew then that he meant to get me, to get me utterly. I knew then that I had to get him. My premonition at the beginning of term had been right; war to the death was the name of our game, but still I did not know why.

He turned and I watched his back, his shoulders, his legs and the black clipboard under his arm heading out into the gloom of the corridor. I felt a surge of unutterable hatred for him and whatever it was he was, which as yet had no name.

He had succeeded where my family had failed. He had made me feel hate as suddenly, totally, potently and as powerfully as love, love at first sight.

I stared after him.

From that moment I knew that if I could get him I really would.

'Sit down, Rova,' said Mr Job somewhat breathlessly, as if something had taken place that was out of his control and somehow beyond his understanding. '*Now* . . .'

'Of course, Mr Job, sir.'

Distantly, I heard his voice.

*Ehh!*

*Ihh!*
*Aaa!*
*Ohh!*
*Uuoo!*

But by then I was sitting on a stone bench somewhere far below my class, in a cold land, chains of hatred forged around my ankles and my wrists, and chokingly tight around my neck.

*Ehh! Ihh! Aaa! Ohh! Uuoo!*

I felt myself move beyond pain to indifference, and from there to laughter. I heard my inner voice as if it was someone else's.

*Ha, ha, ha!*

For the first time I felt something of Michael's indifference and aloofness in me too. Then I no longer heard Mr Job but sighed and doodled on the paper before me and stared out of the window at a leafless sycamore.

My mind disengaged from where my body sat and began a new journey while still seeming to engage on an old one, the first that true survivors learn: into imagination. But the new journey was more subtle, more insidious, potentially far more dangerous than any journey I had embarked on before: it was the journey across the land Failure, in deepening despair at ever finding a signpost that would point me a better way – in the direction of Success.

# 17

# LESSONS OF HISTORY

When Ma moved to the North End she took us into the streets and lanes where our town began its seafaring life, and it was a better school to me than the one I had to drag myself to every day by foot and train over in Stannick, seven miles away.

To me, the bricks of our house and street, the cracked kerbstones, the broken iron railings, the closed shops and the abandoned boats and rusting capstans up on the shore breathed a life of the past that I did not know was history. It was simply what had been, and in among its shadows and mysteries I sensed I might find something to give meaning and comfort to the dark life I had.

Before living in the North End, history was what school taught: interesting but confused, all jumbled up and out of order, with no connection between one time and another. Bad King John and Alfred burning tarts, Romans and Vikings, Henry VIII and his six wives and 1066. Bits and pieces from all over the place.

At grammar school the bits and pieces were even more mixed up and history was even worse. It became dead kings and queens and getting dates wrong. It was all old battles and forgotten treaties, with dates attached. I knew no way to travel down those years; 1066 meant nothing to a boy born in 1944 except an arrow in the eye.

Mr Boys in Stoning Castle told things in their proper order, one thing happening after another. But by the light of the cold eyes of Mr Deller, our history teacher, impatiently tapping his metal ruler on my desk, I could not make sense of things. I was a stupid boy for not knowing what I could not understand.

'1476 is when he died, Rova, not when he was born. Cross it out. Read the board . . . Your brother Michael never had trouble with dates.'

History was many a misery under Mr Deller, but what made it worse was the feeling the North End and its rich sense of the past gave me – that history might be worth knowing if only someone could come along and give me the golden key to unlock its secrets.

Instead history was the feeling of forever not knowing something that I should and forever forgetting things I could not remember. The dates we wrote down and the people whose names we had to learn had no meaning for me because I couldn't see them or touch them or smell them. I needed someone to turn history into the pebbles on my shore so I could pick them up for myself and turn them in my hand, see their colour and put them in my treasure box.

As it was, we did the Tudors one term, the Romans the next, and the Normans after that. There was no rhyme or reason to it; it was in bits from the start and school never taught me how to put the pieces together so I could feel safe with it and begin to learn.

If Mr Deller had started with *us* in his lessons he would have got a lot further. Yet occasionally he said something that showed that he too was one of us, something that resonated in my mind and made me dare raise my hand in class. Sometimes the dark clouds separated and for a moment I saw the sun.

One November, in my second year, wearing a bright red Remembrance Day poppy in his lapel, he suddenly said for no reason, 'My father was killed in the First World War.'

That was the moment I knew that Mr Deller was a human being. There was a look of loss in his eyes which I recognized but to which I couldn't have put a name.

My hand rose up despite itself and I heard my voice say, 'Sir, there's iron girders on our beach and *they're* from the First World War.'

Granny once said while talking about Grandfather, 'Jimmy, you can take a horse to water but you can't make it drink.' Mr Deller might have seen that my iron girders were a pool of sparkling clear water at which we could have drunk together, but he didn't know how.

Instead he said, 'Really, Rova?' in that cold, sarcastic way he had, and another little bit of me died.

It would have been exciting if he had drunk of the water I offered him. But I didn't give up, so great was my need to escape my miseries and so great my love of the past.

Doing the Romans once, we got on to fighting and I felt my right hand go up in the air again.

'Sir! Sir!'

Not so far from our school was Richborough Castle, an early Roman fort which had some of the highest Roman walls left in Britain. I knew that. I also knew how they used it for fighting.

'Sir!'

My hand came down and I waited for the teacher to mention Richborough, but he never did.

I impulsively tried again . . .

'*Sir!*'

'Be *quiet*, Rova! You'll just have to wait until the end of class.'

He thought I wanted to be excused. My hand came down as if it had been bitten by a dog and I nursed it on my lap.

Mr Deller talked about Hadrian's Wall, which was in a far-off place I never went to on my bicycle, so I couldn't get it into my mind, but he never mentioned Richborough.

All he needed to do to put the excited light of learning in our eyes was to say, 'Boys, forget the lesson about Hadrian's Wall and come with me to Richborough and I'll show you what they did just up the road from where we're sitting now.'

He could have given a lesson then that would have made us want to learn. But he didn't. He made us draw turrets of Hadrian's Wall and colour them in, in red and black and brown. He made us do something that held no meaning.

He had thought I wanted to go to the lavatory. But I wanted to say what I knew about Richborough, and how the Romans guarded it and went on fighting expeditions from its impregnable gates. I wanted to say how they introduced concrete to England, which I learnt from Mr Mee, and that I had half a Roman tile at home. I wanted to say that before there were boats at Stoning there was a port at Richborough.

I never got the chance, and I kept the knowledge to myself until the time came when I never bothered to put up my hand, never said a thing, but looked out of the window, watched the clock ticking its way towards the bell for break and gazed at the swallows in the sky.

Then, one day, the darkness of my learning was lightened when Arthur Sanders arrived and liberated history for me. He came to our house to mend the door to our cellar. He brought his toolbox, which held chisels and screwdrivers, a plumb line and a fret saw, and row upon row upon row upon *row* of golden keys into history, which over the weeks and months and years he gave to me one by one as I became ready for them.

It sounds grand to say there was a boathouse attached to our house in Compass Street, for it was anything but. It was just a side door onto a brick-built lean-to, but that side door was wide enough for a boat to be wheeled down the street from the beach and squeezed round and in. It was a long time since it had been home to a boat, but there were still boaty things aplenty, as in those days things had a habit of staying where they were for years. Hanging on nails were lengths of rope, a boathook, a tangle of cork floats attached to a tarred rope and a capstan's windlass. There were even more bits and pieces up in the draughty little loft at the back of the boathouse, whose doors and wooden walls were painted in flaky lime paint. People had moved on, and died, and left those things behind, and no one bothered to remove them.

I made my den up there, with two candles to light it and a canvas-covered cushion I found to sit on. I had some stones, my treasures from the sea, which now included fishing weights and lobster-pot corks, and one or other of the volumes of Mr Mee's encyclopedia given to me by Mr Boys. It was my refuge and retreat and Michael knew never to come there because like a dog in his kennel I would attack him if he did. It was the one place my things were never disturbed.

I was up there out of the cold and wet one day, lying low from Ma who was angry with Granny for saying something and with herself for breaking a milk bottle on the dirty quarry tiles of our kitchen floor. I heard our door knocker: *knock! knock! knock!* The wind was blowing up enough to rattle the heavy gate of the boathouse when suddenly *bang!* it flew open, and a man was standing there with Ma.

They didn't see me but I saw them.

Ma showed the man the coal door down into the cellar and how it was off one hinge. She talked and he listened, nodding his head and not saying much. When she was gone I watched him secretly as he moved his toolbox, which was made of varnished wood and had a leather handle, to give himself room to examine the hinge.

He was old and wiry with thin white hair and his cheeks were so worn by wind and time that the blood vessels showed red. He knelt down and examined the door, opening and closing it gently, as if it was a bird with a broken wing.

'Hmm,' he said to himself, in a way that indicated more than just thought, it showed care as well.

Then he got up and stood back and looked at the hinge and then the door and then his toolbox and then back again, weighing things up. He said 'Hmm' again and opened his toolbox and rummaged round inside. He brought out a hinge and tried it against the door, and then another one.

His toolbox was not big but it was magic. It always seemed to have everything in it he needed for the job in hand. He could have built a house from its contents, and a garden shed as well, if that was the requirement.

He seemed satisfied with the third hinge he produced, so he took off his jacket and hung it on a nail near the floats. Then he positioned his toolbox where he could reach it, before kneeling down and beginning the job.

He never let on that he heard me watching, but after a while he carefully downed tools and strolled over to the wooden steps up to my loft and called out, 'Hello!'

I didn't know whether to lie low or show my face, but he sounded friendly so I poked my head out of the little loft door and looked at him.

'Hello!' I said back.

'Hello, lad!' he replied.

I just stared, sizing him up. He had twinkling eyes and wrinkles. He wore brown overalls braced up with silver clips. His hands were rough and strong, and part of his right forefinger was missing.

Some people look good, some not. He looked good.

'You're Mrs Rova's lad, I take it?'

I nodded.

'Want to come down and give me a hand?'

He got me to hold on to the cellar door while he worked the broken hinge loose, so that the door wouldn't put any strain on the other hinge.

'Now,' he said, giving me the hinge as he took the full weight of the door, 'you hold on to this. Never throw broken things away. What's broken for one purpose may be in apple-pie order for another. Also, someone could hurt themselves on what they don't know you've discarded. My name's Arthur Sanders and you can call me Arthur.'

'My name's Jimmy,' I said.

Exchanging names seemed proper with Arthur. He was a man who did everything the right and proper way.

He nodded and turned back to the job.

'Hmm,' he said, thinking about how to put on the new hinge. Arthur seemed to work slowly but really he worked fast. He didn't waste time and he always got his jobs finished when he said he would.

'And last but not least, Jimmy,' he said a bit later, 'you can pass me that dustpan and brush.'

His box had *everything* he needed, including brown paper bags for the last bits of dust and dirt his jobs created.

Ma appeared.

'Would you like a cup of tea, Mr Sanders, er . . . or a mug?'

'A mug, please,' he said, 'and milk and two sugars, Mrs Rova, if you don't mind; and a mug of tea for my apprentice here.'

He winked at her and grinned at me, and Ma, who was always as sweet as pie in company, smiled back, understanding before I did that he meant me.

Apprentice is what I became that day, in an unofficial way, and as the weeks and months went by, and eventually the years, I learnt which tools to pass to Arthur Sanders, and which to put away, and I learnt what it meant to see a job of joinery or plumbing, of decoration or repair, well and properly done.

But that first day he also gave me my first real history lesson.

'Now,' he said as we supped our teas with milk and two sugars, sitting on boxes and admiring the way the cellar door hung on its new hinges as it should, 'did you know who used to own your house? It was Captain Henry James of the Dover Jameses who had the paper mill. He was a good and generous man, always doing favours and expecting no return. Payment was in heaven, he said, if there was one, not on this earth. He was a big man, and strong, but his boy died at sea. He started shrinking after that, and turning in and looking at the ground.

'In his retirement he had half shares of a lugger on the Reynolds' pitch opposite George Street, and in here he kept a skiff for light work. I stood at that gate as a boy and by then he was already old. He was a man of sail, was Captain James, whose last command was the dried-out skiff in this boathouse. He had sailed round the Horn. Not many even then could say that. I don't suppose you know what the Horn is?'

He was surprised and gratified when I said I did. Mr Mee had told me about it and about running under sail. But I said I would like to know more.

In a long diversion, of which Arthur was a master, he told me about the Horn and the days of sail, so I learnt some geography as well as history, with social studies thrown in.

He sipped his tea, thinking. From talking to Granny I knew when to ask questions and when to stay silent. I watched memory play across his face and in his eyes. There was a wind at the gate, and dust swirling down our street, but where he was there was the stillness and peace of the ages. After you'd talked to Arthur you went back into the world feeling better, and feeling you could cope because you had learnt about others coping before you.

He took out his pocket watch and consulted it.

Hmm.

'What's a skiff?' I asked, not wanting him to go.

'A rowing boat to get you there and back again.'

'What happened to it?'

'Captain James's?'

I nodded.

'The last voyage it went on was on wheels, carrying his coffin to St Andrew's Churchyard where you'll find his stone propped up and broken on the north-west side. He wanted a burial at sea but it wasn't allowed. After the funeral Arnie Reynolds and the boys who crewed his lugger took the skiff down to their pitch. Then at low tide, that same night, they took it to the edge of the sea and set it on fire at the turning of the tide. The tide came in and the tide went out and Captain James went with it like he always wanted.'

I thought of my little paper boats and that it would be good to set one on fire and commit it to the waves.

'Did you see it burn?'

'I saw more than flames down on that shore. I saw the silhouettes of a crew of men saying farewell to one of their own. They had beer in their hands from the Three Compasses but when the flames took they stopped supping and fell silent, each paying their respects in their own way. Then one by one they said their toasts to wish the Captain's spirit well on its journey across the sea. By morning the tide had taken away all signs of the skiff, but memory lives on for a time, and sometimes for ever.

'Not many to remember now, though. Me and Freddie Hammel and a few others. And now *you*, lad!'

He stood up and looked around the boathouse.

'His skiff was called *Evening Tide*,' said Arthur Sanders, 'that's why his men knew when to burn it. He was the last of Stoning's captains under sail. So your mum did well when she bought this house. There's the spirit of the open sea about it.'

He got up and gave me his mug.

'Say thank you to your mother, Jimmy, for the tea.' He knew to ask the question I dared not ask. 'Want to help me again, lad?'

I nodded.

'You can, then.'

Then he was gone, leaving behind the memory of a skiff called *Evening Tide* to fill the emptiness that had been our boathouse, and a memory of the boy who was Arthur once, looking in at our gate long before I was born; and down on the beach, opposite George Street, memories of a burning boat at night and sombre men.

That was how Arthur Sanders populated the North End for me and taught me history: bit by bit, after jobs were done, supping tea in the rest times, passing on memories to me which were not just his past but all the history that surrounded it. Each lesson was a golden key which, once turned, became my memory and gave me the means to begin my own journeys back into history to find the places from where I came.

He taught me that no street in the North End is ever empty, no day without incident, no night without whispers, no breeze, no wind, no rain, no rising sun. It all comes out of a past it still carries, where others like me once went, and Arthur Sanders, Granny and Ma, and men others admire like Captain James, and other people they don't.

One day during the first December after I met him I came across Arthur working on a house in Anchor Lane. He was plastering, so he had his handcart to help him carry the bags of plaster powder there and to carry away the broken lathes and plaster from the ceiling that had fallen down. Plastering was not a job he did on a large scale any more, but a small area like a lavatory or a bit of a bathroom he would do, for a friend or an old client.

As the sea was rough that day I had combed the shore with Mr Bubbles until the tide was almost in and it became too dangerous. I left Mr Bubbles to the very last of the treasure and went to kick stones into one of the shelters, dodging the spray of the bigger waves and watching the herring gulls huddling down against the wind on the promenade, which they did only when things were going from bad to worse.

With an hour still before tea, I wandered past Dragon Street to get out of the wind and spitting rain and I saw Mr Sanders's cart down Anchor Lane, outside No 5.

A voice came out of the grating at my feet: 'Hello, lad.'

He was taking the opportunity to clear out the grating and repoint the brickwork which doing the plastering offered him. Mr Sanders liked to use his time well. He always did more than he was asked; it was part of his service.

'Hello, Arthur,' I said to the ground.

'The front door's open; come on down and look in here! I've something to show you.'

The house was like ours only derelict. Painted canvas hung off the wooden panelling, as it had when we moved into Compass Street. The back part of the house, where the scullery was, was half open to the wind from a wall falling down. Somewhere up the spiral stairs things rapped and rattled. The floorboards were filthy with muck and old newspapers.

After I had explored and poked my head out into the yard, which was filled with rusting mangles, some rotten cartwheels and three hooped barrels, I went down into the cellar, but carefully. The wooden stairs were rotten, and some were missing.

The cellar seemed bigger than the house above it and Mr Sanders had rigged up a light to see what he was doing. Its woven flex hung in loops from the rafters, low enough for me to have to be careful not to catch them and bring the light crashing down. The first cellar was knee high in damp junk, the second, on the street side, was covered in coal dust. It was the third, a little room adjacent to the street but with no window or grating to light it, that Arthur wanted to show me, bringing the light in on the flex and holding it as high as he could so we could see all the better.

'This isn't a room at all, properly speaking,' he said. 'It's the foundations and those are the footings.'

He pointed to where brick arches, supporting the house above, plunged into stones.

'Shingle,' said Arthur, 'that's just shingle. They didn't bring it here, Jimmy; it was here already. Stand on it . . .'

I crunched on the grey shingle, whose pebbles were of the bigger kind you get at low-tide mark and halfway up the beach.

'Listen, Jimmy, listen to that shingle shifting, and you're listening to how Stoning began and to the sound that gave it its name.'

We listened to the sea grating pebbles not many yards away, to the sound of Stoning, and heard and then felt vibrations. It was the distant thump-drag of the rising sea.

I picked up a pebble or two and found they were grey, grimy with the centuries of dark confinement under the house.

'You're standing on part of the shingle bank that the sea threw up long before there were houses here. In those days the centre of Stoning was half a mile inland, where St Mary's Church now stands. But before that, two thousand years ago, before Julius Caesar came, as you may know . . .'

I nodded: the memorial of his landing on our shore was not far from our town.

'. . . before even that there were people here, fishermen, sheltering in shacks built against the wind, hauling their boats up from the sea then launching them back down the shingle bank when the tide was right. The sea threw up a bank of shingle and that bank gave protection to the land behind it, which turned from marsh to salt flats and then dried out. Beyond that, up on the chalk, was where old Stoning was built, well out of harm's way. You're standing on what made the modern Stoning possible. You're holding a pebble that maybe a boy like you threw high in the air two thousand years ago.'

I put that pebble in my pocket to throw in the sea on my way home that evening.

Later, his job finished, night falling and me late for tea, we went up to the ground floor. Arthur dug into his old khaki army haversack and pulled out his thermos flask. It was tin, the tartan pattern on it worn shiny with use, the plastic top that served as a cup yellow with age. But it was always clean, always orderly.

We sat in the scullery surrounded by bits of a new kitchen that was being put in. A canvas sheet that covered the hole in the wall where a window was going shifted quietly, like a sail in idle wind. Arthur pulled it to one side so we could see the coming of night and the first stars.

He poured me a tea and rolled himself a cigarette.

'Ever been to the Dunes, Jimmy?'

I shook my head. The Dunes lay beyond the North End, where the houses stopped at Rampart Road. There were the remnants of a castle there, now no more than yellow bricks set in concrete at the end of the sea wall, a buttress against the sea.

I had been that far but no further. The empty spaces of the Dunes and the golf links scared me. Michael said wild dogs roamed there and that it was the home of the Haunted Highwayman. I had enough on my plate getting to grips with the North End.

'You go up there and stand on the shingle bank that runs above the high-tide mark all the way to Stannick Bay and you'll see what Stoning was like before the fishermen came and the houses started. Go up there and look at the sea, and then turn round and look at the marshes beyond the Dunes, and you'll know the kind of ground on which our town was built. Feel the shingle beneath your feet and the spray in your face and you'll know what the people who came before us felt. Bit by bit was our town made, Jimmy, bit by bit. By hands like these . . .'

He reached out his hands and took one of mine in his own. He meant our hands, young and old, but it was his worn hands I saw, with their calluses and cigarette stains and nails thickened and blunted by a lifetime's work.

Arthur was not just the maintainer of the fabric of our town; he was the Keeper of its past, the teller of its tales.

'Time to lock up and head off home,' he said.

We loaded his cart with the rubbish and his tools, he locked the house up, and I walked at the side to stop things falling off. Into Printer's Square and down to its bottom corner, where Arthur had his little yard.

'And what are we walking down?' he said, kicking at the tarmac and cobbles beneath his feet.

'The shingle bank thrown up by the sea.'

'And what's over there?' he asked, indicating the houses and gasworks towards Middle Stoning Way.

'Salt sea marshes,' I said.

He fell silent.

'There,' he said when his cart was safe and sound, and his tools and toolbox safely into store.

I slipped away, imagining I was trudging up the shingle bank that lay lost and forgotten beneath the streets and alleyways of the North End. Up and up it into the wind I went, back to the Front, there to gaze across the wild darkness of the sea to the distant lights of ships hove-to against the gale before throwing the pebble I had found, out into the waves.

Then I battled my way along Prow Street – along the top of the shingle bank – and allowed myself to be blown halfway down Compass Street to our front door.

'Jimmy? Jimmy . . . your supper's under a cover in the kitchen. Granny's upstairs. I've got to go out to a Committee Meeting. Heat it up and go and have it with her.'

Ma went out and I had my supper, but I took it on a plate down into our cellar and ate it under the light of a bare bulb, staring at the grey grimy shingle that lay beneath a damp brick I prised out of the floor. Above my head as I ate, the light sometimes shuddered to the thump of the waves on our seashore.

It was beef stew, cabbage and mashed potato that I had, but huddled down there in the cold I was a fisherman in a shack eating winter codling cooked on a spit stuck into a driftwood fire, long before Captain James, or Arthur or Ma; even before Granny. Back in the time when the North End began, back in its history time.

'Jimmy? Jimmy!'

It was Granny coming down the spiral stairs above my head, wondering if she was alone in the house. Granny lonely and beginning to be afraid.

I hid the plate for no good reason and went back upstairs. She was wandering down the corridor towards our front door, looking lost.

'Granny! *Granny!*'

My shout towards her deaf ears was more sharp than loud, because if I made it too loud it startled her.

'*There* you are, my dear,' she said, turning round. 'I was beginning to think I was alone in this house.'

'I was in the cellar,' I said, but I didn't say why. 'Will you make me a cocoa?'

'I will, Jimmy,' she said. 'You come on up in a moment and keep me company. You can tell me what you've been doing all day.'

I did, and told her all about the cellar in Anchor Lane and what was there before the North End was built.

Granny said, 'If we're not conquering people we're conquering land, but it's usually both. Just look!'

She pointed at the front page of the *Daily Telegraph*, which was the newspaper she always read. That day some blacks massacred a white farmer and his family in Southern Rhodesia where she once lived.

'I'm not sorry to be old, nor will I be sorry to die,' she said suddenly. 'I'm only sorry I'll not be there to see you grow into a man.'

Another day Arthur told me about Julius Caesar and his coming to our shore.

'No one knows exactly where they landed but one thing's certain, up the shingle bank he had to march with his trained soldiers. Our people at that time were primitive by comparison. The Romans killed some men and caught others and these they crucified along our shore, up on crosses and posts and stakes stuck into the shingle and propped up by staves. These crosses, and the men that hung from them are long, long gone, but they say their screams and groans can still be heard in the cries of herring gulls. You listen, Jimmy, and you'll hear them. You'll hear those cries, or cries like them, wherever there's been conquering, which is to say just about anywhere you care to go along our island shores.'

I told him what Granny had said, about us being conquerors not about dying.

'One way or another we're all invaders, whatever we say. You listen and look and in time you'll see what I mean.'

I listened, and I did hear the cries on the shore, then and many times afterwards; and it seemed to me that the dying chunter of the black-winged cormorant flying fast offshore were those dead men's last farewell.

One day I wandered beyond my usual territory, across Low Street, down Regent's Lane and then along West Street into what started as no more than an alleyway. It was called Church Lane but there was no church there that I could see.

As I walked along it and it widened into something more substantial, with eighteenth-century cottages on either side, I realized from its route that it crossed over the old salt sea marshes and was heading up to Upper Stoning, the oldest part of our town. I knew I was on the original lane that ran from the old town down to the new, what became the North End. That was long before it was housed and paved, when rushes grew along its lower parts, and bushes and trees higher up, and fishermen came with their fish in the direction I was going, and pedlars too.

I was walking a path of history, where old time and new melded into one, and that day I discovered the magic that lay in learning to read the signs that allowed me to walk back in time.

But it was not kings and queens, nor treaty makers, nor even armies that I discovered. Just a little road made by people whose names and dates were long since lost but whom Arthur's stories helped me bring to life for myself. At the top of the lane I found the gate into St Mary's Church in Upper Stoning, so it was not hard to work out how Church Lane got its name. The shape of my town was broadening and expanding in my mind and its past was coming alive.

Halfway back down I stopped dead, because between the houses I could see the Dunes stretching away in the lee of the old shingle bank. And the golf links. And in the blue distance there was the sea and Stannick Bay and beyond even that were the chalk cliffs of Thanet on which Cliftonville had been built, below which lay Ramsgate Harbour.

I stood and stared. Once, long ago, I had lived over there, long ago in my Darktime. In the years when the things happened to me that I could not quite remember but which I still needed to know. Looking at it now, it did not look so dark any more, what with the passage of years and me learning the lessons of history. Nor so far away.

One day, I thought, it would be possible to go back and discover the truth of my past, the bits before I was born and the bits soon afterwards. Maybe it would be possible to find my dad.

There are some hopes that never die because you can never bear them to, however impossible their fulfilment may seem to be. Like the Misses Gallagher in Fitzroy Square, who Granny said still believed their brother was going to come back from the First World War one day, even though he was now no more than a red poppy growing on the battlefield of Ypres.

'What else have they to live for, Jimmy?' she said.

My eyes withdrew from the far distance back to the Dunes, and from Church Lane they no longer looked so formidable. My time to start widening my horizons was coming.

# 18

# LISTENING TO TIDES

The North End is a treeless place.

There are none along the narrow streets and alleys, none in either of the two open spaces – Printer's Square to the north and the car park behind the Fisherman's Rooms opposite the Pier, created after the levelling of the ruins created by German wartime bombs.

No trees, just tarmac, paving stones and granite kerbs, and brick houses in dark reds and murky yellows that front directly onto the dark narrow streets, some no more than twelve feet wide, where sun slants down in secret places.

Once in a while, following a gale, a tree from Norway is thrown up on the shingle beach, dead, sopping, the soil in which its roots grew long, long gone, the roots themselves dead fingers pointing to the waves and sky, the bark stripped, the white and red of the wood laid bare.

So when the winter settles in and the winds begin to blow, having no trees, only brick walls and kerbstones and dank, wind-filled alleys where dustbins rattle, the North End can be a bleak place; as bleak as my first years at senior school.

But even if there were no trees, there was always the sea, stirring its sound around the houses even on the quietest of days; and the tides, ever changing, bringing their hope of better things to come each and every day, to those who can see and those who know how to listen.

As it was autumn when we moved to Compass Street and I was still a stranger, it was too late for me to discover where the North End's secret glory lay: beyond the high walls, in a thousand secret gardens full of honeysuckle and stunted apple trees, with pink valerian on the walls, and hoverflies a-hovering among the scented tomato plants and over the York-stone flags, caught in the light of the bright stars of yellow saxifrage.

Gardens tended secretly, lovingly, by men and women who were growing old, whose lives had seen far better days, whose young had fled the area for jobs on the ships out of Dover, or at Billy Butlin's in Margate, or up the line to that place from which few ever returned: London Town.

Like Mrs Simms next door, who one day yelled over our garden wall for help.

There was no one about but me, so I climbed a chair to look over the wall and there she was all fallen down and tangled with her raspberry canes.

'Is that you, Jimmy? Come and get me out of here! Blessed things have got a mind of their own. Ouch! You'll just have to climb over the wall and fetch me free! I can't very well open the front door, now can I? Come on! Look lively!'

Mrs Simms had been in charge of land girls in the War, so I did as she said and clambered down onto her rockery.

'Don't step on the pinks, they've been there twenty year!'

Her woollen cardigan had caught in the thorns and her slacks were all thorned up as well. Though she was younger than Granny her hands were swollen and bent with arthritis and her legs all bowed. But somehow she managed to garden and turn what was no more than a courtyard into a jungle place, full of colour.

'I'm too old for this,' she declared when I had set her free. 'You can pick 'em for me and we can eat 'em together here and now.'

I did and we did.

'Peggy loved her raspberries,' she said, 'and Jack it was who first put them in two years before he died in bed and I never fetched the doctor till the morning because Jack would have said what was the point? Peggy's coming back for Christmas and . . .'

It was the beginning of my helping Mrs Simms and, through her, helping her friend Mr Shaw, whose garden off Nore Street consisted entirely of pots – big, little and enormous – full of a hundred thousand flowers, it seemed to me, all intertwined and rampant, and all needing watering and pruning and talking to.

He paid me money to help but she never did and I wouldn't have taken it from her if she had offered. Her payment was her talk and her frequent shout over the wall, 'Jimmy! Is that you, Jimmy? I need you!' My being needed was the payment she gave; and her stories about Bolton, where she was raised to be a mill girl before the First World War.

Mr Shaw didn't need to pay me money, but somehow we both felt better if he did. Like Mrs Simms, his children had left for London Town and now only returned for short stays at Christmas and Easter.

I listened to them talk and learnt that when their children came back they were mysteriously changed for the worse by the world beyond our town and were restless and uneasy in the North End, fretting to leave as soon as they arrived.

But when I met them I saw they were children no more, stooping now to pass through front doors that once towered above their heads, impatient with outside loos and latches made of bent and rusty nails, with gas-fired Geysers in the bathroom that let in fumes when the wind was in the east; and inveighing against the dirt that coal fires generate, scolding their ageing parents for not installing electric.

They did not understand that in the ritual of coal scuttle, paper and kindling, tapers and matches, of the clean grate, of the tongs and poker, of the flame and the fire and the ember, of the warmth that requires an effort and some skill to create, the ritual of their beloved coal fires, there is an abiding comfort and a reason to live.

They did not understand, as I was beginning to, because I watched Mrs Simms grow old and Mr Shaw begin to let his lovely pot garden go, that as age and winter hems an old person in, boredom and a final sense of pointlessness is kept at bay by the ritual of the range and the hearth and the fire.

They did not understand that when Christmas is over and youth has fled back to town, a new electric fire that apes the real thing offers cold comfort and does not warm arthritic hands.

In my own house and the ones I was allowed into I saw the generations grow irritable, one with the other.

It was this older generation, abandoned by its children and time, raised through years of austerity, cutting up old newspapers and threading it with string out of habit now rather than to avoid having to pay for lavatory paper, that created the gardens behind the walls through which at first I could not see and through whose high solid gates and modest Regency doors it took me years to find my way.

For the time being, as the winds gathered strength and blew me from corner to corner like an empty half-pint milk bottle that had fallen off our step, rolling round and round from dusk to dawn and keeping folk awake with its noise, the old high walls rose far above my head and stopped me seeing what lay beyond. The gardens and flowers awaiting me in the years ahead were only hinted at by the dead stems of Russian ivy, and the broken branches of buddleia, the pink valerian, peeping over walls and scratching around above me in the wind; and the errant rose, dusky pink, voluptuous cream, beckoning where I could not yet go.

Even the window boxes gave no clue as to what would come: they were cleared of their summer flowers where the owners cared, dried up and forgotten where they did not.

The only plants that grew of their own accord in open places available to me were down through rusty gratings in the street, there to let light into the damp cellars below, but also letting in enough litter and dust over the years to make a spoil out of which grew hart's-tongue fern, whose luminescent green shone beneath my feet.

These were the wonders that Mrs Simms and her friends taught me to see and love.

The only public trees in our neighbourhood were the oaks and ash in St Andrew's Churchyard.

When I returned to school after each summer, that was where I used to watch the autumn blow its days through to December, as the air grew cold and wet, and the winds fretted at my face, and the sea began to roar up on the Front with winter rage. That churchyard was my experience of autumn for years to come.

For me, each fallen leaf scuttering across my path in the morning, lodged to rot in among the propped-up gravestones by the evening, marked one more bit of my failure at school. Because it was bit by bit I failed, leaf by leaf, until I was left leafless, my arms, my hands and my fingers stretched out in silhouette against the evening sky, immobile, helpless, impotent, a forgotten sapling, almost dead before its time, lost in a corner of a churchyard.

But out of uniform, out of school, back in the safety of the world of the North End, away from the despair and hatred of Captain Flax, where there were no French masters to sneer, or maths masters to confuse, or history lessons made up of litanies of dates and people and places that had no meaning, I learnt more and more of the lessons from the alternative curriculum unwittingly provided by the adults of my community.

Mr Bubbles and I became good friends, but it was on the beach we would meet, usually when there were storms; and it was two years after our arrival in the North End before he invited me into his little house in Budd Street to meet his wife. She was French, and my first lesson from her was peeling shallots.

She thrust a knife into my hand and sat me at her kitchen table while she brewed us the strongest tea I ever drank. When I looked helplessly at the awkward shallots she said, ''E'll show you, Jimmy', and Mr Bubbles tried to do so, fumbling with his great hands and grumbling darkly.

'Here, *I'll* show you,' she said finally, when the tea was done, and she took up each one with love, admiring its sheen and colour, and showed me what to do, teaching me that food did not have to be the chore that Ma made it but could be a pleasure.

Meanwhile Mr Bubbles, still wearing his great overcoat and mock-protesting that he had been relieved of a task he could do perfectly well if only he was left alone, supped his mug of tea and smiled, flecks of orange light from the flames of their coal fire dancing in his dark eyes.

'*Je m'appelle Véronique*,' said Mr Bubbles's wife suddenly, '*et toi?*'

'Jimmy.'

'*Je m'appelle Jimmy*,' she said softly, the 'Jimmy' spoken with a soft 'j' and a long 'i'. 'Jeemy' could not do her version of it justice.

'*Et toi?*' she repeated.

'*Je m'appelle Jimmy Rova*,' I repeated, no more aware than she was that what began then was a natural process of healing for both of us.

For her it had to do with loss of language and culture, living in England as she did; for me it was a healing of the severe wounds inflicted on my love of language, especially French, by Mr Job. From that day I began visiting the Bubbleses' cottage regularly and it was far, far more than French that I learnt in that tiny parlour. It was a feeling for quietness and content, domestic peace and the meaning of devotion, one person for another.

FISHING BAIT SOLD HERE, it said on a wooden plaque Mr Bubbles had put up himself: black words on cream paint, the same paint he used to colour the inside panels of his black front door, and the big lintel above his wide front-room window, which opened right onto the street.

Mrs Bubbles used to make her French food right alongside the lead-lined vat of lugworms in the kitchen, chopping, stirring, tasting, humming, talking to herself.

Mr Bubbles told the fishermen he sold his bait to that the special secret of his worms' success in attracting fish was the secret recipe for the dark brown liquid in which he kept them. He said the secret would go with him to his grave: except I knew what it was – paraffin and the oil he used to keep the fishermen's capstan engines sweet and sea water with sand in it.

But Mrs Bubbles said he had it all wrong and that the special secret ingredient was the perfume of wild garlic that her home cooking put into the air, a plant that Mr Bubbles habitually collected on his way across the Dunes when he went bait digging in Stannick Bay. Her husband's worms were flavoured by the scents of French cuisine.

'*De temps en temps* . . .' she would whisper, '. . . sometimes, when

Monsieur is cruel and dark and not so good, I think I might put a few of those fat worms in his stew, but then . . . then . . .'

Then she would smile and wink to say it was a joke, her joke, *our* joke.

I learnt the look of love from Mrs Bubbles and longed for the day I would be able to put such a look in a woman's eyes. It was when she was grumbling and pretending to complain, and thinking of Mr Bubbles, that I saw it: the crinkles at the corner of her eyes and the half smile on her lips betrayed the depth of her love and respect for him.

'. . . then I think that it would be unkind on those poor worms to be cooked with lamb and eaten by such a man. In the sea, on hooks, they have a chance to get away to *la liberté,* but from his stomach they would not escape.'

Years later, learning about the French Revolution, being told about *Liberté, Egalité et Fraternité,* it was her gentle voice that gave substance to the revolutionaries' clarion cry in my mind, and those worms that were French citizens seeking to be free.

'So I never have and of course, Jimmy, be sure of it, I never will!'

The smile, the look of love, the little affectionate laugh, the touch.

Mr Job could have given a hundred thousand lessons but never come near to the power and the potency of the things that Mrs Bubbles taught me about French and France, starting with her deep love and longing for the country of her birth to which she felt she could never now go back. During the War she had committed a crime far worse than murder in the eyes of her fellow citizens in her Normandy town. They had liberty; she was punished by a lifetime of exile.

All those years later, she still suffered from dark moods, particularly in the winter, when the sea crashed up on the beach and shook their cottage. There would be whole days and weeks when she would just sit in the shadows of her front room.

'Jimmy . . .' she would whisper sometimes when I came round, sent by Mr Bubbles to sit with her because she was feeling low. 'Jimmy, *mon petit chou, aidez-moi . . .*' reaching out a hand to touch my arm. And she would lean on me as if she was an old woman and I would help her prepare the vegetables, a job that in her low times she would put off all morning, but in good times she would do in seconds.

In time I learnt to make up the fire, and put a blanket over her shoulders, and talk to her as I talked to Granny, about the things I did and the things I saw. Just talk, just be around, and sell the bait to the fishermen who came knocking at her door: 9d half a score, one and six a score and two shillings for twenty of Mr Bubbles's Specials, the fattest of the lugworms, which he kept in a fine wire cage at one end of the vat.

Others stood in when Mr Bubbles was digging in Stannick Bay and I was at school, Freddie Hammel among them. But it was my presence that calmed her best and brought back a smile, until she was ready to send me home.

'It's better for her here than Blackstone,' Mr Bubbles would say softly, remembering the only time he had followed doctor's advice and allowed her to be put in the local mental hospital over on Blackstone Hill.

Often I heard of how he had pedalled the six miles there through the night, woken by a sudden urgent sense that she needed him and could not live in that place a moment longer. He had banged on the great doors in the night, pushed past the warders, as he called them, made his way to the women's wards and picked her up and took her out into the fresh night air, with everyone too afraid to stop him. He perched her on the crossbar of his bicycle in her nightie and dressing gown, and took her home to Budd Street. From that day on he swore he would never let a doctor get his hands on her again.

The memory of Blackstone Hospital continued to haunt her, but only little by little did I understand that her sadness and her fears had to do with what she had left behind in France when Mr Bubbles rescued her.

The walls of their front room were cream-painted canvas nailed to the wood panels underneath. Mr Bubbles had put up pictures and other things, hung on nails. There was the steamer he served in as apprentice ship's engineer before the First World War, and a bill poster offering five pounds for information about some stolen whisky. The poster was an heirloom from the past – Stoning's not Mr Bubbles's. He had bartered it from Mrs Jacoby who had it in the window of her junk shop at the bottom of Smithy Lane, in exchange for helping her move goods once in a while. His real past remained a mystery, divulged to no one, not even his wife.

Mrs Bubbles had not had time to save anything from her past in France that famous day Mr Bubbles and Freddie Hammel had rescued her by boat from a place near Calais called Wissant, except for one thing: a black-and-white photograph from before the War. It was of her and her twin brother Philippe.

She would take it down and say, 'Mon pauvre Philippe a été tué par les monstres.'

Germans were monsters to her because they killed her brother.

'That's what that means,' explained Mr Bubbles, 'but it don't mean they actually killed him dead. What they did was worse, because he was put into a loony bin like Blackstone near the place he lived and she knows that was the real death of him.'

But whatever had happened for Philippe to suffer this fate neither of them would tell me, except that it was nothing a brother should ever have to see.

It was Freddie Hammel who told me the truth, that Mrs Bubbles had saved her brother's life by collaborating with the Germans so that he might be allowed to live in peace in a time of war in their town's equivalent of Blackstone Hospital until he died. But even then I sensed there was more to it than that, something worse, but they wouldn't say what.

They were more willing to talk about the rescue itself, though their different versions varied, and over the years they changed and it was years before I got at the truth.

In the snapshot she stood with her arms around her twin brother, he grinning, she smiling, and behind them were the cliffs of Cap Gris Nez. The sun shone bright upon it, as it did on their faces when the photo was taken by their father.

The photograph was framed in silver, and the darker the day in her front room the brighter the silver seemed to shine, as if to say there are always memories to keep you going even on the darkest day, and they bear promise that better days will come back.

With the coming of April and the return of the sun Mrs Bubbles would stir herself. For a few days she would be busy around the home, spring cleaning, sweeping out their little backyard, putting away winter clothes, bringing out her summer frocks and polishing the windows until they shone like new. April was the birthday month of Philippe and herself, the time when her own spirits began to improve.

It was usually after Easter, at the end of April or, in a bad year, at the beginning of May, with the first warm day and the true coming of spring, that Mrs Bubbles put on her best frock and set off out into the wide world once more. With a flat-bottomed basket on her arm she would make her way sunwards along the Promenade to the chalk cliffs of Southdown, two miles away.

She would go at low tide so that, when she climbed up the cliff path to the cliff top itself, she could look across the Channel and see the white cliffs of France. They were easier to see when the tide was low. Then she would pick a posy of spring flowers, celandine, violets and anemone, and down in the hollow by the road she would seek out the last of the snowdrops and a touch of May blossom from the hedge if she could find it.

These few things she brought back and put on the mantelpiece alongside the picture of herself and Philippe, and she would light a candle and softly, gently, sing the annual birthday song for him...

> *Bon anniversaire*
> *Bon anniversaire . . .*

She liked others to be there, for it was her birthday party too. Freddie came, and Mr Cox the Chemist, Mr Boys from the Castle and a few others, as well as me and Mr Bubbles. They would drink rum and I would be given pop, and amid tears of memory and gladness that spring had come once more, and heartened by the friends around her and the man who loved her, her winter sadness would be driven away for a time.

Then, week by week, as she grew ever more cheerful, she would regularly walk the long way to Southdown to gather a fresh posy, letting the sea breeze blow the cobwebs from her mind. Sometimes she would take me, and so it was that from her I learnt the names of wild flowers, and had my first lessons in French vocabulary: *ajonc, géranium sanguin, oeillet, coquelicot, valériane, casse-pierre, violette, anthyllis vulnéraire, menthe et estragon.*

All the flowers of the shore, Mrs Bubbles flowers, which grew the spring and summer through along our coast and, as she told me, across the Channel in the Pas-de-Calais. Each one of which was a link to the past and the time that she and Philippe used to pick flowers for their *grand-mère*, who was blind, but who could feel them with her fingers, and sniff them with her nose and talk of days when she too was young and picked flowers.

So it was that Mrs Bubbles's dark mood used to disappear like morning mist as the year advanced. Mr Bubbles would sometimes bring her wild grasses and flowers from the Dunes. Bulrush he would bring, and the yellow flowers of thorny gorse, and scabious and wild garlic, the flowers of the heath; but never poppies.

'Too beautiful to pick are those, Jimmy my boy, and if you do they drop their heads and die, however much water you put in the vase. Each one is a fallen soldier come alive again so you'll never catch me picking 'em.'

Mrs Bubbles taught me more than just French words and phrases, she taught me too about history, and war, and the pity of it. So that when we had history at school, even down there at the bottom of the class, when Mr Deller taught his lists of battles and kings, I could think my secret thoughts of those who fell but did not die, who lived on in other people's minds – mothers, brothers, sisters, twins. I could remember them, the ones our teacher forgot to teach us about, or didn't know how. I had seen their photographs and seen the tears they left behind in the North End; I had seen the tears of war on

Mrs Bubbles's cheeks and the pity of it in the lines of Mr Bubbles's face.

But we were never set essays about any of that, or questions in tests, so I never got any marks for what I learnt.

One day, up on the Front, after I heard Granny crying again from an argument with Ma and wanted to get out of our dark house, I walked the long way up to Southdown and picked her some flowers like Mrs Bubbles and her brother used to pick for their gran. I hid them in a brown paper bag I found littering the shore, in case anyone saw.

Not that I had any real friends to make me embarrassed. But boys saw and told about such things, and sniggered from across the railway carriage, and down the long school corridors. So I hid them all the way home, put them in a jam jar with some water and said to Granny, 'They're for you.'

She sniffed at them with her long nose and then felt them with her old bent hands, the fingers shaking. In the dark light of her room I saw that her once clear grey eyes were now rheumy and growing white. That was the day I learnt Granny was going blind, and I discovered that blind eyes still shed tears.

'Oh Jimmy!' she said, reaching out a hand for mine. But I was growing up. I fled from her gnarled hand and her old tears and lost myself again along the beach.

Another thing I learnt was all about the tides, but it was many subtle things in one and never written down in books. They come in and they go out, each day differently yet each day making up a pattern eternally the same. That's the thing to remember about tides.

Once, back at school after the Easter holidays, I tried to write about the tides for our English master. The essay title he'd given us was: 'Describe something you did in the holidays.'

Our English master was Mr Hamish McRae, who taught all the lower forms English in their first four years at the school. He was in fact the games master whose qualification to teach was merely a cover to continue to play rugby, which was his passion. He was Scottish, and had once briefly represented Scotland in an international, as a reserve, which achievement and memory he wore as proudly as the tartan tie he sported on St Andrew's Day.

Under him for those four long years, those who were not neat and tidy, obedient and team sport-orientated, and that included me, could not thrive, and did not. They grew restive and bored, conscious only sometimes that somewhere in the texts Mr McRae taught so badly and the compositions he marked down for untidiness but never marked up for ideas and imagination, were things worth preserving and making note of, things that needed encouragement.

Every essay had to have a name and the date and that was easy. I could write that out as neat as anything and without a blot. There had to be a title and I thought a long time about that up in my room until it came to me through the window with the sound of the sea: 'Listening to Tides' was my title.

That was what I had done every day of that holiday, morning and night, and often in the day up on our wild seashore.

It seemed a good idea for an essay.

I remember how my pen flew over the paper, telling what I heard and what I thought, and how you could tell the state of the tide by the sound of the sea and the direction of the wind and what gulls were flying and how the ships would orientate themselves at anchor. You could tell all sorts just by listening in my room. And by sniffing at the air. Once it's in your blood from walking the shore, you know what the tides hold just from listening. I had never written such a long essay in my life and I handed it in first, before anyone else, eagerly.

When the day came for the marked essays to be handed out, he held mine back, which he did when he had something to praise. The clock behind his head said five minutes to twelve and there was a spider in a corner of the window waiting for a fly . . .

'Now, Rova II,' he said at last, but I saw his eyes were not filled with praise and my heart thumped and something more in me began to die.

He held my book out so its pages flipped open to my essay and where the sound of the sea was held together by my words. I watched and I heard the eternal sound of the sea fall silent, and saw the restless waves come to a halt and the sea grow still.

Sniggers and titters and my heart battering inside with its hurt and shame.

Red ink lines crossed my essay right out, from its title to its ending.

Mr McRae said, 'Rova, listening is not doing. What did you *do* in the holiday, not what did you hear. *Read* the essay title, then do it again. Write about sport, or . . .'

His words faded away before my misery. Down there in the vale of failure, you die a lot of deaths but no one hears your cries. You are mute to the world, and it is mute to you, and you walk alone in its darkness, giving up all hope that you'll ever see a light. You don't know what to do to get things right.

I had been in Darktime when I was little, now I was somewhere that felt the same, where right answers are wrong and you don't know why or where to turn.

That evening I said to Ma, 'I thought listening was doing something.'

She saw I was unhappy. I told her about the essay.

Ma said, 'Let me read what you wrote.'

She read it once and she read it twice and she made me make a fresh pot of tea before she said anything.

'Jimmy,' she said, 'what you wrote was good.'

Ma rarely said such things but I didn't feel better.

'Mind you, there's a few mistakes . . .'

'He didn't even read it,' I said.

It was this that had upset me, that my words had never even had a chance.

There were tears in my heart but not in my eyes. Darktime taught me not to show my tears except to myself.

'Well . . . the man's a fool,' she said finally.

She said a lot more, and even hugged me, which Ma rarely did. But at the end of it all I knew two things only: I was still down there in the void, and I had another essay to write.

'What *did* I do in the holidays, Ma?'

'Er, um . . .' said Ma.

She didn't know.

'He said I could write about sport or going away for Easter or swimming and even about a film I've seen. But not listening to tides.'

'Humph!' said Ma.

Sport?

I had no friends to play sport with.

Going away?

We had no money to go away. We never went on holiday.

Swimming?

Only the Royal Marines had a swimming pool in our town and it was only open for children on Saturday mornings in the summer holidays.

A film?

I had no money for the cinema.

*Listening to tides* – that's what I did in the holidays.

'What about fishing in a boat?' said Ma.

'I've never been. Not in a boat. Not fishing.'

'Make it up. He won't know the difference. If a teacher's a fool today he'll still be one tomorrow.'

But I didn't make it up. Instead I went to see Mrs Bubbles.

Mrs Bubbles knew sadness when she saw it.

I couldn't cry for Ma but I could for her. I sobbed in her arms although I tried not to. Then I told her about listening to tides and how I had nothing to write about because all I had done through the holidays was that.

'Ma said to write about catching a fish in a boat, but I haven't.'

'Then *certainement* you must,' she said. 'You must catch a fish in a boat today and say that's what you did in the holidays.'

'But . . .'

'Sometimes a little lie is not so bad.'

She spoke to Mr Bubbles. Mr Bubbles spoke to Freddie.

That very afternoon Freddie Hammel took me out onto the great blue sea in his motorboat and there we sat, looking back at my town and the Pier, tossing about and me turning green, threading Mr Bubbles's specials onto hooks and dropping them on a hand-line over the side.

'Best bait this side of Lowestoft, is Mr Bubbles's specials,' said Freddie, puffing his pipe.

He watched me for a bit and came over to where I was sitting and took the boat rod from my hands.

'No, lad, the best way to feel a bite from a boat is to forget the rod and hold the line in your hand like *this* . . . For big 'uns it's different but today there's only tiddlers about.'

It took an hour but when it happened it would have been worth waiting twenty-four hours for. *Bang! Bang!* The tugs were like bangs in my hand.

'Strike 'im . . . *pull* 'im,' cried Freddie, but he didn't take the line from my hand. He was too good a teacher for that.

'It's just seaweed,' I said when the vast weight on my line appeared at the surface.

'Missed 'im,' said Freddie. 'You've got to strike harder and faster when they bite.'

Next time I did.

I caught a three-pound codling and then some whiting and was sick all at the same time, and was proud and glad when we got back to shore. I felt as right as rain in no time.

I showed the fish to Granny and I showed it to Ma, but it was Mrs Bubbles who cooked it, along with some bigger ones that Freddie caught, with herbs Ma never used.

'Nothing like fresh-caught fish,' said Mr Bubbles, taking a nip of his rum.

'Nothing like Mrs Bubbles's cooking either when she's a mind to it,' said Freddie, with a twinkle in his eye.

We feasted on the fish we had caught ourselves, Freddie tucking his napkin under his chin, Mr Bubbles putting on his thick reading glasses that made his eyes bulge big so he could see the bones, and Mrs Bubbles sitting down only when she had served us, and then only to talk. We were not a family, but sometimes I think that was the first meal ever to give me a feeling of what a family meal might be like.

That evening I wrote my essay about what I did in the holidays, or rather what I hadn't done. There were blotches and spelling mistakes. I got a better mark than usual but it was marked perfunctorily, without comment. But by then Mr McRae's reaction did not mean much to me, and I never really came to understand why an answer written truthfully was wrong, while one written as a lie, however white, was right.

I cut the essay about the tides out of my book because it was painful for me to have it there with those red, raw crossings-out. I went down to the shore, sat on the shingle, and made paper boats with it. I often let the sea take away my troubles and unhappiness. It was still the best friend I had. Even with Granny I could not say everything, but the sea heard everything, my cries and sobs included. Those came suddenly, usually unexpectedly, up out of the dark void of the past whose truths I did not know, or how to find, or how to rid myself of.

'Soldiers don't cry,' people used to say.

But not Ma. She said men did not cry enough and that if they cried more maybe they would understand women's tears.

I did not understand her or tell her that on the beach, when I was alone, and lonely, my sobs were drowned by the sound of waves and the shingle in the tides, and that my cries were sometimes so loud they could have been heard above the surf.

I was not a soldier or a man but just a boy on a beach.

That day, with the torn pages of my essay turned into boats in my hands, I bent down to the great sea and floated my boats off, lighting each one with a match because I was thinking of the farewell to Captain James. Watching them until the paper went soggy and the flames went out and the charred remnants of my words were overwhelmed by the waves. I watched them sink, and I cried.

But not for long because in my heart my paper boats sailed on; and after that I often saw them, lying in bed with the window open, listening to the tides in the dark – sailing, sailing, sailing over the sea, looking for a light to guide them to a safer berth than any I then knew.

How often I scanned the horizons of the night in search of that light. But it is hard to find something when you don't know what it looks like for lack of ever having seen it before. I would study the pebbles at my feet and then, not finding what I sought, raise my eyes to search across the open sea as, in my imagination, my paper boats went on ahead of me.

# 19

## MUSIC LESSONS

In my third year at our grammar school, Michael began his O level year. He had long since become a boarder so I never saw him at home, except fleetingly in the holidays; while at school the fifth-formers never mixed with third-formers. Even when we passed each other in the corridor, or out on the playing fields, he never spoke to me, not once in all those years. Having a brother in silence is almost worse than having no brother at all.

Ma said he boarded because it was the best way for him to concentrate on work. Everybody said he was so brilliant he was going to get a record number of O levels. But there was something not being said, something darker and more sinister to it – about the work, and being a boarder. Ma's stories about the reasons shifted and changed and there was mention, by Granny, of him being unhappy at home and in the North End. There were secrets I was not allowed to know about some of the men I sometimes saw him with: men whose names I did not know and who I never saw visit our house or talking to Ma.

Whatever the reasons, it meant that with his bedroom next to mine now empty, I rattled around in the top of the house by myself, for nobody ever came to stay in the guest room, which was up there too, except my cousin Hilary sometimes. Ma had no friends to speak of, or none we ever saw.

There was Mrs Fortnell in Southdown with whom she sometimes had tea, and Mrs Barnby, who was the mother of a boy in my form. There was Angela Lowe née Piddick, as Ma called her, who was a friend from wartime in Oxford, but when she came she stayed at the Monarch. Angie Lowe always had a different man for a companion, who she would send off for walks along the Promenade while she and Ma talked over tea about the perfidy of men and the vileness of teenage boys. Their voices would drop when I came into a room, and they would exchange meaningful glances. Angie made you feel she knew far more than she let on. She knew Ma before I was born. She was a woman whose lips were sealed.

So it was that I lived on the top floor all by myself. Granny was on the floor below, and Ma on the ground floor in the room by the front door. The Man Who Wasn't only came at Christmas, and for some weeks in the summer vacation, when his landlady in Oxford turfed him out so her own relatives could stay.

Despite Michael being Michael, I missed his presence. Better the devil you know than no company at all. It was not his conversation I missed, because after I stood up to him that time and he couldn't bully me physically he did something worse: he sent me to Coventry and never spoke to me. But he couldn't stop me listening to the sound of him playing the piano next to our big mirror in the sitting room.

He would play his music and with his lovely voice sing songs whose words I learnt to understand and love. Often I listened on the stairs, imagining he was the brother I had lost and now had found again and his songs were for me.

That piano was the only friend of his I was allowed to know. The others, the human ones, were secrets he never allowed to be revealed. But through that friend, listening in the corridor outside because he would not let me in the room itself, I met Mozart, and Chopin but most of all Bach; and Michael's voice, treble once but freshly tenor by then, was my introduction to 'Jesu, Joy of Man's Desiring', and, at Christmas, 'Quem Pastores Laudavere'.

Those times were good, maybe the best, when I could share something of Michael and know him as he really was. That kind of music was Michael to me and when I heard it then and sometimes at school, it put within reach for a time the brother I knew was there but who never let me near.

But with his departure to the boarding house our house fell silent of music, silent of almost everything but Granny's moans, Ma's rages and the perpetual wind rattling at the casement windows.

Through my years of walking to school I read and learnt off by heart the words carved into each and every gravestone in St Andrew's Churchyard, wondering who they had been whose names were inscribed there. It was my favourite way to and from the station. But when we first came to the North End I could not have imagined that my twice-daily walks would make me part of a community; and that, for a time, I would become someone people set their watches by.

From behind lace curtains they saw me passing by on my way to school through my years of growing up, still in their dressing gowns, and glanced at their wind-up clocks. They saw me walking by their shop doors as the vegetables were set up and the fish were laid out and wine and beer were delivered at Stoning Wine Vaults, established in 1816 when trade to France opened up again, past which I went if I chose the route up Macaulay Road.

'Morning, Jimmy,' Mr Shuter the dentist would say, as he set up his fearsome drills and polished his spectacles ready for another day repairing teeth.

'Morning, young Jimmy,' Mr Cox called.

'Marnin!' Colin the Grocer would say after he set up shop in competition with the man who was his boss, always speaking to me because Ma took her business to him, though Granny did not.

Over the road from the churchyard was the Salvation Army, who were in business to make friends with passing men and women and boys and girls who might otherwise fall into evil ways, if they have not already, and recruit them for God's Army.

There was never a member of the Army there in the morning, but on my way home, especially if I stayed late at school for games, the Salvation Army Hall's door was sometimes open and the lights on with men and women going in and out wearing funny hats. Occasionally someone I didn't know would say, 'Hello, Jimmy. How's your gran?'

Granny wasn't one of them, but she wasn't against them either. She believed that people who followed something were better than people who followed nothing. She was a Baptist herself but she had seen General Booth, who founded the Salvationists, in the flesh in the days when people still pelted him with rotten eggs and tomatoes.

Then late one afternoon in my third year before my voice broke, when it was nearly dark and I was tired from rugby, I saw a lot of Salvation men and women arriving with brass instruments: trumpets, trombones, horns and a piano accordion.

I stood watching and wondering, because since we had moved to the North End I had missed the sound of the Royal Marine bugler waking me up every morning with his reveille call. I missed the Marines on Sunday marching from the Garrison Church back to their barracks, playing their marches and beating their drums and twirling their drumsticks.

Seeing the Salvation Army band assembling in that Hall in the North End brought happy memories back to me. So I stood for a while and stared at the trumpets and the big trombones. There wasn't much to call me home now Granny was getting so old and tired. Ma was out a lot, so often my supper was waiting congealed and cold on a chipped white plate for me to heat up and eat alone by a guttering fire.

'What's happening, mister?' I asked a man who was carrying a shining trumpet.

Another man, fat and with a red face and greasy hair, said, 'Hello, Jimmy, there's a band competition in our hall tonight. All are invited.'

I stared at him blankly, wondering how he knew my name.

'He means you can come if you want,' said a woman near him. She knew I didn't understand what 'all are invited' meant.

When I got home Ma asked, 'What did you do today?'

As usual she didn't wait for me to reply before telling me my supper was on the stove and shoving her nose into a book. Sometimes she did make an effort to listen but her attention soon wandered and I would lose the thread of our words, because words spoken into silence soon die. Words need the nurturing of someone else's receptive mind.

That day I was going to ask if I could go and hear the bands but when Ma's hand reached out to pick up her book before I had even spoken I didn't bother.

Later on, after baked beans on buttered toast, bread and butter pudding and tea with three sugars, I just slipped away so no one noticed, out into the night, up Macaulay Road because the church-yard was scary in the dark, and over to the Salvation Army Hall. There was a woman at a desk by the door collecting money, so I started walking away.

'It's all right, you can come in for free,' she called.

It was the woman who had spoken to me before.

'Have you come alone?'

I nodded.

'What's your name?'

'Jimmy Rova.'

'Do I know your gran?'

'Probably,' I said. 'She knows lots of people.'

Unlike Ma, who knew hardly anyone.

'Got any brothers or sisters?'

I nodded.

'There's Michael,' I said, not offering much, just enough to make her curiosity go away.

'Oh yes,' she said strangely, 'I know him.' Then, after a pause, 'Does your mother know you've come tonight?'

'Yes,' I lied, adding to make it more convincing, 'and she said to come straight on home afterwards.'

'Go on in then, there's no need for money.'

The hall filled up with people talking and blowing on musical instruments and making them huff. They wore blue-black uniforms with maroon epaulettes. The men had peaked hats like railway guards, and the women had funny hard black bonnets with a band of maroon ribbon round them. Granny said they were to stop them having their heads bashed in by orthodox Christians and the working classes who are easily offended and inclined to violence.

No one looked at me much, except the friendly fat man I had seen before, who came and said, 'Jimmy, you sit here near the aisle at the back where you can see and won't be in the way. Can you play an instrument?'

I said no and he said it was easy and there was always someone willing to teach those ready to learn. Would I like to learn the cornet, which was like a trumpet? When he was gone I sat quiet as a mouse and kept out of people's way. They probably thought I was one of the bandsmen's sons come to watch. I decided if anyone asked me who I . . .

'What's your name, sonny?' a man asked me.

I said I was Jimmy and my dad was a bugler in the Royal Marines. It made me feel better saying that. I was thinking of the bugler Granny got to come to my hospital bed years before when she first came to live with us and saved my life.

The man said, 'He must be a good player then,' and went away. He had slidey eyes and I saw him glance at the fat man, just quickly, like a tongue flicking out of a newt's mouth in the pond by South Stoning Castle.

Then a man called everyone to attention and we all stood up and said a prayer and sang a song, while I looked at the legs of the woman in front, which were black with her stockings, black like her shoes.

> *In quietness of heart and mind*
> *By depth of thought and act of will*
> *I choose your better way to find*
> *And in my life your plans fulfil*

The prayer they recited was up there on the wall above my head, painted onto a wooden plaque. The plaque was varnished brown and the words of the prayer were in black. In one place the varnish had dripped down the wood and solidified into an eternal shining tear.

After the prayer and song we sat down again and after more talk and a clattering of chairs, one of the bands got itself into position and a man stood up at the front, clutching a white baton. He was the conductor.

He held up the baton and we all fell silent.

Then the band started playing marching music like the Royal Marine Band, but they did not play so well. They played raggedly, and their uniforms were not as smart as the Marines'. They were just fat men and women with greasy hair and pimples. They were soldiers of Christ but the Royal Marines would have mown them down in no time with the smart rat-tat-tat of their kettle drums.

The bands changed several times, there was tea and cakes, and outside the sky went from dark to black and it felt late. The man with slidey eyes came up to me and said, 'Sonny, you could learn an instrument so easily – look, he's no older than you and he's in the Dover band.'

He pointed at a boy with Brylcreemed hair and a uniform. He was at least twelve. The man put his hand on my shoulder and smiled.

'We give junior lessons on Saturday mornings before band practice. You could come if you liked.'

I ran all the way home that night, but a few weeks later when I had nothing to do one Saturday morning I went up Macaulay Road looking for that man. He was there ready and waiting.

He said, 'You can't just do it without your parents' permission. Did you say your dad was a Royal Marine?'

I said, 'He's gone away.'

He grinned.

I think he knew I didn't have a dad, not counting the Man Who Wasn't.

He said, 'I'll come round and sort it out with your mum.'

I never told him where I lived so someone else must have done, because there he was knocking on our door a few days later, smiling, his fat cheeks shining.

As usual Ma was in a hurry and didn't listen long before saying yes, if I wanted to.

'Who was that?' said Michael, who happened to come in while they were talking. He was home for one of his rare weekends.

I said proudly I was going to learn the cornet with that man and he was with the Salvation Army, but it did not matter that I did not believe in Christ and God. He was going to let me borrow an instrument.

'Humph!' said Michael, frowning. 'You'd better practise in the downstairs WC where no one can hear you!'

We had a lavatory through the kitchen, right at the back of the house. It used to be outside but they filled in the door and knocked through the wall by the kitchen cupboard so you didn't have to go outside in the rain to have a piddle. One of the other funny things about our kitchen was that the rainwater gutter ran through from one side to another above the kitchen sink, so it roared like a river when it rained outside.

Then Michael was looking at me with more than a frown. There were points of doubt in his eyes. I thought he was jealous, but I couldn't have been more wrong. He was worrying about me, and that was something new.

I went to that man three times in all and learnt to play three notes, C, G and F.

The first time he showed me how to hold the trumpet and how to blow. He had to touch my hands and my mouth and he smelt of cigarettes and plastic, from his smoking and his work in the plastic factory at the top of Printer's Square. That time the fat man was there in the big hall putting up notices.

'Well done, laddie,' he called out when I sounded my first notes. 'You've got natural born talent, I can see that. Eh, Seddy?'

The man teaching me was called Cedric and that's why everyone called him Seddy.

'He'll be a good little player if he's willing to apply himself,' said Seddy, and that made me so pleased that I ran all the way home to tell Granny and show her the instrument he lent me. It was bright and shiny and I was proud of it.

'Good,' she said, 'it's good to learn a musical instrument.'

Ma asked, 'What notes did you learn?'

'C,' I said.

Ma looked into the distance beyond the kitchen wallpaper and I asked, 'Why didn't *you* learn an instrument? Granny says . . .'

'I'm sure she says a lot of things,' said Ma sharply, 'and anyway, I did. The viola. Scrape scrape scrape, just so your Uncle Max and Aunty Ellie had their trio.'

'Oh,' I said, shocked at her bitterness, not wanting her to say more. Ma could spoil my present with her past. Her words were like tears and stung like salt.

In the second lesson I learnt to play half a tune and Seddy and the other man said I was coming on fast. Seddy came up behind me to show me how to hold the trumpet better and I felt his tummy press into my back, which I didn't like. But once he had finished showing me it was all right and I blew better.

'Very good, young Jimmy,' he said.

The Hall was big and echoing and I didn't like the fact the door was closed and just the two men were there with me. This time the other man was sweeping the floor.

'There's always work to do,' he said, 'and I like to keep occupied, oh yes.'

When the lesson was over Seddy said he had a present for me. It was a junior Salvation Army uniform: trousers and top.

'You can try it on now if you like.'

I remember those words like ravenous rooks sitting in a tree waiting to swoop on crushed and dying animals; and Seddy and the other man's watching eyes as they waited for me to pull down my shorts and change.

I did not want to change in front of them like that.

I said, 'No!' but it sounded rude and my heart thumped.

'Not to worry,' said Seddy, patting my shoulder.

'No hurry,' said the other man, grinning. 'No hurry at all.'

The trousers stayed where they were.

Instead, we cleaned the spit out of the trumpets in silence.

'Don't you want to wear the uniform? Most boys do,' said Seddy softly a little later on.

I can remember his voice now, sliding back and forth in my memory. It was more a feeling than a sound, like the run of a finger with a dirty, uncut nail down my cheek, softly threatening.

I wanted to say I didn't believe in Christ and God but there was a holy picture on the wall and that felt rude too. I wanted to say I just didn't want to.

I was glad to get away at last and the sea air made me forget about it. Later at school, miracle of miracles, Michael came to me and asked me about my cornet lesson. I told him how they had said I was good and how I didn't want to try on the uniform.

'What uniform?' he asked, frowning.

I told him about the trousers and not wanting to change in front of them.

Michael frowned.

'When's your next lesson?' he asked.

I told him and he went away.


The third lesson arrived and we hadn't got very far before two things happened.

First Seddy came up behind me again to show me how to hold the instrument and I couldn't move forward to stop his tummy pressing into me because of the music stand. This time the other man wasn't there and Seddy's tummy pressed harder, so I could feel the push of his privates. I breathed more easy when he moved away and I played the notes really well.

For a moment I even felt like the bugler I used to hear from the old house.

'Very good,' said Seddy, 'but you're still holding it wrong. Let me show you again.'

As he came nearer again I felt as if my breathing was beginning to stop. The room seemed dark and the windows were high, high above and moving out of reach. He was pressing against me again and I was scared, but I didn't know what to do and his privates were pressing harder still against me. I wanted him to move away. I wanted to run. He seemed to get angry and held on to me as his hands ran down my front and gripped me and he pulled me into him and I felt him hard against my bottom.

Spit dribbled out of the trumpet mouth onto my knee.

'Like this,' he said, his head bent down so close to mine his fat cheek touched my ear and I could smell the smoke on his breath, and the plastic from the factory.

I felt paralysed, floating, giving in, and I heard him say, 'Yes,' and felt his hands gripping and floating as my cornet slipped down and down and down onto the ground and he took my privates in his hand and then felt for my flies.

Then the second thing happened.

The street door opened and someone said, 'Jimmy, you're to come here. *Now!*'

It was Michael.

He sounded angry and his voice was shaking.

'You're to leave him alone, mister,' said Michael to Seddy, coming in and grabbing my arm and his foot making contact with the cornet, which scuttered over the bare wooden boards of the Salvation Army Hall. 'You're not teaching him any more.'

I could suddenly breathe again and there was light in my eyes as Michael pushed me out of the hall and into the street.

His cheeks were white and his lips blue and he looked as cold and angry as winter shadows.

I didn't argue, I just started to run into a great world of relief without looking back.

'Not Jimmy,' I heard Michael say back to Seddy as if he knew him, 'not *him* . . .' and I knew he was protecting me, but I did not know from what.

I knew Michael needed courage to come and get me and that's why his voice was shaking. But he overcame his weakness and his fears to save me.

From that day on I loved my brother Michael and forgave him all he did to me. He was weak, but that day he was strong for me.

I never asked him why he came, or what it was he was saving me from. He knew but I did not, not then.

I was learning to climb the sycamore but there were parts of it where dangerous branches led away from the light to darkness, which I knew nothing about.

A long, long time later I thanked Michael for what he did. But by then it was too late. When he had needed someone as I had needed him, no one had come, and he had been forced to climb the wrong branch and it proved so thin and weak it broke and plunged him into darkness in his life.

The day Michael helped me escape from Seddy I ran up to the Front and then onto the beach and along it, far from Seddy and from Michael, to where the sea wind could clean away the shadows that had tried to envelop me and the filthy feeling of Seddy's body against mine.

After that I only ever saw Seddy sometimes across the street, or in the Salvation Army band, playing in a circle in Lower Street, collecting money. Other boys joined the band but I never did.

He always grinned and said, 'Hello, Jimmy,' as if he had taken something of mine I could never get back.

He had.

As it was, I forgot about the cornet and playing in the Salvation Army band, except that I made sure I never again walked on the far side of Macaulay Road on my way back from school, when darkness was falling and the lights were coming on and the Salvationists were plying their old trade; and if I heard the *rum tum tum* of brass instruments playing it was not the Salvationists I chose to remember but the Band of the Royal Marines.

# 20

# BREAKDOWN

By the time we moved into Compass Street the truth was the North End's little shops and businesses were in decline. They had been in decline since the mid-nineteenth century, the glory days, when sail was still king and steamships were just a mad idea. In those days, back in the time before the Crimean War, when Florence Nightingale became famous, ships used to shelter by their tens and hundreds in the Downs off our shore, and it was the boatmen of the North End who serviced them and brought Stoning its trade.

In those days Stoning buzzed like a beehive and Ma claimed that every other house was a drinking place, and every house in between was a house of easy virtue, which sounded nice to me, not knowing what it meant.

Granny pursed her lips and said, 'That can't be true because it doesn't leave any room for groceries and hardware, not to mention haberdashery for elastic.'

Granny was always setting off to buy elastic for her pink woven cotton knickers, and for garters for me to stop my socks falling round my ankles. She made so many in her idle moments that I tied them together and used them for catapults.

Granny said, 'Michael's tidy and so would you be if you did not allow your socks to fall down your legs like concertinas. As for drinking places and houses of easy virtue, if that is true your grandfather would not have approved. Sometimes decline is no bad thing. It is another word for progress.'

It was around then that I began to wake up to the fact there are bad things in the world, and personal bitterness.

Every Christmas morning we gathered in Granny's room and she opened a brand new bottle of the most alcoholic drink she knew, which was Blackthorn Cider. She poured each of us a glass and she proposed a toast: 'In memory of Grandfather, a lifelong member of the Temperance Movement.' Despite the fact that it was Christmas there was not much of a twinkle in her eyes.

As I grew older I began to see that this was Granny's idea of a joke. I don't know what happened to the bottle afterwards but I do know what happened to its contents: Granny drank them, down to the dregs, which was why at present-giving in the afternoon she sat by the fire with two red cheeks, and the firelight in her eyes, grinning mutely.

But when I grew older still I saw that Granny's joke was a veil that hid a lifetime of married bitterness. Grandfather was a bully and imposed his will on his family just as he did upon his students, only more so. The house he made Granny run was a house of tears. It was the precursor of our own. The sins of the father were visited on the grandchildren.

It was only with me that Granny was able to give the love she would have given her children if she had been allowed. I was the beneficiary of my mother's maternal deprivation.

Granny knew what decline and breakdown was because she had lived so long and seen it in so many ways. Now she herself was declining, and she knew it. Her hands were growing stiff and her eyesight had all but failed, and she was deafer by the day. She still went for her daily walk, though, whatever the weather, just to keep herself alive. Knicker elastic was an excuse to get outside.

The more I ventured south along Lower Street into the centre of town, the more I saw what she meant by the North End being in decline. The shops in the High Street were getting bigger and brighter every week: Marks and Spencer came and Brogue's Haberdashery went, old wooden shop fronts and awnings were pulled down and replaced by plate-glass windows and swing doors. The older people who had served in one shop all their lives gave way to young girls who flitted from one shop to the next and then right out of town.

The new shops sucked the life from the old, taking so many customers from the few corner shops left in Nore Street that they struggled to stay afloat and when each one closed our quarter felt a little more dead.

At the bottom of our street, on the corner with Middle Street, was Fender's, a grocery store that sold liquorice and sherbet dips and bread in greaseproof paper for ninepence a loaf.

It was run by Mr and Mrs Fender without any help, and like Granny they were getting older. Just before the start of my fourth year at grammar school Mrs Fender fell down the shop steps when opening up for the day and broke her hip. She lay in the street moaning until the ambulance came and took her to Stoning Hospital.

Mr Fender had to run the shop by himself after that, even after Mrs Fender came home. She sometimes came down to sit behind the counter, serving customers as best she could while he went out. But she could not climb the wooden steps to get things from the higher shelves, and she found it hard to pick up goods left by delivery vans. She could not load the shelves.

The hair on Mr Fender's head grew whiter and thinner, and his face went grey from the worry of looking after both his wife and the shop.

Ma, who had a book-keeping qualification, came back from buying bread one day and announced, 'It's just a matter of time.' Ma thought she was a doer but really she was a wry observer of life and not much more. She had an eye for tragedy and an ear for grief but she did not have hands that helped. She did not have the gift of loving kindness. Grandfather drove it right out of her.

Arthur Sanders said of Fender's, 'That shop started out before the War as Eddie Fender's pension; now it's a millstone. But I doubt he'll give it up except over his own dead body. The shop's keeping him alive not killing him and that's something that others don't understand.'

After another big store selling food opened up in the High Street, I helped Arthur Sanders put in a new counter in Fender's, and make a new step, and some shelves, to try to compete. Arthur would take no payment, not even for the material.

'It's all right, Eddie, it's all right . . .'

One day Mr Fender hurt his back and couldn't open up. He was confined to his bed for a week and after that the doctor said he would have to go easy on the lifting. Freddie Hammel sent his nephew Frank over to do the heavy work each morning and evening so Fender's could open again and stay open.

'And no argument,' growled Freddie, who could be fearsome, when Frank complained. 'If you knew . . .'

When ABC Bakeries said it was not going to supply bread to Fender's any more because it was not worth the cost of delivery, Mr Goldfinch, the baker in Dragon Street, started sending his own bread round so Fender's still had stock. Every loaf of bread and bun and pastry that Mr Fender sold after that was profit lost to Mr Goldfinch. But he never complained.

'If you only knew . . .' he said as well.

'Knew what?' I asked Arthur many times, until eventually he told me.

'In the war years, when there was rationing, Eddie Fender could have sold goods on the black market at ten times their cost to him and not have to be working today. Many others did it and grew fat on their pickings, including the Linnells, but he never did. He did no favours for customers who had money in the bank and food in the larder, however loyal they had been to him. No, he gave his surplus to the ones who had nothing, the families who couldn't cope, of whom there were many in those days. Come Christmas and Easter, it was him who organized the boxes of goods that many of the poorer families up Rampart Road way found on their doorsteps on Christmas Eve so they and their kids did not go without.

'It was him who organized the coal for those who had no connections with the colliery and made sure the old people were warm. It was him who arranged doctoring for mums who wouldn't have got it otherwise. Eddie and Dottie never got a medal, not even one to share between them, but they never expected thanks, which often they did not get either. They were nonconformists who believed in helping others because it was the right thing.

'Well then, Jimmy . . . now hard times have come their way, and will get worse, and those of us who have got memories that go past yesterday will always see Eddie and Dottie Fender right, and don't you forget it. Your time being strong on this earth does not last for many years. One day you'll be weak and frail as well, like they're becoming, and like your granny already is. The strong help the weak: that's the beginning and the end of things so far as a community goes. Your time to help will come and you'll know it when it does. You're a good boy, Jimmy, so you'll do the right thing.'

Maybe I didn't understand all he said then. But I would come to. Arthur's words on many things had a habit of biding their time until I was ready to hear them right.

So it was that breakdown and decline was all around me.

On the next corner along Nore Street going into town, where Smithy Street cut through from the Front, was Lambert's General Store, which had a tragedy attached to it mirrored by nearly bare shelves.

Old Mrs Lambert and her daughter Eileen ran it, but having hardly two halfpennies to rub together they could not afford to stock the shelves with much. In the summer and autumn there were vegetables and fruit, grown by Mrs Lambert's nephew on his allotment off Upper Stoning Road. In winter there were tins of pilchards and baked beans, and lard and sweets.

I went to Lambert's for the bubble gum and because Ma said it was our social duty to shop there sometimes. When you pushed open the door a bell on bendy metal tinkled above your head, and the flies would rise up buzzing. Mrs Lambert would appear from her back parlour, staggering on her lame leg, and say, 'How many?'

Mrs Lambert's tragedy was the loss of her husband, who was run over in Dover and died a lingering death; and the fact that Eileen was simple. She was fat and had a big bosom and used to grin, but her teeth were bad. Ma said things about men taking her to the Dunes and taking advantage of her simplicity.

'The question to ask,' Ma said once, darkly, 'is what happens to the babies?'

It was true.

One minute Eileen would be her normal porky self and the next she would be so fat that all she could do was sit in a wicker chair outside the shop in the sun, grinning. Next minute she was thin and gaunt and serving in the shop again.

Ma got darker still, liking gossip of the malicious kind.

'The other question to ask,' she said, 'is what is the mother's role in all of this? You don't think the girl does it for nothing?'

Michael, who was good at maths, said that there was a direct correlation between the disappearance of Eileen's 'babies' and the appearance of plump pork sausages in her shop window, which I did not understand.

'Sweeney Todd,' said Michael with contempt, as if I should have known. Eventually I found his name in a book called *100 Most Gruesome Murderers of the last 100 years*. He was a barber who colluded with the butcher next door to turn his customers into meat pies. He cut their throats with his big sharp razor while shaving them and dropped them through a trapdoor onto a conveyor belt that took them to the cellar next door. There they were minced, turned into sausages and put out for people to buy. Michael said that Todd's Best, as they were known throughout the south of London, were made from the fat bums of his rich victims, their flesh made succulent by eating too much veal and quail washed down with port.

'It's only a matter of time before Lambert's closes,' said Ma.

I never saw it close, though. One day Eileen and her mum were gone and the shop was for sale, the next their shop was a front room with lace curtains with Londoners using it as a holiday cottage.

'Our area's looking up,' said Ma.

But to me, and the old people who had supported Lambert's through the years, it felt like breaking down.

Further on still was a fishing tackle shop that sold some of the bait Mr Bubbles dug. It had red fishing reels made by Abu in the window and rods and lead weights and paternosters on display. But the shop was only open on Fridays and at the weekends for visiting fishermen.

'Used to be open all the time,' said Freddie, 'until Rod & Fish near the Pier took away his trade.'

Decline was in the air and on the wind.

One day Ma announced shocking news, which she read in the *East Kent Mercury*: 'Marines to leave Stoning after 100 years.'

The Marines were part of our town's tradition and a source of pride. You rarely saw their men in uniform out of barracks because they got into fights with fishermen, but they were there all the same. Their famous band, which you could hear practising at all times of day and night over the wall of the barracks in London Road, their squads of men in white singlets, their punishment runs up and down the shingle, the boom-boom-boom of their guns on the ranges up by Southdown . . . they were part of the fabric of our life.

Granny was upset.

Ma talked about the need for change.

Arthur Sanders said they had survived the threat of the Marines leaving before but that it was bound to happen one day.

'Nothing stays the same – a community and a town is made up of little changes happening all the time. If it stayed the same it would be dead.'

He was right, things didn't stay the same.

Three days later I came back from school and found two policemen in our house.

'Sit down, Jimmy,' said Ma.

Granny was hovering uneasily.

Ma looked exhausted. Her face was the colour of coal ash after the fire has died.

'It's your brother Michael,' she said, and in my heart there started a scream of fear that he was dead. A scream whose echo faded but did not die away.

'Michael's gone, disappeared. Now, Jimmy, you must try to tell these two gentlemen everything you know about when you last saw him.'

I felt the hand of one of the big blue policemen on my shoulder and felt myself slipping towards Darktime.

'Sit down, sonny, and tell us in your own words.'

'Try your best,' said Ma.

Ma's voice was quiet, like an ill person's, her eyes haunted. The air was dirty with feelings and emotion.

My heart beat so loud I felt I would explode. My voice would hardly come out through the fast tight breaths I took, and when it did it was frail and it shook. My hands shook too.

*Michael's gone*, and with those words my world changed, and with it something about me and the North End.

'I didn't see him at school,' I said. 'He wasn't in assembly.'

Because Michael was a boarder I only ever saw him in assembly and just occasionally through some door or other with his friends. But him not talking did not mean he was not my brother. That's what he did with me, Michael, not talk. That was him *being* my brother.

Since he had left I rarely had reason to go into his room, which was right next to mine. When I did it always felt cold: neat, clean, tidy, hardly anything there, nothing out of place and bitter cold. He never had a treasure chest like I did and on his windowsill there were no stones or pebbles from the beach. His drawers were closed and half empty when you looked inside and his bed made like a prisoner's who expects to get told off if it is so much as a hair's breadth out of line.

That was Michael for you.

Even then I had most of the pieces of the puzzle of what he was in my hands. I was not yet ready to put them together.

'Did you see him yesterday?' the policeman asked.

I shook my head. The last time I saw him he was laughing with another boy at the far end of a corridor. Then he saw me and stopped, stared coldly and disappeared round a corner.

'Which boy?'

I told him.

'Did you talk to him?'

I shook my head, staring at Ma. There was a haunted look in her eye and now her face was turning haggard yellow like the pages of one of her paperbacks that had been too long in the light.

I was asked some more questions and then sent out of the room and upstairs, where I sat on my bed.

Michael gone. That left me alone with Ma, with only Granny for support, and she was getting older all the time. Sometimes I heard her talking to herself in her room, strange disjointed words that were thoughts not sentences. In the night I had heard her weeping cries. She missed the African Gentleman but it was only in her sleep her loss was allowed to express itself. Granny's life was done and the only thing that made waiting for the end less painful was her love for me. It was Ma who was in the ascendant now, like a terrible blood red star.

Michael's going meant I had to fight Ma by myself. I sat in the dark, feeling sad and terrified. Before this Michael's silence always held the promise that it might be broken. Now it had become absolute: he had abandoned me.

Michael never did come back to Compass Street and I finally lost my brother: not a good one, but loss is loss, whoever it is who's gone.

There was a phone call that afternoon to say he had been found in a park in Ashford. He must have gone by train and spent the night there. He said he could not remember anything, and in his pocket was a huge bar of Cadbury's Whole Nut chocolate, untouched. Nobody asked, 'Why Ashford?'

The doctor sent him to the mental hospital in Canterbury to be examined and for tests. Ma said we had to visit him, 'we' being Ma, me and our cousin Hilary, who came down from Oxford especially for the occasion, being close to Michael.

We went to Canterbury by bus and then to the hospital by another bus. It had gates like a prison, and it was built of grey-yellow brick. The lines of men inside, with their hair cropped short and their dark ill-fitting clothes, looked like prisoners of war or refugees. A line of men came walking by.

'*Jimmy!*'

It was Ma telling me not to grin at the staring men but I was just trying to be friendly; they looked so sad.

My cousin went white with fear. Maybe she thought she was going to be attacked, but all they wanted to do was touch her to see if she was made of flesh and blood like them. They never saw people like her in there. Maybe they wanted to touch the woman of her, and taste the food of femininity they were denied all the years of their lives.

We waited in a room with a hatch, behind which sat a man in a white shirt wearing a peaked cap. He had Brylcreemed sideburns and a great ring full of keys. There was a radio playing pop music behind his head, and a board with papers drawing-pinned to it. He said for us to sit on one of the benches opposite and wait. There were magazines and a calendar which said OXO and a magazine called *John Bull* with a story I wanted to read because it said in big letters *Transvaal – where pioneers battle against a witchdoctor and two girls fight for the love of an adventurer*. The room, and the rooms beyond it, and the vast high corridors through which we walked, echoed with cries and shouts and smelt of polish, disinfectant and urine.

We were shown into another room and Michael was there on a chair next to a man in uniform.

He looked small and thin and pale.

His hair had been cut short and he was in strange ill-fitting clothes. He looked like a Barnardo boy.

Behind him there was a great metal window going up and up with cords hanging from it with turned wooden handles. They were for opening and closing the top of the window, which was open that day. The only sound in the room when we entered was the handles on the cord rattling on the window frames as the wind caught them.

My brother Michael looked frightened.

I wanted to run to him and protect him – from the man and from Ma and from our embarrassed cousin. Michael was my tormentor but that day he was weak and needed help; just like I needed help the day he rescued me from the Salvation Army man.

Ma did not go to him but stopped and stared, and so did I. I could see hope die in Michael's eyes, but hope for what, I did not know. In its place there came a look of indifference.

A man in a dark suit entered and spoke in whispers to Ma. She nodded and said, 'Yes, yes, of course.'

I was sent back to the first room, then my cousin followed, brought by the man who had been with Michael first.

'Ma's with Michael and the psychiatrist,' Hilary said.

Her voice was high and tight, not like the voices of the people in the North End I had got to know. She had grown since I had hit her so hard that distant day when we were young and I refused to carry her case any more. She had grown up into a world different from mine. She smelt of nice soap and perfume and, though I did not recognize the odour then, of city life. She did not smell of the sea or the eternal movement of tides and stars. She was a stranger to me.

There wasn't much to do or say except to listen to the pop music and smell the distant smells and hear the distant cries. We waited a long time and the worst thing was we did not see Michael again, so I never got a chance to say the things I had planned to tell him.

I wanted to tell him it was all right about everything. It didn't matter, any of it, if only he . . . *If only you . . . if only*. But I never got to say those words.

I simply wanted to try to say I loved him.

Ma eventually came back and said, 'That's settled then; it's for the best,' and I knew her words were words of abandonment and that we were going to leave Michael behind in that prison place. I wanted to say that I would rescue him but I didn't know the words, and I was scared.

Michael had been scared the day he rescued me, but he overcame it and knew what to do. I was scared that day he needed me, but I didn't know what to do.

On the bus journey back to our house I saw the great black wheels of the lifting gear above the shafts of Nunnestone Colliery turning again, one set going one way, the second going the other. It was then that I cried, my head pressed against the window glass so nobody could see. That was my grief for the loss of Michael.

With the turning of those wheels against each other, black on black, my world stood still. All around the sky was grey and the landscape bleak, the fields empty of their crops, ploughed and furrowed for the winter, the soil grey-white where the chalk showed through.

My cousin went back to wherever she'd come from and the house was silent but for Granny moving about and talking to herself, and Ma tidying up, between cups of tea by the fire and her library books.

Nobody mentioned Michael, not at home, not at school. It was as if he had never been, but I knew he had. For days I would sit on my bed looking at the black latch on the door into his room, wondering if I dared go in there again.

One night, when the wind was quiet and I could hear the swishing of the sea, I couldn't sleep. From my bed, above the radio, at an angle, through the open window, I could see the sky and clouds drifting. They were pale and soft in the moonshine.

I stared and stared until slowly I felt crying come into me, huge like the clouds, a sobbing all through my body. It was much more than in the bus.

I had to struggle to rise up beyond my cries to get out of bed, to raise the latch in the darkness and go into Michael's room. I stood by his bed sobbing a long time before I dared to disturb its neatness, pulling down the sheet folded over the blankets, to climb in and cry. I cried with a fist in my mouth and teeth to stop the sound. I cried for Michael and for me and for my loneliness.

I cried because I had been left alone with Ma.

I cried for the brother I left in the prison place, sitting in a chair, looking so frightened, so much in need of help.

I cried for not knowing what to do.

But all that night Michael's sheets and his bed stayed as cold as ice.

In the morning I woke and remade his bed so not a thing was out of place. Nobody would have known I had ever been there. The last thing I remember is walking back across the freezing linoleum to his door and raising the latch so no one would hear, then going back into my untidy room, back into my bed, which was soft and warm.

Lying there, I made a resolution.

From now on, I decided, I would keep my room as tidy as Michael's. Everything neat, not a thing out of place. And that's what I did and never stopped doing. I began to find comfort in order.

*   *   *

'Jimmy, Jimmy, you're going to see Michael today.'

It was six weeks later and Ma was springing one of her surprises. Michael had left the hospital and they had found a place for him in a School for Maladjusted Boys and I was to visit him.

'By yourself,' said Ma. 'It's better for you both that way.'

Ma was good at justification, at arranging things to her own advantage. She didn't want to see Michael, and with me gone for the day she would be free. By then, freedom was her watchword. Granny and me were the last people in the way of it.

'You're to stay until Monday as there's no train back on Sunday at a sensible hour, so I'll pack you a bag. I'll make you some sandwiches for the journey. There's also a parcel you're to give to Michael.'

The sandwiches were Ma's usual salty scrambled egg, which made the bread foul and soggy, so I threw them out of the train window. But there was a Penguin, and as I had some pocket money, I bought some sweets and more chocolate.

It was the first time I had made a journey like that by myself out of Stoning. The sun shone and I heard birds singing through the train window as we rattled along.

A woman in the carriage said, 'And where are you off to?'

'To see my brother.'

'That's nice,' she said so warmly that I felt I really did have a brother in the normal way.

The special school he was staying in was just a big old house with other boys. It had high hedges and a huge garden leading on to woods. There was a gravelly drive and a boy saw me arrive and took me to Mr Lyward, the headmaster.

He was in the kitchen with an apron on, stirring a huge pan of soup.

'You're Jimmy, Michael's brother,' he said. 'Here, you stir this and I'll find you something to eat while Alan here explains how Finchden Manor works, or doesn't, as the case may be.'

He cooked me eggs and bacon and fried tomatoes and fried bread on the kitchen range, and sat me down at a great big table to eat, while boys came and went. The sun shone through the windows and outside boys ran and shouted and laughed themselves silly at something I couldn't see.

He made me cocoa with three sugars and he talked to me while I ate. Or rather I talked and he listened. I told him about Ma and Granny and something about Michael. He came and sat down and had a cup of tea. He listened so quietly that I spoke for a long time. I felt he listened to every single word.

But I never told him about the night I cried in Michael's bed. And I never spoke about something that happened to Michael in the long ago near the time of my Darktime, which he had only ever told me about once. I didn't want to mention it because he was ashamed; and, anyway, I had forgotten it until that hour of talking as if I couldn't stop; and he never told me everything. But at least in talking to Mr Lyward there were lots of other things I remembered and was willing to talk about, as if they had been waiting to come out.

'Mmm,' he said, sipping his tea, 'yes . . .'

Then he would fall silent, almost as if he wasn't there, and into that deep silence I found myself talking even more, as if it needed filling up to stop it being silent.

But I still kept quiet about the biggest thing, the thing that happened to Michael in the long ago in Ashford, which was the place Michael was drawn back to like a moth to flames when he had his breakdown, where Michael said 'things happened' but I didn't know what he meant. I wanted to protect him.

So I didn't say a thing about that, just a lot about other things, better things, as I ate the fry-up Mr Lyward made, which was one of the best meals of my life, sitting in the sun from the window, having a second helping of fried bread and tomatoes, not having to do anything or be anything but what I was. Just sitting and talking. It was like a dream.

Later Alan took me to find Michael. He said he was up in the woods with other boys, making a swing. I said to Alan I could find him for myself. It was as if I was on the beach at home with the tide coming in. I wanted to see things change at my own pace. I wanted to come back to Michael in my own way.

'Oh, but . . .' said Alan.

'It's all right,' I said.

'Anyway,' he said uncertainly, 'they're making the swing up there in the woods . . .'

I waited for him to go and then I drifted towards where the sounds of the swing-making were coming from. When I caught a glimpse of movement through the trees I slowed and skirted round, pausing sometimes, listening, not wanting to come out into the open, wanting to watch for a time, unobserved.

But this time I was in the no man's land between isolation and company and I was playing with the pleasure of it. I had all the benefits of being alone and all the benefits of joining in, while having the disadvantages of neither. I was in command. I dropped down to the moist soil, in among the mossy roots of trees, sniffing the rich smell of growth and decay, listening to an unseen trickle of water, catching glimpses of the blue sky above, listening to the distant *coo-coo* of wood pigeons.

'Higher!'

It was Michael's voice.

'Loop it higher, one two *three* . . . !'

Except it was not a Michael that I knew.

Then I saw him between the trees, with two other boys his own age, all much bigger than me.

He was in charge and they had a long thick rope high up a sloping branch, and with pulls and flicks, under Michael's direction, they were getting it as high up the branch as they could.

When Michael was satisfied he said, 'Get the tyre!'

The difference in his voice was made by happiness. I had never heard or seen him as he was in that wood that afternoon.

He tied one end of the rope to a lower branch and then they worked out how best to tie the tyre to the other end so it could swing. The place they had chosen sloped down, so that when the tyre swung out it went a long way, and it rose ever higher over the falling ground.

Michael had khaki shorts on and a short-sleeved shirt. He looked well and strong; and he laughed, quite loud, distinctively, and he did not seem like the brother I knew.

When I emerged from the undergrowth I did so shyly, not certain what reception I would get.

'Michael,' I had to say more than once to get his attention, 'Michael . . .'

'Jimmy!' he said, and for once he seemed glad to see me. 'We were expecting you!'

He introduced me briefly to the other boys. It was the strangest thing: he did so with pride, as if he really was proud of me. He had never showed that before. They carried on playing while I watched. I found a tree stump in the sun and sat and breathed easy. It seemed the best place in the world to be that afternoon.

I shook my head when one of the boys asked me if I wanted a go. 'Later,' I said.

'Jimmy likes doing things in his own time,' said Michael.

It was the first time he ever said anything about me that was not rude and showed he knew me. 'He's happy in his own company,' said Michael, but that was half the truth. I would often have been happier in his.

'You're like each other then,' said one of the boys as he swung back and forth, 'and you look like each other too.'

Later, when the boys had gone and Michael and I were left alone, I had a go on the swing.

'I'll pull it back so you get the highest start possible,' said Michael.

'Do we?' I asked as I swung out into the void. '*Do* we look like each other?'

'We must do,' said Michael, smiling.

There was never very much in my bank vault of the memories I have of Michael but those three words together are solid ingots of gold to me.

'Let's try swinging round in a circle . . .'

He tried, I hung on too long and we ended up rolling down the slope in a tangle of arms and legs. Laughing.

\* \* \*

'Ma's mad,' he said much later; 'you do realize that, don't you? Don't say I said so, but that's the considered opinion of Mr Lyward.'

'Mad?' I said.

'Horribly,' he said, and now he wasn't laughing, 'as mad as Flax. It was her or me, or maybe it was Captain Flax or me, come to think of it. Anyway, I had to get away from all of them. It was even the same for Hilary, with Ma: it's the same for everyone in her life. It'll be the same for you one day. You have to get away or her malevolence infects you.'

We left the swing swaying wildly in the wood, in the hope that someone would find it before it stopped and think there was a ghost about. We walked up through the wood and then beyond over a fence to a derelict church and graveyard on the hill above Finchden Manor.

That afternoon we played and we talked and we shared silences such as we never had. For the first time I knew what I had always believed in my heart, that it would have been good to have a brother who was a friend.

We didn't do or say much. We just walked and explored and looked back at the view below, where Finchden poked its roofs and chimneys above the trees.

'How long are you going to stay here?'

'For ever, I hope,' said Michael. 'I never want to live under the same roof as that woman again.'

He looked at me a long time and said, 'You're stronger than me, Jimmy, you always were, so you can survive her. But I'm not and I can't. You *know* that.'

If I did, I couldn't have put it into words. But him saying it made me believe it. His words that afternoon were a secret army that came to my defence in times yet to come.

*You're stronger . . .*

But that night, sleeping in a dormitory with several boys including Michael, making do with a mattress on the floor, I did not feel stronger. Silent tears wet my pillow. They were the tears of farewell. I had been sent not to give comfort but to say goodbye.

* * *

In the morning Michael was his old self again – distant, cold, removed. He left me to my own devices and I eked the day out with Alan for company, and Mr Lyward watching, and listening.

It was Alan who walked me back down to the station on Monday morning, not Michael. For a few brief hours that Saturday afternoon Michael had opened a door to me, and then afterwards he thrust me back outside into the cold and closed it up again for ever.

I never said 'Goodbye, Michael,' not then at any rate. But I thought those words as my train pulled out of the station: *Goodbye Michael, goodbye,* as I stared and stared at the other rail track until it turned into a blur and all I knew was I had left him far behind.

Ma said she would be there when I got home, but I didn't expect her to be and she wasn't.

But nor was Granny.

The house was empty apart from me, wandering from room to room downstairs, wondering whether to light a fire, and then looking in on Granny's. It was only after several minutes that I realized that something was wrong: there was no ticking of her clock. In fact, her clock had gone. And so had other things. There was just a counter-pane, no sheets and blankets; and the pillowcases had gone from the pillows.

I crept from her room, not wanting to believe what I was thinking. I didn't go into Ma's room, but I peered round its door and looked at her solitary bed. The room smelt of her. It made me feel sick.

I wanted a friend to go and talk to, a boy like me. But I didn't know one. Not a single one.

I went up to the Front and down onto the beach and walked along the shore all the way to the ruins on the shore at the far end of the Promenade, where I climbed up on the buttress that was all that remained of the old castle and stared across the Dunes.

I was not ready to go there yet.

I turned and went home, walking towards the last of the sunlight in a cold clear sky.

When I got home Ma was still not back.

I lit the fire but however hard I tried it just guttered and never got warm.

Ma arrived back eventually, after dark.

'You're early,' she said, and lots of other words, explaining, justifying, avoiding.

*Ma's mad.*

'Where's . . . ?' I began.

'Your grandmother's gone into an old people's home which is very nice and the best thing and that was this morning because her mind and body are breaking down and she'll be happier there, much happier . . .'

Granny had gone. Ma had packed me off to see Michael so she could get rid of Granny in peace.

I felt cold inside, icy cold; and I knew I hated Ma and that she was mad.

'What a strange time it's been,' sighed Ma as if it was she who had made all the effort of change. There was excited satisfaction in her voice. The sound of the approach of liberty.

'First Michael with his nervous breakdown and now Granny! What a lot of changes in a few weeks. But things have a funny way of being for the best, hard though it is for the rest of us, and . . .'

As Ma talked on I felt the cold house and its rooms stretching away around me in no particular direction, like the coming weeks and months and years. I felt something breaking down inside me.

*Granny gone.*

There was a feeling of absolute fear inside me and of desolation, unutterable, complete.

Ma talked smoothly on and each word she uttered compounded my hatred.

'Light the fire again, Jimmy,' she said, suddenly changing the subject, 'and I'll make us a cup of tea. I've got some doughnuts as a celebration.'

Her celebration.

This time the fire crackled and burst to life. By its flames Ma's cheeks looked red and her eyes bright.

I had never seen her look so well.

'Is Granny coming back?' I asked.

'I doubt it,' said Ma firmly.

'But some of her things are still in her room,' I said.

'The removal men have taken most of what she wants to keep to her new room in the home. Other things will go into storage and the rest to the Salvation Army. We have to clear the room before Mr Sanders comes to redecorate next week. Your grandmother was becoming unclean.'

It sounded like Granny was an old flea-ridden bitch that had just been put down.

I went up to my room and sat on my bed, not sure what to do.

A nervous breakdown, that's what Michael had.

Unclean, that was what Granny was.

And me?

A nuisance now, until the day came when it was time for me to leave the house for good.

I felt the feeling of breakdown inside, and fear, and the threat of a return to Darktime.

*You're stronger than I am*, Michael had said.

I put castle walls around the Darktime inside me, and I closed up the gates against it.

I opened my window as far as I could to feel the salt sea breeze on my face, and to hear the sound of the sea.

I got into bed and when Ma came up to say goodnight I pretended I was already asleep. Not that she ever did more than stand at the door. She never came in and bent down and kissed me.

I pretended to sleep, but really I was listening to the sea, I was breathing the air and I was suddenly thinking a terrible thought: *I bet she's got rid of Michael's things just like she has Granny's.* My heart beat painfully at the idea of it.

The moment Ma was gone I jumped out of bed and poked my head round the door into Michael's room.

Everything loose was gone, including the curtains and the blankets and sheets and mattress off the bed. I looked in one of the drawers: empty. There was never much of Michael in that room but now there was nothing at all. Just the dry, clean smell of him and that was on the way out because she had left the window open to get rid of every last trace.

I stood in my bare feet on the linoleum floor and knew for sure that he had gone for good. It felt as if a murder had been committed and I would for ever be alone.

I went back to bed and had another thought: finding a friend would be good, because I was going to need one now that Granny had gone.

*Jimmy, you're to wake me up . . .*

It was Granny's voice from my memory, and it made me smile. Ma could not crawl inside my head and stop my thoughts and memories, or pack them up and put them out for the dustbin men. There was a point beyond which even Ma could not go.

But I was wrong. I didn't know that a mother can haunt a mind or that a ghost needs exorcism.

Darkness fell, and the sound of the sea grew and grew.

Directly below me, where Granny had been, was just emptiness in the dark, a place where an old lady would never again weep in her sleep for the African Gentleman; or ever again make cocoa and crumpets for the grandchild she loved.

I lay listening to the sea until another thought came into my mind: *Granny's in her new bed tonight and I bet she's lying awake and thinking of me, I bet she is.*

I lay thinking and listening until the rush and the swish of the sea round my room, and the thought of Granny thinking of me, put peace in my mind and swept my bed away and me inside it, out across the open sea, right across it, for ever away from Ma.

# 21

## FLOWERS OF THE DUNES

For many months after Michael's disappearance I suffered a sense of abandonment, even though he had never given me much cause to feel wanted.

Another winter came and Ma and I had Christmas alone, except for a brief, unhappy visit from Granny. The dark gale-ridden winter along our shore mirrored my mood.

But then there came the miracle of spring when each extra moment of new light, each moment of unaccustomed warmth, eased my mind and put into me a growing sense of liberty; and that special, magical day, which comes each year when nature suddenly finds the strength to run on ahead joyously, freeing itself from winter's darkness.

The day when, along our shore, the sea begins to gleam again, and the shingle sparkles with the new-born light.

I got up early and eager, hurried my cornflakes, gulped down a cup of tea and ran up to the Front.

Out to sea on the eastern horizon, towards the Goodwin Sands, steamers came and went, their black smoke trailing. Some went north towards the Thames estuary, others south down the Channel, towards the open Atlantic, and from there on to the wide ways of the Seven Seas. Above and around me seagulls flew wildly. Like me, they saw a day so wonderful they could not decide which way to go.

It was a day for exploration and discovery and after sitting down on a bench and breathing it all in for a while, I jumped off the sea wall onto the shingle with a crash and headed north along the beach, clambering over each groyne as it came, watching the small waves retreating ever lower to reveal the sand-with-pebbles that lay at the low-tide mark.

Gulls rose screaming at my approach, while two hundred yards offshore, necks thrust forward like black spears, cormorants skimmed south past me just above the waves, towards their staging post, the Stoning Bank Buoy beyond the Pier, their feathers green-black in the sun.

I crunched on along the wet shingle towards the Dunes, clambering over groynes, skimming stones across the sea, picking up the flotsam and then discarding it, stopping to stand and stare, stand and smell, stand and breathe, oblivious of time.

That first day of spring when the world of people felt old and weary from winter but nature was young again and filled with hope, I stood between the two and chose to venture where I had not been before.

In turning northwards I had made my choice: it was time to discover the Dunes. I was big enough to do so and I wasn't afraid of the open places any more. I reached the ramparts of the old castle ruins, climbed up them, and looked across the grassy sand hills of Stoning Golf Course, ran down the shingle bank onto a sandy pathway, and headed out into my new world.

I heard it before I saw it, high, high above my head: the trilling of a bird, flapping, rolling, floating against the bright sky. I climbed a slope to get a better view but it only drifted further away, further north, further across the Dunes.

Walking on the golf links themselves was not allowed, because a big notice said so, but there was no one there to see and the wires of the boundary fence along the path by the shingle had long since rusted into decay and broken.

That day the Dunes became part of my world and offered no barriers to me.

I walked through the fence and with craning neck I followed the bird onto the golf course until I realized that it was merely keeping its distance ahead of me, no more than that. I was not following it; the bird was leading me on.

I stopped and stood still, then I dropped right down by some gorse, and at once the bird dropped fluttering down below the crest of the dune ahead. I crawled up to spy on it and there it was, frail and speckled, hard to see, tail wagging, uneasy at having lost sight of me.

Then, growing impatient with being still, I rose and ran through the grass, crested the slope, ran helter-skelter down towards the bird, then up another and on, on, running and running, the bird rising up into the sky in flight once more, running and running and feeling the freedom of the sea air and leaving the shadows of the North End far behind until it was being out of breath that forced me to stop.

Panting, breathless, half laughing, I crouched down. Then suddenly, breath recovered, on and up the next dune after the bird, reached the top and starting the run down again . . .

'Oh! Oh!'

I almost tripped over a woman, or maybe she was a girl, kneeling on the ground looking at something through a magnifying glass.

'Oh!' we said together

I thought I was going to be in trouble, but she seemed all right. Somewhere above me the bird started to trill again and my eyes were drawn back to the sky to find it.

'You're trying to catch the skylark! You'll never succeed!' she said with a laugh, following my gaze as we both shielded our eyes against the bright sky. The bird now had a name, and knowing its name, I felt as if I had caught and stolen something of it.

'Um, yes,' I said, and then, not knowing what else to say, I wandered on.

She wore glasses and a tweed skirt and something I had not seen since the days of Uncle Max and Auntie Fiona: walking boots.

'I . . .' she began, but I felt awkward there and the bird was moving on, singing high into the white of the sky

'Well . . . bye!' she called after me.

'Bye!' I said.

That was my first meeting with Harriet.

In the weeks and months that followed I began to discover the life that lived in the grassy sandy shadows of the Dunes – the birds, the mammals and the flowers of marsh and shore. Slowly, I discovered the amphibians, newts and toads and frogs; and when I dared venture north and west over the barrier ditches and dykes filled with water, I discovered the slippery eel and the vole; and further still over distance and time, in the desolate reaches where the River Stane met the sea, I watched the passage of migrating birds, and the busy life of river mud and shelly shore, which looks dead only to untutored eyes.

The Dunes stretched inland from the shingle bank for less than half a mile, to the ancient highway that ran from Stoning to Stannick.

They went five miles northward from Rampart Road to Stannick Bay. Its northernmost piece of land, the lonely windswept Staneflete where the Stane wound its way to its estuary and the seabirds roosted undisturbed, was almost too far to walk from Stoning in a single day.

These things I knew from Ma's Ordnance Survey map, which I taught myself to read. There were so many things to find out there across the sand hills to the sea when I found the courage to venture that far alone.

Meanwhile there was everything to discover among the dunes closer to home, the greatest thing being space, vast secret space, in which there were a thousand places to hide, and watch, or lie on my back in the sun and watch the larks before trying to track down their nests.

There were rabbits to chase, golfers to watch, golf balls to find, and here and there, already rusting and crumbling away, and becoming more deeply buried under brambles with each passing year, defence works and gun emplacements from the War.

Apart from golfers on the links, there were few people about. Shore fishermen used the path on the lee side of the shingle bank to reach their beats, rather than trudge along the heavy shingle of the shore itself. A few bait diggers came and went from Stannick Bay, though Mr Bubbles was the only regular one from Stoning, and there was the farmer who worked his fields and livestock on the marshy fields on the far west side of the Dunes.

Sometimes children came with kites, but they stayed near the Rampart estate, and once in a while I saw the girl I had stumbled across who knew the name of birds. She waved to me and I waved back, but we skirted round one another, respecting each other's privacy. But I liked it when I saw she was about because it was like finding a friendly traveller on the road.

But apart from us and those few others, the Dunes was not a popular place: too desolate, too lonely, too far from the comforts and securities of the town.

When she discovered I was going there nearly every day, Ma said, 'There's strange men on the Dunes, so be careful.'

'Strange men?' I repeated darkly, thinking of Seddy the Salvation Army man who tried to teach me to be musical with his hands on my privates.

'And unpleasant men,' she added, liking to dwell on her own fears. 'Do not forget Eliza Mayne.'

Whoever she was, I didn't. I found her first on the OS map on which her memorial stone was clearly marked, and one day set off to find it. Her stone rose among the grass on the spot where more than a century before, it said, she had been 'most foully done to death'. The wind stirred in the husky marram grass and I looked over my shoulder quickly but saw not a soul in sight. At dusk, as shadows descended, there were many ghosts of people like Eliza Mayne who had had reason to cross the Dunes over the centuries, hurrying along in fear of what followed behind, anxious to get their journey done and reach the safe lights of town.

You could hear the shuffle of their feet along the ancient highway and in the rustle of the grass in the ditch alongside. While on the narrow concrete track nearby, made for the Volunteer Observer Corps and no more than two and a half feet wide, you could almost hear the rattle of the Raleigh bicycles of the aeroplane spotters and gunners if you closed your eyes.

'Jimmy, Jimmy, where have you been?' Ma would ask when I drifted home after dusk in the evenings of that first summer across the Dunes. But there wasn't much interest in her voice.

Even if she had been interested there was no easy answer to give, for when I had roamed so far and seen so much I hardly knew myself where I had been or what I had seen; and anyway, what I saw and experienced shifted and changed in my mind. I was not time's servant, but time played tricks with me and my perceptions.

*Where have you been?*

*Across the Dunes* was the only answer big enough.

I discovered only slowly why it was so few children ventured out alone upon the Dunes. They were scared off by the gangs of rough Secondary Modern boys who came out of the Rampart estate by the nearby gasworks on bicycles, with catapults and kicking balls. They didn't live in the North End so, not knowing them, I wasn't scared of them.

Anyway, they never got far. Their bikes got clogged up with sand, and footballs got lost in the inaccessible ditches. They chased me once or twice but by then I had made the Dunes my own, and I ran like a fox, back and forth, in and out of sight, following the paths I knew or had made for myself. Until, puffing, I lay on the ground and watched them disappear in the wrong direction. They taught me to keep my eyes open and watch out for myself.

I often lay on the ground, using the vegetation as cover, protected from the winds, warm in the sun. I would stare at ants and flowers, the ants the little red ones that lived in the sand, the flowers special to the dunes.

My favourite was a yellow one that grew close to the ground and had a flower no bigger than a daisy. I had seen it before but not on the dunes, and it annoyed me that I could not remember where. It was like an old friend from good times gone but whose name I could not remember.

One July day, lying on my tummy looking into the yellow depths of that tiny flower, a shadow fell across the grass around me and I could not make my escape.

'Botanising?' the person said.

I could not see the face against the brightness of the sky above me, but the voice said it was a girl.

I sat up, not knowing what to say.

'Do you know its name?' she said, squatting down. She was the girl I had first met, and seen so often since, dressed in a green tweed skirt and wearing flat shoes that day.

As she squatted opposite me and looked at the flower, my eyes caught a glimpse of brown stocking tops, and the white of knickers. I didn't know where to look after that, but I knew where I wanted to.

She always carried a khaki haversack and wore a scarf over her head against the wind. She looked like a teacher but was younger than any that ever taught me. She looked healthier too and her stride had more purpose than theirs, as I knew when I had seen her and then not seen her disappearing amongst the nooks and crannies of the Dunes, and amongst the vegetation of dykes.

*Do you know its name?*

I wanted to lean forward and touch where her suspender pressed against her thigh.

'Er, no,' I said.

'Hello again! I often see you on the Dunes.'

'Yes,' I said.

'Don't you have any friends?'

She said it warmly, as if surprised, so I gave her an answer that told no lie but avoided the truth: 'Not any that want to come on the Dunes.'

'I'm the same,' she said, adding, 'and that flower's called tormentil.'

She caught me staring and moved from a squat to a sideways sit, becoming decent once again.

'Tormentil,' I repeated, shifting from one small excitement to another.

That was the first wild flower whose name I learnt in English, except for the obvious ones like daisy, daffodil and dandelion, stinging nettle and wild rose.

'Herbalists used it to stop pain, hence its name,' she said.

I didn't know what a herbalist was. Or exactly what 'hence' meant. But I could guess.

'So it's a medicinal plant.'

'Oh,' I said.

'Every plant has a name and lots have medicinal uses.'

I stared into the rich warm yellow centre of the tiny plant and whispered 'tormentil', not knowing a new door to knowledge had just been opened up for me.

'Every plant has a name?' I repeated.

She nodded, smiling. She moved to the grass next to me, opened her haversack and produced a well-thumbed book. It had page after page of pictures of flowers, hundreds of them. I leafed through them and I smelt her scent and her. It was so good.

'What's that?' I asked, pointing to one I knew and hardly daring to breathe.

'Bladder campion.'

'It grows across the Dunes where the shingle starts,' I said, feeling a mixture of things. Her mouth was red.

'Yes, yes it does,' she said as I looked at her red mouth moving. 'It's got a little puffy bit like a bladder underneath the flower, hence *its* name.'

Her voice was soft.

I worked out what 'hence' meant.

'And this one . . .'

I pored over the italic print.

'And . . .'

'These are flowers of the dunes,' she said. 'They've all got names.'

The world had swirled about my head for a time what with her being so close, but I came back to normal again.

We sat together in silence staring across the Dunes towards the rise of the shingle bank, to where the flowers of the sea grew.

'Is this a flower of the dunes?' I said, nodding towards the tormentil.

She hesitated.

'Partly. It's a flower of heath and mountain and it survives where others don't because its flower can grow so close to the ground that rabbits and deer can't crop them.'

'Mountain?'

'Mountains really,' she said.

The word stirred me as if I had heard someone calling my name from a place I once knew: 'Jimmy, Jimmy, *Jimmy* . . .' Then a restless breeze seemed to come through me and I stood up, unsettled, looking about, seeking something I had only just then realized I had lost but whose name I did not know.

'I climbed a mountain once with my Uncle Max and Aunt Fiona and it . . . it . . .'

I remembered them leaving me near the top and walking off a little way with the wind and talking and laughing. That was the moment he asked her to marry him and standing there in the Dunes I remembered that between me and them, on that mountain, was short green grass all speckled with hundreds of the tiny flowers of tormentil, a carpet of golden stars.

I missed Uncle Max and Auntie Fiona, and I missed the mountains, which was strange because I had only ever been there once and barely thought of them since.

'It was called Moel Siabod where this grew, where I first saw it,' I said.

I felt the call of the mountains so strong it was somewhere halfway between pain and pleasure.

'I never went back, and they went to America.'

The girl looked at me, not recognizing the name Moel Siabod, but I recognized something in her. That something was what Auntie Fiona also had. It was warmth and naturalness. From that day I could place the feeling, though I had no word for it, that would be part of the treasure I was looking for, part of the home I wanted to find once more. That place would have the warmth of a girl-woman like her.

'You know a lot about flowers,' I said.

'I'm doing biology for one of my O levels at Dover College, the only one in my year who is. Part of it is botany. I'm doing a project about the flowers of the Dunes.'

'How old are you?'

'Sixteen,' she said.

She looked about thirty to me.

'And you?'

'Fourteen. I'm at Stannick Grammar. My name's Jimmy Rova.'

'I'm Harriet Fosse.'

She reached out and we shook hands as if relatives had introduced us; but it didn't matter – we had touched more deeply already over the flowers of tormentil.

Almost all the friends I ever made were made suddenly and without meaning to, like on that day. I would be on a road, the road turned a sudden corner and there they were waiting to be found, as if they had been there fully formed since eternity waiting for me to come along. From that moment on those friends journeyed with me, if not in person, then in memory.

That moment remembering a lost scene in Wales was such a moment when the road turned, and she was there, one way or another, there for ever.

'Got to go,' I said, suddenly embarrassed. Close to, I did not worry so much how old she was.

'Um, well . . . I expect we will meet again,' she said. 'Bye!'

'Um, bye.'

I walked back across the Dunes and by the time I reached the Promenade again, and then clambered down onto the beach to throw stones in the sea, I thought I had forgotten all about her.

# 22

# TIDAL CURRENTS

That same year I met Harriet a hand-me-down bicycle came my way. It was a light blue racer with drop handlebars, nearly falling apart. Arthur Sanders showed me how to check the brakes, adjust the saddle and orientate the handlebars. Even so, it was a stretch to reach the pedals and I wobbled around on it for a time until the day came when it seemed suddenly to shrink about me and fit.

Things were changing quickly and there was something in the air that year which put strange and sudden moods into me like squalls across the sea. I would grab the bike and shoot off along Nore Street towards the Dunes. I would race along the concrete wartime cycle track, cycling too fast, rising up and down and flying in the air, crashing on the broken bits, veering off up dunes and then bumping and wobbling back towards the path, the wheels getting buckled with sand in the chain

I did mad things, strange things, whooping and shouting into the wind and up towards the larks, but croakily, because my voice was beginning to break.

At home, with Michael gone, there was nothing I wanted to say to Ma or to her occasional friends.

'It's a stage they go through,' she would say of me, frowning or smiling, depending on her mood. We argued often, with hours and sometimes days of silence in between.

I refused to go out with her to the shops, I refused most things: *You can't make me . . . You can't . . .*

'But you could have been there and back to get the bread in the time it's taken you to refuse.'

'I won't and you can't . . .'

Her red raw hitting hand would rise up sometimes but I was quicker now and I dodged and paused at a distance, daring her to try again.

'Bloody boys,' she would say in a voice that combined hatred with boredom. 'Bloody, bloody children.'

I used to come home longing for the welcome that was never there. Instead, there was just a note on her kitchen table about the food she had made, or half made, which had her grey hairs in it sometimes and made me feel sick.

Ma could be nice but usually she was not. She grew hot and bothered and there was sweat in the hairs on her upper lip and she had to sit down a lot. It was best to keep out of her way. She had always been mad; now she was getting madder still. She did not say that life had passed her by and her best opportunities had gone, not then; and if she had I doubt I would have listened or been interested.

Yet, sometimes, in the evening, by the fire in winter and out in our yard in the summer, when she was mellow like sun-warmed bricks, she talked about her past: my aunt and my uncle, Grandfather, Oxford, punting on the river with fellow undergraduates, Howard Scupple and his friends, cycling to the Rose Revived; and Spain in the early thirties, where she went when her student days were done and to break away from Howard for a time.

I would listen then and ask questions.

'Can you speak Spanish, Ma?'

'Oh yes . . .' she would say, her face creasing into a mask of smiling memory of things I was too young to understand, or things she never talked about because to do so might mean she lost the memory of them for ever.

'I know the Spanish word for "oranges",' I said once. 'It's *naranjas*.'

'Oh,' she replied, 'ah . . .' but made no more comment than that.

The memories Ma shared were the dark ones she wanted to get rid of. The best, the deepest, the ones that sustained her long life of living and half-living in Stoning, she hoarded for herself in her own heart, unshared. It would have been hard to guess that it was the things she did not talk about, the years she never mentioned, which were the war years, the time of the conception and birth of Michael and myself, that were the ones that mattered most to her.

How could I know that among those wild and scented flowers that she kept alive in her too-secret garden was the truth about the people that had mattered to her, including the Man Who Was?

The last time her hitting hand was put to use on me was during those vibrant moody months when I met Harriet and had my first bicycle. It caught me straight and hard across my face and blood came from my nose.

It was in her filthy kitchen with the smell of fish and cabbage in the air. She had been in a mood all week. I smirked once too often and she hit me. I stood in shock, looking at her, blood trickling, blood on my sleeve and hand, blood dripping onto the grubby quarry tiles below in among the grease and woodlice.

We stared at each other in silence and I knew a boundary had been crossed that put me on one side and she on another, a boundary between two countries, one of which was about to declare its independence from the other.

'I'm going to the Dunes,' I said, and from that moment they became the heartland of my inner life. I had outgrown the loft in the boathouse and my bedroom, and now I had outgrown the house.

I went there on my bike, pedalling stolidly, not wiping the blood from my nose and mouth, carrying my war wound, caught in a spiralling mood of anger and hurt, frustration and loneliness and self pity.

*Bloody, bloody Ma*, I thought, and then retreated from my ironic smirk at echoing her so cleverly, uneasy that I could subvert her voice inside myself so well. I felt it was she herself inside my head not simply my idea of her. I had a first inkling that it might be harder than I thought to be rid of her.

I had a realization of why Michael had had to have a breakdown to escape. I had the first sense of an inner battle looming. Meanwhile, I needed the windswept Dunes to clear my head and cleanse myself of her. So I raced on.

'Hello, Jimmy,' Arthur called out from Coastguard Mews, but I ignored him.

Nor did I respond to Harriet's waves across the Dunes.

I cycled until I grew too tired to push against the sand and tussocky grass, and then pushed my bike to the seventh tee, above which the highest dune of all rose up. I dropped the bike and climbed the dune to stand facing the wind and roar my croaking boy-man roar, trying to expel Ma out of my head via my mouth, and thinking that I had.

*Bloody, bloody . . .*

I broke free of the foul taste of Ma and ran down the dune and over the grassy rises and falls to the foot of the shingle bank. Then, pretending to be a Marine being punished, I ran up and up it as hard as I could, legs ever more aching, feet ever more tired, until, arriving at the top, I stood heaving and breathless and surveyed the whole of the world beyond the North End – out towards the vast sea, then north and north-west beyond the dirty chalk cliffs of Thanet along the wiggly eastern edges of the map of the British Isles to places whose names I knew but to which I had no hope of ever going: the Pennines and Scotland and Cape Wrath.

Then south and west, along the shingle shores to Dorset, and on along the rugged shoreline of Devon and Cornwall and out into the sea across the Atlantic to America, impossible to ever see so far except in my mind's eye.

Then finally, south and further south over the Seven Seas, south towards the sun and the light and the lands of warmth where Arthur Mee had sometimes taken me on camels in the desert, and by motorboats upriver, and by dhows towards paddy fields.

Up there on the shingle I stood, the vision of my solitary journeys from the North End crumbling even as I first grasped them, slipping away, dreams as fruitless and hopeless as the desiccated seaweed that lay broken at my feet, disappearing into the shingle whose stones had long since lost touch with the tides.

Until at last, summoning up some final energy and faith that I might one day escape, I looked much nearer, towards where I knew

France lay, though it wasn't visible that day, and said to myself, 'One day I'll go there and put the sea between Ma and me for good.'

It was a promise of a kind.

I retreated down to the Dunes and back to my real world.

I set off northwards to walk further across the Dunes than I ever had before, leaving my bike in some gorse bushes to pick up on my return. I walked steadily, my voice half boy but my body half man: strong, wiry, feeling its coming power. On and on to leave Ma further behind and alone in our dark house, until the Dunes turned into a posh golf course where the fences were repaired. I was forced back towards the shingle bank and up it to discover I had reached Stannick Bay and that there on the stretching sands with their shallow pools and seaweed – darker, taller, broader than all the other bait diggers – was someone I knew: Mr Bubbles.

'Hello, lad,' he said. 'So you finally made it here. You've taken your time!'

It was four years or more since he had saved me from the waves off the North End and in all that time I had never been to see where he plied his daily trade. He had often asked me to come and join him bait digging but until then I never had.

His voice was as deep and shifting as shingle at night. I grinned with pleasure to be with him where he worked. He showed me how to dig lugworm from the sand with his short-tined, long-handled fork, specially made. He worked fast, for the worms were fast as well, now digging, now bending to catch and tin them, now moving to another spot, the rusty tins he put them in left behind in each area of digging to be retrieved later. He dug for the worms in long trenches down the sand, towards the sea.

The holes he made filled almost at once with sea water and became sky reflections in the sand. Black-tipped, sharp-winged terns flocked over the places he had worked, hoping to find a scrap of worm, or hovered over his paint tins, too timid to risk diving down to rob the contents but almost doing so again and again as they weaved and dropped and encouraged each other to take the plunge.

'Watch out for herring gull, though,' he warned. 'They're not so bashful as the terns. Here, lad, bring them tins up here; the gulls are coming right on cue. Quick.'

A couple of juvenile herring gulls were sufficient to displace the whole tumbling flock of terns, though reluctantly. But at the sight of a marauding greater black-backed gull they all evaporated into the bright air towards Ramsgate and Cliftonville.

'Take 'em to my transport and cover 'em,' said Mr Bubbles, 'and I'll be with you in a jiff to have a bite of lunch.'

I hurried to grab the tins and took them to his bicycle where I covered them with his black felt coat, stained with a thousand such misuses. Mr Bubbles did not trouble with the new when the old would do.

I wiped rust off my hands and watched him dig his last trench. I did not know the word 'balletic' or the meaning of perfection, or that Mr Bubbles was on the biggest, most beautiful stage in the world doing what he did best, better than anyone.

He danced the dance of the bait digger before my eyes and his orchestra was the sea and the wind, his stage the sands.

A short walk, the briefest of stares at the sand, the quick first plunge of the fork and then the rhythmic digging backwards down the sand towards the sea, bending to pluck up the worms and drop them in the tin, so fast, so efficient, so perfect.

He straightened up one last time, paused to look about him and then over his shoulder towards the sea, and then came slowly up the beach. His boots were the biggest man ever wore.

He bent over the tins and studied their writhing, heaving contents and seemed well pleased. Then he leant closer to one and removed a lugworm, bigger than most.

He took it back to one of the earlier trenches he had dug and dropped it in the water there.

'The one that got away,' he said. 'There's always one. It might be me, it might be you. Remember that. Now . . .'

It was his ritual, his version of fate, to liberate one of his own captives.

He had propped his bike up against the wooden remnants of a

groyne whose vast length seaward from where we sat had mostly been swept away over decades of gales, leaving only a few black stumps in a line towards the sea. Tied tightly to the bike's crossbar was an ancient and cracked woman's shopping bag made of once-shiny American cloth. He untied it carefully and set it down as if it was the finest bag in the world. He took a white embroidered cloth from it and laid it on the shingle before me. Then he took out a succession of packages wrapped in brown paper and tied with white twine, with an order and precision that made them seem like gifts for a god.

Which they were. They were his lunch – delicate white sand-wiches, a twist of salad, a small bottle of dressing, sausages of a kind and rich scent I had never known, seemingly a hundred things – made by Mrs Bubbles, his Véronique.

He cut the string of each package not with the fish gutting knife he always carried in his belt but with the silver blade of a pearl-handled fruit knife so delicate that it looked as if it would fall apart in his thick, stained fingers. Then he took out a half bottle of white wine and a glass tumbler sturdy enough not to break on his daily journey across the Dunes. He laid the food and wine out with great care, so that when it was all finally set and ready it looked in perfect harmony with itself, and the cloth, and the seashore.

'There,' he said, 'help yourself. Try the sausage. Try the tomatoes. Try 'em together as intended.'

We sat surrounded by the sounds of sea and sky, and by tins of lugworms, entwining wetly, and had a meal that taught me the beauty of food that is made with love.

'Try some. French boys do.'

He handed me the tumbler half filled with wine.

It was the first I had ever tasted and in its taste, as in the memory of it, was the tang of the salt sea wind and a man who held in his great, calloused, rusty hands the many secrets of happiness.

'The days she does not make my lunch I know not to come away for worms but to stay nearby in the North End doing jobs with Freddie, for she may need me. Or if I must, I make sure there's someone near in my place. Freddie, or . . .'

And he named the names of friends he trusted until he came to the last one: '. . . and in latter years, you lad, you too. You've done your turn.'

We sat in silence and I basked in the compliment he made so naturally, of counting me a friend.

'What do you have for lunch when Mrs Bubbles doesn't make it?'

The question came from me without warning and for a moment I wished I had not asked it.

But he laughed and said, 'Spam or corned beef in cut white bread from Fender's and a bottle of mild from the back door of the King's Head.'

He winked and drank the last of the wine, tilting back his head for the last drop, like a priest at the end of Holy Communion.

'There's blood around your nose,' said Mr Bubbles finally, after he had packed it all up again and studied me awhile. He liked to take his time.

I said nothing.

'Who have you been scrapping with?'

'Ma.'

'You need a friend of your own age to fight with, Jimmy, not your Ma.'

'I know,' I said.

'Well then . . . as for scrapping . . .'

I look up at him, and then at his great hands.

'Do you remember my advice to you on your first day at school?'

I nodded.

'I did what you said once or twice, but that's all I've needed to. No one ever bullies me.'

He nodded appreciatively.

Then he frowned.

'From what I've heard, school's not favoured you much, lad, has it?'

A gull screamed above our head and in my heart.

I said nothing.

'Well . . . stick at it, lad. It'll come right. You'll be glad of your education one day. Now, it's time to get on. Where are you headed?'

I shrugged, not knowing. I looked across the bay, towards Staneflete where I knew the Stane joined the sea.

'It's further off than you might think. Hours away by foot, impossible on transport without destroying your machine. Salt and sand are the enemies of ball bearings and chains. Not a place to get benighted is the Stane, the sea comes in and catches you out. One moment it's a baby asleep, the next it's a gang of villains at your heels. Be careful going that way, Jimmy. Start early and stay near the high-tide mark.'

He stared towards far-off Staneflete.

'Mind you, the tidal riverbanks there have got the best ragworm in the whole of East Kent. One of these days I'll take you. Best not to go there alone the first time, especially if you've had a scrap with your Ma and are all topsy-turvied in your head. Now . . .'

After that day I often crossed the Dunes to seek out Mr Bubbles where he worked, in summer and in winter, fair wind or foul. He got me a fork like he had so I could dig bait too, which he sold for me, giving me the profit. That was the first real earnings I ever made, not counting the money Mr Shaw gave me for tending his plant pots.

Often we barely talked. Sometimes I wandered off, a little way towards the Stane, as I too called it now, until, sensing he was staring after me and concerned, I would turn back.

He taught me to dig bait.

He taught me the names of all the seabirds and the difference between the migrants and the indigenous species.

He showed me where the wartime defences had been.

He showed me how to tie a fork to a bike so it wouldn't impale me if ever I fell off.

He showed me the places for night fishing, where a yard or two, one way or another, or in the length of a cast, could make all the difference to having a catch or having none, depending, that is, on the wind and the state of the tide and one thing and another. Rough though he seemed, Mr Bubbles taught me the meaning of finesse.

One day I said, 'You never told me about how you rescued Mrs Bubbles in the war.'

'Didn't I, lad?'

'No.'

'Hmmm,' he said, 'I don't s'pose I did.'

It was Granny who taught me when to be silent and I stayed silent then. He ate a bit more of his lunch and he drank a bit more of his wine.

Still I stayed silent.

He glowered at the terns and then at me, but I didn't say a thing.

Then he said, 'Fish don't stop biting because of war, Jimmy, so Freddie and his brother weren't averse to a bit of fishing work under cover of darkness on the grounds south of the Goodwins. Nor were the Frogs, and when they met mid-Channel it wasn't for idle gossip and it wasn't fish they exchanged.

'Course Freddie's brother was never one to smuggle, so once in a while I went along to a rendezvous.'

'I thought you never went in boats.'

'Wartime's different and a spot of contraband is different again. Still didn't like it, though, so when I was working the boat with Freddie I pretended I was on the Dover bus. Anyway, in 1941, by when Jerry occupied north France, Freddie got word of a cargo of wine and along I went. Pitch black and fog, spitting with rain – just Freddie's cup of tea, except he got lost, the silly bugger.

'Ever seen a mine close to? Well, don't. It's got bits that stick out which you're not to touch. "What's that, Freddie?" I asked. "A bit of flotsam," he said.

'We ended up safe and sound and in one piece on the rocks below Cap Gris Nez and guess who's trading the wine? Jerries and Frogs together. Talk about bloody collaboration. And guess who they've got with them looking like death? Mrs Bubbles, that's who. "She comes with the cargo," they said.

' "Bloody hell," said Freddie, who is not given to swearing, "she's not coming with us. I'm married!"

'Well, I looked at her and it was foggy and there was no light to speak of, so all I could see was the shape, which was womanly. I never was any good with women but I knew treasure when I saw it.

' "I'm not," I said, and I heaved her in along with the wine and laid her down in the bilges out of sight. Couldn't see her face till dawn when we were approaching Stoning beach and I never saw a sadder sight. Like a winged bird on the shore, waiting for death.

' "What are we going to do with her?" said Freddie.

' "Get her off before your brother sees her," says I, "because he wouldn't approve and she'll be carted off as a spy."

'So we beached the boat upwind of the usual pitch and I picked her up and told Freddie to send his missus to Budd Street when his business was done. Then I carried her down as quick as I could by way of Anchor Field and Nore Street to my place and when I carried her over my threshold I looked at her and she looked at me and that was all the vows took and ever needed, that and no more.

'I put her upstairs and Mrs Hammel tended her for months on end and hardly let me see her.

' "What's wrong with her?" I asked Mrs Hammel.

' "Not your business, nor Freddie's, nor anybody's now. She'll be all right if you leave her be. She'll talk in her own time."

' "She don't speak English," I said.

' "Then teach her."

'So I did, starting with that framed photograph she had, because it was all she looked at in them early days. "Photo" wasn't difficult but "brother" was harder, I seem to recall. Anyway we taught each other what we could and one day she got up and made a meal of some fish I'd caught and I never tasted fish done like that before and I thought, "This is more than treasure, this is gold."

'Stoning in wartime was filled with all sorts of itinerant folk, and not just military. They came and went and Freddie put the word about that Véronique was all right and not to be commented on. His missus got her a job in the canteen in the High Street and after that she fitted in and made a life, a life with me. My luck was in, that night we found her on the shore in France. They don't come in better quality gold than Mrs Bubbles.'

He was silent a long time after that, a nice companionable silence. There was another question I wanted to ask him but I put it in the form of a statement.

'You never had children, Mr Bubbles.'

'No,' he said, 'me and Mrs Bubbles never did. She couldn't, you see, Jimmy, not after what happened in Wissant. That she couldn't do. No, she couldn't, so I couldn't.'

He looked strange so I didn't say any more.

The gulls wheeled about us and he threw them a scrap to see them dive.

He talked to me then of the birds of the shore and the currents of the sea. All sorts of things. Then and later, all sorts of things. Until one day, up there having our picnic lunch, our digging done, he finally answered that question I shouldn't have asked him.

'Mrs Bubbles wasn't the only thing made of gold I found along the shore.'

'Wasn't she?' I said, not understanding.

He shook his head and grinned and patted my arm, which he didn't often do, though he did more after that.

'You never had a dad, Jimmy, and I never had a boy. We can count ourselves lucky we found our treasures on the shore. Can't we, lad?'

I grinned and nodded and I said we could.

We never said more about it than that.

It was all that needed to be said.


On those days when he wasn't there, at the end of my bike ride along the concrete path, or my trek over the sand hills, or my trudge along the seashore finding wood and popping bladderwrack, I felt disappointed, and sat watching the sea, wondering where a boy found a friend of his own age.

One gusty, dangerous October day, I went to find Mr Bubbles but he wasn't there. Our house was full of anger and old hatreds because Granny had been allowed to visit for lunch and had not liked what she found had happened to 'her' room. I carried on walking past the lugworm place, on towards the Stane, hunched against the wind, and though the wet sand sucked at my boots I did not care whether I lived or died.

On and on as the afternoon light faded and darkness approached me from the north and the first lights of Thanet came on and the first lightships began to flash from the open sea.

Somewhere on the sands, not having reached my destination and with the sea roaring now to my right and the first star in the sky, I stopped, unutterably alone.

But not lonely.

For long moments a dark weight lifted and I watched as the first solitary star turned into a myriad, all shining ever brighter. I just stood in the fall of night and discovered the freedom of being still, glad of the people that I knew.

Then I turned back home in the darkness along the top of the shingle bank, in awe of the stars but comforted by the lights of the hurricane lamps of fishermen down along the shore.

# 23

# DROWNING

---

The September of that year, our last before O levels, we had glorious weather, a true Indian summer. Balmy days of warmth, millpond seas, men still in summer trousers, women with bronzed faces and hair tinted blonde by the extra sun.

Mr Gelato kept his ice cream hatch for serving passers-by open long after he normally closed it. At weekends visitors appeared and inhabited the beach, the sea and waves staying unusually warm, and so, unusually full of swimmers. Freddie Hammel, who normally returned his little hire fleet of skiffs and rowing boats into storage after the August Bank Holiday, kept them out on the beach by the Monarch Hotel.

The skiffs made a cheerful sight out on the sparkling sea, people larking about in them and laughing, women trying their hand at rowing, girls screaming as boys splashed them. All the fun of the family that I didn't have. I would sit on the beach in my swimming trunks, feeling bad about homework, wondering what kissing was like. It grew so hot that all of us were waiting for the weather to break, but it didn't. The sun just carried on shining and everybody laughing.

They were easy days and as school wore on my old sense of continuing failure got pushed into the background. I was able to carry on walking the Dunes in a T-shirt, and when that got too hot I went back to the beach at the top of Compass Street and lay on my back, the shingle softened by a towel, and let the sun warm my brown body as I tried not to think about girls between bouts of squally gloom inside my head that belied the sunshine all about.

\* \* \*

One Sunday morning, lying there, I was brought out of my slumber by a sudden shout of warning. It was Freddie's voice and I sat up at once. It had carried over the chatter of the many people on the beach because old Freddie was not one to shout in anger, only emergency.

At once I looked towards his white hut. He was standing at the edge of the low sea wall. He had cupped his hands and he was bawling across the milky surface of the water at a man who had rented a skiff. The man was no more than a hundred yards out and he had two children in the prow of the craft clutching its sides. The tide was halfway down, which explained why his craft was drifting northward parallel with the shore.

Freddie was shouting because the man, dark haired, had left the oars loose in the rowlocks and had done what no one is meant to do in a skiff: he'd stood up, legs apart, and started to rock the craft from one side to another.

You could hear the knock of rowlock and oar on the wood, you could hear the slosh of the water – so calm was the day, so gentle the onshore breeze. You could hear his laughter, which seemed to mock the children's sudden screams.

Because the boat, tipping too far one way, began to fill with water and the man, trying to straighten it, tipped it too far the other. The water that had been shipped inside sloshed across to the other side of the craft and the screams grew frantic. Freddie shouted again and suddenly and terribly the boat turned turtle and the man and the children disappeared into the sea.

Yet even then the chatter on the beach continued, and kids laughed in the waves along the shore. Only a few of us had seen what happened and understood why it was that old Freddie had started running down the beach. He ran to the skiff nearest to the sea and leant his weight into its stern and manhandled it straight into the water.

As its bow made a wave he ran alongside, leant over to keep it balanced and got himself in, his old arms and legs finding a young man's strength. No one knew better than the former coxswain of our lifeboat that seconds counted. As his boat pushed on out into the water he knelt at the oars, got them set in the rowlocks and then did something I had heard about but never seen. He stood up and rowed the oars short and fast, more vertical than horizontal, directing the skiff straight towards the stricken craft. You could tell he was rowing not only for a man's life and those of two children, but for his own as well.

For I had seen what only he knew: it was his shout of warning that had made the man turn and probably made him tip the boat too far. If Freddie had stayed silent the boat might never have capsized.

I had started to run to help him but Freddie was too fast for me. So instead I ran down to the shore, climbed the groyne to get a better vantage point and stared hard at where the boat floated, bottom up.

No more than twenty seconds had passed, perhaps thirty, but in our strong current that's twenty yards. Freddie would need someone onshore to tell him where to look because out there in a boat with a current flowing there are no easy reference points and you're too low down to make sense of things.

Of the children I could make out neither sight nor sound. Of the man there was just a cry, again and again – 'Help! Help!' – as he clung on to the drifting prow of the boat, out of sight on the seaward side.

I saw an oar in the water. I hoped he had the children safe on the far side of the boat with him, but in case not I searched the surface of the water down-current of the boat, as Freddie made his rapid way towards it.

Then I saw it, unmistakable: the surfacing of a child's shoulder, the reach backwards and upwards of a hand, an arm flailing as it turned helplessly, then all gone again.

'Thirty yards down-current of the boat!' I shouted to Freddie. 'Thirty-*one* . . .'

I counted the seconds because that was how Freddie and Mr Bubbles used to follow the progress of something carried by the current which was now in sight, now out of it, their eyes sliding along the surface of the sea with the beat of their counting to keep up with where it ought to resurface.

Briefly he looked my way, and nodded. As he was rowing he could not wave acknowledgement. Then he turned back to face the way he was rowing and was presented with an impossible predicament: whether to save the man at once or begin searching for the children.

Lifeboatmen are trained to save the lives they can save before searching for the lives they may not be able to. So while Freddie went for the man I continued to follow the drift of the water and knew just where that child was. I saw him, or her, surface, not once but three or four times, turning, reaching out, struggling, growing weaker.

Somehow Freddie got the man aboard the skiff, no easy thing for an old man, but he did it. Then, still standing, he turned towards me and I shouted, 'Sixty yards down now, Freddie, sixty-six . . .' as I saw that child again.

Others had seen what was happening by now and started swimming out, but a hundred yards is a long way, especially in currents, and it takes skill and knowledge to know what path to follow through the water to reach a place that's moving all the time. Freddie knew how to do it, which is why he made it look easy rowing a boat out.

The swimming rescuers didn't know, so they were all going too high or too low or not far enough and on a colder, rougher day most would have endangered their own lives. Knowing that and how Freddie worked I stayed where I was, up on the groyne where Freddie could see me, and hoped I could direct him to where he needed to be.

He rowed his skiff hard and fast parallel to the shore, using the groynes as his measure, and then started searching the surface of the sea, but even for him and with me directing it is no easy thing to work out distances or a bearing when you're drifting in a skiff: distances seem further, currents slower, and the sky and the sun cast reflections that dazzle.

Freddie turned the boat too soon by three or four yards and I shouted again but by then he was too far off to hear me easily. Others were shouting too, which didn't help. As he searched the wrong part of the sea by a few short yards and despite our frantic shouts, the child drifted on and under and didn't come up again.

As for the second one, he, or she, was long gone out of sight.

The whole crowd now knew that something was wrong, and suddenly, high above our heads, the first of the lifeboat rockets went off. *Bang!*

Its sound reverberated among the red-tiled roofs of the North End. Then a minute later *Bang!* again.

All I could do was watch the flow of the drifting surface until my eyes ached with the strain of trying to see so far, and my heart and my mind numbed into disbelief and horror.

A motorboat appeared, one of the fishermen's, and then another, and eventually the lifeboat. They all searched back and forth, fanning out northward, drifting with the current, hoping to find the children still alive.

Eventually, unable to stand it any more, I retreated into the hushed and gathering crowd and slipped on my trousers, T-shirt and shoes, as if standing in a swimming costume on a beach in the sun did not seem right. Yet others, perhaps oblivious to the tragedy, carried on their day, growing bored with watching, and went back into the water to swim.

With the other boats now out searching, Freddie hitched his skiff to a motorboat and together the two boats brought the one survivor back to shore and I went to help beach his boat. Freddie's face was grim and grey with effort and he looked ill. Yet it was the man who had capsized the boat whose face I remember most. It wore a mask of horror, of utter loss and wretchedness, of shocked hopelessness, of grief.

Later our local paper said who he was and who the children were. He was the uncle, they were his nephew and niece. That man had been larking about, trying to give them a time of pleasure. If they had been me, they would have known how to swim ashore. But they were them and so that man drowned his brother's children. No wonder the horror in his face etched an image and feeling that never died.

But I too felt guilty. Just by seeing it happen I felt bad. As for Freddie, he was consumed by grief and shame, thinking that if he hadn't shouted that man might never have turned to look and so not tipped the boat into its capsize.

Mrs Bubbles arrived and it was she who insisted on accompanying Freddie to hospital for a looking over. An ambulance took the sole survivor. It was me who closed the forgotten door of Freddie's cabin and put his table, his chair and his biscuit tin full of takings inside too. Somewhere among the change was the money the man had paid.

I went home but Ma was out. I wanted to talk to somebody. I went to find Mr Bubbles but he was out too and Mrs Bubbles wasn't back yet. I drifted around the North End, not knowing what to do. I wanted to cry but there were too many people about. I didn't want to go to my favourite places. I kept thinking of those children's bodies in the water, slowly drowning, as once I nearly had. I thought of their arms and hands turning this way and that with the current and I knew I could have saved them if I had been there in the water too.

I wanted to say to someone that I had tried and tried to tell Freddie where to go because I could see where they were drowning and if he could have heard my voice better they could have got them out in time.

I wanted someone who knew me to say, 'Jimmy, Jimmy, it wasn't your fault, there was nothing more you could do . . .'

But there was, there was, there's always something if you know how to find it. There's always a way not to die if you know the key. I wanted to save them and stop their endless drowning in my heart, their fear and isolation in the great open sea so near to the shore, an isolation I could have borne so much better than they ever could. Or so I thought.

I wanted to cry and scream and guide them back to where they would be alive again.

But there was no one I knew to whom I could say those things. So I just walked and walked, sniffing back tears I never quite shed, thinking that maybe if I had run straight into the water and swum with all my strength, I might have got to them in time and taken those children's hands as once Granny took mine and guided them to safety.

In the end it was to Granny's nursing home I went, but she was asleep.

'You can sit with her if you like.'

So I did, sitting and snivelling and looking at Granny's yellow face and her mouth wide open and toothless, a dark and horrible void.

Eventually I left, not wanting her to wake up and find me there; not wanting to say words in the end, because the moment had passed and my grief for those children was locked inside.

I went home, but still Ma wasn't back. So I got on my bike and I headed for the Dunes and then cycled out along the concrete path to Stannick Bay.

As it was low tide by then, Mr Bubbles was far out on the sands, staring out at the searching lifeboat and other boats. He was big and dark and as usual wore his black coat despite the sun and his big boots. Around him were the usual seagulls and piles of black wet sand he had dug and his paint tins full of worms.

I laid my bike on his for comfort and then I started the long walk across the sands towards him. The gulls saw my approach and rose squealing. He turned and saw me and I started to run. I was blubbering and crying and he put out his great arms and I ran into them and he held me as I cried and struggled and hit him with my fists.

He held me as I told him what had happened and said, 'They didn't need to die. They were just two kids. I could have saved them.'

'You can't save the world from its grief, Jimmy,' he said. 'You can't save every life.'

'I could have saved them. I should have swum straight out to the one I saw, I should . . .'

'You did the right thing showing Freddie where to search.'

'He missed them.'

'You couldn't have done more than you did, Jimmy, and Freddie'll say the same.'

'I could have.'

'You couldn't.'

Later we stood on the sands watching the boats search.

'Where will they be by now?' I asked him.

'At this state of the tide?'

He screwed up his big beetly eyebrows and his bronzed oily brow. He scratched his stubbly chin. He wet a finger and held it in the air. Then he shook his head.

'A bit further out than the lifeboat I'd say, more Ramsgate way. They'll drift out in a great loop and back again but further out. In this wind they're not coming back to shore in Stannick Bay.'

'Are they searching in the wrong place?'

'Probably so,' said Mr Bubbles. 'But if you couldn't see them on the surface on a day like this with your good eyes, Jimmy, you can reckon they've drowned. Let the sea have 'em for a while. But folks don't need to drown.'

'Is it true what Freddie said once, that you survived a fall into the sea?'

Mr Bubbles nodded but he didn't smile.

'It was in 1924 off Dungeness, off the coaster *Pomeroy* out of Medway. My fault.'

'What did you do?'

'Floated and made a decision.'

I waited.

'I decided if I got out of the water alive I'd never set foot in a boat again.'

'And did you get out alive?'

He looked at me and I looked at him.

That was the silliest question I ever asked anyone in my life.

Mr Bubbles chuckled and I began to laugh and we stood there in Stannick Bay holding each other up as we laughed, tears rolling down our cheeks; while the boats offshore carried on their search for those two dead children.

It was only the gulls stealing Mr Bubbles's lugworms that stopped us.

'Little buggers,' he said, breaking free of me and chasing them.

'But you got into a boat again, didn't you – otherwise you would never have rescued Mrs Bubbles from France.'

'War and saving lives is different, Jimmy. It makes you break such promises and find courage you never knew you had.'

We stood some minutes longer thinking our thoughts before he said, 'C'mon, lad, come and have something to eat.'

So we sat up on the shingle by our bikes and had the leftovers from his lunch. Later we cycled home together, me carrying one of his tins of lugworms from my handlebars.

Mrs Bubbles said Freddie was in hospital for observation from the strain, so Mr Bubbles went to see him and I went home. My shock and grief had found its proper place in my heart by then.

'Supper's ready,' said Ma. 'What did you get up to today?'

I grunted.

'The lifeboat was called out today, for two children,' she said.

I grunted again.

Ma returned to her book and her pot of tea.

The following Thursday, when it was in the *East Kent Mercury* about the man being the uncle of the two children, Ma said, 'A terrible thing. I doubt that the family will ever recover. Imagine, a man takes his brother's children out for the day and they drown but he survives. Things can never be the same. You cannot forget, nor perhaps ever forgive, that kind of thing, even if it wasn't his fault.'

I knew it was but I never said a word because Ma liked to dwell on such matters.

'There are some things a family never recovers from,' she said.

Her words hung in the air of our chaotic home like a flypaper covered in flies.

Mr Bubbles was right about where those children ended up. One was round on the Margate sands past North Foreland and the other was caught in the sprat nets in Pegwell Bay.

They were not the only ones who died.

Not long after Mr Bubbles knocked on my door, which he never did before and never did again. He didn't want me to go reading it in the local paper before he had a chance to tell me himself.

'We're going baiting,' he commanded me.

We walked that long way to Stannick Bay, him pushing his bike in silence.

When we got there he said, 'Jimmy, I've got something bad to tell you, something very bad. Freddie Hammel died last night. He died of grief for those two kids. He blamed himself. He was a man who saved lives not took 'em. He was a great man and a strong man, but last night he died of grief.'

I sniffed and snivelled and so did he.

We dug lug and when we were done we put them all back.

A few weeks later they auctioned off his hut and boats and all his goods and every last chattel. People stood in a ragged circle on the Front because you can't take five skiffs into an auction house no more than you can put a great man and all his goodness and strength into a coffin.

People said that Freddie Hammel was the last of our great life-boatmen but Mr Bubbles didn't agree.

'They're all great, they are,' he said, 'past, present and future. But one thing's sure: next to Mrs Bubbles, he was my greatest friend.'

Life had changed. It seemed more sombre, while some things were less important now than others.

Ma said, 'Jimmy, I want you to do some shopping.'

'Must I?'

'Yes. You never do anything to help.'

'Okay, Ma.'

I didn't argue, I just did what she said. Some anger had gone out of me; something better had replaced it.

But before I did her shopping I went up to the Front and stood on the sea wall above that part of the beach where Mr Bubbles first met me. I stood there knowing who it was I had needed in the hours after I saw those children drown.

I had found Mr Bubbles but really I had needed a dad, a real one.

I stood looking at the sea and wondering where he had gone off to long ago and what made him go there.

I stood with my eyes streaming tears and holding my body stiff and strong because otherwise it would have cracked like glass.

I stood angry because he wasn't there. That was the first time I shed adult tears and they were bitter and angry and sharp on my face, like bleach spilt on the back of your hands which you wash away but carry on feeling for a time; the first time I felt the pain of the blood that seeped from the rock I tried to be all those years of forgetting Darktime.

# 24

# GRANDFATHER'S LEGACY

In those dark and lonely years after Ma got Michael and Granny out of our house, before I too left, there was one thing I did willingly enough: listen.

Between arguments and silence, between going off in huffs, in among the brooding and the bitterness and the sense of time lost, there was our parlour, and endless pots of tea. There was also the fire it became my task to clean out and reset, a ritual with kindling and coal which never ceased to amaze and fascinate me with its power.

You can turn a dirty, cold grate into a thing of life-giving beauty in no time at all and that's what I did day in, day out, especially in wintertime, when the gales were blowing fit to break the windows and Ma put towels along the bottom of the doors to keep the draughts out.

Her chair was to the right of the fireplace and mine to the left, and behind me on the wall there was a blue plastic electric clock, which was Ma's idea of modernity. We had no television, only books and an old Roberts radio, as well as the one in my room, which went back to the war years and needed to warm up before it made a sound.

But we had ourselves: or rather, Ma had an audience – me.

Outside the house things were different. I didn't like being seen out with her, shopping or at school, as to me she looked big and untidy and badly dressed – bigger and untidier and worse dressed, that is, than other boys' mums. They looked neat and tidy; they didn't lumber along and their hair was nicely done and their make-up good.

My Ma always seemed to wear her glasses crooked. They were grimy too and her shoes were scuffed and dirty. When she smiled her creased smile all I saw was that she had stains on her bottom teeth from drinking too much tea. It was a mystery to me that she had any friends at all, let alone male admirers, of which there were a lot. So in public I tried to pretend she wasn't my Ma and we weren't together at all; and I hoped that if we did meet anyone they would be blind.

But when we were in our home, away from prying eyes, it was not what she looked like I noticed but her voice and her words, melodic and precise, dramatic and infinitely descriptive; and her eyes and expressions, ever-changing, ever apposite to the story she was telling.

So I sat and listened, gripped, my doubts about her as a ma and as a person falling away before the power of her presence and her words.

Ma's general theme was the unfairness of the world and the perfidy of men, and her approach was wry, witty and only obliquely bitter, though that strong current ran deep. She told her stories so many times, each time a little differently, that it took me a long while to realize that she was wrestling to find exactly where the truth of her past lay.

She talked fluently, with humour, and though we argued, I was generally a benign audience before which her words flourished and took glorious flight. Granny had taught me to listen and taught me to talk, but Ma taught me her version of the ways of the world of men.

In the company of others who doubted her, or questioned her or challenged her facts or pointed out that they were different from before – people without humour, who did not understand that her references to literature and history were not clever but just the language she had been trained to use – she froze and fell silent.

Among the sort of women I wanted her to be – who spent money on hairdos and clothes, and had unscuffed shoes and properly applied make-up – Ma retreated into the shadows of inferiority.

In the company of dominant men she never even bothered to start to talk, seeing the ghost of her father at their shoulder, and the frown of his face.

Before her children, however, one to one, distanced though we were, she flourished and gave to us the stories of her life. Or some of them, the ones she wanted to reveal. And being the last at home, I had the longest and greatest feast of her talk. Through those long winter evenings of her soliloquy I learnt what made her and why she was the way she was.

No one likes to suffer the unkindness and cruelty, selfishness and bitter acts of a ma like Ma, but there is a cold comfort in understanding where they come from and perhaps the beginning of forgiveness.

Ma could, and did, claim three countries of origin. She was born in Denmark in 1908, her mother was English and her father was German and it was a story she told many times . . .

'My mother, who you call Granny, was Laura Margaret Fairbairn, a member of one of England's leading Nonconformist families. That means they weren't Church of England and that they took their religion seriously.

'She met Father while she was a member of a choir from England at a Church Convention in Hamburg in 1893 at which he was lecturing. Herr Dr Gustav Theodor Drickner . . .'

Ma always said this with a frown, pausing to sip some tea, making clear she hated him. She said 'Drickner' as if it was a dirty word. She would take another sip and glance at me to see if I was listening and had taken her point before continuing.

'I may have told you, Jimmy, he was a north German, one of the leading Lutheran theologians and Old Testament scholars of his day. They married in 1895 following Father's first appointment as a minister – in Stralsund, which I believe is a large village fishing on the German Baltic Coast with a strong tradition of Nonconformist worship. Reading between the lines of a little memoir I have of him, penned before the Second World War and printed in Germany's horrid and nearly unreadable gothic script, he did not go down well. Which doesn't surprise me.

'I imagine that his sharp intellect, overbearing nature and rigorous scholasticism made him as impossible as a minister as he was as a father. He was probably impatient with ordinary parishioners and had no interest in the daily round of a parish and its congregation.

'His Church, thank God, saved his flock from too many years of his ministrations but also had the wit to recognize his strengths. After the publication in 1897 of the first of many books on the Old Testament, they moved him away from real people into a job at the Lutheran College of St Anthony in Hamburg, where he became Director of Studies. That means he was doing what he liked doing best, taking charge and telling people the error of their ways.'

'Granny says that sometimes, "the error of their ways".'

'Well, you'll find there's a great deal in common between your grandmother and your grandfather.'

'But she didn't like him.'

'Quite so,' said Ma meaningfully, allowing a pause to let her point sink in. 'He moved to Hamburg University in 1900 and by 1905 had moved on to the Theological Department of Berlin University. After failing to gain the advancement he thought he deserved in Berlin he ruthlessly switched loyalties to Oxford, England, which by then had a growing reputation in Nonconformist theological scholarship. He was a visiting fellow at New College in 1911 . . .'

'What's a fellow?'

'Somebody, in those days invariably they were men, who knows a lot about a little and teaches, in exchange for which he gets food and lodging in an ancient building. It's nice work if you can get it, which most can't.'

'Could I?'

'I doubt it very much indeed, Jimmy. Now . . . in those days, when Father came to Oxford, there was a lot of anti-German feeling in England but his reputation as a scholar overcame that. He gained a Readership at New College and rose steadily, securing election to the prestigious Chair of Comparative Theology in the mid-twenties, which position he held until his retirement in 1939. He died in 1945, a year after you were born, in fact on your first birthday, which was inconvenient of him, but that was Father for you.

'At the funeral, of course, Oxford being Oxford, everybody said what a wonderful teacher he had been and how his students loved him.'

Ma let out one or her tight little laughs which told me that wasn't how *she* saw him at all.

I poked the fire and put on a few lumps of coal while Ma poured herself more tea. Then I settled back into the chair to enjoy the coming onslaught. Ma was like a cat playing with a mouse when it came to a good story: gentle at first, vicious at the end, but in control throughout.

'The truth was not spoken at the funeral; it never is. In fact he was a cold, self-centred man who put his work first and his family, and most particularly his womenfolk, last. He was ruthless and strict to the point of cruelty . . .'

'You weren't allowed to talk in the house after nine in the morning; Michael told me that.'

'If we so much as made a noise that study door of his would open and he would be standing there fixing his gaze on us over his reading glasses while we froze in terror.'

'So he was like Captain Flax at school?'

'Worse, Jimmy, far, far worse. Does Captain Flax's moustache bristle?'

She knew about Flax from Michael and me and she knew he had a moustache.

'I don't think so . . . I'm not sure what you mean.'

Ma took off her grubby specs and leant forward towards me, eyes fierce, moving her mouth and cheeks in a strange way.

'Your grandfather had a beard and when he was angry, which was often, it bristled.'

'Bristled?'

'Moved like it had horrible electric current running through it that would burn you: his eyebrows too. Quite horrible. You see, to him, as to many academic Victorians, women were a lesser species, so he not only treated Mother badly, depriving her of love, affection and care, but Ellie and myself as well. For example . . .'

Ma had a thousand examples of Grandfather's cruelty and I never grew tired of hearing them because each time she told her stories they were slightly different, slightly more horrible.

'. . . did I tell you about the photograph?'

She had but I shook my head. I was happy to hear it again.

'Mother's brother Monty, who was a very successful retailer in Bath – Father despised retailing, of course – was in Oxford one day and decided to pay us a visit without warning and just knocked on the door. Grandfather was furious. He did not like his morning disturbed by one of Mother's relatives. Ellie and I loved Monty – he was a big, sociable, handsome man with twinkling eyes, a breath of fresh air in our dark academic household.

'Father got rid of him as fast as he could but not before he had entertained us girls with some conjuring tricks, the climax of which – Father had to look on in silence, bristling his moustache and beard – was the production of a five-pound note from Father's left ear. That was bad enough – what was far worse was that Uncle Monty, obviously taking pity on us and probably knowing how mean Father was, presented us with the note, insisted that we took it and told us to spend it on "something nice and non-educational" for ourselves.

'The moment he was gone, Father demanded the money and, unable to deny it was ours, insisted on how we spent it: we had to go to a photographic studio and have a photograph taken of us, which we sent to Uncle Monty with effusive thanks. It cost five pounds, so we never saw a penny of the gift. Not a single penny . . .'

Ma's silence at this point was always eloquent, her expression angry, her sigh bitter. Finally she would say in the thin, whining voice of an aggrieved adolescent, 'And that was the only money I was ever given to spend on myself until I was eighteen! A bloody photograph. I'm sure Uncle Monty was appalled and furious, except that I doubt fury was part of his nature . . .'

When Ma spoke like this, reliving her past, she soon forgot that she was talking to a boy of twelve or thirteen and used language and expressed ideas more suitable for an adult. She was frank, too, in ways most parents never are; and being an historian by training and interested in psychology and the way people learn, put what she said in a wider context.

So it was that I came to understand why she grew up without personal confidence, fearful of men in authority, yet over-trusting of them too, and with certain qualities that at the time were disadvantages in a woman – not because I worked these things out, but because she said them herself in ways that would be hard to forget.

On her disadvantages as a woman, and those of Ellie too, she was as clear as crystal. First of these was her considerable conversational skill, allied to a wide and varied knowledge of literature and books, which she said made her seem formidable to men, who preferred a less challenging, 'feminine' woman.

'The other thing is an inability to make the best of my personal appearance, which I freely admit. I never could get the hang of lipstick. It's hardly surprising when I spent my childhood being criticized for being ugly by the only man in our house and laughed at for trying to improve my appearance . . . and, incidentally, your Uncle Max never joined in Father's criticism of women and the belittling of us. He spent most of his youth as a boarder in a public school and when he was at home kept himself to himself and well clear of Father.'

'What was the house like?'

'Tidy to the point of perfection,' said Ma, frowning, spilling tea and dropping bits of biscuit on the rug by the fire as she poured herself some more. 'Oh, leave it alone, Jimmy; there's no one but you and me to see . . .'

Only slowly did I begin to read between the lines of her description of her past in Oxford and interpret for myself things deeper than she said.

For the deepest and most harmful effect Grandfather had on Ma was that he so dominated her as a child that she never managed to escape him as an adult, and so free herself of the anger and hatred he engendered in her. It was this malevolent passion that she visited on Michael and me in particular and from which Howard Scupple rescued Hilary in Oxford, by keeping her when he had to look after her, well away from Ma.

Thus, like Michael before me, I gradually came to some conclusions of my own as I sat year after year listening to Ma's own analysis. By the time I was fourteen I had begun to understand that Ma's tears in the face of reasonable personal challenge, her habit of retreating from difficulties, usually into a romantic novel, and her sudden irrational rages were symptoms of the little girl who was trying to escape from the shadows of her childhood and her father, who, never having himself been loved, never quite learnt to engender love in others, who in consequence never quite learnt to love themselves.

In her acid descriptions of our behaviour, and this included the mainly absent Hilary, of our supposed moodiness, taciturnity, forgetfulness, ingratitude, bloody-mindedness and even cruelty, and her dismissive 'You really are so predictable, Jimmy!' and 'This is really very tedious!' – in all this I heard the voice of her father, alive once more.

In the months and later years after Granny's forced departure, I began to see that Granny's slow decline had helped Ma formulate her own radical approach to old age. She often talked about it, fearfully, but it took a while to see exactly what she was afraid of: not death but the passage to it. The real nature and depth of her fear only became clear as I understood how hard she had had to struggle to gain independence from Grandfather, and how passionately she did not believe in the God of whose existence his professional life as a theologian was meant to be the witness.

At about the time she had been preoccupied with getting Granny into a home there were stories in the newspapers concerning the shocking conditions in some old people's homes. Every day, it seemed, she would wave the *Daily Telegraph* under my nose and read out another revelation about the brutal and uncaring treatment of the old.

'I don't want to be treated like this when I'm old, do you? Eh? *Do* you?'

'Er, no, Ma.'

'Well, you better think about it, hadn't you? It's more important than Lonnie Donegan and that bloody, bloody pop music . . .'

'What music do you like, Ma?'

'That's not the point. The point is . . .'

Not that Ma's care and concern for Granny herself was improved by her new preoccupation with old age – it was what was going to happen to herself in old age that the need, as she saw it, to find a home for Granny brought into her consciousness.

The debate with which she engaged was Europe-wide and Ma, her background being what it was, was able to follow it in several languages at once. It made her an advocate of voluntary euthanasia and led her to a chilling decision, one in which in her obsession and self-absorption she wrongly wished to involve me.

It was an argument, a position, she rehearsed many times in our parlour, over cups of tea, with the air filled with the smoke of the cigarettes she'd taken to smoking in those years.

She believed that her experience of medical authority, most particularly of *male* medical authority, as well as common attitudes to the individual liberties of elderly patients at all levels in the long-stay hospitals and wards towards which her declining physical state was rapidly leading her, gave her very good reason to be afraid.

She knew well how easy it is to forget that the old ladies and gentlemen who sit so forlornly alone in the public spaces of old people's homes, their bent heads and vacant stares often an expression of a final despair, were once young, vibrant and hopeful. Through those many dark days and nights of one-way conversation Ma left me in no doubt that she believed that once that fundamental truth is forgotten such people soon cease to be human beings in the eyes of their carers: and in the wake of that forgetting comes indifference and its consequent cruelties.

There lay her fear.

She was frightened of finally becoming an object on a conveyor belt leading to a dump which seemed different only by degree from the lime pits into which in some places, in recent periods of history, the dead have been thrown.

She wanted to die with dignity, at a time and in a place of her own choosing, still in touch with the people and the different worlds she had loved, and with something left of the many selves she had fought so hard over so many long years to create, to reinvent and to protect.

The fear – and sometimes the terror – that began to gnaw at her through my last years at home was that if she allowed the long-term care system to get hold of her she might at the very end of her life, having fought and won so many battles in the cause of her own freedom and independence, lose the war.

Disempowered, she would have to live surrounded by people and things she did not love. She would have to sleep in a room and a bed not her own; and probably suffer the words and deeds of people she did not respect, like or trust, or, worse still, of people she did not even know.

Helpless, she would have to watch herself deteriorating and suffer the misery of doctors trying to prop up the edifice of herself which she now wanted to fall down. Then she might have to face the prospect of suffering pain, indignity and loss of control, knowing – perhaps knowing to the very end – that she might have avoided it if she had had the courage to take her own life while she could.

She had a deep fear of the do-gooders, the reassurers, the mealy-mouthed, and of medical consultants, who she knew were duty-bound in the cause of her own good to deny her the freedom to die. She knew there were some doctors who might ease her death, but she could not rely on them.

In short, she feared she would be trapped in life and ultimately faced by her idea of hell – a doctor who assessed her declared wish to die as evidence that she was no longer competent to adjudicate on her own life. It was the circularity of the argument she hated – if a person decides they no longer wish to live and asks to be helped to die then that is evidence enough that they are incapable of making that decision.

I sat evening after evening as she told me her fears, often with homework left undone, because I had to listen.

So it was she came to believe that one of the final challenges of her life was to see to it that she avoided being cast into that geriatric hell by remaining in her own home, where she had privacy and the means for a self-inflicted death always available, until the last possible moment.

But there was a problem.

She knew, because she had seen it with her own eyes among certain of her friends, that if she left it too long, even by a day, age might muddle her mind and rob her of decisiveness and so of her final victory. She therefore needed an ally she could trust to speak the truth when the time came lest she herself had become uncertain.

The person to whom she entrusted the task of telling her when that time had come was myself.

One day at breakfast she received paperwork from an association promoting voluntary euthanasia, which she read in silence. It was then she began to spell out for the first time her firm intention to kill herself when the day came that she was no longer able to look after herself.

She talked matter-of-factly and without sentiment, and I knew she meant every word she said.

'I expect that day will come some time in my seventies and if you asked me now when it will be I would reply that I intend to kill myself when I am seventy-five years old.'

My mother was in the habit of being straightforward about life, people, sex. Now it was death's turn.

'However, when the time comes I may be too old, too doddery, too senile to remember what my real wishes are any more. So . . . when I'm *getting* too old but not yet there you'll tell me, won't you, Jimmy?'

Naturally, I hesitated, not from deep thought but blank astonishment and incomprehension. I could not imagine her ever being old or unable to make decisions. She was my mother and I had no father: she *made* the decisions.

'*You will, won't you?*'

I was only fifteen but in that moment I felt like a man, though I knew nothing about death, or about the meaning of half the things Ma said.

So . . . I said I would, and in so doing I knew I had made a promise as inviolable as one of Grandfather's Old Testament vows and an unexpected despair descended on me.

'Of course,' she added darkly, 'you won't talk to anyone else of this. It is . . . a mortal confidence.'

She might have used the word 'secret' instead but in saying 'mortal confidence' she added significantly to the weighty sense of moment and responsibility.

I was too young to say that this was no reasonable thing for a parent to ask a fifteen-year-old to agree to. For one thing, it is not a promise that one so young can properly make. For another, it locks a child into a dark vow it may be very hard to break, especially if it is sugared with the notion, as this was, that of all her three children I was the only one she trusted with so special a task.

Worse still, and most insidiously, it alters for ever that child's perception of his parent's life and being, and so perhaps his own: if he truly believes, as I did, that his mother really is going to kill herself one day, and in some way he will be involved, it gives an unnatural and dangerously collusive foreknowledge of one of the key stages of adult development – the death of a parent – which even an amateur psychologist could predict is likely to be damaging.

In making that youthful promise I became party to an unnatural and terrible contract, which was effectively a time-bomb that would explode one day and perhaps destroy me. Certainly it would have a fallout that was dangerous and unpredictable.

The stage was set for a countdown whose exact timing would be a function of my mother's fine judgement and my own, about when, exactly, she might lose the ability to look after herself and a last chance to kill herself: a countdown to her suicide.

I bore this burden in silence and seemed to bear it well. But it haunted me and was one of the darkest shadows of those years: a burden that might eventually wear me down.

It did not help that I was vowed to silence on this subject and that when, inevitably, I confided my secret to someone the results were catastrophic for me and for them.

# 25

# CAPTAIN FLAX

Our school was one third boarder, two-thirds dayboys. But as vast tribes and communities in Europe and Asia were made subjugate to the Roman minority, so we dayboys were made subjugate to the boarders.

The reasons were similar: we were a state of disunion, they a state of order, training and leadership. From their first coming to our school the boarders were put into special boarding houses at the far end of the school's considerable acreage, into whose grounds, and through whose doors, few of us dayboys ever penetrated, not least because it was against school rules to do so. The rules perpetuated the division.

In this secret place, unseen by us, the boarders were subjected to the regulations, stated and implicit; the mores, brutally learnt and self-serving; and the unpleasant rituals, mercilessly imposed by the brutalized older on the innocent younger, which are often the nature of residential communities, particular male ones.

So the boarders became close-knit early on, and were trained in the tribal skills of mutual survival and the moral imperative of internecine warfare. The fact that they lived on the premises and had to be kept occupied meant that they did more group activities, particularly sport, than we dayboys. At the end of every day, while we travelled back to our homes all over East Kent, they trained. The boarders were therefore fitter than us, and had more team spirit, and they felt superior to us. Their houses and their teams and their individual champions won nearly everything. They expected to win; we expected to lose.

The evil genius of this culture, its Master of Ceremonies, was

Captain Flax. As Head of Boarding Houses he laid down the rules and set the tone for the boarders from the start. Under him the anti-sneaking ethos flourished into something dangerously institutionalized and punitive for those who dared transgress it.

Flax saw his two boarding houses as army regiments which owed their first loyalty to him and their second loyalty to themselves. This meant that those within them must never, whatever the cause, carry their complaints outside. Instead, whatever their sufferings, whether simple homesickness, mild bullying or something more serious, the boys in his houses had to complain directly to him.

Here they faced a dilemma, of course. The anti-sneaking code was such that the very act of complaint to Captain Flax made the complainant guilty in his eyes and thereafter a subject of suspicion. Real boys, he seemed to feel, real little men, should deal with such problems themselves. He preferred, and actively encouraged, the boys to solve their own problems, make their own judgements and inflict their own punishments.

When these failed, however, or were disputed, Flax himself became the final Judge and Executioner, and such was the malevolence of his presence that even our worst imaginings could not offer any real idea of what his final punishment, if he had one at all, might be. All this helped create the climate of fear and secrecy surrounding Flax and his followers of which we dayboys were aware, but whose nature we could only guess at.

From time to time there came to the boarding houses boys strong enough to resist the culture of intimidation and violence imposed by Flax, but they were few, and generally they left the school early. Captain Flax hated these boys with a passion, for he saw them as insubordinates, deserters and traitors. I did not know it then, but it happened that Michael was one of these few.

When he became a boarder, Michael might, on the surface, have seemed ripe for victimization at the hands of Flax and his schoolboy strong guard, for certainly he was physically weaker than many others and he had no interest in sport at all. But Captain Flax's regime had met its match and Michael wasted no time in declaring war on the system.

He had hinted of this when I visited him at the boys' home he was sent to after absconding from school. Much later, he told me what had happened.

Michael's battle against Flax began when he refused to participate in the weekly swimming sessions which it was Captain Flax's pleasure to organize for the boarding houses at the nearby army swimming pool, part of a complex of barracks built out on the Stannick marshes for training purposes in the twenties and thirties.

Michael had never learnt to swim, and there was something about cold water that seemed to cause him almost physical pain. He always avoided it and the uncovering and exposure to the elements it involved. In any slightly cold conditions, his face quickly turned white and his lips pale blue.

Flax was unsympathetic to Michael's request not to go swimming the first time it arose, and even less sympathetic when Michael was taken ill two swimming days running. Rightly believing he was feigning it, in the third week Flax insisted that he go, and deputed three of his bullyboy favourites to ensure that Michael stripped off and went in.

This was a mistake. Michael had an inner strength and courage it was not wise to provoke. He also had a calculating ruthlessness which, as it turned out, outstripped even that of Captain Flax. As the school bus sped along to the swimming pool, with Michael's minders all about, and Flax himself sitting in the front seat impassively, Michael realized that he had to find a way of dealing with the situation once and for all. He waited until they reached their destination so that he could see the lie of the land before deciding what he must do. Perhaps his first thought was escape, but the isolated location and the central position of the pool within the vast camp itself made this impractical.

The coach stopped, the boys tumbled out and he was taken into the Nissen hut used for changing. The open-air pool lay somewhere behind it. By now he was weak with fear, but it was not just the fear the non-swimmer feels at the thought of being out of his depth in water; nor even fear of the bullyboys at his side.

It was far deeper than that, and its roots lay in a different, viler violation of him that had taken place when he was seven: the act, or rather acts, which explained his lifetime dislike of physical exposure. It was only from the nervous, excited, ill-informed backchat of us boys at school – tales of queerness and sometimes, more often than we cared to admit, of things that had actually happened to some of the boys at the hands of parents, or brothers, or relatives in general – that I put two and two together and made the four that had been Michael's horrific experience when he was seven and I only five.

'Take off his clothes, the lot, he's going in,' Flax's Head of Year commanded the other boarders.

Despite his initial shouts and struggles he was debagged in the Nissen hut, roughly and unpleasantly. This was a process we dayboys only rarely saw, and then in its least harmful form – the stripping off of shorts or trousers, but leaving the other clothes untouched, most crucially underpants.

This natural veto on going too far was not part of the boarders' ethic, not when there was no one to see but themselves and they had the excuse of a boy's unreasonable unwillingness to swim in a nearby pool and the tacit approval of a member of staff.

Michael's shirt and vest came off, his socks, and finally his pants, until he was naked, his white skin, his genitals, exposed to the laughter and rough mockery, verbal and physical, of the boys around him.

Fearful though he was, appalling though the memories this experience triggered, it was nevertheless a dark place Michael had been in before, and an inkling of how to survive it suggested itself to him. He went suddenly passive and limp.

He was dragged out into the open air through a jeering crowd of boys and hauled to the side of the pool.

'The deep end, sir?'

Captain Flax, sitting in a chair by the side of the pool as was his custom, nodded. It did not occur to him that Michael could not swim and it was Michael's extraordinary, courageous, tactic not to tell him. Michael, in recalling this for me, remembered the details.

'He sat smiling by the pool, neat and tidy as ever, especially his shoes, which were their usual highly polished brown.'

Michael was taken to the deep end.

The stripping, the exposed nakedness, the hands of boys at his genitalia, had triggered in Michael a response whose nature few if any there could have understood. It was not a wish to survive, but a fearlessness of death. It was a response whose dark tunnels, whose voids, whose pitch-black shadows, Michael had long since explored and become familiar with. He was prepared to risk his life to win and in taking that decision he was going far further than Flax himself would have dared to go.

Seeing the pool, and most particularly that there were no steps down at the deep end, Michael saw what he could do.

*The deep end, sir?*

'Throw him in,' said Flax, 'for his own good.'

Willing hands pushed my brother in.

I was not the only one of us two to know the extremes of loneliness, of being finally cast out. He knew it worse, far, far worse than I.

Michael crashed into the water, felt it rise briefly above his head and did the one thing that for a non-swimmer requires the greatest nerve and courage: nothing.

His arms went limp, he rolled front-down in the water, and he lay there, his head nearly all beneath the surface, his mouth and nose completely so.

Around the pool the boys watched gleefully, their mirth only slowly dying as their laughter gave way to uncertainty.

Michael, naked, simply lay floating, half submerged in the cold water. Only a boy with a death wish and a head for mathematics could have done it.

As he lay there he counted, one and two and three . . . for he knew perfectly well how long he could hold his breath.

'I just counted my way towards the moment of drowning,' he told me blankly, meaning it.

The Head of Year looked uneasy, then suddenly desperate, and turned around to Captain Flax.

'For God's sake, boy . . .' Flax began, rising as all around him his subordinates waited for a command, not knowing what to do. The prospect of fun had turned to a prospect of murder.

'Get him out of the . . .' shouted Captain Leonard Flax MC DSO, beginning to run.

And it was he who was forced to jump into the water first, he and the Head of House and other Seniors, forced to look silly and jump in to grab Michael, turn him over and stare in horror at his loose mouth and his blue lips, and the water that flowed from his mouth.

It was not easy getting a limp body out of the deep end. They swam at Michael's side, pushing him, trying to lift him, shouting, Captain Flax's clothes sodden, his hair dishevelled, his calm shattered, until they finally got him to the side, where hands reached down ready to heave him out.

Michael was always the clever one, the one who could lie, who knew when to act.

He heaved his chest, he coughed, and as they started to pull him out he showed how much of a match he was for Flax. He kicked his right foot straight into the head of one of the senior boys, really hard, and smashed it into the side of the pool. It was nearly hard enough to kill. Then, in the commotion, Michael managed to roll over on top of the stricken boy and let his arms and legs get in the way, so that the smashed boy's face slipped under the water unnoticed and blood spread out into the pool and the boy drifted from the side, his limpness for real, his life genuinely in danger.

'Sir, it's Yates, he's . . .'

And Captain Flax had a real problem on his hands with two boys almost drowned and one of them concussed as well.

The swimming session broke up in disarray as Flax, sodden and cold, summoned an ambulance for the second boy, and Michael, warm and dry, affected a frailty he did not feel. Both went briefly to hospital; both soon recovered. Michael was never made to swim again and nor did any boarder ever try to harm him; while he and Captain

Flax agreed to a stand-off, one that lasted until Michael went missing from school three years later and never came back.

It was this swimming-pool incident that lay behind the viciousness of Flax's comment at that first French class: 'another little Rova to deal with'.

Still, despite his hostility to us Rovas, the boarders left me alone. I had learnt how to fight back at my previous school and through what Mr Bubbles had told me. When one tried it on I just hit him as hard as I could. When he fell down I bashed his head on the woodblock floor. It was just as well it wasn't concrete. There was a ruthlessness about me too, an anger, which others sensed and instinctively avoided provoking.

Just how far victimization was allowed to go at our school was shown by what happened to a boy who joined our school in the same year I did. His name was Ramsey and he came from Southdown, so he travelled on the same train as me, though he got on at an earlier stop. He was clean, fresh-faced, open, but he was not on the face of it a brainy boy. He was in the lower form, so I first noticed him when I was demoted there halfway through my first term.

Ramsey was one of the few who did not snigger when I so miserably appeared in that lower class. Instead, he looked sympathetic and came and said hello at break. That same term a boarder took and broke one of his model cars and he, not yet knowing about sneaking, having come from a gentler more benign first school, reported him. The boarder had an older brother and he got Ramsey the next day. Nothing much, but enough for him to miss school for a day and come back bruised about the face and pale. It would have been better if Ramsey's mother had never reported what had happened to our headmaster, naming the culprit in the process; it might have been better still if they had never let their son return to the school.

Ramsey became the victim of our year, our generation. Constantly got at, first by older boarders and then younger ones, and finally even by us. He grew pale, with rings under his eyes, and he went through school with his head down, his posture submissive. He scurried about, hurt, afraid and lost on the periphery of our life. No good at work, no good at games, unhappy, picked on by boys and masters alike, and eventually cast down like me, but for different reasons, into perpetual failure.

As time went by we learnt that there were better ways of hurting him than physically. Ramsey was a naturally neat boy, orderly and organized. So when he returned to school in the second year and his satchel was shiny new, we scratched and cut it. His shoes were always polished, so we always scuffed them. His shirts came ironed and clean so we flicked them with ink. He was useless at games, so we never passed the ball to him and he was forced to stand in the cold winter wind out on the wing, in a far corner, un-used, ignored, pale in baggy clean shorts, shivering: ostracized not only on the playing field but later in the changing room, where we refused him access to the warm bath and showers and hid his clothes.

By being our victim he taught us all how to bully, and the more he did not hit back, the more he took, the more we thought of ways to make him suffer. And sometimes, for lack of anything better to do, we just hit him for no reason, and bruised his eye or bloodied his nose. He became our violent habit.

Yet after that first time, never once did he sneak or tell, and never did his mother complain.

Even the masters were part of his victimization, and most especially Captain Flax. We knew he hated me, but I stood up to him. Ramsey did not and so Captain Flax's treatment of him grew into something worse: it became a study in public sadism which bordered on the criminal.

'Outside,' he said to Ramsey once, for no reason that any of us could see.

Ramsey hesitated.

'When I say outside, boy, I mean *outside*, where I can see you.'

It was January, and the sycamores around the tarmacked play area were covered in hoarfrost. The sky was an ugly grey, and that morning on the way to school I had tried to break puddles of hard black ice, and failed. It was the coldest day of the winter so far.

It was a cold made worse by the nasty little breeze that was stirring.

Ramsey went outside and stood in the playground where Captain Flax, and the rest of us, could see him suffer the cold, and the humiliation, and the loneliness. Shuffling his feet at first, blowing at his hands, glancing again and again into the window for some sign from Captain Flax that he could come back in.

He declined slowly into a hopeless huddled shape, his face blue-white with cold, his eyes downcast. He was almost destroyed before our eyes, those of us who could bear to look, which was not many.

Yet there he still stood, staring, waiting, patient, terribly sad, but surviving. The sight of him through that long hour made me feel a shame so palpable that I wanted to be sick and I resolved never to be part of the bullying of Ramsey again, *never*. While my resolve to win the battle against Captain Flax gained new strength and purpose. It was not just for me that I would find a way to destroy him, but for all of us boys who were his victims, of whom I was sure there must be more.

So there Ramsey stood, growing ever colder; and I, who wandered the shore, knew what cold was better than most. When break came and Captain Flax dismissed the class, I went out to Ramsey despite what others might think and led him back into school lest some of the boarders should add to his agony and try to stop him getting back inside to find some warmth.

He was so cold he could hardly move.

He was so cold that the lukewarm radiator in the changing rooms to which I led him seemed to scald him.

He looked at me without hope of friendship or any kindness beyond what little care I had shown in bringing him in and there were tears in his eyes as his shivering mouth uttered a single word, the ancient, oldest question of innocent victims: '*Why?*'

For a time I regretted what I had done because it turned me into one of his few safe havens. After that he felt he could sit near me on the train to and from school, and sometimes at breaktime. This embarrassed me by association. I never encouraged him, or talked to him much, but he persisted in staying near, perhaps sensing in me another survivor, and one who, like him – though I did not know it – might have hidden depths.

Yet I never discouraged him either, not in so many words, because the truth was that I secretly admired him. I now saw that he had a strength to which I could not put a name. It grew slowly through the years, his strength, and it became an aura about him, evident perhaps only to those of us who suffered failure too. He was our martyr and seemed saintlike. With the months and years of his torture it was as if each time he was bullied and did not respond, he gained and we lost.

Until there came a day that I found I looked for him because I liked him sitting near, because I too had no friend, no company. Another day, too, when someone came to punch him and I rounded on them.

'Leave him alone,' I said, squaring up to them in his place. And they did.

Once he said, 'Jimmy, they never hit you.'

'I'm Rova to you, Ramsey,' I replied. I usually let him call me Jimmy, but others were listening and I could show no weakness.

'Sorry. But they don't,' he whispered.

Everything about him could be annoying, including his persistence.

'Why?'

'Why what, Ramsey?'

'Why don't they hit *you*?'

'Because I hit back. It's what you should do.'

'I can't,' he said. 'I'm not made that way.'

We began to realize that this victimization of Ramsey was as nothing compared to what happened to some of the weaker boarders in the secrecy of the boarding houses.

A group of us boys who hung about together were standing on a rugby touchline watching one of the boarding houses perpetrate its usual rout of a day house when we noticed a junior boarder near us, apart from his own crowd. He was snivelling.

'What's wrong with you?' one of us asked.

The boy did not clear off but said, 'It's Flaxy.'

'What about him?'

'Can't say.'

'Can't say what, you twerp?'

'*No one* dares say anything.'

There was an utter wretchedness and despair in his eyes and stance that I recognized only too well.

'What's your name?' I asked, breaking my usual brooding silence.

'Ryan.'

On the far side of the pitch Captain Flax, surrounded as usual by his acolytes, suddenly glanced up and seemed to stare at us, as if he had heard every word.

'Nobody dares say anything about what?' I asked.

'The punishments in the boarding house. They're wrong.'

'Complain,' I said unsympathetically.

The boy looked at me crookedly.

'I have. No one believed me and now they're going to get me . . .'

His voice trailed off; some boarders were approaching. The rugby supporters resumed their shouting, and the ball was suddenly kicked our way, bounding and bouncing over the rucked and muddy playing field. The players came after it and we stepped back from the touchline as a line-out took place.

'Come *on*, boarders! *Faster!*

'Here, Moore, here!'

'Make an angle, boy, make . . .'

Play moved away from us once more, the boarders as aggressive and vocal as ever, the dayboys dispirited. Ryan had moved on and was standing alone now, too far away for us to talk to, the picture of misery.

'What did he mean?' said Ramsey.

I thought I knew, or knew something. There was the look of Michael about him when he said, 'They're going to get me.'

I remembered Seddy, from whom Michael had rescued me, and I felt an urge which I did not act on to go and find Ryan again, to try to help him. Mr Bubbles may have been right to say to me once that you cannot save everyone, but you do not forget the ones you failed, not ever.

'Somebody ought to do something,' I said, without much conviction.

'Yeah,' said someone else.

'But *what*?' said Ramsey.

We had no answer then, individually or collectively.

A man like Flax froze the collective soul of the school. No wonder us dayboys, distanced though we were from the horrors of boarding, were helpless at school and silent at home about the things that mattered, like bullying and victimization, like mockery by teachers in the class, like lonely boys who desperately needed support.

As it was, Ryan's brief and hopeless attempt to seek help came back to haunt us all. And too late we learnt the truth about him.

He was a boarder who, like Michael, had incurred the displeasure and contempt of Captain Flax. He was perhaps weaker than most, certainly more sensitive. In his first year he was perpetually homesick. In his second year he was often ill and in the school infirmary. In his third he became simply blank, sad, depressed, the butt of his boarder peers as Ramsey was the butt in our year, but without Ramsey's resilience.

With no one to turn to, he declined into a hopelessness. The rumour was that he had been tried in a kangaroo court of the Seniors in the boarding houses and had been sentenced to an 'ultimate punishment', one about which so many dark stories abounded. It was about this, whatever it was, that he tried to talk to other masters before the sentence took effect, but either they did not believe him or none had the courage to confront Captain Flax.

It was about this he tried to talk to us.

A few days later, one Wednesday evening, only days before the end of the winter term, twelve-year-old Richard Ryan walked out of our school grounds. He made his way through Stannick, past the Christmas lights in the shops, and along the side roads for a mile and a half to the railway embankment to the north-east of the town. He waited until at least two trains went by and it was almost dark. Then he lay on the line, face-down, and let the next train pass over him.

He was decapitated and his feet cut off. The trunk of his body was dragged and rolled under the trains and broken up. Parts of him were found more than three hundred yards down the line. He was not missed officially that night because the boys in his dormitory decided not to report his absence. His remains were found by a railway worker at first light the following morning.

These details were not known to us immediately, but were reported over the next weeks and months in the local press. Meanwhile, a hushed morning assembly heard only that there had been an accident and that Ryan was dead. A strange, heavy, nearly palpable sense of shock descended on us. The shock turned into two days of thrilling, awful talk as bit by bit the fact of his suicide emerged. Then the mood grew more sombre as rumours spread about what it was he had feared so much that he killed himself.

The boarders seemed unaffected, but after Ryan's death, among us dayboys, the old fear of Captain Flax developed into something new: contempt, hatred and righteous anger. We did not realize it, but Ryan had become a martyr in the same cause as Ramsey, the same one I had so long espoused: to get rid of Flax, to destroy him.

Now I had allies. It was simply a matter of time and the right circumstance, but I did not know that its success would need a solitary, unexpected, extraordinary act of heroism.

# 26

# MR WHARTON

Time is deceptive. What seems in the present may be past. A star shines bright to those who are far enough away, but to those who are near it has already died.

The war years had receded and time was catching up with those who rose to ascendancy in wartime, like Captain Flax. They had almost had their day.

Ma got a better job, as administrator/book-keeper on a big farm near Stannick, and made the acquaintance of people with boys at Stannick Grammar.

One day she came home saying, 'A little bird tells me that your headmaster Bernard Smiles is retiring soon, and not before time. Let's hope they find someone younger and more progressive than the old guard!'

Time's changes come about when new generations start to overthrow the old, and that's what began to happen at our school, stuck as it was in the old ways in education, not yet understanding the new.

With the start of my O level year departure from school into the real world became an imminent possibility. For those who had slunk about in the bottom half of the lower stream for so long, failures in every subject, any hope of staying on at school into the sixth form to do A levels had all but gone and most had already begun to have interviews for jobs.

Yet a few us, failures all, still had a hope, barely expressed, that somehow, even at the eleventh hour, we might find a way to pass the examinations our teachers had so long predicted we would fail. The trouble was, never having experienced success before, we had no idea what it looked like, where it hid or how to find it.

Ramsey and I were not the only ones to harbour this secret hope. There was Jowett, our year's fat boy, who had not an ounce of unkindness in him and was the greatest failure of us all; Thom Brody, unnervingly strong and mature for his age, who was harmless if not provoked. He came from a broken home and rarely talked to anyone, but when he did he showed himself to be quick, intelligent and ruthless. The boarders had never troubled him. But he had never done well at anything. Finally there was Templar, who was always ill, suffered from acne and had a laugh that annoyed people.

There was a common sympathy among us five which had grown over the years but never been expressed, and of us five only Ramsey and I – and sometimes with Thom too – were friends. The others were too alone in their own ways to know how to be friends, or even to believe they might have come commonality with others.

Yet as the years had passed perhaps some sense of common feeling had developed. The boarders left us alone now because ever since the Ryan incident we somehow came together when there was trouble, though without quite acknowledging each other. Ramsey had always stayed near me, but now Jowett would shadow us, and Brody, feared by all for his violent unpredictability, loomed close if there was trouble.

As for Templar, girlish Templar, ugly of face, crooked of teeth, weedy of form, we protected him, circling like a quartet of parents round a threatened child. Except he was not a child, nor yet a man, but like us, something in between, awaiting that sudden transformation for which, though we did not quite know it, we all waited and which had already begun.

There was another boy who liked to be with us five and who we did not reject: Goddard, top boy in our class in almost everything, yet lacking an ability to make friends with any but us lost ones. He was a swot and maybe that's what isolated him from everyone. But we knew loneliness when we saw it and with us he was in safe company.

So it was that come breaktime, or the journey home, or watching a match played by senior boys, we six made a group and no one else touched us or came near.

* * *

The O level year began badly, like all the rest before.

Masters came and told us that we had to work and if we did not we would fail and have to leave, job or no job. We felt a growing sense of panic and dismay. Whether we tried or did not, it made no difference, the only thing we were good at was failure.

After a month the first orders came out and for us six it was just as it always had been: five of us down the bottom and Goddard at the top, unable to explain how he did it. He was apologetic but we didn't mind and in our friendship and acceptance he found comfort.

Then Mr Tranter, our English master, left and our maths teacher was off sick, so for weeks we drifted further off course in two of the most important subjects. In maths, we had to settle for a succession of fill-ins until one of the least inspiring of the junior teachers filled that spot. As for English, it didn't really bother me because, no matter who taught me, I had long since given up the struggle to find a way out of the confusing mire of failure and loneliness.

When we sat in class doodling, trying to focus on one irrelevant text after another, the only image that came to my mind, and it recurred so frequently and unstoppably it was like a nightmare, was those children I had witnessed drowning, and the feeling that I was one of them as well.

I felt a grief for things and only the *crunch crunch crunch* of my feet over the shingle of our shore served to numb my mind and let it drift darkly with the sound of the sea. I even stopped acknowledging my friend-of-the-Dunes, Harriet.

In those weeks when O levels began to loom, my sense of grief was building slowly into a vast unremitting wave, which I could sense but not yet see on the far horizon, advancing slowly towards me. It was inside me, too, mounting, darkening, inexorable.

I had no strength and no defence against it now. I sat through class after class of failure, attentive only to the feeling that something was going to engulf me from outside and from inside, but not knowing what to do or who I might turn to.

I was back at the edge of Darktime and I was frightened, because if I let it overtake me again I knew I might find it hard to escape a second time. Worse, perhaps, was the feeling – the insight – that even if I did escape, Darktime would never, ever go away completely, but would be an affliction I must suffer always, a fear I could never escape. Like rain.

'How was school?' Ma would say.

'Okay.'

But it was not. Every day I was there I was confronted by what I could not do and felt I would never be able to do. Every day. I even stopped joining our group at breaktime and turned my back on Goddard; and when David Ramsey tried to talk to me I walked off.

It all seemed pointless and often I stood on our seashore waiting for a wave big enough to come and take me away to where there was no more pain.

My face was brown from the sun and wind and my body strong but inside my head I was not well. My tears were not just for me but for life and those children I saw die: but their faces and expressions were those of Michael and me.

It was on the Monday morning of the sixth week of that crucial term that our new English master appeared, the replacement for Mr Tranter. No rumours preceded him, nor any knowledge of him at all. Nothing.

On Friday Mr Lothian, who normally taught history and was filling in for O level English, simply announced that from Monday a new teacher would be arriving.

'What's his name, sir?'

Mr Lothian shrugged indifferently. 'I know no more than you.'

Monday came and there he stood, fiddling with textbooks at the master's desk when we arrived back in our form after the mid-morning break. His appearance was unpromising. He was slight, he was shiny faced and rather red, he wore round golden spectacles of an ancient design and he looked like a swot grown up. His start was nervous and hesitant.

'Well . . .' he began, 'er . . . um . . . good morning.'

We glanced at each other, thinking we knew a weakling when we saw one, not realizing we were in the presence of a giant. A lightness came to the eyes of some of us, even a malicious levity.

He spoke again: 'I said, "Good morning",' and levity suddenly fled the room.

There was an unexpected edge to his voice, made all the sharper and more effective by the blandness of his round face and specs, and his thin, crinkly auburn hair.

'Er, good morning, sir.'

'Um, good morning, sir.'

'Yes, well, it is, I suppose,' he said, glancing out of the window. 'My name is Wharton and I had better go through the register and see who's here and if I can remember your names.'

He did so, rather slowly, each time looking up to gaze impassively on whoever answered. Disconcertingly, he held that gaze for a few moments before dropping his eyes to find the name of the next boy.

When this job was done, we expected him to close the register and open up some book or other and ask us to do the same. To find a page, to pore over an exercise, to grow bored once more.

But he did not.

He stood up, came round the desk so there was nothing between us, and said, 'Now, let us see if I *can* remember your names. There's no point in saying you'll remember something if you don't, is there?'

A hush began to fall as he began to run through the register and link the names to each one of us from memory, 'Aitchison, Anderton . . . that's you. Baldry . . .'

It was extraordinary and unforgettable as, for the first time in our school lives, a master put his own mental ability to the test before us.

'Brody . . . Cooper . . .'

A slight smile came to his face as with increasing confidence he repeated our names, all of them, looking each of us in the eye as he did so. Each one of us noticed, remembered, acknowledged.

'All present and correct?' he said in conclusion and someone said 'Yes, *sir!*' and we grinned.

Ramsey glanced at me in amazement, as I at him. Something had happened, something new. Somewhere a new clock had begun to tick away old things and somewhere else old footsteps receded down a corridor. Here, in our room of failure, a new master had arrived and with him, we sensed, a whole new world. We were not wrong.

'This is the first lesson I have ever taught anyone,' he said, 'which means . . .'

The silence in the room grew yet more profound. We had no idea what the fact that he had never taught before meant but he somehow made it seem important and there was not a boy in the class who did not want to know.

'Which means, I think . . .' he continued, allowing a sudden brief smile to part his thin lips, 'that all of us, you and I, have . . .'

Have *what?*

Mr Wharton's pauses were the most pregnant of any master that we ever had. We leant forward to hear what was coming as one. We had become an audience hanging on his words.

'. . . which means that we all have *everything* to gain.'

Whatever it meant it sounded positive, in fact it felt like the first positive thing any master had ever said to us in all our time at the school. That inclusive *we*, that joyous *everything*, followed once again by that shyest and briefest of smiles.

'Now,' he said, pushing aside the textbooks he had been holding, 'now . . . I have been told that as a class you are "not very good at English" and might find O levels "difficult". Let us deal with this misconception at once.'

We stared.

'Is there anyone here who does not understand what I am saying now? The word "misconception", for example. What does it mean?'

We said nothing until finally Goddard raised his hand. 'It means not understanding something right.'

'Exactly, Goddard. Well done. But let me put it more simply . . . and, *please*, at least nod or shake your heads. It is not nice speaking to a vacuum.'

Again that edge, that sharpness. That slight impatience.

'Is there anyone in this room who does not speak English?'

As one we shook our heads.

'So you *all* speak it?

We nodded our heads.

He looked questioning.

'Er, yes, sir,' said Goddard, suddenly our official spokesman, 'we all speak English.'

'Do you realize that adults come from all over the world to England to *learn* English? They pay large sums of money for the privilege. And they find English *very* difficult. But I doubt that a single one of those adults, however intelligent they may be, even after ten years of study, would be able to speak English even *half* as well as each one of you already do.

'In short . . .' he continued, after the slightest of pauses to allow what he had said to sink in, 'each one of you is an *expert* at English language, so good in fact that people would pay each of you a great deal of money if *you* could teach them what you know.'

We sat thunderstruck.

No one had ever told us we were experts at anything.

No one had talked to us as equals, as he was doing.

'So I see *no* reason why in eight months' time each one of you should not receive through the post a letter from the school announcing that *you* have passed your English Language O level. Indeed, it would be quite amazing, would it not, if an expert in the subject did not pass so simple an examination? Eh? *Well?*'

'Er, yes, sir!'

'Um, yes, sir!'

'But, *sir* . . . ?'

It was Jowett.

'O levels aren't, er, *simple*, are they?'

'Oh but they *are*, Jowett, they are *very* simple.'

We stared at him, even more dumbfounded.

'You seem to have difficulty in believing what I have just said.'

'No one ever said O levels were easy before, sir,' growled Brody dubiously.

'No, Brody, I don't suppose they did. People like to make examinations seem difficult but really they are not. Unless you choose to think they are. Now, kindly repeat after me these simple words: "I am going to pass my O level in English language next year." '

We did so, but in a stumbling way, mumbling the words, at once embarrassed and amazed.

'Louder, please,' he said.

'I am . . .'

And louder still . . .

'I AM . . .'

Soon we were shouting the words in a rising roar that grew more enjoyable and rewarding the louder it got.

'I AM GOING TO PASS MY O LEVEL ENGLISH LANGUAGE NEXT YEAR!'

The classroom door suddenly slammed open and Captain Flax stood there, looking surprised and extremely angry.

'*What* . . .' he began, gazing around the room to bring it to an icy stillness before fixing the new master with a glare as his voice slowed to a terrifying purr, '. . . is going on?'

Our eyes switched from the senior man to the junior in expectation of that retreat and backing down that we had seen so many times from other masters.

Captain Flax raised his eyebrows slightly, and his eyes narrowed.

'Eh, Wharton?'

Mr Wharton's eyes grew unexpectedly steely behind his spectacles before he smiled and shrugged slightly.

'I am very sorry if we have disturbed you, Captain Flax,' he said so sweetly that he seemed to be stating the exact opposite. Then he added, 'Youthful enthusiasm: why not put it down to that?'

Then he did the unthinkable: he turned back to us and thereby somehow consigned Captain Flax to the shadows.

The door closed, leaving behind a mute declaration of war. Mr Wharton glanced back towards the door, and to our surprise and pleasure there passed across his bland face the briefest of looks of intense dislike, to be replaced almost at once by the same, strange, even frightening, steely resolve we had seen moments before.

'Sometimes,' he said mysteriously, 'discretion is the better part of valour. I suggest it would be unwise to be quite so vocal next time . . . What do I mean by "discretion is the better part of valour"? Eh?'

In the silence that followed my heart thumped loudly because I knew the answer. It was an expression that both Granny and Ma used from time to time, Granny in the context of Grandfather, Ma in the context of men.

'Think before you act because you might find it's better not to act at all,' I found myself suddenly saying aloud, before adding, 'er, sir.'

'Yes,' he said, 'it might very well mean that, exactly that, in some contexts, er . . . Rova. Well done. On the other hand, let us think about it for a moment, for it could have other meanings too . . .'

*Well done.*

Two words that felt like the first words of praise I had received in all my years at Stannick Grammar. *Well done*, I repeated to myself, savouring them.

So it was that in his first lesson with us Mr Wharton began the transformation of our academic lives not only individually – as by some alchemy he made each one of us feel special and full of new possibilities by the end of that first class – but collectively as well.

'Before this lesson ends,' he said, interrupting himself on the subject of Shakespeare, which was the subject of his first lesson, 'let me return briefly to the subject of O levels, and in particular the two I am responsible for with this class: English Language and English Literature.

'I want to make something absolutely clear to each one of you. There is an expectation that the pass rate in this class will not be high, and certainly not so high as in the Upper Fifth. But I do not like failure, because generally it is completely unnecessary, especially among a group of experts on the subject such as yourselves.'

He smiled and we grinned, conspirators together.

'More importantly, I like the feeling of success. It feels good. It breeds *more* success. I have very little interest in how this class may perform in other subjects, but in *my* subjects this form will do better than the Upper Fifth, *better*. That will require extraordinarily hard work. It will require new levels of neatness and application, but more important, new ways of thinking and of using your imaginations. It will also require that you find ways to help each other. It will require that you do homework. It will require . . .'

At this point he began to lose us, because we knew, we *knew*, that success in the sense he meant was out of our reach, however hard we tried.

Mr Wharton let his voice trail away.

'But I see you do not believe that as a *form* you will do as well as the Upper Fifth, for which I do not blame you. The belief will come only with time, of which unfortunately there is not much.

'But it will come and you will succeed. One by one you will succeed, just as, a long time ago it now seems to me, *I* began to succeed after a long time of not doing so.'

A shadow crossed his face and revealed to us, or to me at least, that he knew what he was talking about because he had once been where we were.

'It will start with one of you, self-belief. Then it will come to another and another. That's how it will be in the so-called *Lower* Fifth, at least as far as my subjects are concerned. Understand?'

He stared keenly at the class as the school bell went to mark the end of the period. There wasn't the usual rush for the door, but nor was there any rush to answer his question positively.

'Eh. *Do you understand?*'

He seemed suddenly to doubt himself, retreating before our continuing doubt and silence.

The bell stopped ringing and hundreds of feet rushed down the corridors outside and into the playground below our windows. But our class sat mute, stunned, unable to speak; wanting to believe that what he said was true, wanting to understand.

All but one of us, that is, but as Mr Wharton had just suggested, only one was needed to start things rolling. That brave individual was the last one any of us would have expected to speak out. That he did so helped mark a turning point not only in his life but in that of our form as well.

'*I* understand, sir,' called out David Ramsey clearly, revealing for us all the deep truth that lay in Mr Wharton's words: that we need be victims no more; and showing a courage we did not know he possessed.

'Good,' said Mr Wharton, picking up his things and going to the door, 'that is what I like to hear.'

He turned to look back at us.

'Good,' he said again with a satisfaction that communicated directly to us all. 'I think we may say, may we not, that in this class today we have *all* begun?'

'Yes, sir,' said Brody, speaking for us all.

Inevitably we called him 'Warty', but never was a master's nickname spoken with more affection or respect.

It soon came out generally that he expected the Lower to do better than the Upper in his subjects and an extraordinary battle began, both spoken and unspoken, whose effect was to unite our form for the first time in a common educational cause whose objective was success.

Homework was done, boys participated, set books were read, and Warty put into us the belief that we would succeed. Where Flax commanded by fear, Warty did so by engendering respect, perhaps even love. Where Flax punished, Warty praised. Where Flax frowned, Warty grinned.

And time, instead of dragging, began to race.

It was Warty's habit to give us a break from set books once in a while by reading something to us just for enjoyment, or interest, or to challenge us. Sometimes a bit of a novel, sometimes a speech from a play.

One day it was a poem.

Until then, such had been the brooding darkness in me, that I contributed little to Mr Wharton's classes, though I liked him and I listened to what he said. But I rarely said much and I never admitted I read the set books ahead of the class. I did not let him draw me into discussions, though he tried.

But like the others, I enjoyed it when he read to us because he read well, introducing us to things we had not heard before. The afternoon of the poem, the poet unnamed, the subject unexplained – he finally found a way into my heart and mind just as he had with so many of the others in so many different ways.

'As usual,' said Mr Wharton, 'I'll read the piece without comment and then we can discuss it, or not, as the case may be. This is one where you just listen to the sound of the words. Let those sounds lead you to this great poem's meaning.'

I put my head on my hand and my elbow on the desk and I picked at the edge of an exercise book. I stared out of a window.

*No worst, there is none.*

I straightened up, I don't know why. *No worst, there is none?* Inexplicably, I felt a prickle down my spine.

*No worst, there is none. Pitched past pitch of grief,*
*More pangs will, schooled at forepangs, wilder wring.*
*Comforter, where, where is your comforting?*

The image of those drowning children came to me. Then of me watching them; and then, finally, I thought of the loss in their uncle's face when Freddie brought him ashore.

*No worst, there is none. Pitched past pitch of grief,*
*More pangs will, schooled at forepangs, wilder wring.*
*Comforter, where, where is your comforting?*
*Mary, mother of us, where is your relief?*
*My cries heave, herds-long; huddle in . . .*

The great wave of despair these words created in me was the despair

I imagined in the heart and mind of the man who drowned his brother's children, and it was me. Breath seemed to leave my body and not come back and breathless I found myself at the edge of shining black cliffs, sheer as fear.

The poem continued and I could not stop it or the welling of the flood within me.

> *My cries heave, herds-long; huddle in a main, a chief*
> *Woe, world-sorrow; on an age-old anvil wince and sing –*
> *Then lull, then leave off. Fury had shrieked 'No ling-*
> *ering! Let me be fell: force I must be brief'.*

The words flowed over me and into me, filling me, and there in Room G, surrounded by thirty other boys and Mr Wharton, I acknowledged the spirit of another sufferer, the poet, and allowed him to turn me to face his grief-stricken desolation and so face my own.

> *O the mind, mind has mountains; cliffs of fall*
> *Frightful, sheer, no-man-fathomed. Hold them cheap*
> *May who ne'er hung there. Nor does long our small*
> *Durance deal with that steep or deep. Here! creep,*
> *Wretch, under a comfort serves in a whirlwind: all*
> *Life death does end and each day dies with sleep.*

A silence followed.

'So . . . ?' said Mr Wharton eventually.

People started to say things, wrestling with words and meaning, struggling with the strangeness of the sentences and the made-up words, puzzling. But I knew the words and the feeling as I knew the sea, wordlessly.

Before meaning there had to be feeling. That was at the root of what Warty had been teaching us.

The discussion continued but I took no part in it. I sat overwhelmed, wanting to weep and cry out, to run from the room, to be alone with my tears – but more, more than that, I wanted to cry from relief, that I was not alone and had seen at last another figure on the shore I had trudged along alone so long. I had glimpsed world-sorrow, and understood there might be more than just my own.

So I simply sat and waited for the period to end, staring sightlessly at my desk, and Mr Wharton, sensing something was wrong but not guessing the depth of it, left me alone and asked me no questions.

Until the end.

Then, as he summed up and asked rhetorically what the poem was about, I found myself putting up my hand.

'Yes, Rova?' he said gently.

'It's about desolation, it's about that.'

I could hear the stormy seas upon my winter shore; I could see the sadness that overtook Mrs Bubbles in the winter; I could hear Granny weeping in her room.

No one spoke, least of all Mr Wharton.

'It's about loss of hope,' I added finally. 'It's about loss of love.'

There was a long silence and somewhere a door opened in the school.

'I think it is, Rova; yes, I believe it is.'

I looked at him and I knew he understood, absolutely. In that moment he acknowledged me, who was the Boy With No Shoes whose name was Jimmy Rova and who was someone who existed, really existed.

I stared at him and he at me and then I looked down again, down at my worn desk, down at my grubby fingers intertwined with all the stress of years of misery – *cliffs of fall, frightful, sheer, no-man-fathomed* – and when the bell rang for end of school I carried on looking, trying not to cry, as boys got up, desks banged and people pushed past and the corridor outside filled with noise, until I felt a hand on my shoulder as David Ramsey stood protectively over me so others might not see I had begun to weep.

'Sir,' I heard Goddard say, 'it's Rova, I think he's, I think . . .'

'I know,' said Mr Wharton softly, and I knew he did.

A boy came to the door looking for someone else.

'Get lost,' said Thom Brody, looming and closing the door against the world.

They let me cry, the five boys who were my friends and the master who stayed back in that class: Goddard, Ramsey, Brody, Templar, Jowett and Mr Wharton.

They let no one else come in and they let me talk and tell them all about the drowning of the children and how I could not help them and how their dying bodies turned in my mind; and about my despair, which was fear as well; and about the darkness I was in, the place of failure where I did not want to stay but from which I did not know how to get out.

Brody said, 'I've been down in that place Jimmy says he's in. I'm down there.'

One by one we said it, one way or another, as my tears dried on my cheeks and I felt life and light flooding back into me with the rueful feeling that comes after crying.

Mr Wharton had sat listening and I swear that in those bright eyes of his I saw the glistening of tears.

'I was in that place as well,' he said, 'and it was not so long ago. The question is, how to get out of it, eh? That's the question, isn't it?'

We nodded.

'How do you get out of it?' he said, standing up and going to the window to look out at all the boys in the main playground heading off back home or to their boarding houses.

'Yes, sir,' said Brody, '*how?*'

He turned to look at us and if ever a teacher had a group of boys who wanted to listen and learn it was Warty Wharton then; and if ever a teacher rose to an occasion he did so that afternoon.

'Well, you start by realizing that the mountains you think you have to climb have been put there by other people and not yourselves and that they are imaginary. There are no mountains, only a succession of simple challenges. For example, examinations are not difficult. The amount you have to learn to pass them is hardly anything at all.'

'But sir . . .' began Jowett.

'*Really,*' said Mr Wharton, going back to the front of the class, digging in his case and pulling out a thin little book. 'Do you know what this is?'

We shook our heads.

'It is published by the Oxford Local Examination Board, which is the board that sets all the exams you will be taking at O level. There's another one for the A levels. What this booklet contains are the syllabuses for all the subjects.'

We looked blank.

'A syllabus is the material you will be examined on, that's all.'

'Do you mean that book contains all we've got to know in English Language and Literature, sir?' said Ramsey.

'No, not just those two subjects, but all of them.'

'*All* of them?' said Templar disbelievingly.

'All of them – all the fifty or so O levels for which the board sets exams.'

'Just in that little book?'

'Yes, Rova. Which means . . .' he opened it up and turned to a page, 'that as far as my subjects are concerned, all you need to know is on these three pages . . . well, two and a half, actually.'

He showed us.

'In fact, it's rather less than what's on this page, since we have certain options – which bit of Chaucer, for example, which Shakespeare play and so on . . . It's not much, really, is it? It's not the mountain you all seem to think.'

'Can we see the page for Physics O level, sir?' said Goddard. That was his weakest subject.

'Of course,' said Mr Wharton.

We took the little book and pored over it, looking up subjects, comparing notes, amazed and dumbfounded by the simplicity of it all.

In a few short minutes Warty reduced a vast mountain range of worry to a few foothills.

'Mind you, it does not help,' said Mr Wharton eventually, 'if you don't know how to revise or how to sit examinations. The latter I intend to leave to another time and the whole class, but you may be interested to hear my views about revision.'

We were.

'Most people skim through their notes unmethodically, which is what I did until I worked out the Method.'

'The Method?' murmured Ramsey.

'Cribcards,' said Mr Wharton.

'Cribcards?'

'They're just a way of checking whether or not you know a subject. Like the characters in *A Midsummer Night's Dream* – their names and who they are. You work out a question and write it on the left side of your card. You write the answer on the right side. Then you can check what you know for yourself whenever you like. So . . . How many characters are there in *Dream*? That's on the left side. Answer: Twenty-one. That's on the right. Next question on the left side: name the six main characters. And you write down Oberon, Titania, Puck and so on, on the right . . .

'That way you can reduce everything you need to know to questions and answers which you can easily check whether you know or don't. No need to skim through hard-to-read notes in a mad panic, just check through cribcards. If you've done the work on the cards properly and can answer the questions you've set yourself for every topic in your O level then you can't really fail that examination, can you?'

'Er, no, I suppose you can't, sir,' said somebody.

'Try it,' said Mr Wharton, smiling. 'I will teach the Method to the whole class next week. Thank you for suggesting I should. Now, I regret I must go home. And Rova . . . ?'

'Sir?'

'The poem I read was by Gerard Manley Hopkins. Your brief summary of what it is about was as good as any I have ever read or heard. Here, take my copy, in fact keep my copy, because you've earned it. The "No worst" sonnet is number 65, but there are others you might like to read . . .'

'Thank you, sir.'

'And Rova, I trust you will now begin to contribute rather more to class discussion. You have things to say we all wish to hear.'

'Er, yes, *sir*.'

Then, with a smile, he was gone and with him a once unassailable mountain of worry and doubt.

Time raced ever faster now but we had been shown a way to run faster still and as we began to use it, to enjoy it, we found we were no longer running from failure but racing instead towards success. Not just in English but in everything else too, as we saw that if we could succeed in one subject we might dare think we could succeed in all.

The exams finally approached, but so powerful was Warty's sway on us that as a group we abided by his advice not to swot late into the night, especially during the three weeks of the examination. The first days of the exams were full of fear but as, one by one, we emerged feeling we had not done so badly after all, and Warty's Method had prepared us far better than we imagined, a new mood overtook us: it was one that combined new hope with a determination to get through successfully.

Six thirty in the evening was our cut-off for last-minute revision and as the hot weather of that June made indoors uncomfortable we decamped our post-exam meetings to the beach near the Pier.

Templar's mum, getting into the spirit of things, got together with Goddard's and they brought drinks and sandwiches down to the beach after our cool-off swim at the end of each examination day. We never said as much, but for all of us it was the happiest of times, combining a companionship we had never known before with new-found confidence.

Then, one Friday afternoon, the exams were suddenly over and only the dog days of that summer term stood between us and the holidays. For worse, for better, our time as children at that school were done.

If we came back it would be to the sixth form, sixteen going on seventeen, almost adults, allowed to discard our blue blazers for grown-up grey tweed jackets and straw boaters, the uniform of Seniors. Too big to be bullied, moving into a world where the masters treated us more cautiously and with more respect, as we began to discover that learning consisted of elusive ideas as well as the facts we had struggled so hard to memorize until Mr Wharton showed us how easy it had always been.

In mid-August, on a fine warm summer's day, our results came through. Our success was dramatic. I who had once hardly dared to hope for five O levels had nine. David Ramsey too. Goddard ten. Brody nine. Templar, who was going on to do art in Canterbury, had seven. And Jowett?

'Eight,' he told me in an excited call.

'Which did you fail?'

'Arts and Crafts,' he said, adding, indifferently, 'cribcards don't really work for woodwork.'

But my nine! I couldn't believe it.

I called David again, just to talk, for the world seemed ours that day.

'My mum says she wants to talk to you,' he said eventually.

Mrs Ramsey sounded tearful.

'I just wanted to thank you, dear,' she said, as if I had done his work for him. Then she added, 'His dad would have been so proud.'

Later, in my room, while I dressed, the first euphoria over, I felt a sudden blizzard of bleakness in my heart and the old fatigue. I had a brief pang of self pity, wondering if *my* dad would have been proud, wanting the feel of his hands on my shoulders telling me he was. Wanting what I could never have.

Instead I went to Mr and Mrs Bubbles with my good news. He had been there to wish me well that long-ago day when I first went off to big school. I wanted him to know.

FISHING BAIT SOLD HERE, the notice said and as the tide was in, so was he. You can't dig for lugworm in Stannick Bay when the water's covering the sands. I showed him my piece of paper with all my O levels on and he showed it to Mrs Bubbles.

'You read it out, m'dear,' he commanded, 'I've got the wrong specs on.'

Mr Bubbles could hardly read or write but no one ever let on they knew.

So Mrs Bubbles read out that list, dwelling on each subject for what seemed an hour at a time.

'*Félicitations, mon petit,*' she said when she got to my pass in French, giving me a hug and a kiss on both cheeks.

They sat me down and made me their thick sweet tea and Mr Bubbles looked like the cat with the cream. He kept patting me on the shoulder and saying he always knew I had something between my ears.

'What now, lad, more learning?'

I explained about A levels and how we had had to make choices. I had put myself down to do English, history and geography, thinking I would never get the sciences.

'What do you really want to do, Jimmy?' asked Mrs Bubbles.

'Maths and English,' I said, 'and for number three . . .'

I remembered German, which I had spoken once.

I remembered French, which had been the subject of humiliation.

History I loved because of Arthur Sanders, and geography because once long ago with Uncle Max and Auntie Fiona I had stood on top of a mountain and wanted to know about the world.

But now with my success at O level the sciences had opened their door to me, which had so long been shut. They weren't so bad after all, nor so hard.

I thought of biology and Harriet and the flowers of the dunes, but something made me shake my head.

'Physics,' I said decisively, because it went with maths and over recent weeks I had begun to enjoy the challenge of it. Also I liked the master who taught it at A level.

'There you are, the lad knows his mind,' said Mr Bubbles. 'Now get your Ma to go and tell the school that you want to change now you've got your results. She's good at talking is your Ma.'

He reached out his vast hand to me and we shook on it.

'And I tell you what. The day you come through that door with another sheet of paper with your A level you'll be old enough to celebrate good and proper!'

'Mr Bubbles!' exclaimed Mrs Bubbles, as if he had gone a little too far.

He disappeared out into his yard and dug about in the shed.

He came back with a bottle of wine as dusty and dishevelled-looking as an abandoned house.

'It's one of several as fell off the back of a boat,' he said, winking at Véronique.

It was red and I read the year rather than the name.

'1940,' he said, 'four years before you were born.'

'Jimmy, Mr Bubbles is not telling the truth. It did not fall off a boat, no, not at all. He took it and he put it on the boat when he took me. He stole it from France.'

'Humph!' said Mr Bubbles, pretending to be grumpy. His thick dark brows beetled but his eyes smiled.

He took it back to its secret place.

'There's more where that came from out in the yard, but not many more. We'll drink 'em when we know the time's right, eh? You better keep on working, Jimmy, work yourself all the way to college and out of this town, because education is freedom.'

I looked at him and I thought to myself that I never knew a freer man. I also thought that one day I would find a way to say thank you to him, a real thank you in a way that he would know came from all of me.

I didn't know the words then so I didn't use any. We just drank tea, and had some more, and laughed a bit as they chided one another, as they always did. Then it was time for me to join David on the beach, which was something we had all arranged for our celebration.

There were ice creams and pop and larking about in the sea, with Templar's mum and dad and Goddard's and Brody's two little sisters. Between us all, and calls made to other friends from our year, we worked out who got what results.

We six did best out of our form, and best out of the year but for a few swots in Upper. Best of all, we worked out that the Lower had done as well if not better than the Upper in English Literature, but not Language. Honours even. It was a better result by far than anyone could ever had predicted, even if it did not quite reach Mr Wharton's high standards.

But we needn't have worried.

By the strange and special alchemy of that day, Mr Wharton himself suddenly appeared, dressed in a pale linen suit, wearing round sun spectacles and white shoes.

We cheered him and he sent Goddard off with some money to buy more ginger beer and ice creams.

'Well done, everybody,' he kept saying, visibly moved. 'Oh, well done!'

That day, out on the beach, we strutted a new stage and took our curtain calls. It was a day of joy.

Then, as the evening drew in, we began to go our separate ways. Our little cast of characters had had its triumph and would never reassemble, not in that form, nor perhaps quite so joyously.

'I hear you're doing English, Rova,' Mr Wharton said as he headed off home, leaving just David and me on the beach.

'Yes, sir. But I want to change from History to Physics and Captain Flax won't like it.'

'Leave it to me,' he said coolly; 'I can deal with Flax.'

Then he too left for the evening, a giant in our lives, though by the evening light of Stoning Beach he seemed small and vulnerable in his crumpled linen suit.

'Well,' said David, '*well!*'

'I don't want to go home,' I said, 'I want today to last for ever.'

I walked with him the two miles to his house and then, after supper there, back to Compass Street.

My friendship with David had gained all the comforts of familiarity and trust, its early, difficult start having led to a deep, unspoken bond which the years and separation could not break. That night, walking home alone from his house, I knew David would be somewhere near for always. I knew the true comfort of having a friend.

# 27

# HARRIET

Examinations and my time of despair after the drownings got in the way of my friendship with Harriet Fosse, but they didn't undermine it. It was there waiting to be found again when the pressures were gone and the days grew hotter still with the late August sun.

A few days after we had celebrated our O level success Harriet called by to go for a walk. Really it was to tell me her A level results: she had three straight As with a distinction in biology.

We sat in the shelter on the Front to keep out of the heat of the sun as we looked across the Channel to France. In the months since we had last seen each other she seemed to have grown far older than me. She talked eagerly of her college life to come and of all the things she had to buy and do, and half of what she said I didn't really understand.

She didn't touch her legs to mine like sometimes before and she kept her bulging blouse all done up, despite the sun. My ache for her was old, it came and went between affection and fierce desire.

'I want to celebrate,' she said suddenly, touching my arm, 'you know, do something to mark the occasion of our successes. Any ideas?'

As it happened I did. For years I had saved the money I earned here and there from helping with people's gardens, bait digging with Mr Bubbles and helping out on the boats. Granny occasionally gave me some too and I put it all in a National Savings Account. Sometimes I dreamed of what I might do with it. That day with Harriet dreams began to become reality. My dream was to go on holiday away from Stoning. Most of my friends used to go on holiday but Ma and I never did.

I said, 'Harriet?'

'Mmm?'

'What are you doing between now and the start of term?'

'Whose, yours or mine?'

Mine started at the beginning of September, hers, being college, was one month later.

'Mine, I suppose,' I said.

'Nothing much.'

'I had an idea a long time ago to go on holiday, cycling and staying in Youth Hostels. Thom Brody did it with his dad.'

'Oh. Who do you want to go with?' she said, frowning.

'There's only one person I ever wanted to go with,' I said, my heart thumping, '*you.*'

This was not quite true, but it felt like a sensible lie. I had thought of going with David Ramsey but he was playing a lot of golf by then and was never free for more than a day or two. Anyway, sitting in that heat, her bosom so near, Harriet seemed to offer more interesting possibilities.

I remembered what Ma once said: 'Take your opportunities or someone else will take them for you.' And maybe a look came to my eye.

Harriet blushed despite her tan.

'My dad'll want to talk to you and talk to your Ma.'

'Is that a yes?' I asked.

'Oh yes,' she said, and she hugged me. That was the first time her bosoms touched my chest full on and I don't know how but her lips and mine got stuck fast and our teeth didn't get in the way.

In a rush, I said, 'Let's go to the Dunes.'

'What about the cliffs?' she replied. 'I think they would be better because they're high up and more . . .'

'More what?'

'Um, private.'

She blushed and I went hard. Ma once said, 'The art is to let men think they're making the running. It makes them feel better and more masterful. God knows why.' It was obvious to me that Harriet had been thinking about the cliffs and us going there.

'We'll cycle,' I said, thinking it was easier to hide my bulge sitting on a saddle than walking along the Promenade. Getting on my bike without her seeing was my only problem.

We found a secret place on the cliff top, the high summer grass all about our heads, and we lay there all afternoon, floating together at each other's touch. Sometimes I think that afternoon started the happiest weeks of my life, when I was in love and it never rained and I touched her bosoms outside her frock and then inside it. The excitement between my legs made me so hard that sometimes it was painful. My pants were damp with it.

Her dad and Ma talked about our idea for a youth-hostelling holiday and it was agreed, provided we kept to the route we planned, which was round Kent and Sussex, and she phoned her dad every night.

That was a good time but I remember clearly only the beginning and ending and the sun, which seemed with us all the time.

The beginning was outside her house, with her dad at the door and our bikes all packed and ready.

Her dad said, 'I've given Harriet five pounds extra spending money, and I'm giving the same to you. Here . . .'

He gave me five crispy pound notes and I put them safe in my rucksack.

'Look after her,' he said. 'She's all I've got.'

He had tears in his eyes.

'I will, always,' I said.

I don't know why I said that word 'always' but I did. It seemed right at the time. When Ma had said goodbye half an hour earlier she closed the door before I was even gone. Harriet's dad stood waving until we were out of sight, because that was how he was, caring. Ma's goodbye meant she didn't mind you going, wouldn't be thinking about you when you were gone, and did not much care when you came back.

Mr Fosse's meant he would be there waiting with a smile and a welcome when you came home and be worried sick all the time between.

Home is not a place or a building but the people inside who give it warmth and meaning and the eternal longing to return. That's why with Ma I never had one. Yet often I've felt that longing to return as if someone had put it in me: often, too, searching the shore, I thought that that was the treasure I was looking for.

So it was that Mr Fosse's loving farewell was the beginning of our holiday.

The sun that I remember was warm and bright and ran ahead of us all through Kent and Sussex. It was filled with laughter, that sun, and it was like nectar to drink or long grass to roll in or conversations that flow on and on from one thing to another, from dawn to dusk. It was the sunshine of friendship, mutual desire and carefree days, far from the shadows of the North End and Ma.

Each night, before we went to our separate dormitories, Harriet and I kissed a long time. I never tired of it and nor did she. Sometimes our hands strayed where they shouldn't, especially mine, but never far enough for me.

'Best not,' she said after a lot of sighing.

'Yes,' I reluctantly agreed.

Harriet taught me what being loved by a woman felt like. It felt good, like I imagined coming home should be.

The sun shone on us all the way there and all the way back and when we got home it was the end of the summer holiday. I had the sixth form to look forward to and she had her college to go to.

We coasted back down from Dover Heights into South Stoning by way of Star Hill to Harriet's front door. Warm was the welcome from Mr Fosse, like butter in crumpets, like a hug in the night. But I didn't stop long because I was feeling so good that I wanted to get home and tell Ma all that that we had seen and done.

I waved and was gone, back to the North End and life with Ma. I should have learnt long since what to expect, but Ma's surprises were often like slaps in the face. When I opened our front door the house smelt of powder and perfume and I heard a woman's laughter, like a young woman's, only it was Ma's. There was a bunch of flowers in a vase, and a different rug and the world seemed strange about me. As I advanced down the corridor a sudden silence fell.

'Ma? It's me!' I called.

'Damn!' I heard her say, and then more fiercely, 'Oh damnation!'

I was already apologizing before she opened the kitchen door and came out frowning, ready with a lie.

'A friend called by,' she said.

The pleasures of my holiday that I wanted to share with her fled away. She looked flushed, dishevelled and annoyed.

'It's all right,' I said, wishing I was not there, 'I'm going fishing on the Pier, with . . . er . . . David . . . all night. I just came back to get my things.'

It was something we had long said we would do but that day it was a lie.

Mr Filbert, the farmer she worked for now, appeared from the garden. He was in his shirt sleeves.

'Hello, lad,' he said, not looking me in the eye.

There were food things on the parlour table, and a white table cloth I had never seen before and the remains of a candle in a green wine bottle, the wax all dripped and solidified down its side as if it had been left to burn the night before.

Mr Filbert eventually eyed me and I eyed him.

'What time are you coming back from fishing, Jimmy?'

'Not till morning. It's *night* fishing, Ma. Our last night but one of the holiday. I *said*. That's why you thought it was tomorrow I was coming home.'

Another lie from me, but from her not a question, only relief at the prospect of me leaving again as Mr Filbert dug his hand in his trouser pocket and offered me twenty pieces of silver, to get some fish and chips.

I didn't want to take a single one but felt I had to.

I changed, put some warm clothes on, got my fishing gear, grabbed the Thermos that Ma, now good-humoured, had made, and went off into the evening, with no one to tell about my cycle trip. Not Ma, nor Granny, because visiting was not allowed after half past five.

I stopped on the Promenade and threw the money Mr Filbert had given me out onto the shingle.

That night on the Pier the whiting were in and I caught a lot. But what was the point? I chucked them back in, one after another through the night, until in the end, when I was too tired even to think, I cast without any bait so others would think I was fishing and sat on the seat huddled against my rod, well wrapped up in the shadows of one of the shelters, staring at distant lights across the open sea, and went to sleep.

The sound of the waves and the rhythm of the tides was all the music of my world when I was young.

It was a common tune that could mutate itself into a symphony just like that. A ballad that could change into an opera with a shift in the wind; it was a jig at dawn that could turn into a dance of death with the fall of night or into a requiem. That's the music I heard in my troubled sleep that long uncomfortable night when it was convenient for Ma to choose to believe her son's lie while she lay in a man's eager arms; as once, in the last year of the war years, she must have lain in the arms of the Man Who Was.

I drifted home some time next day, which was Sunday.

That night, the last before the start of a new school term, and the last of that hot summer, Ma snapped that I still had not got things tidied and my uniform ready and one thing and another. We had an argument and she slammed her door tight shut and left me to sort things out myself.

I made my own supper.

I went up to a cold bed.

She did not make me breakfast. So I made my own and then, filled with foreboding, I set off to the station for the start of my time in the sixth form.

I saw Harriet twice more before she went off to college and her new life.

The first was three weeks after the start of my new school term. She called on the phone and we met on the Front.

'I just wanted to say goodbye because I'm going to university tomorrow.'

She looked at me and she looked grown up.

It was as if we had become strangers again.

'Good luck,' I managed to say.

Then I remembered something.

I remembered Mr Bubbles meeting me unexpectedly in Nore Street that first day I went to school, just to wish me well.

'When does your train go?'

'Tomorrow morning, just after nine.'

Tomorrow was a Saturday.

'Not long then, Harriet.'

That was when I started to know how much I would miss her.

'Goodbye then,' she said.

'Goodbye.'

Come Saturday morning, I got up early and I went to the Dunes. I knew where to find what I was looking for because over the years Harriet had taught me. Even though I was up early I nearly missed getting to the station in time. I raced on my bike all the way there.

When I reached the station yard I slowed down so I could walk the last bit and gather my breath. I didn't know exactly what I was going to do or say, I only knew it was important.

She was not hard to find because the train was already in. She was leaning out of the window and saying goodbye to her dad. Harriet had had her hair done. She was in a suit. She had stockings and new shoes on. She didn't look happy and didn't look sad. She kept looking anxiously towards the signal, so she didn't see me coming.

'Hello,' I said.

Her dad smiled and backed away and Harriet turned and saw me. The look on her face was joy and sadness, excitement and fear, hope and trepidation; and it was gladness to see me.

'I came to say goodbye,' I said. 'I picked these for you this morning so you'd have something of the past to hold on to for the future.'

I don't know where those words came but they're what I said.

I gave her all the flowers of the dunes, scabious and campion, wild garlic and tarragon, sea thistle and lesser knapweed, all the names she taught me; and nestling in amongst them, to say that one day I hoped

I'd see her again, was tormentil, the first flower she taught me, whose yellow light is the warmest and the richest I ever knew. I was lucky to find one still in bloom – the other flowers were nothing but dried dull husks of their former glory, but I knew she wouldn't mind. I tied them together with red twine I found on the shore. It had been hunting for that among the flotsam of high tide that made me nearly miss her train.

Harriet took them from me and looked at them and smiled. Then she looked at me again and even though her dad was there she reached out a hand and drew my head towards her and kissed me and I kissed her, like I had always dreamed one day I would kiss someone. Free and easy, like stars did in the films; just like that.

The signals changed and the train jerked and pulled away.

'Good luck!' her dad cried. 'Ring me tonight!'

'Goodbye, Dad,' she said.

'Goodbye!' I shouted.

'Goodbye, Jimmy!'

After that she just waved and smiled and her eyes were filled with tears of sadness and of happiness.

*Goodbye, Harriet,* I whispered as the train moved round the bend, and we could see her waving no more.

'So . . .' said her dad, '. . . so, Jimmy, she's left us now.'

'Yes,' I said.

'She thinks the world of you, Jimmy, the world. She always has. When she needed a friend she found you.'

He had tears in his eyes from saying goodbye to Harriet.

I looked at him and he looked at me and we walked together from the station, youth and age, future times and past, one getting stronger, the other getting weaker. I going one way, he another.

When we parted he reached out and shook my hand.

'Your A levels started this year, didn't they, Jimmy?'

I nodded.

'Good luck,' he said, 'I hope you do as well as Harriet.'

'I'm going to try,' I said.

# 28

# TOP CUP

Jowett started work in Dover in the lorry business and after that summer we saw him only occasionally. When we did he looked leaner and tougher than most of us, and he wore better clothes. Goddard, like Ramsey, did arts subjects, so our two paths crossed less and less at school. Ramsey and I just carried on as before, though he too changed.

That August day on the beach I had noticed when he stripped off to swim that he was hairier than me and more muscular. His shoulders and forearms looked thick and strong. Maybe it was the golf he played so much, maybe it was just growing up. No one would ever bully him again.

Golf had become his passion and in our first sixth-form year another boy, Gareth Fylde, joined the school who was a golfer too and lived in South Stoning near David and the golf course. The two played together every weekend and I began to see David much less out of school.

But Thom Brody did maths and physics like me, plus chemistry to my English. He never said much, not then nor later, but he and I trusted and supported each other. We worked as partners in the labs when practicals demanded it and what little edge I had on him in maths he had on me in physics. Together, still mindful of Warty's Method, we helped raise each other's standard for exams.

The months raced by into winter and another season of gales, and then straight on through to a wet spring. Time never seemed to stop, or go slow, not like it had when we were young.

A wet summer term took over, with teeming rain that washed out sports fixture after fixture, including the golf matches David played for his club. Even up on the chalk the greens were too soft.

My fear of rain, until then only rarely a problem, suddenly deepened that year. More than once I found myself caught in a downpour along the shore I still beachcombed when I had nothing better to do. It was not so bad that I avoided venturing out when it was wet and windy outside, but it made me uneasy and sudden heavy rain, of the kind that sometimes sweeps unexpectedly inshore from the sea, froze me where I stood. If there was no shelter, as there was not across the Dunes and Stannick Bay, or no time to reach any, I might be stuck for tens of minutes, an hour or two sometimes, getting wetter and colder, the fear and dread in me so great it numbed my mind and bent my posture.

Ma knew about this problem but offered no solution except the vague reassurance that one day I might grow out of it. At school my weakness was simply tolerated as an eccentricity, and perhaps because I was able to walk in the rain when I was with others, their company seeming to break the awful spell, no one saw how serious it was. Only David and Thom understood heavy rain's real power over me. They never commented on it much, but they were the two who could be relied on to wait for me if rain threatened, or began, and walk at my side to and from the station. Many a time that wet May and June one or the other saw me home.

'Okay?' Thom would say.

'There you are!' was David's way of saying goodbye.

On rainy mornings Brody would sometimes come for me too, since he lived nearer.

'Okay?'

'You don't have to,' I'd reply, but the truth was that with each episode my fear of rain was getting a little worse and the numbing of my mind more intense. I dreaded being caught out in a situation where my life was in danger, in the middle of the road or on a railway track. Like a mountaineer, I began to check for escape routes along the way – a doorway, a group of trees, anything into which I might retreat. I dreaded wet and thunderous immobility.

Yet still I walked across the Dunes and along the beach, but forever eyeing the clouds now, filled with potential fear.

'Why?' David asked once. 'What are you afraid of?'

I didn't know. It was a dread, a phobia, though that word was hardly known to us. It was a feeling of helplessness in the face of certain loss; it was a feeling of not knowing, a disorientation so extreme I did not know what to do and so did nothing. It was the sound of the rain as well as the feel of it that paralysed me: its drumming, its drumming, its drumming drumming down.

That summer term our long-time Headmaster, the weak but affable Reverend Bernard Smiles, retired through ill-health just as Ma had told me that he might. He had been so long under Captain Flax's thumb that we barely knew or noticed him except at morning assembly, when his role was marginalized by Flax, and on Speech Days, when he took the podium and introduced the guest who was going to present the prizes. There were plenty of rumours about his likely successor, but inevitably the front-runner was Captain Flax who, as Smiles's deputy, had taken over as Acting Head after Smiles had left.

A new chill came over the morning assemblies. The phalanx of begowned masters, Mr Wharton among them, now sat obediently in a row behind Flax, staring ahead impassively as he took assembly, standing for the morning prayer, making their small announcements when called on, dancing to the Captain's tune.

He rapidly grew into his new part, seeming more expansive and slightly more benign. But the menace never left him and he needed only to glance to one side of the hall or another, or at a particular row of boys, or even at a master of whom he disapproved, for that fearful hush to fall as our uneasy glances went to and fro, a flock of sheep wondering which of us the dog would snap its teeth at next.

Ma, who as secretary of our local National Savings Committee heard all sorts of gossip, said that no one wanted Flax to get the job but everybody was afraid of him and the Chairman of the Governors, himself a military man, was in his pocket.

'A nasty man, Flax,' said Ma, 'but that's the world of men, weak and self serving, wanting to lead but yearning to be led. Flax is not bright enough to be Head of such a school . . . Only harm can come of it.'

It was true. Time had moved on and memories of the war were receding fast. The sixties had begun and a BSc and an MA carried more weight now than an MC and a DSO. But at our school no one had the courage to act on the fact and Captain Flax, greyer now, thinner, but still formidable in neat tweed jackets, pressed twill trousers and his polished brown shoes, reigned supreme.

Prize Day, traditionally the last Tuesday of the summer term, loomed, a grand ceremonial occasion that would offer an opportunity for Captain Flax to shine. It always took place in the Great Hall, with the small boys squashed up cross-legged on the floor in front, parents behind and the rest of us on seats at the back. Except for Seniors like me, who stood at the sides, helping people find their seats, keeping order if need be.

Shining down upon us all from the side walls were the vast varnished boards that listed old head boys and scholarship winners in golden letters; and the respective winners each year of the Victor Ludorum for sport and the winner of Top Cup, the best all-round senior student of the year. None of our names were there but Templar's uncle's was, who was Victor Ludorum before the war. A perpetual reminder to Templar that he could have done better. Proud parents were always there but ours never were, having nothing in us to be proud of or to celebrate.

So it was that our last but one Prize Day approached with the expectation of nothing much at all, among our small group, at least. The Chairman of the Governors would make a speech, the prize-winners would receive their prizes from some bigwig, who would also make a speech, and the sound of congratulations would be heavy on the ears of the majority, who by definition were failures, more or less.

Year after year, boys like Ramsey and I, Templar and Brody looked on with no chance of a prize. Among us six who had worked so hard, only Goddard had ever received anything and they were just subject prizes in the lower forms, book tokens not cups. Because it was cups that mattered, the big and the more silvery the better, and the best of all was Top Cup, donated in the thirties by a former head boy and awarded to the boy who did best all round in academic work and sports. In all my time at our school it had always gone to a boarder and we already knew it was going to be a boarder again that year. Nothing changed much in our school. So there was no hope for us and our role would be simply to look smart and clap.

That year's Prize Day was widely expected to be the moment when Captain Flax's position as Headmaster would be made official. For all the dayboys, and probably many masters too, this was not a prospect to look forward to, which explained the subdued feeling that settled over the school in the days before.

Yet nothing could quite take away from the mounting excitement that always heralded prize-giving time – a combination of the end of exams and routines being broken as the school wound down and prepared itself for the long summer holiday. Not that it was Flax's style to let things go as much as the retired Head had done, but we Seniors were taken out of regular periods and given tasks like clearing out cupboards, sorting chairs, humping tables and generally helping get the school spick and span.

Some of the boys in the Second-Year Sixth disappeared off for job or college interviews and others were taken off in coaches all over Kent for the serious matter of inter-school sports fixtures and the final tennis and cricket matches of the season.

Even David Ramsey was allowed off school to compete in a golf competition with Fylde at St Andrews in Scotland, but the best Brody and I managed was a trip to the school printer in Stannick with one of the masters to help bring back the summer issues of the school magazine and programmes for Prize Day. Which meant that since the printer taped a copy of the programme to the outside of the box in which the copies had been placed we got a sneak preview of who the prizewinners were.

'Humph!' said Brody. 'The usual!'

The winners were the familiar names and, as ever, Top Cup had been awarded to a boarder, just as we expected: Gardner. Captain of

Cricket and a past winner of the Science Prize and now winner of Top Cup.

Knowing this took something away from the day for us and it could not come and go fast enough, as far as we were concerned.

Finally that last Tuesday arrived and the absentee sixth-formers returned from interviews and fixtures to swell our ranks again: boys from open days at Oxbridge and a couple with posts in the Army and Air Force successfully lined up, while Ramsey and Fylde arrived back at the last moment from their golfing jaunt.

There was tea on the Headmaster's Lawn, served by us Seniors, and rumours about who had won what prizes began to circulate, if only because of whose parents had turned up, or from form masters who gave the game away.

Captain Flax was sporting a brand new academic gown, confirmation if any were needed that he had the Head's job. Mr Wharton wore a white summer blazer and a red carnation. Conversation and laughter, handshakes and warm hellos, all were bright on the summer air and helped dispel a little of the gloom we felt at Flax taking over. While Brody and I, until now affecting boredom, magnanimously agreed that despite everything there was still a certain excitement to Prize Day, even if we were not among the great and the good.

Yet, that year there was something else in the air, something strange. As the final countdown to our assembling in the Hall began a special excitement spread in the school, a rumour of a surprise, the suggestion that something extraordinary was going to happen.

But what? Ushers now, we helped herd boys and parents in due order out of the sunshine of the lawns into the School Hall, wondering what might be going on.

As the Hall filled up a whisper went round and we saw at once what was behind it. For there, on the table that bore the silver cups and prizes, was a cup of a kind we had never seen before. It stood next to Top Cup, but was even more silvery and it made Top Cup look small. Indeed, it was surely a trophy rather a cup and it had great bulbous handles and a lid. Whatever it was, it was the finest we had ever seen. A new cup, and one that displaced all else and which might well make Gardner feel aggrieved.

We craned to get a look at the inscription that might tell us what it was, but the platform was too high and the cup was facing the wrong way. In any case, the sun was shining directly onto the platform and that cup which, like some Holy Grail, seemed to dazzle us and make it difficult to see.

A hush fell as the masters processed in and sat down behind it, half hidden as it seemed. Then the governors and Captain Flax and finally the Chairman of the Governors filed in, accompanying the bigwig who was to present the prizes.

Inevitably, among us boys, the entire proceedings that long afternoon were dominated by mounting speculation about the new cup, the unparalleled trophy: what it was for and who was to receive it. The obvious way to find that out yielded a disappointing result.

The winners of the prizes traditionally sat in the front two rows, in order of their awards, most junior first, Top Cup last. They were ushered up one by one on the right side of the stage to shake the bigwig's hand and receive their prize. The cheers and claps would grow progressively louder, the loudest being preserved for the Victor Ludorum and finally Top Cup when, by tradition, boys stamped their feet, called out and clapped as hard as they could.

On seeing the new cup, most of us immediately worked our way along the prizewinners to see who was sitting there who wasn't listed on the now-public programme. But there was no one extra, and no clue in the seating or the programme itself about the cup.

Perhaps, then, another boy who had already had a prize was to get that last and most glorious as well. Gardner maybe.

As the prize-giving progressed the mounting excitement became palpable, the whispers animated, the guessing extreme. Perhaps, after all, it was merely a cup presented to the school as a whole, a general thing without the glory associated with an individual.

Meanwhile, Captain Flax looked increasingly assured and relaxed, almost cheerful. He it was who announced the winners' names, a signal for them to come up onto the stage. He, too, who directed them off the stage and back to their seats once the bigwig had given them their prize and shaken their hand.

At last came the Victor Ludorum and a frenzy of stamping and cheers. Then finally Top Cup and more frenzy still, especially from the boarders. We dayboys clapped but we were half-hearted and we didn't stamp the floor. Until, at last, with that one glorious new cup remaining, its purpose unannounced, a silence fell, one heavy with expectation.

Only Captain Flax appeared calm, almost smug; even the Chairman of Governors seemed restless and excited.

'I will now ask the Chairman of the Governors,' said Captain Flax, 'to make his traditional address to us all . . .'

He led the clapping as the Chairman stood up.

He was not the most fluent or engaging of speakers. He had the clipped accent of an upper-class military man of the old school and that afternoon he seemed ill at ease. Perhaps he was simply out of kilter with the sense of excitement – almost unruly – that had gripped us boys and some of the parents at the coming presentation of the mysterious trophy.

He said something about the achievements of the school, something too about various decisions the governors had had to take, most about money and new building. He thanked certain masters who were leaving, conveyed regrets concerning one, recently retired, who had since died; and the death as well of three old boys whose attendance at the school dated back to the Edwardian age.

'But the most important decision governors ever have to take, and we do so in consultation with the educational authority, concerns the appointment of a new Headmaster. As many of you will know . . .'

He said some words about our recently retired Head, mention of whom elicited sympathetic applause. He said some more about the high standard of those who had applied for the job and how on such occasions the decision was difficult but . . .

His glance at Captain Flax left us in no doubt that he had the job.

Yet he had something else to say first.

'Before I announce the name of the new Head of our great school we have a rare, in fact a unique, award to make . . .'

We had come at last to the new cup, the one that mattered. So deep was the silence that we hardly dared breathe.

'. . . but since it is not, as you can see, part of our normal prize-giving, indeed not a school prize at all, I have asked the Head . . . I mean to say the *Acting* Head . . .'

This little slip attracted amused conspiratorial titters and a flurry of whispers and even a clap or two as the parents of boarders in particular nodded and nudged each other to affirm what everybody already knew, that Captain Flax was to be the new Head. He, however, maintained his composure, though a certain flush of pleasure suffused his normally pale face.

'. . . I would like to ask the Acting Head to announce this great achievement and present this very special cup.'

Captain Flax rose and did not beat about the bush.

'It is a rare honour and privilege for an Acting Head . . .'

Again the gentle laughter, the tacit understanding.

'. . . to be able to make the announcement I am about to make. I have looked carefully through the school records, the earliest we have for such matters dating back to 1865, and I can confirm that we have never before had a boy or boys achieve a *national* honour on behalf of the school. But I am pleased to say that this is now the case.

'Some three months ago the then Head was approached by a certain boy, who is here today, for permission to represent the school with another boy at a sport and in a tournament in which we had not been represented before. In which, indeed, we have no track record at all, nor one would have thought, any chance of significant success.

'It was almost the last decision Reverend Smiles was to take before his illness forced his resignation. Needless to say, as Acting Head, I was honoured to abide by that wise and generous decision and to encourage that boy, and another with him, both from the Lower Sixth, to do the best they could on our behalf.

'They were competing with all the schools in Britain in a competition which has never before been won by a state school but which had been the preserve of the private schools and, if I may say so, of more privileged boys than most of ours.

'Into that competition these boys went with no expectation from any but themselves that they would be able to achieve more than represent the school.'

He paused and looked at the great silver trophy in front of them.

'Well, I am pleased so say they competed brilliantly. No, they were not merely among the top few, nor were they third or second. Those two boys *won*.

'Ladies and gentlemen, boys, please show your appreciation to the two boys who yesterday afternoon, at St Andrews in Scotland, beat all-comers to take the title of British Inter-school Open Pairs Golf Champions: David Ramsey and Gareth Fylde.'

In the last moments of Captain Flax's speech I had begun to guess at something of the truth. Now I looked at David in astonishment as he leant over and whispered in my ear as the applause and the stamping and the cheering began, 'The Method wins again!'

I laughed and shook his hand and shoved him on his way along with Fylde towards the platform.

If his back was sore from the thumps of praise it received during his slow progress to the stage, it was because I began them. I cheered and I clapped and I stepped forward from the side as others did, as we all did, all of us who had never won a thing, all of us who had only ever watched the winners shake the hand of the bigwig, and especially all of us dayboys.

For now, from out of our midst, a winner had come, a real winner, a *national* winner, who had dared take the challenge far beyond the close and limited confines of our school.

A dayboy.

Once a weakling.

A victim turned victor.

It was not just for Ramsey we clapped, but for all of us who, truly, he and Fylde represented.

So infectious were our cheers and claps that the masters stood up as Ramsey mounted the steps, and then the parents too, and the two were carried in a storm of noise and shouts up the steps onto the stage to take the cup of cups, a *real* Top Cup, the first any of us had ever seen.

Knowing David as I did, and having seen the smile of pure delight as the announcement had been made, I was surprised to see that, as he climbed the stairs and Captain Flax took up the cup and reached out his right hand to shake his, David had gone pale. He was taller than Flax, and looked every inch the winner, but suddenly he appeared nervous, not cheerful at all.

He seemed preoccupied and looked at the cup not Captain Flax. The cheers died in my mouth, and in Brody's too at my side. Yet from everyone else they got louder still as, seeming to forget to shake Flax's hand, or refusing too, he simply took the cup, held it up for Fylde to hold as well and stood, pale faced, ill at ease, never smiling once.

The cheering went on and on – and on. Until from among the parents there came the call 'Speech! Speech!', which was immediately taken up by everybody.

Boys never made speeches. It was unheard of.

Masters made speeches, not boys.

Captain Flax stepped forward and tried to usher the two boys off, but David did not move.

'Speech!' we cried and younger parents too. You could begin to smell rebellion in the air. A revolution was happening before our eyes.

We saw Flax frown, the smile leaving his face. We saw him lean close to David's ear and utter what appeared an order to move.

Still David did not shift his ground, the cup held low before him as he seemed to struggle with something that was on his mind. Then our cries began to die and an expected silence fell.

'Go on! Speech!' someone cried again.

David looked round at the Chairman, ignoring Captain Flax.

The Chairman wavered, looked from a now grim-faced Flax to a still hopeful audience, wavered a moment and then nodded his head at David and gestured for him to step forward, which he did, cup in hand.

Those in the audience who were still standing now sat down again, while those of us who had moved forward settled back. Suddenly the stage was David's and, pale and awful though he looked, he took sudden and unexpected advantage of it, with the same ruthlessness and courage he must have needed to win his cup.

'I'm sorry,' he said, his voice quite clear, his eyes on the audience, more man than boy, 'but all I have to say is that I do not think that Captain Flax should be the next Head of our school.'

He paused, he hesitated and then he said what no one had dared to say: 'He interferes with little boys. He shouldn't be Head of this school. I'm sorry . . .'

There was a strange and terrible gasp, a frisson of shock that turned at once into something far more.

'Get off the stage, boy,' ordered Captain Flax in a low and terrifying voice, suddenly a commander under fire, '*now!*' His face was livid, his eyes terrible, his mouth cruel. He was anger incarnate.

Ramsey did not move, less perhaps from courage now than surprise and shock at what he had done. The mood in the Hall had shifted from triumph to horror and disgust, but like a swirling, shifting storm, the anger seemed directed at Ramsey, for upsetting the day, not at Flax.

'Get him out of here,' hissed Flax, his voice suddenly a model of control and confidence.

A games master, one of Flax's minions, rose with determination and advanced behind Ramsey to grab him and pull him off the stage.

The Chairman stepped forward, trying to upstage David, and began to smile and speak inanities.

The crowd faltered and began to chatter with embarrassment. David had done something that seemed unforgivable and the sooner he was gone the sooner he, and what he had said, could be forgotten.

I saw that Ramsey the hero was about to be transformed by a master's hand at his collar into Ramsey the villain, the spoiler, the victim once more. I saw the old fear return to his eyes. He had made his stand and now needed support if he was to survive.

He looked around for that support, the cup hanging heavy in his hand. He looked from one part of the audience to another until finally he looked at me, as he had done so often in our early years at the school. At my back I felt Brody's hand, pushing me gently forward. I did not resist.

'It's true what Ramsey says,' I heard myself say and then more loudly, 'it's true. Captain Flax interferes with little boys. We all know it in this school. None of us want him as our Head.'

The hush turned to ice, unspeakably unpleasant. Nearly unbearable. The master, Flax's minion, faltered behind David, his grip on him weakening while the Chairman opened his mouth and no words came out.

As I stepped forward Captain Flax stared slowly at me. I knew it was the moment I had so long waited for.

'You know it's true,' I said, and I did not even need to raise my voice. Indeed, the voice that came out of my mouth was not my own but Michael's: it had its toughness, its cruel incisiveness.

Then, moving in for the kill I had so often dreamed of, I said again, 'You *know*.'

He opened his mouth to speak and still he might have turned the crowd and found a way out of it. But then something happened to stop him, something unanswerable, something that turned the darkness that hung over that Hall and all our school into light. We heard and we saw the simple voice of truth, which cuts through everything.

Among the little boys sitting cross-legged at the front, one slowly stood up. I did not know his name, and he was so junior I barely recognized him.

He rose and stood still among those who sat about him. He was just a little boy as I had once been, and Ramsey and my brother Michael.

'It's true, sir,' he said.

It was to the Chairman he spoke.

'It's *true*.'

Then one by one, now on the right side, now on the left, now at the back and now at the front once more, other boys rose, boarders many of them, each one in some way a past victim of Captain Flax.

The Hall fell silent and that afternoon it seemed we saw the wrath of God; or if not of God, of Truth, and the meaning of revolution.

Captain Flax stood staring, the blood gone from his face. He looked thin and drained and suddenly old.

More and more boys rose in support of those who had already done so, until the whole school was standing.

Then another whisper started, as cruel as Captain Flax's mouth. Begun almost silently by Brody at my side, it quickly spread around the room and came back to haunt Captain Flax.

*Ryan ryan ryan ryanryanryan . . .*

It was the surname of the boy who killed himself on the railway line. But somewhere in its utterance, somehow, it became sibilant and turned itself into something more dreadful yet, a hiss, a fearful hiss, foul as the stench of death, awful as the thought of a boy in such distress that he lies down on a railway line and waits for a train to come.

Then, as Captain Flax stood there speechless, still hoping to ride out the storm, there was action behind him. Quite suddenly, but without drama of any kind, Mr Wharton stood up and with a strange shrug, a look of distaste, he simply left the stage, shaking his head. After him the ranks of the masters broke and one after another they followed him, voting with their feet their lack of confidence in the proposed new Head.

He stood there a short time longer, a pitiful, lonely figure, his power drained out of him before our eyes until, yielding suddenly, a spent force, his face yellow, his eyes haunted, Captain Flax left the school stage for the last time.

As for David, he stepped down and the boys made way for him in silence as he headed back to Brody and me and our protective custody.

That was the terrible end of that Prize Day. People left in silence, parents leading their children to car or train or bus without a word, while us senior dayboys headed for the station and left others, the boarders perhaps, to clear up what we were not going to touch.

Not much was said, not then or later.

No further accusations were made, nor any charges brought. When we returned to school in September it was as if Captain Flax had never been. Three other masters had also left, but we never knew why.

Mr Wharton stayed.

Another man came in as Headmaster, younger, brighter, full of the joy of learning. He had nothing to do with the boarding houses. Captain Flax's old house was closed down and used for something else and the division between the boarders and the dayboys became blurred.

Ma said Captain Flax was forced to retire, unable to get a job because he was unable to get a reference.

But later, talking to Michael, I learnt different.

He told me that Flax had moved to another part of England and got a job as deputy head in a preparatory school.

'But he . . .' I protested.

'Believe me,' Michael said, with one of his hard and cynical laughs, which expressed his lack of surprise at the world's cruelties, 'that kind look after their own.'

I did – believe him. Because by then I was sure that Michael was one of that kind too.

# 29

# TORMENTIL

The departure of Captain Flax ended an era at our school and an era for ourselves. The weight of failure had been lifted from our shoulders and we could raise our heads now and look towards the outside world. With each week that passed it seemed to beckon ever more, taking our friends from us one by one to job and college and to university, leaving fewer and fewer of us hanging on behind waiting impatiently for our individual summons to leave.

A levels did not hold the same awe for us as O levels had done, least of all for those of us who had followed the Method and knew it worked. Having won through once we intended to do so again. We had discovered self-motivation the hard way and its discipline was not hard for us to maintain.

Ramsey, Brody and I were the remaining rump of our little group: Jowett and Templar having left the school, while Goddard, into arts subjects, made different friends.

He gained an early exhibition to Cambridge, subject to good A level results, and after that we hardly saw him. Brody applied to read engineering at King's, London, and gained a place on the basis of grades he could now easily achieve, while Ramsey and I, firm friends now, gained a place each at Bristol.

Our world was filled with hope as our final summer term started. The A levels came suddenly and went as fast, all in a flurry of nerves and excitement, and finally fatigue. When they were over we had sufficient confidence to believe that each of us would do well enough to continue our studies at college afterwards. We drank a few secret beers, we lusted after girls but had neither courage nor opportunity to take it further. The days seemed filled with sunlight, endless and unstoppable.

David's golf was taking more and more of his time and at the beginning of July he got himself invited to America with some other up-and-coming young golfers to tour college campuses playing golf. Even then he had his sights set beyond simply playing golf.

'It's only a game,' I had chided him when he seemed to be taking it too seriously.

'No, Jimmy, it's not a game, it's a business. I want to own a golf course of my own one day.'

He saw into his future far more clearly than I did into mine.

David finally left our school quietly one day before the end of that last term. Only I knew he was not coming back.

'Well,' he said, as we got off the train at Stoning together for a final time, 'I'm glad *that's* over.'

He meant his school career and no one knew better than me how he felt.

Then: 'Jimmy, you were the best thing that happened to me in all my years at school.'

I felt embarrassed but he continued in the old persistent way he had, the same way that made him win at golf: 'If you ever need my help, Jimmy, I'll try and be strong for you. You taught me how.'

'Show me how to overcome my fear of rain then.'

'Can't help you there,' he said, biffing my arm.

It sometimes seemed that David had been the only dependable person in my whole life apart from Granny and Mr and Mrs Bubbles who, like him, loved me as I was.

But Granny was old now, and as good as blind, clinging on to life in her nursing home and fighting all the way. While Mr Bubbles had had a turn the previous winter, collapsing on the beach, and though Mrs Bubbles did all she could to look after him, he was no longer as strong as he once was. His great black coat hung from him now as from a scarecrow.

The future was for David and me and our few friends.

* * *

With David gone off for the summer to America, Thom Brody was the only one of our group left behind with whom I could wile away the time waiting for our results and confirmation that our future was set fair.

Like David he had filled out, but he didn't have David's lightness. He never said much about himself but nobody I knew ever made me feel protected quite like he did. I had felt that since that day in Mr Wharton's class when I broke down: it was Thom who had stood guard at the door to make sure no one else came into the room.

Thom never said why he understood me but he never needed to. I could tell that he had dwelt in Darktime too. How or why or where or when I did not know, but its mark was on him as it must have been on me. We did not need to talk about those things.

At the start of that last summer holiday Thom Brody found himself a girlfriend. He didn't say much but there was more to it than holding hands. Meeting them promenading, hand in hand, up by the Lifeboat Station, a grin on his normally dour face, I saw he had found a new confidence.

'If you had a girlfriend we could all go to a dance in the Palais,' he said.

'I'll watch out for one,' I said heavily.

In fact I had done nothing else for months, but no girl appeared because in truth my heart wasn't in it. I harboured a secret love for Harriet Fosse and admitted no one else into my heart.

She came down from university to Stoning sometimes to see her dad. She would call me and we walked and talked but we never kissed again. I wanted to but I seemed to have lost the art of doing what had come naturally before. Also she made a point of talking about boys she knew at college. They sounded older and more experienced than me. She didn't want me any more.

Mr Bubbles used to say you only had to ask but my vocabulary for asking dried up when Harriet was around. Then, too late, when I had worked out the words she was off back to college again.

So there was never a Palais dance for me with Thom and his girl. But when he wasn't walking around with his girlfriend he came on the beach with me and somehow or other we started helping with the boats at Stoning Sailing Club up by the Lifeboat Station, which had taken over what used to be three fishermen's pitches. That was how we learnt to sail. When boats were free we sailed them, or in the evening when people had gone.

Soon Thom's girl began to sit on the beach and watch us as we laughed and larked about, sailing together and then against each other, falling in the water and climbing back out; learning the art of righting a capsized boat.

In those short weeks when the sun shone and we were waiting for our results we seemed to be more in the sea than out of it. From then on whenever I saw the wind on sun-filled waves, or tasted the salt sea spray on the wind, or spotted an old-fashioned clinker-built dinghy, its varnish worn, or heard the flap of a sail and the slap of wire against masts when the boats are all pulled up the shore for the night . . . I saw Thom and myself that delicious summer, bronzed by wind and sun, our hair turning blond, our grins wide. So brown were we that you could have laid us down on the shingle and you'd have lost us in its myriad colours and walked right over us at the waves' edge, thinking we were the shingle and the sea. You'd only have known we were there by the sound of our laughter, and our rough and tumbles, and our splashing in and out of the blue salt sea.

Thom's girlfriend, who had a job in Gelato's before she went to college that coming autumn, took to bringing us free ice cream and colas, wrapped up in old newspaper to keep it cool. She would come and sit up by our towels and wave frantically, ice creams in hand, and that was the signal to head on in.

Day after day that summer, evening after evening.

'You ought to find yourself a girl, Jimmy,' she used to say, her hand in Thom's, her thighs together, leaning against his.

'He's got one and her name's Harriet,' said Thom.

'No I haven't.'

'Yes, I heard,' said his girl darkly. 'She doesn't know a good thing when she sees one. If I meet her I'll tell her . . .'

'You won't!' I said.

'I will, I promise!'

'No you won't!'

But she did.

One bright afternoon, two or three days before our results came through, when Thom wasn't there, someone capsized not too far offshore. They weren't in trouble, just wet and inexperienced. I ran along the beach far enough that I could swim out and reach them without being swept past and back towards the North End.

I knew our currents so well by then that I could judge where things were drifting at any state of the tide. Mr Bubbles and Freddie taught me how to do it and that summer completed my education in the art. It's a matter of knowing how the water runs and what your strengths are; a matter of walking that beach as many years as I had; a matter of learning how to hear the heartbeat of the sea and feel its flow within.

I always went to capsizes if I could, even if they didn't need me. I swam or I sailed, got myself near, watching over them. I did it and so did Thom. It was our unofficial job that year and one of the reasons the club gave us the run of the boats.

There weren't official lifeguards on our beach then, nor warning signs, nor regulations stopping things. Just us.

But I liked to be there for my own reasons.

I never wanted to hear a call for help across the water again.

I never wanted to witness another drowning.

I would rather have drowned myself than know that pain again.

Those children drowning that summer day when I was young, and that man's face, were never far from me.

I wanted to be able to do what I had not been able to do for them. Sometimes I cried from sadness and frustration at that memory. But you wouldn't have known if you'd seen me in a boat that summer: I looked as strong and solid as an ox.

So that day, Thom not being about, I swam the long way out, describing a beautiful parabola with my body in the sea so I reached that craft dead on, popping up like a miracle.

'Hello!' I said.

He was a man in his thirties and he was tired.

'I thought a rescue launch would be on the way,' he gasped, trying to make a joke of it. 'I'm a visitor.'

He was cold as well. But at least he had a life jacket on, even though it was too big.

I told him what I was going to do and seeing as he was a heavy chap and it's harder than it looks getting someone out of the sea into a dinghy I told him what to do as the craft righted itself.

'Not too soon and not too late – I'll give you a shout.'

He obeyed my orders like I was a sea captain. It was Mr Bubbles and Freddie who gave me that kind of confidence. Freddie was dead but a bit of him lived in me; Mr Bubbles was alive, though ailing, but he was there as well.

I had hold of the lanyard and climbed up on the daggerboard and – One! Two! Three! – we were up and he was scooped right into that boat in a mess of sail and seawater; then, with a heave, I clambered in as well. We bailed most of the water out and I told him where to sit. I turned the craft to the wind and eased it round to fill the sail and take us off.

'We're going offshore,' he said in puzzlement.

He was shivering with cold.

It was summer and a very warm day but that's how dangerous the sea can be if you don't know what to do.

'We're going out to get back in the right place,' I said.

'It's a long run.'

'Has to be, because the current's strong,' I said, telling a half truth.

For the whole truth was that it was a lovely day and a fair wind and a good sea and I fancied a long run in, so I went a long way out. That was my reward for getting him home in one piece and his shivers were his punishment. He wasn't going to die of cold in any craft I sailed.

We sailed out, made the tack and started the long run back to shore, him happy now, me happy too.

I could see all of Stoning bathed in the evening sun, red roofs and grey, and the white cupola of the Royal Marines' Barracks.

I could feel the sun on the side of my face and the wind on its other side.

I could see our first house in Stoning, the one the Man Who Wasn't had owned with Ma, and the sycamore I climbed up that day when the African Gentleman came to see Granny and confirm their deep love.

I could see the Monarch Hotel and the warm rich red Kent peg-tiled roofs of the North End.

I could see the shadowy top end of Compass Street in whose shadows I had lived so long.

And far off along the coast, past the houses, I could see the Dunes stretching away to Stannick Bay, where the water shimmered in melting air.

The dinghy keeled into the wind, the shivering man clung on, and I felt my body's strength as I held the tiller and the boat steady and kept the line for shore.

I could see all the places of my childhood and I could see that now I was a child no more, but strong and purposeful, my days in Stoning numbered, not far off the numbers of my fingers and my toes, which was twenty.

We raced at an angle towards the shore, the wind just right, as if we were going to crash into it. But at the last moment I eased us round to slow and let the last wave take us in so the craft's bow just nudged the shore, no more than a kiss in the shingle.

I jumped into the shallows, helped the man off and heaved the boat up with the aid of a couple of waves. Someone came and gave me a hand and we were soon out and up the beach, salt water running down my trunks and legs, dry salt in the hairs of my arms, my hair tousled and dry, the sun warm on my glad face.

'Hello, Jimmy.'

She was sitting where Thom's girl normally sat on the shingle, her legs bare and her knickers showing as the wind caught at her summer frock.

I didn't have to think what to do or say, nor worry much about what I wanted, which was her. I felt good and confident and her eyes were filled with light.

'Hello, Harriet,' I said. 'We could have a walk tonight and a swim tomorrow.'

'Yes, Jimmy,' she said.

I knelt on the shingle, my legs astride her lap as I had seen Burt Lancaster do and I put my lips to hers.

'Oh!' she gasped, pulling away a little to get her breath.

I collapsed on the shingle beside her, front down, laughing. It's not a position you can hold very long, kissing a girl like that, and I had grown hard with excitement, which must have showed in my trunks. That was why I was laughing. With Harriet there was suddenly no embarrassment any more. It was like the old days.

My bulge took a long time to subside before I could roll over on my back, and then only just. The shingle had left strange red indentations in my chest like monstrous smallpox, that's how long I lay on my front before I could roll over.

'I'm so glad to see you,' she said, snuggling her head to my temporarily blotchy chest.

'What about the boys you see in college?' I said.

'There weren't any, Jimmy. I just made them up. There never has been a boy, in fact . . .'

Her hand slid down the side of my face and my excitement came back again, so I had to roll on my side and press myself close in case passers-by saw. I knew what she was saying.

My excitement was painful between my legs. It pressed against her thigh and when her hand slid from my face to my chest and then further down I thought it was going to explode with a great big bang, an explosion big enough to send shingle flying and a few dinghies and me and Harriet up into the air.

'Jimmy!' said Harriet and laughed, so I laughed too. We pressed against each other, leg to leg, then front to front.

'I can't move,' I said, 'somebody'll see.'

'Then we'll just have to lie like this until you can,' said Harriet, putting her arms around me. I felt her bosoms on my chest, and the point of one of them, proud through her dress, was near my mouth and I wanted to put my tongue to it, so I did, wetting her frock with my spit.

'Jimmy!' she said, her voice filled with desire.

So we lay in the late afternoon sun, me slowly drying and getting cold and eventually subsiding.

'There's only been you, Jimmy, just you.'

For the first time in my life I wanted to say 'I love you', but I didn't.

We kissed for a long time and then we just lay there, hot and cold, dry and moist, the shingle lumpy and uncomfortable, but me feeling we were in seventh heaven, and Harriet as well.

'Where will we walk?' she asked.

'The cliffs, like before,' I said, 'and tomorrow there's the swim . . .'

'Have to be later in the afternoon; there's relatives,' she said.

'Okay,' I said and I was glad because it gave me time to act on the idea that came to me. I told her my plan. She said it was a good idea, and it was, because the cliffs, what with their smelly bomb shelters and dogs and strange men walking, wasn't the best place for our first time, which was our unspoken intent.

Our special place was the Dunes and it always had been. That was my plan.

So that evening we just walked, right up into the stars at the top of the cliffs, taking care not to fall over the cliff edge and bring our lives to a sudden end. We sat in the rough grass with the sound of the sea we loved far below, and the ship lights across the Downs stretching to the dark horizon, punctuated by the sweeping lights of the lightships of the Goodwin Sands.

We talked of everything, did Harriet and I, high above it all on the cliffs, so near to the stars we could almost touch them. We talked of everything and too much, with sex and desire in the evening air. We stood up, hands to bodies, lips to lips, and then cheek to cheek we stared across the dark void of the sea to the twinkling, nearly invisible lights of France.

Then we turned to each other and sank back into the grass. For the first time I felt the soft moist woman of her, past her stockings and beneath her knickers; and she felt me, which was moist and hard, and she sighed and groaned and shoved herself all over me and said 'Yes, yes' and 'Oh!'

She unbuttoned her dress and I got her bra free and her bosoms, which I had wanted to touch with my tongue, I now enveloped with my mouth, playing her nipples with my tongue.

She sighed and moaned and I gasped, 'Don't touch me down there!' because I could feel what was going to happen.

But suddenly she did and what with her nipple in my mouth and her hand rubbing me up and down, I came as she did, trying not to make a sound but uttering grunts and groans as if we were strangling.

We lay then, did Harriet and I, panting and kissing and touching and finally talking of so many things. But there was danger in the intimacy and confessional of our talk, but of a kind we could not have known.

For a long time I had wanted to break my silence about Ma's suicide plans, but I had made a promise not to. There, as we lay in the grass in the dark, unseen, unheard, Ma a world away, I finally told Harriet all about it and about my juvenile agreement to tell Ma when she could no longer look after herself.

I talked and I felt bad. Maybe I cried, maybe a tear just coursed down my cheek. But I had no idea it would shock Harriet so much.

'That's awful,' she said, sitting up. 'That's appalling. Someone should . . .'

'Don't ever tell Ma I mentioned it,' I said hastily. 'You've never seen her when she's angry.'

'I've never seen her when she's happy either,' replied Harriet tartly.

Maybe we talked a bit more about it, maybe. Maybe we just talked of everything and too much.

The next day Harriet brought her bag of things to my house and that was the first time she'd met Ma in a long time.

You could tell they didn't like each other and I stood between them, first in the corridor and later in our yard, feeling I was between the devil and the deep blue sea; between Scylla and Charybdis.

I should have taken that as a warning.

Ma was strange that year, and particularly strange that day, which was the day I got my A level results.

I got all three, two As and a B – the same as Thom and the same as David. I had been on the phone all morning until Harriet came.

The moment she arrived I told her the news and she hugged me close and that was Ma's first sight of her and she didn't like it, though she smiled.

'How do you do?' she said, formally in the corridor. 'One teaspoon of sugar or two?' she said, in our little garden.

'None at all, thanks,' said Harriet, smiling and beautiful, eyes only for me.

Ma didn't like being Number Two in her own back yard. Ma fought for her independence from men all her life but now it was a woman displacing her in her special chair facing the sun and she didn't like it one bit.

'Supper's at seven,' she said, 'and we'll celebrate your success.'

'Er, I won't be here.'

'But I've bought the food.'

'I'm going out,' I said.

'With *you*, I suppose?' said Ma, looking at Harriet.

Harriet could be fierce as well and she was.

'Yes,' she said, not giving an inch.

'I see,' said Ma and she got up and went, leaving behind the stench of ill feeling and madness.

But I had warned Harriet about Ma and she knew most things, so I thought no more about it.

'Only two more weeks,' I said, 'and then I'm going to Bristol to sort out accommodation.'

'We could go walking,' she said.

'Where?' I said.

'In North Wales. We could go and look for tormentil. Remember?'

I remembered Uncle Max and Auntie Fiona and that happy time away from Stoning and from Ma.

'I haven't much money,' I said.

'You don't need much to walk,' she said.

'We could stay in Youth Hostels again,' I said.

So it was decided, there in Ma's yard, our way of enjoying those last days before I left home.

Our plan for that night was this: I would take our bags, which held clothes and towels, some food and some nightlights, across the Dunes on my bike and hide them in a place I knew up near the shore. Then, as darkness fell, we would change into our swimming costumes at Mr Bubbles's house and walk up to the Front and then down the shingle to the shore and swim out a little way into the sea. We were going to let the current drift us past Compass Street, past the groynes, past the old castle, all the way along the shore to where I had hidden our things.

I had one doubt and Harriet another.

Hers was being seen walking up Budd Street in nothing but her costume.

'It'll be murky,' I said.

'Even so . . .'

'I'll get Mrs Bubbles to lend you her dressing gown and she can take it back when you're on the beach.'

'Well . . .'

My worry was that there might be night fishermen after ling and flatties along by the castle. I didn't want us to be caught by hooks, but I didn't want to go too far out to avoid them. You could only swim so far off our shore before the current took you and made it hard to get back in. I decided to sort that out when we came to it, and just hope that if there were fishermen there they didn't cast over us.

Evening came and we changed liked a couple of excited children in the Bubbleses' house.

'I don't know,' said Mr Bubbles, shaking his head. 'The sea was for fishing in when I was your age, not larking about in.'

'Mr Bubbles can't swim,' explained Mrs Bubbles, 'so he is afraid for you, Jimmy. But I have seen you swim. I have watched you all the summer, swimming like a fish.'

Then, feeling foolish but excited and shivering with the feeling of it, Harriet in a dressing down, we went up the road with both Mr and Mrs Bubbles coming to see us off.

'Daft, you are,' said Mr Bubbles, but he was grinning. 'And you, young Harriet, dafter still. But one thing I know: this lad'll look after you and see you safe home, there's no doubt about that.'

Harriet got on as well with Mr Bubbles as she got on badly with Ma.

Then, in semi-darkness, shivering with desire not with cold, we set off into the sea for our swim, to float with the current all the way to the darkness of the Dunes.

'Oh!' said Harriet and we swam out on our backs and held hands, not too cold, being in love, and not too far out, being sensible.

We watched the shore and the houses over the Promenade float by, as it grew darker all the time. Lights coming on in houses, streetlights flickering into life, the first stars coming out – magic happened before our eyes. Once we came in near enough to shore to feel the sand and pebbles on the bottom, but mostly we were out of our depth, and waves rolled in from behind as we faced ashore, lifting us up and letting us down.

'Oh!' sighed Harriet and 'Aah!'

There were no night fishermen, though I saw one setting up and another cycling along the Promenade to do the same.

There were just the houses floating by, the lights, our hands and arms touching in the cool embracing sea and our hands and bodies sliding, touching, in the secret darkness of the night.

'It's not cold at all,' said Harriet, her bosom to my chest, her salt wet lips to mine, as we floated and floated along and I kept an eye on the shore.

'I could do this for ever,' I said, my feet reaching down into the depth of the sea and feeling nothing but nothing, and then rolling in the dark water and looking up and saying, 'Harriet! Look at the stars!'

Out there, far enough from the shore to feel freedom but not so far to feel in danger, she and I floated, lost for ever in a moment when the world seemed to be ours, its joys a compensation for our occasional sorrows, its vast strength our comfort and our strength.

After a time I said without thinking, 'We need to head for the shore now, Harriet.'

My voice trembled and so did her reply: 'How do you know, Jimmy? I can't see a thing but stars.'

'By the silhouette of the shingle bank,' I lied, for a show of confidence seemed best that vibrant, potent night.

But I did know, without quite knowing how, from the familiar push and drift of the sea in my flesh and bones, and the touch of the seabed at my feet when it came, sandy just there, and the waves and water about my body, all part of me and me of it.

Oh yes, I knew.

In that magical, starlit darkness, Harriet and I rose out of the waves like Adam and Eve and we stumbled hand in hand up the shingly shore. Then up the shifting bank within a few feet of where we should have done, which was where, next to a clump of yellow sea poppies, black in the night, I had hidden our bags.

I found her towel and mine and we held each other close until, wanting to get warm, we began to towel each other's shoulders and necks and heads.

It was Harriet who slipped the straps of her costume down her shoulders and I whose hands pulled them lower. Harriet who put my hands to her bosoms and nipples, I who slipped her costume off and dried her with my towel where she lay sighing, before bending down and wetting her with my lips and tongue as she opened her legs. I had never done that before, but I knew what to do. I tasted the taste of her, which was salty and good, and she sighed and sighed and finally moaned.

In that darkness, beneath the world's great sky, with the sea murmuring down on the shore behind us and the rustling of the breeze across the Dunes in front, we explored a new world neither of us knew.

'Be gentle,' she whispered, reaching up to me, her lips to mine, her nipples hard at my chest, her hands running down my back and pulling down my costume before her fingers played with me in front and I stiffened even more in her hand.

The darkness of the night gave us freedom, the Dunes reality, the sea our slow but urgent strength, one to another.

The towels became our bed as I knelt before her and her thighs and the secret darkness between and felt the strength between my legs, and her hand, gentler than mine, guiding me into her.

That brief moment before, of being there but not inside, at the tight moment of her opening, when I felt the world sliding open before me, when she gasped with brief discomfort and almost-pain and then sighed 'Oh' and 'Ooooh!' and her arms came round me and held me close . . .

That moment held no memory, no reference to anything. No one but she and I were there.

No running, no gate closed shut, no Ma's red raw hitting hand, no lost shoes, no Darktime, no Granny, no long years of failure, no loneliness, no fear of rain and what it meant, which was unutterable loss.

That moment was now, and love in each other's arms and the storming ride of passion, and the gentlest violence that I ever knew: that was what that long moment meant as together we defined for each other for ever the meaning of making love.

'Oh,' she sighed, 'oh, oh . . .' her hands on my buttocks as she climaxed and I came too, 'ooooh . . .

Then we just lay as one, complete and at peace.

Later, growing cold, I pulled the clothes from my bag to cover my legs and back and she pulled out hers as well and made me snug, her petticoat across the last part of me that bore the cold, my shoulders.

'There!' she said, warm because I was on her, in her, there.

I felt the feel of her clothes against me and the scent of silk and perfume, and a memory came, elusive, of that time before Darktime when I knew the woman in the room, distant, the feel and presence of her there but nothing more; except that outside against the window pane was the relentless drumming sound of rain.

I wept then and Harriet, holding me close, asked me why.

I tried to explain but the drumming rain of memory was elusive and I couldn't see the face of the Man Who Wasn't, only feel his hand holding mine; and the woman whose scent and softness I had longed to find again all my life seemed to drift away and out of reach, lost in the arms of Harriet, who held me.

Then she wept too.

Happiness? Ancient and lost.

Happiness: present and found.

The sweet safe contentment of being home.

The rain far away and not yet come again. All I knew for certain was that the rain marked the beginning of all my ills.

'Jimmy, what are you thinking about?'

'Not sure, don't know,' I said. 'It doesn't matter. Really.'

We dressed with the slow intimacy of lovers, each watching the other's pale body in the dark, and then I lit the nightlights and by their flickering light we had the feast I had asked Mrs Bubbles to make for us.

Sweetmeats and patisserie, chocolates and almonds, and a bottle of red wine that long before had fallen into Mr Bubbles' hands and which Mrs Bubbles gave us without him knowing.

''E will not mind, Jimmy. But bring back the corkscrew!'

There we sat, woozy now by candlelight and stars, watching the lightships, discovering the easy, magic, seductive world of the aftermath of love.

We played with fire that night and other nights, thinking only of the present, not of what might happen.

Then Harriet got sensible, and I responsible. The God of Fortune and Cupid, smiling on us, let us go without a consequence.

For our walking holiday we took rucksacks and boots but not many clothes, as well as a tent and anoraks, our Youth Hostel cards and what money we had, which wasn't much.

The morning we left, Mr Bubbles borrowed a Kodak camera from a neighbour to take a photograph of us, all togged up and ready to go.

''Ere, Mr Bubbles, you are better at digging worms than taking photographs,' said Mrs Bubbles, who knew about snaps because she had got her dad to take the one of her with her brother Philippe which was always on her shelf. She knew the importance of memory and the meaning of *souvenir*.

She touched our cheeks and said we looked like children, and told Mr Bubbles to stand behind her and make us smile. It was then she took the photograph of Harriet and me, arm in arm, young things about to walk off into life. Harriet's hand was on my arm. I looked strong and she looked beautiful.

'It'll be here for you when you get back,' Mrs Bubbles said.

Then she stood with him and they looked at us with pride and love. No bride and groom could have had a better send-off than we did for that holiday.

We went by train to North Wales and walked the hills and valleys of Snowdonia, the land of tormentil, the depth of whose rich yellow, its quietness, its surprises, its modesty, its warmth, was like our love.

Again, we talked of everything and too much, including those forbidden secrets to do with Ma it would have been better to keep silent about. Which Harriet still could not forget or understand or even leave alone.

'You just can't make such a promise,' she said, 'it isn't *right*.'

I shrugged.

'We have a right to die,' I said.

'We have no right to take life, only to make it.'

We made love differently after that, the passion diluted. We had journeyed on. Even though the stars and the moonstruck shingle and the candlelight were still there in memory, they did not look the same.

Harriet and I came back to discover that summer had fled from Stoning and autumn had settled in.

We had only a day or two to pack for university, she for her final year and I for my first.

That night, back in my cold house, anxious now to leave for ever, I found Ma had already begun to clear my room even before I had gone. Like she once cleared Michael's.

My things were in brown grocery boxes ready for the attic.

'I left out what you might need for university,' she said.

I should have expected it, but Ma's cruelty never ceased to surprise. And I should have realized there was worse to come. The things she did made me ashamed to think she was my mother.

That night she came up to my room just before I turned in for bed, my cases packed.

'Oh, I forgot to tell you,' she said in that innocent way she had, 'you know Mr Bubbles in Budd Street? The bait digger?'

My heart thumped in pain and dread.

'He died. They found him on the beach at Stannick Bay . . .'

Her words, her cruelty, faded away to a silent cry of grief.

I just stared at her, just stared.

She stared at me, knowing what she had said but affecting not to as I held back my grief and tears. It was her punishment for my bringing Harriet to the house and having someone to love and go walking with. It was a jealous punishment. I knew that because there was a guilt about Ma's expression and tone and a sense of satisfaction like Michael used to have when he inflicted punishment on me.

That year, those months, that time when I left home, the coming of Harriet, our happiness – all that disturbed Ma. She was not well. She had gained her independence too late, for the tide of time had turned against her and her body and she was suffering shifts of change and mood. My longed-for going, which once she must have looked forward to as liberty, had come just as her body was failing her. Maybe she had finally reached up high enough to grasp the chalice of freedom and found there was nothing inside it but a poisonous dryness and sterility.

When she was gone from my room and I was alone again I stood, numb.

Mr Bubbles dead.

I felt a great cry of loss in me but I did not utter it. Instead I opened the door of Michael's old room and there, quietly, I sobbed on Michael's empty, blanketless, sheetless bed, finally sitting and rocking as outside, the Stoning autumn reflecting my mood, it began to rain.

* * *

Next morning I braved the drizzling streets to visit Mrs Bubbles in Budd Street. She opened the door and we stood silently in each other's arms. Then she took me inside.

'Oh, Jimmy,' she said, so small in her big chair, glancing at Philippe on her mantelpiece, making me tea with what seemed withered hands. 'Oh *mon petit chou*. I did not know where to write to you, I did not know . . .'

When they needed me I was not there for them.

I would have found him on the beach in Stannick Bay when he did not come home. I would have known where to go and where to run for help.

As it was, Mrs Bubbles had to get people who did not know him to go and find him and he was brought back to Stoning Hospital, not to his home.

They buried him up on the heights of Dover Cemetery, far from the sea.

We got a bus at once and I went to say goodbye with her at my side. The grave was freshly dug and there was no stone. Just a few flowers, already faded. I wanted to do something to mark the occasion, to find some better way of saying goodbye, but I could not think of one.

'Oh Jimmy,' she said, taking my arm, 'I had so many years of love.'

Then, typically thinking of me and not herself, she said, 'Now you are going to your college to learn new things,' she said.

'Yes, later today,' I said, 'I must. Will you come and say goodbye?'

'Your mother . . .'

'No, you,' I said, '*you*.'

By the time I had got her back to her house and gone up to the Front to walk the few streets home for the final time it had started to rain more heavily, beginning to drum on the pavement at my feet, drumming fear into me and a sense of coming disaster.

I felt the old paralysis beginning to come on.

It got heavier and heavier and the cage descended over me. My feet grew heavy and my legs heavier still until I had to touch the walls of the house to move myself along, inch by inch, terrified. I felt the old darkness and a sense of paralysing loss, my steps heavy on my childhood pavements as I turned at last into Compass Street.

What is a nightmare?

The feeling there is nothing you can do, nothing at all, so that what is happening will happen and you can do nothing, unable to run, unable to act, unable to escape: your cries of warning silent and unheard.

I struggled down Compass Street and then I saw them out on the street by my front door, Harriet and Ma. Mad Ma and her red raw hitting hand.

Oh Ma.

I knew at once what Harriet had done.

She had gone to see me but I was out, so she'd found herself sitting with Ma as they waited for me and then what I had revealed about my pact with Ma over her suicide must have come out. Harriet must have said something, probably to try to rescue me from my promise.

I knew that's what it had to be.

Through the bars of the rain I saw Ma raise her hand as she raised it to Michael and raised it to me: I saw her raise her hand to Harriet, their hair streaming with rain, the drumming in my ears stopping me shouting, just stopping me.

Unable to move, I watched as she hit Harriet, not once, not twice but so many times that she fell down. When she tried to get up I saw Ma hit her again.

'Ma's mad,' said Michael once. He was right.

I saw their mouths and teeth shouting.

Then, and it was the last time I ever did, I saw Ma's red raw hitting hand crack the fallen, kneeling Harriet so hard across the face, so hard.

I saw Harriet's blood streaming down her face in the rain.

Only ten yards away, I stood paralysed, unable even to hear their anger and their cries, unable to move, unable to do anything but watch the silent horror before me as, for a lifetime as it seemed, they fought and Ma won.

Harriet got up and then fell again, blood from her nose washed down her chin by the falling rain and onto her frock. She fell again and that was when she looked at me.

*Help me,* she cried without uttering a sound.

I was unable to move.

I could not get through the drumming rain.

So, helpless, I saw my love breaking before me, I saw the end of love.

'Help me!' I heard her broken bloodied mouth finally scream, but I could not because of the drumming in my ears. I was unable to move even though my love was breaking.

Ma, turning from the fallen Harriet, looked at me, her hand at the ready.

But she did not strike again. She saw the murder in my eyes.

'You shouldn't have told her,' she screamed in a voice whose potency was madness. 'It was not your right to tell her. You promised me. It was our secret that you told. You promised. She had no right . . .'

There was darkness then, and a girl, my girl, running away as once I ran, running from the man with shears, who had turned into Ma, my girl disappearing round the corner of Compass Street in the rain as Ma slammed shut our front door and I, unable to move, unable even to cry out my grief, just stood there.

Unable.

Disabled.

Crippled by the rain that fell down about me in a hundred thousand bars as I tried to reach out to find a hand to guide me out of the darkness I was in.

It was David who helped me and got me away to safety and the new beginning of my life.

The rain eased, I moved at last back into the reality of the now empty street. Having nowhere else to go I went to Harriet's house, but there was no reply.

So then I walked on along the old Promenade of childhood

towards the cliffs, there to climb perhaps, there to get away from Stoning and Ma.

I found myself that grey day knocking at David's door, knocking and crying, broken.

His mum took me in.

*Jimmy, Jimmy . . .*

I wept for grief.

She calmed me down and called the clubhouse and David abandoned his final game before university for me.

'It's all right, Mum,' he said; 'it's all right now, Jimmy . . .'

So I told him.

'I should have thought when I first felt the rain today,' he said, 'I should have *realized*. I won't let it happen again.'

'No,' I said, 'no, David . . . it's something I must learn to beat. Harriet . . .'

We called, he went around, she wasn't there.

I drank tea and sniffed while he called Thom Brody. No one could find Harriet. We even rang the hospital.

We waited and waited until the time came when he had to go.

David got my cases, going in the side entrance of Compass Street because Ma had made herself scarce as I thought she would. The side gate was not hard to force. He went upstairs and rescued my things. Then he got me to the station by taxi.

Thom met us there with news of Harriet.

'She's home. Her dad's going to see your mum, Jimmy. They don't want to see you. Leave it a bit . . . I'm in Stoning a few more days; I'll sort it out.'

He was never able to. Nor was I, despite my letters and my calls. Ma's hand killed Harriet's love for me for ever, for what woman can love the man who fails to protect her from his mother?

'This is it then,' said Thom: 'you two today and me next week.'

David's mum was also there, fussing to the last, proud and sad that the great day had come.

Then the train came, with its screech of brakes and hufty-puff and hiss of steam, great clouds of it. When they cleared, I saw Mrs

Bubbles there as well, to say goodbye and hug me, her skin and bones all filled with love.

'Goodbye, my Jimmy,' she whispered, 'one day things will be good for you and you'll forget the bad times. Goodbye!'

'We'll see her home,' said Thom, David's mum nodding that they would.

Mrs Bubbles reached her hands to mine and held them, she kissed me three times and then gave me a buff envelope from the pocket of her old coat.

'You make me so happy,' said Mrs Bubbles as the train heaved and moved, 'so so happy, and Mr Bubbles he is happy too; where he is he is happy. You were his own true boy. Bye bye, Jimmy, bye bye.'

Then we were gone off under the bridge.

To the last I hoped that Harriet would come as once I came for her in that same place to say goodbye. But when she had needed me I did not go to her and now our love was a broken thing, lost and left behind upon the shore.

When the waving was over I opened the envelope that Mrs Bubbles had given me and it was the photograph of Harriet and me that she and Mr Bubbles had taken.

David and I sat down and he looked at me as if he expected tears. But they did not come and my eyes stayed dry.

'I wish *I* could cry,' said David, half laughing, seeing the funny side.

'I'm glad you don't have to,' I replied, grinning.

I laid the photograph on the seat and looked out of the window at Stoning disappearing from my life.

The train gathered pace and plunged into the first of the tunnels on the way to Folkestone as faster and faster we began to leave our home far behind.

'Well, we made it to university,' said David.

'Yes,' I said, 'we did, we did.'

The train rattled and rumbled along through the Kentish countryside, we two rocking in our seats with its rhythm as we headed inland into adulthood, away from the sea and from Stoning and from all its griefs.

'I'm glad we're going to college together,' I said.

'So am I, but I'm sorry about Harriet and your mum . . .'

'I'll get used to it,' I said. 'I got used to all that sort of thing from Ma a long time ago.'

'You don't fool me, Jimmy,' he said, punching my arm.

The train travelled on, faster and faster, and new horizons came our way, the past receding so that even when we leant out of the window and strained to look, our hair beginning to recede, our faces more lined, we couldn't see it clearly any more.

PART THREE

# LOOKING

# BACK

# 30

# CROCODILE

David always knew what he wanted after university, but my vision wasn't so clear. In fact I didn't have one.

He worked for a while for a company that made golfing goods and did so well they sent him to study the American sports goods market. Then he set up on his own and he never looked back.

'Come on over and see for yourself,' he said to me time and again. 'This is the place where it's going to happen.'

What's going to happen? I would wonder, shaking my head. I wasn't yet ready to venture across the sea and risk the troubled waves. I was tied to my country and my past by chains I could not name; except that when you put them together they added up to fear.

'One day I'll come to America,' I said.

'One day's a day too late in America, Jimmy!' David replied.

It wasn't hard for me to get offered a job because like David I had a first-class degree. But as my ambition was third class I had no focus and I couldn't choose between the opportunities presented to me. So I finally settled on a job with no future at all, just to gain respite.

I found a job working for a charity that raised money for poor students overseas. It paid just enough for a bedsit in Notting Hill Gate in London Town, and food. There seemed so much time stretching out ahead, enough for me to do nothing of much consequence while I found where I wanted to go.

Often, especially when it rained and I felt the familiar fear, I just sat on my bed watching the grey sky until it cleared and I was able to go out. But the roar and filth of London closed in on me and sometimes, seeing the clouds race above the high stained buildings and the few trees sway in wind and rain, I longed for Stoning Beach and the Dunes; I ached to sit on the shingle bank above Stannick Bay with Mr Bubbles and watch the swooping gulls.

I wanted to be that single lugworm to which it had been Mr Bubbles's habit to grant liberty. I felt the need for freedom but I hadn't yet learnt that the only real freedom is that which you find for yourself. People can only show you the way. The day has to come when you set off for yourself and don't look back.

But me? I just yearned to crawl away into the vast nothingness of a beach covered daily by tides and to be swept out to the open sea beyond. I didn't put the name 'sadness' on what I felt, or 'loss'. I just knew the despair of being among ancient shadows from which I could not escape and of living with a loss that seemed constantly to renew itself, which I was unable to let go.

I did not know that I was ill, what might now be called mentally ill. I did not know that 'depression' and 'obsession' might apply to me and had never even heard the word 'therapy', or have any idea that it might offer me a way out.

I did not know that I had not escaped Darktime after all and that the sense of loss, so deep, came from the time before when the Man Who Was left me and never came back. No one told me that if I failed to close the doors on the past, or at least learn to live with it, I might never be able to get on with my life.

So it was I was drawn back inexorably to Stoning, a moth to a light too bright, blinded to the better, safer, redeeming lights beyond.

During my university years I had felt no need to go back at all, though occasionally I made the trip there, to visit Granny and Mrs Bubbles. Ma I never saw in those years and never wanted to. But later, stuck in London, I began going back to Stoning routinely and found dark solace there.

I liked to walk my childhood streets, to count the kerbstones in Pilot Lane, to wonder at the changes in the High Street and the continuing closures of corner shops and pubs in the North End and the sale of houses whose inhabitants had been friends, to strangers who came only in the holidays.

Like me now, like me.

I always visited Granny, who was still clinging on, and Stannick Bay, to remember Mr Bubbles and remind the lugworms who was boss; and if I dug any there for some night fishing along the shore I never forgot to let one go free. We all need to know there's a chance of freedom.

I visited Arthur Sanders too, remembering old times. He wanted to give me all his tools because he was too infirm by then to pick up his toolbox, too arthritic even to turn the screw of his mole wrench.

'You have 'em, Jimmy.'

'Nowhere to keep them, Mr Sanders,' I would say.

'Your Ma . . .'

'She'll throw them all away. She throws everything away.'

'Fine woman, your Ma.'

'Mad,' I'd say.

'You mustn't speak like that, Jimmy lad. One day she'll be gone and you'll regret saying those things.'

'I won't.'

'Did I ever tell you . . . ?'

Arthur Sanders never stopped teaching me. He and Mr Wharton were the best teachers I ever had.

I also went back to visit Mrs Bubbles, who had retreated with the years into her life of a recluse in winter and reawakened less and less when springtime came. I sent her a birthday card every year for her and in memory of her twin brother Philippe and a Christmas card too. I worried about her more than anyone, more even than Granny. She had been much loved and without Mr Bubbles she was adrift.

Her little cottage was rising in value but she said she did not want to move.

'Where to, Jimmy? This is where I have been loved.'

She kept Mr Bubbles's black coat hanging by the door. You had to squeeze by it and brush against the rich scent of sea and sand, salt and sweat. She kept his great bike out in the yard, along whose crossbar I had retied the short-tined fork he had used so long for lugging. Mrs Bubbles would touch the saddle and caress the fork. Without her man to look after she felt she had nothing in her life and did not know where to find a purpose again.

I had long since cleaned out the tank he had kept his lugworms in and taken the mess down to the beach at low tide in bucket after bucket where it disappeared back into the shingle and sand like ancient blood as the sandhoppers had a feast. He would have been pleased at that.

I often stood on the beach, missing him, aching at his memory, wishing I could have thought of a way to give him what he gave me.

'Give it to others, lad,' he would have said, if he had said anything at all.

I just wished I had something to give to Mrs Bubbles to bring her the joy and happiness he had always given her.

One day, a year into my cul-de-sac London job, I found myself at the top of Compass Street and impulsively turned down it to knock at my own front door.

'Hello, Ma,' I said.

'Oh . . . it's you,' she said, staring at me and not immediately inviting me in.

She hadn't changed much: she was still big and overweight with her hair badly done and her glasses grubby and skew-whiff. But she looked well in her face and her eyes were less tired.

'You'd better come in,' she said eventually, adding as we headed awkwardly down the narrow corridor towards the parlour, 'you only just caught me. I'm off tomorrow.'

'Off?' I said.

She nodded and then sprung one of her surprises. A surprise so great, so astonishing, that you could have knocked me down with a feather.

'Oh yes,' she said casually, 'I work as a cook these days, a peripatetic one. Cook-housekeepers are hard to come by for the upper classes, people in their seventies and eighties now who used to have servants. I advertise in *The Lady* and can get temporary jobs whenever I want them.'

'A cook?' I repeated in wonder, thinking of all those grim tasteless meals she had made me, those congealed plates; and not wanting to think of her filthy kitchen and the lack of hygiene.

'Yes,' she said brightly. 'It takes me out of Stoning and brings me a nice little income. Shall I make some tea, and you can stoke the fire like . . .'

I think she was going to add 'like the old days' but wisely she thought better of it.

I remade her smouldering fire and she served tea in the same stained and chipped teacups on non-matching saucers I remembered.

'This is nice,' she said when we were sitting in our respective positions again. But we looked guardedly at each other and for most of the time the conversation was strained.

She brought me up to date on news of Hilary and Michael, Howard Scupple and Uncle Max. He and his doings, on which Ma waxed amusing, gave us something safe to laugh about.

It wasn't so bad that visit, but it wasn't so good. Whatever hatred I had felt for her seemed suddenly gone, to be replaced by . . . nothing, no feeling at all, except distaste. If we were mother and son it did not feel like it.

'I ought to go,' I said finally.

'Yes, and I had better get on,' she said a little too hastily.

There was no love lost because none had been found.

'I'll give you my address,' I said and I wrote it down on a betting slip she had.

'I won't lose this,' she said, 'because I keep them all to keep account. I was nearly ten pounds ahead last year and am ahead of the game this.'

The visit seemed to ease things in my mind about Ma, to put her in her proper place, to make me think less about my past with her.

'I'll pop in next time I'm down if I've time,' I said.

'That'd be nice, Jimmy, if I'm here.'

So from time to time we had our cups of tea by the fire and our occasional laughs, but things were never the same, never. Even if she had chopped off her red, raw hitting hand for shame we couldn't go back to the time before she smashed Harriet into the ground.

Rain troubled me more and more, not less. When it came unexpectedly I was forced to shelter in doorways until it had passed. Its steel bars still checked my passage. But like someone who cannot read, or is dyslexic, I learnt to hide my disability, so hardly anyone ever knew.

Nor did my dark secret keep me from going walking, which was my only interest outside work. I grew used to hunkering down in rain on the hills, watching it dripping from my anorak hood; waiting for it to pass from the shelter of rocks or woods. I felt my fear and trembled; but I knew I would not die.

However, it meant that I was forced to walk alone because I was too ashamed to admit to anyone that rain could paralyse me. Even more ashamed to admit I did not know the reason why. Fears and phobias were not things to talk about in those days, they were things to hide.

One May, after walking in the western Highlands, I found myself in Inverness, waiting for the coach to take me south, and saw a headline in *The Times* about the African Gentleman. He had died and the whole of Africa and Europe was in mourning. The article told everything about him from his beginning to his end, except nobody knew the date of his birth; and, of course, it did not say a single word about him coming to see Granny and me.

I knew immediately that the time had come for me to watch over Granny as he'd told me to. There and then I sent a telegram to her nursing home to say that I was coming down to see her. I went by way of my flat in London to get something which I liked to keep wherever I was living. You never know when you'll need such a thing.

I put it in my coat pocket and went straight on down to Stoning by train and by the time I got there night was coming on. As I stood again on the old familiar platform of Stoning Station I could smell the salt sea air and hear that the sea was roughening up towards a gale.

I walked to Granny's nursing home and found her sitting in her room with the window open at the bottom, as she often did. She liked the feel of fresh air. Her only light was a flickering candle.

She used to say, 'If ever I get bedridden you make sure they leave my window open, even on the coldest day.' She said it would be easier for her soul to fly to its last home across the River if the window was left open.

'My soul would prefer not to have to go downstairs and have to fret about finding keys and pulling bolts at a time like that!'

I found her sitting there in the twilight with nothing but a nightlight, which was against the rules. The lace curtains sucked in and out with the strengthening breeze and the candle flickered.

'Is that you?' she said when I called her name.

She reached out her old hands to mine.

'I knew you'd come,' she said.

On her little table with the nightlight was the *Daily Telegraph* open at the photograph of the African Gentleman. All about it she had put the things he gave her: the giraffe, the ebony man and the wooden spoon. It was an altar she had made.

'Come on, Granny,' I said, fetching her thick red coat and her walking stick. 'He said I'd know what to do, and I do. Come on, even if it's late.'

She said she had not been out for days and days . . . but she let me help her on with her coat. She said it most certainly *was* too late in the day now for an old woman like her . . . but she took her stick when I offered it just the same.

'Come on, Jimmy,' she said, as she always did.

Granny did not walk nearly as fast as when I was young, so it took us an age to walk down to Stoning Pier through the night. She held on to my arm all the way because the wind was so strong it would have blown her away like dry seaweed along the beach. Her face was a tight yellow parchment in the lights of the Promenade.

The Pier was open for All Night Fishing at one shilling a go but when the Pier Master saw it was Granny and me he let us on for nothing.

'Jimmy lad, if you're going on the lower deck watch out you don't get wet,' he said. 'The tide's rising fast before the wind and I'll have to close it before too long.'

I was pleased he called me lad; it felt like coming home as coming home should be.

We walked the length of the Pier with the driving wind and sea all about, and men in thick coats and balaclavas with their eyes fast on the tips of their rods for bites, and their hands, slimy with herring and rag, thrust into their pockets. When we reached the bar at the end we turned left into the wind and went down the steps to the lower deck. At high tide on stormy days the sea rose powerfully underneath and sent spumes of water up between the slats.

We crossed over to the lower deck's north-east side, Granny holding on to me for dear life as the sea rushed past under our feet like a threatening flood. On a night like that you needed a pound of lead to keep your tackle down; on a night like that nobody would stand a chance if they fell in and were swept away.

We leant on the railing and looked down at the dark sea and I brought out from my pocket the crocodile the African Gentleman had given me so many years before.

'He's going to need it back again, Granny, if he's going to get safely across the River to the other side,' I said. 'He said this day would come.'

She took it from me and held it over the rails for a long while, the wind doing its best to pull it from her grasp.

She was saying goodbye.

She looked so old I thought the wind would blow the last life out of her, but even in old age there was iron in Granny. She spoke some words in the African language she knew, which was the language of his tribe, which he himself had taught her. It was an invocation and a prayer. She sang a little too, and cracked and old though her voice was, it was the chant of a young woman; but the keening that followed it was that of an old wife who had lost her man.

Then the crocodile began to move in her hands for it knew it had a job to do. It swished its tail, and it opened its mouth in a great wide yawn as if it was waking up.

Then it became too strong for Granny to hold any more and she let it drop into the racing sea below. For a moment we saw it by the lights of the Pier turning round and round in the water searching for the right way to go, which was eastward out to sea.

The sea rose, the sea fell, and the wind and the waves drove on. Then with another swish of his tail the crocodile grew vast before our eyes and was gone, out across the ocean deep, out towards the lights of the Goodwin Sands, and then beyond to find and help the African Gentleman across the River and up into the stars.

As we watched, the sea seemed to rage. Then the wind blew and blew so much that it snatched away the terrible cries that came from my old Granny's mouth and tore the tears out of her eyes. I held her then as he would have done, and as once she held my hand at a hospital bed: I held her with a love I never knew I had. I just held her and let her weep.

'Oh Jimmy,' she said, her hand suddenly touching my face, and I felt a bitterness leave me and a strength come in its place. I felt a healing too.

When she was calm, and so was I, we watched out into the night for a quarter of an hour or more, right until the Pier Master came down to us and said it was time to go back to the upper deck. He had to shout to be heard.

'Come on, Jimmy, get your granny up to safety!'

But he stood with us for a moment or two, holding on to his official peaked hat for dear life, looking out into the raging night.

'It's blowing eight and rising nine,' he said: 'there's a wildness out there tonight.'

We were soaked through by spray before we got back to the main part of the Pier. We paused to look back into the darkness and I knew there was something stronger by far than 'wildness' out there, stronger even than the sea itself. That was the Crocodile and the love of Granny's life, the African Gentleman, as they made their way towards the stars to make ready for the day when Granny was ready at last to join them.

'You'll have to make a crocodile for yourself now, Jimmy,' she said as we began the long walk back to her nursing home, 'for it's your time to venture out onto the River now.'

'Maybe I'll find some driftwood on the beach in the morning and make it out of that,' I said.

For the first time in years the next day seemed to offer something positive and I felt a lightness in my step.

But Granny wasn't listening to my future, for that was beyond her time. She was peering up at the stormy night sky, trying to see the tail of the Crocodile in the stars above.

'I cannot see at all well,' she said. 'My spectacles have been getting weaker and weaker for many years now and I only wear them for show. In fact, my dear, truth to tell, I cannot see at all!'

She allowed herself a cackle of laughter and she was Granny of old again that night as she held on to my arm for support and I saw her safely home.

# 31

# THE OPEN SEA

After that night on the Pier with Granny I felt different, better, even excited, but I did not yet know what to do about it, so I did nothing. I stayed on in my nothing job, paying rent for my nothing flats. I was in that place between the low tide and the high, betwixt and between.

I moved from one flat to another until they all seemed the same: neat, nothing personal except my long-unopened treasure box and Mr Mee's encyclopedia, which I flipped through in the half-light, in search of something I had never been able to find. Its blue sepia prints of old masters were an accurate reflection of my state of mind.

You don't find the love you never had, the love of the Man Who Was, between the pages of a book; and you don't find it in the urban shadows of the capital, hemmed in by rain.

The job changed, my earnings increased and I finally ended up in a reasonable flat in Marylebone: two rooms, a kitchen and a dilapidated bathroom. I cleaned the flat from top to bottom obsessively, as if to clean out the past. When that was done I could not decide what to put in it apart from a solitary bed, a few books to keep Mr Mee company, my dull, carefully pressed clothes and postcards from my latest English walking tour, the previous ones being ritually thrown away so as to leave no trace.

These were little adventures, never very far. Wales, the Dales, the Lakes . . . But never the thought of going abroad. I was afraid of too much change. I feared the rain. I was disturbed by so many things that I wanted the comfort of familiarity.

The new flat was bleak, as empty as that orange box washed up along the shore before I put my treasures in it. There now seemed to be no more treasures of the sea to find. The only thing I kept was money because I could not think of what to spend it on. Maybe there was a touch of Ma in me: my savings grew.

David Ramsey called me once in a while, and wrote, telling of his progress, which was considerable. As well as running his own company in America he was doing an MBA. He saw a future for himself in leisure.

One letter said: *You could do anything, Jimmy, as we both know. All you need is a bright new idea or, failing that, a sound old idea which you can do better than anyone else . . . Let me know when you find one. I'd like to work on something with you – there's so much we could do together.*

Thom Brody came by and we went out for an Indian, a new thing then. Thom was now an engineer and between lucrative contracts. His life was good and he was getting married to an English girl he'd met in Malaysia. They were buying a flat and getting married, in that order.

'No point in paying rent to a landlord when you can pay the same to a building society and borrow enough to buy somewhere, is there? But what about you, Jimmy? What's your news?'

I had none, or not much, and I felt sure that Thom found me boring now.

'We had good times on Stoning Beach that summer of the A levels,' said Thom.

'Yes,' I said, 'yes . . .' struggling to find something more interesting to say.

Thom's mind was on the present and the future not the past. I must have seemed to be a man who was turning grey before my time. I was not even a shadow of the bronzed boy Thom sailed with that glorious summer when we were eighteen.

'Heard from Harriet?'

I shook my head.

'Got a girlfriend?'

I shook my head again.

'Don't often meet girls,' I said.

'They won't come to you,' said Thom. 'You have to go where they are.'

'I'll work on it,' I replied ironically, half smiling, and for an instant I think Thom caught a glimpse of the friend he had once known. I am sure it was then that Thom understood that I was ill; and that I finally had my first inkling of the fact myself.

'Jimmy,' he said impulsively, reaching out to take my hand, 'if there's anything I can do, anything . . .'

My eyes, which looked at him then, were filled with fear and loss.

'Hey,' he said, 'life's not that bad!'

The months drifted by and on my rare visits to Stoning, I stopped bothering to see Ma.

Then one day, after a year-long silence, she wrote. Neat writing on the usual cheap buff envelope, her familiar hand. I left the letter unopened until I made a coffee and felt I had the strength to face her prose.

I cut the flap carefully and to my surprise a cheque fell out: four hundred and forty-three pounds, nearly half my annual salary, more than all my savings. The biggest cheque I had ever had.

Halfway through the letter, trying to pass it off as if it was just another piece of news, no more important than the rest, she explained where the money came from: *Granny has died, as I expect you know by now, and this cheque is your share of her small estate. I was sorry we were not able to get in touch with you at the time as you seem to have moved again . . .*

I stood up, but the scream I screamed was silent; and the tears I shed were dry.

*Granny had died . . . and I was not there to hold her hand.*

My grief, my anger, all the worse for not having known, not having been told.

*Granny dead:* and suddenly the world was a different place without a north or a south, an east or a west.

I phoned work and said I wasn't coming in.

I stared at the cheque and put it away in my file marked 'Lloyds Bank'. I didn't want Granny's money. No life, least of all hers, should be summed up with a cheque.

Finally, as I sat staring at Ma's letter, anger and despair overcame my sudden blank emptiness, my disbelieving grief. I wondered why Ma had not told me. No reason could be good enough for robbing me of being able to say goodbye; and I didn't believe she had been unable to find me – Mr Postman always found me because I lived a neat and ordered life. I always had my post, like my phone calls, such as they were, redirected.

So I was angry but guilty too.

*I should have been there for Granny.*

I phoned Ma.

No reply.

I phoned Michael, or the number I had for him, which was that of a friend.

'Haven't seen him for years,' said a voice with a disconcerting Afrikaans accent, indifferently.

'Tell him Jimmy called.'

'Jimmy? His brother?'

I was surprised I was known, but the man who answered was no more forthcoming than that.

'I'll tell him you called when he shows up again. If he ever does.'

I even thought of phoning Hilary but I had not kept her number and I had no idea where she lived now.

I looked at my nearly-empty book of numbers – it was a shop empty of goods, testimony to an empty life.

So I phoned David and he listened, though it was the dead of night in New York. He listened to my tears and anger that I never knew Granny had passed away.

'Call the nursing home where she lived. They'll know what happened.'

'I want to go down.'

'Then go. They'll know where she was . . .'

'Buried. That's what she always wanted. She always said . . .'

David listened to my tearful memories.

'She meant everything to you,' he said.

*She saved my life in a thousand ways.*

I called Ma again just before I left to catch the train to Stoning and to my surprise she answered. She listened to my anger wearily, affecting innocence and guilelessness, but the guilt in her voice gave her away.

'How did she die, Ma? At least tell me that!'

Ma sighed, a story beginning, a version of the truth.

'Very foolishly, for she was often warned, she had a candle burning. She was always so *wilful*. Her nightdress seems to have caught alight and though she was not badly burnt, hardly at all, they decided that in her effort to put it out she had a stroke. I fear she was in pain. But not for long, the doctor said, Jimmy, and it is better, after all . . .'

Her words flowed away from me then, out of earshot. I felt my hot tears flowing. Then quietly, thankful I was so far away and could do nothing worse, I put down the phone.

I never told her I was coming to Stoning, nor did I visit her. I went instead to the nursing home and talked to the Matron I had met once or twice.

'Can I see her room?'

'Well . . . I'm afraid somebody else has taken it now, but . . . just for a moment then. Mr Caster won't mind.'

Mr Caster never knew. He was a white-haired gentleman in a tweed jacket sitting at the window, staring at nothing because he was blind; hearing nothing because he was deaf. He was waiting for death as Granny had been.

I looked around briefly but everything was changed.

'Where are her things?'

'Your mother asked me to pack them up and give it all away to charity . . .'

My heart tightened with pain.

'. . . but, well, those closest often make decisions they regret so we hold on to things. And anyway your grandmother was particular about certain articles. Please, come with me.'

I followed her down corridors of shining linoleum and mahogany doors and then into the basement. She showed me into a junk room, but a tidy one.

'Of course, the clothes have gone and the jewellery, we insist on that. But . . . there's these two boxes of small effects which your mother left for us to dispose of . . . just knick-knacks really, but they may have some sentimental value to you . . . and, of course, the clock.'

She pointed at a cardboard box on which Granny's name was very clearly written. Against it, covered in a black velvet cloth, leant grandfather's pendulum clock, which she had had in her room.

'She often told me it was for you. She even put a note to that effect on the back of it. Your mother said you'd come and collect it eventually.'

'My *mother?*'

The Matron nodded.

Sometimes words need not be said by near-strangers for them to speak volumes to each other. I think she already suspected Ma had not said a thing.

'Where was the funeral?' I dared finally ask.

'She never told you?'

It was for confirmation of the words unsaid before.

'No,' I said softly. 'Did my grandmother die . . . I mean was she . . . ?'

'She died putting out a candle, which she should never have lit.'

'Granny was always careful . . .'

'She was an old lady, Mr Rova, and I'm afraid she shouldn't have had it. But . . .'

Her eyes crinkled into a smile.

'She was a grand old lady, wasn't she? Independent to the last and never a single complaint. She was a pleasure to look after.'

I smiled too, tears in my eyes.

'Did she suffer? I'd like the truth.'

The Matron could tell no lie and I knew that Granny had, shocked and in pain, her heart failing in the struggle to stop the flames.

'I should have been here to help her,' I said.

The Matron reached out a hand and touched my arm, just like Granny sometimes did.

'I'm so very sorry,' she said, 'she thought the world of you. We couldn't understand why you were not at the funeral. We . . .'

Sometimes it is best to say nothing.

'Where was she buried?'

'Dover Cemetery, but . . . well, she was cremated. I *thought* she said to be buried but your mother insisted she told her otherwise . . .'

It was the final lie and, so far as I was concerned, the last betrayal. After that it seemed that nothing could have any significance.

'The ashes are normally sent to the deceased's next of kin or scattered a little while later,' the Matron said, sensing my distress. 'Oh dear, I'm sorry. Please call me if there is anything else you want to know.'

She left me to go through the box and ponder the things inside, which were not many and all but two of them nearly meaningless. But there in the shadowy darkness of the box marked with Granny's name was the wooden spoon from Africa, the love spoon with which Granny made her chutneys and jams; and a figure carved in mahogany, who looked angry to have been left in the dark so long.

I put these in my bag, but the clock proved more difficult. I could carry it, just, but its bulk made things awkward. A taxi seemed best.

'Where to, sir?' asked the taxi driver.

Impulsively I replied, 'Dover Cemetery and then Dover Priory Station,' and I left Stoning there and then, without even seeing the sea. I suppose it was a statement of a kind, but it left me uneasy, feeling that I had left something unfinished behind, something nagging at my heart.

Still, my numbness of spirit had gone and in its place, very distant yet, was the sense that in death there was a new beginning.

There was no sign of ashes when I reached the Garden of Rest where Ma had given instructions for them to be scattered.

'No one came for the scattering?'

'Often don't,' said the man in the cemetery office. 'The service is the thing, and the committal to flames, and the name in the Book of Remembrance.'

I had seen that, written in copperplate, just a name written by someone who didn't know her on a page no one would ever see.

So I stood alone, the taxi waiting, and tried to say my goodbyes to a stretch of grass and some clipped rose bushes.

Then I felt a spit of rain and I began to tighten up. I knew Granny would want me to go; she had no truck with too much sentiment. So I left and had the taxi take me to the station, imagining as I went the half smile Granny would have given at hearing a description of the sterile place where her unwilling ashes were finally scattered.

*Very vexing, my dear, but I hardly think it is the end of the world,* she might have said.

In the time of waiting for the train I made a call to Matron.

'There *was* something else . . . was her window open when she died?'

'Oh yes, yes it was. She insisted it was always open, summer and winter, but she never told me why.'

'It was so her soul could cross the River and find its way home,' I said.


It was several weeks before I worked out what I had left behind in Stoning and it was Granny who told me, talking in my mind, as I often let her do in those days following Ma's shocking letter.

*Jimmy, the best way to help yourself is to help another,* she told me one day as I sat on my bed, staring.

This was the morning after Michael had phoned. My message via his old flatmate had finally reached him. He came round straight away and insisted on going out. His idea of going out was drinking in a pub and talking ever more loudly; cruel laughter, brittle jokes at others' expense which were funny in their way but got less so as the evening wore on.

Of Granny and her death and Ma's failure to inform he said dispassionately, 'Old people die. So you didn't get to the funeral. Well, she's not going to care, is she? As for Ma . . . the woman's a bitch, a bloody bitch.'

He said it loudly and was aware of people looking.

'Hilary went,' he said suddenly and then, aping a female voice he said, ' "We tried to call you, Michael, and James too, but couldn't track you down . . ." '

He laughed and so did I.

'Bloody bitches, both of them. Fucking women! Except I don't!'

He laughed again, harsh and loud, his mouth full of fillings I never knew he had, his eyes lacking the milk of human kindness. Looking at him then, thinking I must draw the evening to a close, I missed the Michael I once knew. I found myself grieving for him as much as I was grieving for Granny.

That comment about women was the nearest he got then to saying he was homosexual, gay not being a word we used at the time.

He had something more to say and it revealed the reason he had responded to my phone-call message: he was going away.

'South Africa, working on a lumber farm, blacks. Henryk, the person you spoke to, is going too. His father runs it. Jobs for the boys.'

'How long for?'

'I hope for the rest of my fucking life.'

He laughed the cracking, bitter laugh again.

So it was I was sitting on my bed in the twilight the day after Michael left England, without further goodbye, thinking there was now no one left of the family that had never been, starting in the time before Darktime, which I could not remember.

No one to talk to, no one to share.

Even David had gone away.

And then outside it began to rain.

That was when Granny said in my mind, *Jimmy, the best way to help yourself is to help another*, and I knew what I had left behind in Stoning and what I had to do: find a way to help Mrs Bubbles.

Grandfather's clock tick-tocked now in my flat, as it had tick-tocked so for many years in Granny's room. I got up to look at the calendar. In eight days it would be Mrs Bubbles's birthday again, and that meant it would have been her brother's too.

Granny's voice had set a train of thoughts in motion and they led across the open sea to the white cliffs of Cap Blanc Nez, near where Mrs Bubbles had once lived.

But sitting on a bed or standing paralysed in rain, trapped in the chains of the past, never got a kettle boiled and never brought much colour to your cheeks. I had to do something: if I could not get across the sea on my own behalf I could do so on somebody else's. It was time for Mrs Bubbles to go home.

I travelled down to Stoning and knocked on her familiar door. For a time, so slow was her response, I feared she was not there or something worse, but then I heard the rattle of a chain where there had been no chain before, and I knew at least she was alive.

'Oh oh oh oh, Jimmy,' she said and holding her, grieving for Granny, I knew I should have come to help her many years before; and I thanked whoever I ought to thank that I was not too late.

On her mantelpiece by the picture of Philippe, her twin brother, was a fresh posy of flowers from the South Stoning cliffs and I knew that she had not yet given up hope of life.

'I picked them yesterday so maybe something told me you were coming. Something made my heart feel good.'

'I came because . . .' but I knew I should not tell her why because her response would be no and no and no again.

Even on a clear day, when you can see the coast of France, I don't think that Mrs Bubbles ever looked. After Mr Bubbles had found her and brought her to Stoning she turned her back on France for good.

But with his death she had lost her life again and now I had to do for her what Mr Bubbles could no longer do. I had to do for her what Granny had done for me. I had to find a way to guide her home.

I didn't know how and I didn't believe in very much but I knew if I tried then something would happen that was good and meant to be.

'I want to take you back to France, just for the day, just to see . . .'

'No, no, no . . .'

'It wouldn't take long. You could hear French spoken again . . .'

'No, Jimmy.'

'You could pick flowers again along the French shore and put them on Philippe's grave and say a proper goodbye . . .'

'*No.*'

'Please.'

'No, *mon petit chou*, no, no. You do not understand the things that were said in those years when *les monstres* occupied France, especially to women like me who . . . who had . . .'

'It's nearly thirty years ago.'

'People do not forget and they do not forgive. People in my town did not understand why I went to see the Germans and why . . . But at least I was able to help Philippe be given a place where he might live peacefully to the end of his life . . . and if Mr Bubbles had not come I too would be dead. I am not going back.'

'Well then . . .' I began, not knowing what to say in the face of such terrible purpose, 'well . . . do you mind if *I* go on your behalf? I could take some photographs and bring them back to show you.'

It sounded lame but I noticed her eyes grow a little brighter.

'Of course you could go. France is a free country again, like England has always been. I cannot stop you going.'

'Would you *like* me to?'

'I . . .'

But she could not bring herself to say no.

Then, finally: 'When will you go?'

'Now, today, tomorrow morning, early . . .'

'Is it so easy?'

'You can see France from the Front, you know that; it won't be difficult.'

'I have not looked that way for a long time.'

'Tell me about the town you lived in.'

'No, Jimmy.'

'Tell me? It was Wissant, wasn't it, near Calais?'

I knew it was. I remember Freddie and Mr Bubbles telling me about it and I had confirmed it on a map.

'I do not want to.'

'What would Philippe have wanted?'

'He would not have known what he wanted, he could not have known. He was . . . he was . . . so innocent.'

'What would Mr Bubbles have wanted?'

'Ah . . . Jimmy, Jimmy . . .' and she smiled. 'He would have wanted me to talk to you.'

'So talk then.'

'Well, I will tell you a little and then tell you not to go.'

But she told me a lot, all that afternoon and into the evening, more than enough for me to know where to go and what photographs to take when I got there. At some stage, she seemed to accept I would be going, even though, until then, I had not been sure myself.

'Will you let me take the photograph of you and Philippe to help jog people's memories and to prove that I really know you?'

It was her most precious possession but she didn't hesitate to give it to me, silver frame and all.

'I shall like to think that it has been back to where it was taken before the War destroyed our lives. I will not come, not ever, but my picture can travel for me. Bring it back safely, and yourself.'

She gave me the posy to take as well.

'Find the place where they buried him, but if you cannot find that then maybe our old home still exists. Put these flowers there in memory of him. It will be a birthday present for our sixty-first year and my farewell to him. It is the time now to stop thinking about the past, eh Jimmy? Both of us must find something new to look forward to.'

She managed somehow to look like the Mrs Bubbles I had once known again, just for a moment. She looked like that to give me strength. I think she knew that the journey was as much for myself as it was for her.

It really was as easy as I had told her and because I was her emissary I did not worry whether or not it might rain. I set off for France early the next morning, having slept on her sofa and heard her creaking about above, as restless at the thought of my journey back in time as I was.

From the start I had a sense of wonder about my trip, a sense of release. As the dark granite nose of Dover's Admiralty Pier fell behind us, the sun shone clear and I felt the first premonition of escape, of chains breaking, of the past losing its grip. I had a bag with a few toiletries, a photograph of twins, one long dead but the other most certainly alive, and a posy of flowers of the shore.

'*Bonne chance,*' she had whispered at dawn when she saw me off in Lugger Street, onto the Dover bus. As the ferry headed out into the sea I had so often looked at from the shore I felt that good luck was with me. The world was turning that day when I did Granny's bidding and helped another; it was turning my way.

# 32

# THE WORLD TURNING

I felt a new feeling that morning I sailed for France: it was the traveller's excitement of going to a new place, heightened for me by the fact that this was the part of France I had stared at across the water for so many years, wondering what it would be like to be there.

To me that distant land I had longed for was where freedom began. Mrs Bubbles had taught me that hers was a land of liberty, though she herself was one of its exiles. She taught me something more as well, yet until that day of my first coming to her country, I did not know she had put something of her love of it in me.

Disembarking from the ferry in Calais, going to the information office and speaking my first French to get directions for a bus to Wissant, sitting on that bus and journeying through a landscape so like the one between Dover and Stoning . . . it felt like returning to a home unsullied by bitter memory.

Naturally I looked westward when I saw the sea, to try to see England, but the view kept getting cut off by turns in the road until, when I did get a clear look at it, I saw there was a misty haze and nothing could be seen.

But, in truth, I was glad, because like Mrs Bubbles I did not want to look back, not yet. The time was not quite right.

The world was turning but it had not turned that far: I had learnt enough about life not to want to hurry it.

The bus set me down opposite the Mairie, by a memorial to the dead of the First and Second World Wars, just like the ones I had stood looking at so often in English towns. The names were French but the loss was surely the same.

There was more loss still on the walls of the nearby church: the plaques Mrs Bubbles had asked me to look out for, which recorded the deaths at sea of local fishermen. They lined one wall, some complete with enamelled oval photos of those who had died . . .

*Priez dieu pour le*
*Repos de l'âme de*
*Jean-Baptiste Beaugrand*
*Époux de*
*Catherine Honvault*
*Disparu en mer*
*à bord du Laurette*
*Le 18 Janvier 1937*
*à l'âge de 40 ans*

REGRETS

. . . others referring to people and events which, like those so similar ones in Stoning, must by now be all but forgotten, like '*la catastrophe du 12 Mai 1907*'; like the two children I saw drown, wondering now who still remembered them and when in the future the last memory of them would die. Wondering what was the purpose of those lost children's lives and what was the purpose of my own.

'*Regrets*' seemed the quietest of things to say before so many memories, but as I stood staring at the word on memorial after memorial and the words of Edith Piaf's song '*Non, je ne regrette rien*' tried to repeat themselves ironically in my mind, the irony died away and only the word 'regret', in its English form, remained.

I wandered from one end of the small town to the other and then along a minor road to a third way in. The road sign *Rappel* – a reminder of danger – seemed everywhere, thrusting its short stark word at me. *Rappel . . . Rappeler . . .* to remember.

And that morning, each time I did remember, something else of Stoning and my childhood seemed to find its completion and slip away.

The long process of saying goodbye, which had begun with Granny on the Pier when we remembered the African Gentleman together and committed the crocodile to the waves, was gathering pace.

There were other more concrete things about Mrs Bubbles's home town that were familiar. When I went across to the promenade I was astonished to see that the lie of the land, the rise of the chalk cliffs of Cap Blanc Nez, was a mirror image of the chalk cliffs of Southdown. They were littered with the same squat defensive pillboxes and entrenchments of a country expecting invasion, all cracked now and ivy-clad. Like Stoning, too, Wissant had only a couple of streets of shops and the tang in the air was salty and fresh.

The differences were only mildly disorientating: Wissant faced west while Stoning faces east, so the sun rose from behind, as it seemed to me, from over the land, not over the sea; and instead of a steep shingly shore I found an expansive sandy one, ruined now by yellow-walled, orange-roofed holiday chalets.

The road signs seemed smaller, busier, the lamp-posts darker and more ornate; the few hotels were at once more homely and more stylish, the shops smaller and more local. A few of the streets were cobbled and the boats, the *flobarts* Mrs Bubbles remembered so well, were rounder, taller and flatter-bottomed than the luggers of our shore, testimony to a different set of the sea.

The people were different too, to look at anyway: the women older, darker than in Stoning; their hair more worked, their hands more lined; and the men seemed shorter, fatter. Momentarily I laughed aloud: the French, it seemed, looked French!

I went into a seafront bar and sat down; and then after a while I stood up and went to the counter, realizing suddenly that was how you ordered something.

'*Monsieur?*'

My French stretched easily to a *café au lait* and it came with a biscuit. The looks they gave me were brief, courteous and discreet.

I had fallen in love with France almost before I finished that first cup of coffee. I was discovering the taste of freedom; I was discovering life and a sense of civilisation.

As time passed, I relaxed.

A radio spoke French; a man read a paper, in French; a woman delivered some fish that I did not recognize, although I thought I knew all the fish of our shared sea; a man carried a small fridge through to the back and took out a broken one, having a coffee on the way. While outside, beyond the promenade, people walked across the sands.

I felt the weariness of years draining away, leaving me content, without energy but at peace. I knew it would be all right, all of it.

I knew I was doing right.

I even began to dare to believe that the world was turning just for Mrs Bubbles and myself and that the time had come to find where Philippe had lived and was now buried so I could offer up the posy Mrs Bubbles had picked in memory of him; the time had come to say goodbye even to him.

I had been given a town plan for Wissant at the Calais information office and I pored over it again now, as I had on the bus, looking for the street where Mrs Bubbles said they had lived as children fifty years before and the mental hospital where her brother had been sent to die.

Neither was marked.

I wandered the town looking for signs of them, but found nothing. I wanted to ask for someone's help but my French was clearly not quite up to it because when I tried not once but twice the people I asked shook their heads. Not unfriendly so much as indifferent. Maybe they were visitors like me.

The last one pointed towards the Mairie, where the bus had first set me down.

I mounted the steps of a fine double-fronted building with a mansard roof which expressed a civic pride that made Stoning's Town Hall look like no more than a side show.

'*Monsieur?*'

I began to explain and was cut short with a smile and shake of the head and an apology.

'In there will they talk to you,' the woman said.

It was an office-cum-library, a place of books and records.

A middle-aged woman listened to my struggling French and finally said, 'You can speak English, sir, if it is easier. Please?'

I showed her the address I was trying to find and she frowned and then smiled.

'The street name has been changed since the War. We do that in my country to honour our heroes. It is now the Rue Maurice Pippet.'

She showed me on my map where it was.

'And the old hospital that was here in the War, I could not find that one on the map either.'

'Ah, yes . . . *un moment* . . .'

She picked up a phone and consulted.

'It is what I thought . . . it was replaced. It is no more. Those old hospitals were not so good . . . France is a modern country now.'

'Yes . . .' I said, hesitating.

'Is there anything else?' she asked.

It was a day of sunshine, when people gave each other time.

'I was looking for where someone local might be buried. I came from England to put some flowers on his grave.'

'Ah . . .' she sighed, 'I also have made such a journey. *La guerre* . . . *!* If he was a citizen of Wissant it will not be so hard to find where he lies.'

'His name was Philippe,' I said, 'Philippe Dupuy.'

She frowned, picked up the phone and consulted again, longer this time. She glanced at me one or twice and then, putting her hand over the receiver, said, 'Are you of his family?'

I began to try to explain but it felt as if it was coming out wrong. Instinct made me simplify and tell a lie, though it was a lie I liked.

'I am his sister's son,' I said. 'He was my uncle.'

She stared at me, nodded and returned to the phone. Her conversation became more animated. It began to seem I was causing trouble.

Finally, exasperated, she shrugged and said to the person on the other end what sounded to me like, 'Come and see for yourself!'

She put the phone down.

'Monsieur Hubert himself will come now and see you.'

'I didn't mean . . . I just . . .'

'He will talk to you. He will be a little time because he has a meeting to change.'

'I . . .'

'He will not be so long.'

I sat while she worked, glancing at me sometimes.

A big, shiny, oak door opened on the far side of her office and a man appeared. He was bearded and looked like what he was – the Mayor. He had no need of a chain of office to prove it.

'Monsieur . . .' he said, shaking my hand, 'Hubert.'

'James Rova,' I said. 'I am from England.'

He nodded slightly and then stood staring at me.

'You are the son of Philippe Dupuy's *sister*?'

His English was careful but clear.

I nodded.

'You know her given name?'

In all my life I had never spoken Mrs Bubbles's first name, and only rarely heard Mr Bubbles do so. It seemed an intimacy too far, but I said it all the same.

'Véronique.'

'*Dupuy?*' he said with emphasis.

I nodded.

Then: 'I have a photograph,' I said.

'*Une photo?*' he said faintly.

He waited, standing still, while I retrieved it from my bag, silver frame and all.

He took it and stared at it.

He touched the ornate frame as if not believing what he saw and needing the touch of something concrete to confirm it.

'And she is alive?'

I nodded, understanding why he might doubt it. As far as they were concerned she had simply disappeared into the night.

'She had no reason to come back,' I said.

His English, though good, seemed not quite up to this.

He called to his assistant, the woman who had been helping me, saying that she spoke English better than he did. Then he signalled to me to follow him into his office.

Above his desk, on the wall, was the tricolore, and not far below it a black-and-white photo of Général de Gaulle standing at the base of a monument that rose above what looked from the diggings nearby like a solid chalk cliff.

As I sat down I felt suddenly nervous, not sure what I was going to say. Mrs Bubbles had wanted me to say a quiet goodbye with flowers, not announce to her home town that she was alive and living in Stoning, almost within sight of Wissant, just across *la Manche*.

We waited until his assistant came in, carrying some files. She sat down near him and they stared at me like the bureaucrats they were. He looked through the files carefully, checking and rechecking.

'Can you tell me the date of your mother's birth?' he asked eventually, looking up at me.

I had not wanted to sustain the lie for so long but now did not seem the time for the details of that truth.

'April 14th, 1918,' I said promptly. 'The same as her brother's. Every year she places flowers by that photograph in his memory. This year, though it is a little early, she wanted me to come and place them on his grave if I could find it, or maybe near their old home, if I can find that. Mrs Bubbles . . . I mean my mother . . . she doesn't want any fuss. She doesn't want to come back herself . . . she . . .'

They listened to me, staring, nodding, seeming strange.

Monsieur Hubert said something to his deputy and she said to me, 'The Mayor would like to know how she came to England. You see, he thought that she was dead. He thought . . .'

'Well, Monsieur?' said the Mayor, cutting her short.

I told them about Mr Bubbles and Freddie Hammel's night-time trip during the war, and what I could about them finding the woman who became Mrs Bubbles. Then I told them about how Mr Bubbles looked after her.

. . . and then . . .

. . . and then, because Monsieur Hubert's eyes were kind, and he was not a man to whom you would want to tell a lie, because in fact he felt to me like a man you would have trusted with your life . . . and because I was tired, very, very tired, suddenly more tired than I had ever been, I found myself telling them everything . . . and finally that she wasn't my mother at all, but a friend, *like* a mother, like . . .

It was a day when people were good; and it was a day, as Mr Boys of Stoning Castle once said to me, that made the others worth waiting for.

At the end I said, '. . . and so you see, Monsieur, she is afraid to come back.'

'*Afraid?*'

'She says people in France do not forget and they do not forgive . . .'

With a sound of exasperation, Monsieur Hubert stood up at last.

'We are not a primitive country and these things were nearly thirty years ago,' he said. 'Also we are not without sensitivity. People knew then what happened to the Dupuys as they did to other casualties of war in this town . . . they knew very well.

'I was a boy then and like others my parents took me . . . you have a word for this . . . to the south.'

'Evacuated you?'

'Yes, that. They evacuated me to relatives in the south of France before the Germans arrived in 1940. I only heard what happened to the Dupuys when I returned to my village after the War.'

He frowned, his eyes glancing at his assistant and then at me, wondering what to tell us.

Then he shrugged and said, 'You have been direct with us, Monsieur, so I shall be with you. These things should not be forgotten. Do you know what I mean by "*les monstres*"?'

I nodded.

'It's the word the French sometimes use for Germans,' I said. 'Mrs Bubbles – Véronique – uses it.'

'We are all *monstres* in time of war, all of us. But, well . . . the Germans who occupied the region of the Pas-de-Calais wanted to show their strength and that resistance was not a good idea.

'They collected together men who were young and healthy and took them to be interrogated in their centre in Calais. Philippe

Dupuy was among them and he was not able to give a good explanation of why he was here. They thought he was . . . playing, like an actor, you know . . .'

'Pretending?'

'Yes, that. Pretending to be stupid. Unfortunately for him he looked intelligent and he was so, in his own way. He was innocent, that is all, and good. He could not have understood what they wanted.

'They beat him and tortured him with other men. When Véronique discovered where he was and what was happening to him she went to Calais to try to help him. She wanted to explain he was not like others.

'She offered herself in exchange for his life. They took her into the prison and maybe they liked the look of her and they decided to, to violate her . . . in front of Philippe and others, saying this would happen to all their sisters and mothers if they did not tell the truth.'

He paused, unsure whether to go on. If I looked shocked it was not shock I felt, for I had long suspected that something like this had happened, something so violent and horrible that Mrs Bubbles had no wish to recall it, or ever to tell me: it was sorrow I felt to have it confirmed.

'Of course he did not confess because he had nothing to confess, he was just simple, that's all. He wept and felt shame and witnesses said that he repeated over and over again *Oh non, oh non, oh non, non, non, non, non* . . .

'Afterwards she was dragged away and never seen again. The witnesses said they were told she was killed and buried where she would never be found but it seemed that her action and his obvious simplicity in front of his sister's violation saved his life and that of two men from Wissant who were arrested with him, both fishermen. These are the two men who told us what happened.

'Many others were shot but those three were sent home. Maybe these Germans were not all bad, just as we French and English are not all good. Maybe Philippe's crying and sorrow made them realize that he was simple after all. Maybe someone senior took a liking to Véronique and pity on Philippe. A few days after his return to

Wissant, Philippe was put in the care of holy sisters in the hospital for the old or mentally ill that was still here in the War, put there to die.

'He said *oh non, oh non* as if it was his fault in some way, but there was never anything to be sorry for or to forgive, only something . . . something . . .'

He turned to his assistant again and spoke another word or two, this time in French.

'. . . something to praise,' she said, 'what she did for her brother to save his life is something to *honour*.'

He fell silent, looking at me.

It seemed to me that the interview was at an end but at least I felt could take back these assurances to Mrs Bubbles that she would be welcome in Wissant in the hope that she would one day let me bring her home, if only for a few hours, to say her own goodbyes and put her mind at rest.

I reached down and got the posy of spring flowers out of my bag, picked at the foot of the Southdown cliffs a day or two before. It was a little worse for wear but not too bad. Mrs Bubbles had wrapped some wet cotton wool at the base of their stems and tied it with cotton; then she had wrapped the posy in something waterproof.

I placed it on the Mayor's desk. The tricolore loomed, the Mayor stared, and behind him, smiling, so did Général de Gaulle.

It seemed that nothing I could have said or done was better proof of the truth of what I had said, and that Véronique Dupuy was as alive and real as that wilting posy on the shining surface of Monsieur Hubert's desk.

Sometimes words come to me out of the past.

They whispered their way into my mouth at that moment and then seemed to utter themselves.

'*Oeillet, coquelicot, valériane, cassepierre . . .*' I murmured, repeating the names of the flowers as Mrs Bubbles had taught them to me. In fact, the posy I had brought had none of these in it, it being so early in the season, but I said the names all the same.

'She taught me what little French I know, including the names of some flowers, which were and are the flowers of her shore as well as of mine.'

Monsieur Hubert reached over, picked up the posy gently and stared at it and then smelt it, though I knew it had hardly any scent. I saw in him then a man remembering his boyhood, wandering the same shore as Mrs Bubbles once did, as all the children of Wissant must have done, as I did in Stoning, learning things about the place where they were raised, things they could never forget.

His assistant seemed about to speak but he silenced her, a twinkle of pleasure in his eye.

He gave me back the posy.

'Come, Monsieur Rova, I shall show you myself where you should place them. It is not so far to walk. Come . . .'

He told his assistant to stay behind but she demurred, wanting to come too.

So they locked up the Mayor's offices and we descended the steps to stand briefly before the war memorial where Monsieur Hubert wanted to pause. A moment's silence.

'We all lost in the War,' he said, 'and the years since have made us see things differently, better, and helped us understand there were heroes we did not recognize at the time. I shall show you this!'

He turned back towards the Mairie steps and pointed to a small plaque on the wall, its frame worn, its glass grubby with salt, the printed announcement inside stained with damp, its words hard to read.

He began speaking in French and it took me a moment to realize that he was quoting from memory the words framed on the wall. The last two sentences he spoke directly to me, looking into my eyes.

*A tous les Français* . . . the notice began, to all the French people. But a third of a century had passed and to Monsieur Hubert the words had become universal, for all people, though perhaps with the French and the British now first equal among equals.

'. . . *Notre Patrie est en péril de mort . . . Luttons tous pour la sauver.*'

The notice was signed by Général de Gaulle himself and was datelined London, June 1940.

'Véronique and Philippe Dupuy answered the Général's call for help and sacrifice in their own way,' said Monsieur Hubert, 'and our town should be as proud of them as we are of the dead whose memory we also honour. So now, Monsieur, I will show you where you must place your flowers.'

We set off together on foot, as if on official business. He turned left, which was south, walked a bit and then turned left again. People nodded and called out greetings to him, which he acknowledged only in an aloof 'I-am-on-official-business' kind of way as he led us on.

We made our way through the oldest part of town and turned finally into a little street, at the end of which there was a distant view of chalk cliffs: the Cap Blanc Nez.

'This is the street where Véronique lived,' he said, stopping. 'Her house was *that* one.'

He gestured towards a small house, hardly more than a cottage. It was half-timbered, the rendered parts of its walls were painted a faded orange-pink.

There was a tiny garden in the front in which a woman was standing.

She seemed surprised, very surprised, to see our little procession approaching.

'Is he at home?' demanded Monsieur le Maire.

She nodded towards the door, which was ajar.

'*Il n'est pas là, Monsieur,*' she said stepping aside and seeming to sense it was not the moment to be asking questions, '*il est au fond du jardin.*'

'This is the neighbour who looks after the house,' explained Monsieur Hubert. We nodded at each other before she retreated altogether.

We headed straight through the house into the garden, which like the house was as neat as two pins. It was long and narrow and at the far end was a vegetable patch, all beanpoles and neatly dug rows of soil. A man in blue overalls was working there on his knees.

He did not see us and he seemed to move slow and stiffly. His hair, what was left of it, was white.

Then, hearing us perhaps, he got up with some difficulty, turned and stared, a look of alarm and then slow recognition on his face.

He waved but did not move.

He had a trowel in one hand and some seedlings in the other.

He had a face whose features I had seen a thousand times.

Monsieur Hubert turned to me and put his hand on my arm.

'There is Philippe Dupuy, Monsieur, the brother of Véronique. He is the only person in Wissant who believes his sister is still alive. So please . . . give him those flowers and tell him he is right, as he has always been.'

There were tears in his eyes, as there were in his assistant's. In mine there was joy.

How long was that garden? I do not know. Thirty years long, perhaps, or a moment only.

I walked towards Philippe. I reached him. Then, lacking the words to say who they were from, except that I said her name, I offered them to him.

Carefully he bent down and stuck the trowel in the new-dug soil.

As carefully, he laid down the seedlings.

Then he straightened up once more, took the flowers and nodded before touching them, his hands her hands, his eyes hers. He blinked once and then again.

Then, rather slowly, slowly enough for me to understand, he finally asked a simple question.

*Non, non, non* . . . Mrs Bubbles had said, again and again.

'*Oui, Monsieur Dupuy,*' I replied, as her son, had she ever had one, would surely have done; adding, in English because my French was not up to it, 'she is coming home.'

He might have been the only person who believed she was still alive, but I think even he had begun to think that the day would never come when he would see her again.

He stared at me and then began to sob, a child's sobs, and I put my arms around him and held him close, as Mrs Bubbles had sometimes held me.

'She's coming home,' I repeated again and again, 'she's coming home.'

# 33

# LOOKING BACK

French hearts move a great deal more swiftly than their bureaucracy. Despite the best efforts of Monsieur Hubert and his assistant, it was six months before Mrs Bubbles's papers – her passport, her *carte d'identité*, her very existence it seemed – were in order, and official, and acceptable.

Time enough to sell her house in Budd Street and have sufficient funds in the bank to convince the French authorities that she would not be a burden on the State.

Time enough for two people to adjust to the fact that their other half was alive, and well. Mrs Bubbles wrote and Monsieur Hubert read out her letters to Philippe, but it was her he wanted now, not her words. He refused to speak to her on the phone after their only attempt, which distressed him.

He refused an invitation to Stoning.

'*Non, non, non . . .*' it was his turn to say.

But without a passport she was going nowhere and so they had to wait and make do with letters.

Until I suggested she send him a cassette of her talking to him, which she did, describing her house, and Stoning and Mr Bubbles and me. Telling him the story of her life. This tape seemed to satisfy Philippe, and Monsieur Hubert reported that he played it over and over again, listening to his sister's voice and humming as he did so.

Six months is a long time for two people waiting but for me it proved just time enough to decide what to do with Granny's legacy.

I resigned my job, I gave up my flat, put things in storage; I packed my rucksack with the few things I would need and bought a new pair of boots, the first thing I spent the money from Granny on.

I needed a walk to free my spirit – from Wissant to Paris would do, for a start. Once I had no shoes, now I had need of a brand-new pair of boots.

On the appointed day I travelled down to Stoning and was there to help Mrs Bubbles close her front door behind her for the last time and accompany her safely home across the sea.

When we finally arrived in Wissant and were standing on the threshold of her old home with Monsieur Hubert and his assistant, she turned to me and smiled.

'I will see him alone, Jimmy, because . . . because . . .'

But the door opened and there he stood, her brother, her twin, dressed to the nines in suit and white shirt, his trousers so pressed they almost stood up by themselves.

If they tried to speak, no words came. Just the sobs and the cries of two people too long apart.

Until I ushered them in, where they might be out of sight of us all and by themselves.

I remember only her whispers of apology for being gone so long and his whispers back, over and over again . . . *rien, rien, rien* . . .

*It's all right, it's all right now, it's all right.*

. . . before I closed the door on their reunion and left them to their privacy.

Mrs Bubbles wanted me to stay with them for a few days but as I had never in my life stayed in Budd Street I had no intention of doing so in Wissant. I had seen her safely home, as Mr Bubbles would have wanted me to, and there was no more to do or say.

Their world was set aright.

I stayed two nights, courtesy the Mairie, in Wissant's best hotel and might have stayed longer were not my feet and their new boots eager to get started.

Early one morning Mrs Bubbles and Philippe and the Mayor and his assistant and Philippe's neighbour, forming together a little deputation, saw me off onto the official path that runs up to Cap Blanc Nez.

I said goodbye to them there, kisses on cheeks all round, with a hug from Mrs Bubbles and a flower put in my lapel with love.

'Goodbye,' she said, 'goodbye, *mon petit chou.*'

I began the slow climb up to the monument on top of the Cap, where I read the words of remembrance to the French and English mariners who had died in the War in the Channel.

Then and only then did I allow myself to do what I had avoided doing before. I looked back, back across the sea to the land where I had been raised as a boy.

It seemed the strangest of sights.

The sun shone on the white cliffs of the East Kent coast and all along my shingly shore. I stood and stared and thought a long, long time. I remembered a boy running from a man with shears, I remembered a locked gate, I remembered a hand holding mine in the time long ago; and a pair of shoes that I lost and couldn't find.

I stood looking back across the open sea, just looking, until I knew that what I sought lay ahead of me now, not far behind.

Far above the white cliffs of Dover, dark cumulus clouds loomed, threatening with rain.

I hesitated only a moment before I remembered that I was not there any more, but *here*, where I had always dreamed I might one day be. Those clouds did not threaten me here.

Impulsively, I turned away and looked back no more. I put the rain clouds, and the cliffs, and all that happened long ago, far behind me. Then I turned, as the world turned, and set off towards the rising sun.

# ACKNOWLEDGEMENTS

I would like to thank the following, who made the writing of this book possible: Vivien Smith, who opened the door to the story's telling by giving me the love and space I needed to get started; Sue Field and Inger Lunder, for support over many years.

My literary agent Caroline Sheldon was seminal in the creation of the final form of the book; my editor Tim Waller nudged me expertly the extra creative mile; and my publisher Val Hudson turned the publishing process into a pleasure and delight. Michael Rines and Renée Holler helped greatly with the manuscript.

My first-born son Joseph read the first part of the story and his response made me want to continue; Les Cozens, of Deal in Kent, gave me access to his extraordinary archive of our home town's life and history and generously shared his knowledge of it.

I owe my love for history, a theme in this book, to Brian Kennett, an inspirational and much-loved teacher at Sir Roger Manwood's Grammar School in Sandwich, Kent; and to David Warwick, my English teacher there, to whom I owe my recovery of a sense of self-worth when I was failing.

This story is a memorial of a life lived and people who have shared it, most particularly of my brother Barnaby Michael Horwood, who died in 1999. He was stolen from me when I was five but in the writing of this book, I have found him again.

If you have enjoyed this book and would like to know about William Horwood's next publication or wish to respond with your own views about THE BOY WITH NO SHOES then please email the author personally at info@boywithnoshoes.com or write to William Horwood c/o Headline Book Publishing, 338 Euston Road, London, NW1 3BH.